Routledge Revivals

Planning the Mexican Economy

The Mexican economy, like many other economies in the Third World, has grown as the result of a flourishing oil industry. One major problem which faces economic development planners in such economies is how to ensure that development in the oil sector leads on to more general development in the rest of the economy. Often, oil led development may induce agricultural stagnation, increasing food imports, inflation and income concentration.

Planning the Mexican Economy (originally published in 1984), based on original research, looks at how this problem has been and might be faced in the Mexican economy. It uses econometric modelling to chart the relationship between different sectors of the economy and to show how change in one factor—such as income redistribution—affects other factors. It puts forward and compares different comprehensive development strategies and makes recommendations about the most effective approaches and policies.

Planning the Mexican Economy

Alternative Development Strategies

Jorge Buzaglo

Routledge
Taylor & Francis Group

First published in 1984
by Croom Helm Ltd

This edition first published in 2024 by Routledge
4 Park Square, Milton Park, Abingdon, Oxon, OX14 4RN

and by Routledge
605 Third Avenue, New York, NY 10017

Routledge is an imprint of the Taylor & Francis Group, an informa business

Publisher's Note
The publisher has gone to great lengths to ensure the quality of this reprint but points out that some imperfections in the original copies may be apparent.

Disclaimer
The publisher has made every effort to trace copyright holders and welcomes correspondence from those they have been unable to contact.

A Library of Congress record exists under LCCN: 83024792

ISBN: 978-1-032-91394-0 (hbk)
ISBN: 978-1-003-56348-8 (ebk)
ISBN: 978-1-032-91469-5 (pbk)

Book DOI 10.4324/9781003563488

PLANNING THE MEXICAN ECONOMY

ALTERNATIVE DEVELOPMENT STRATEGIES

JORGE BUZAGLO

CROOM HELM
London & Sydney

ST. MARTINS PRESS
New York

©1984 J. Buzaglo
Croom Helm Ltd, Provident House, Burrell Row,
Beckenham, Kent BR3 1AT

Croom Helm Australia Pty Ltd, First Floor, 139 King Street,
Sydney, NSW 2001, Australia

British Library Cataloguing in Publication Data

Buzaglo, Jorge
    Planning the Mexican economy.
    1. Mexico — Economic conditions — 1970-
    I. Title
    330.972'0834   HC135

    ISBN 0-7099-3247-2

All rights reserved. For information, write:
St. Martin's Press, Inc., 175 Fifth Avenue, New York, NY 10010
First published in the United States of America in 1984

Library of Congress Cataloging in Publication Data

Buzaglo, Jorge D.
    Planning the Mexican economy.

    Originally presented as the author's thesis (Ph. D. —
University of Stockholm)
    Bibliography: p.
    Includes index.
    1. Mexico — Economic conditions — 1970-   . 2. Mexico
— Economic conditions — 1970-   — Mathematical models.
3. Agriculture — Economic aspects — Mexico. I. Title.
HC135'B883 1984   338.972   83-24792
ISBN 0-312-61433-0

Printed and bound in Great Britain

C O N T E N T S

ACKNOWLEDGMENTS

In 1978, when examining the problems faced by agricultural planning in Mexico, I perceived the need for studying the effects of
oil-based development -and its possible alternatives- on agriculture and the rest of the economy. Work and discussions with
José Luis Garibay and other economists at the Mexican Department
of Agriculture were conducive to this perception. Afterwards,
this idea took form as a Ph.D. research project at the Department of Economics, University of Stockholm. Successive drafts of
my work were discussed there, in seminars conducted by Peter Bohm
and by my adviser, Göran Eriksson. I have also benefited from
comments of Ake E. Andersson, Ake Blomqvist and Lars Werin.

I am also most grateful to Terrance S. Barker, Arne Bigsten and,
in particular, the late Leif Johansen for their helpful comments
at the difficult stage when the model on which the study is based
was first drafted.

This study would never have reached its present scope and detail without the support I received in Mexico, especially at the
Centro de Investigación y Docencia Económicas (CIDE) and the
Programming and Budgeting Department. Hernán Sàbau made an important contribution to the final version of the model; he also
designed and executed some of the estimations. The collabora-
tion of Valentín Solís was essential in the conception and implementation of the estimation, programming and simulation.
During four months in 1980, it was rewarding for me to work with
the enthusiastic and imaginative group formed by them and by
Arturo Chacón, Antonio Gaitán, Carlos Ramírez, Roberto Ramos,
Guillermo Rivera and Eduardo Suárez. I would also like to acknowledge the help and suggestions of Nora Lustig (Colegio de
México), Pedro Uribe, Jaime Ros and the members of the Mexican
Economy Department of the CIDE. Many other useful comments have
also been received.

In the process of writing the successive versions of this work,
Maj Asplund and Ulla Blomqvist assisted me with both the English and the typing. The intervention of Julie Sundqvist radically improved the form. My friend Carlos Narvaja drew the
figures.

I gratefully acknowledge the financial support of the National
Labor Market Board and the Swedish Agency for Research Cooperation with Developing Countries.

My gratitude, of course, does not by any means implicate the
above persons and institutions in the errors and views contained
in this work.

Jorge D. Buzaglo

CHAPTER 1.   INTRODUCTION

This study deals with the effects of alternative
approaches to development policy. It is concerned
with the relations between development strategy and
the configuration of output and demand over time. The
main objective is to determine the related levels of
welfare, employment and sectoral trade. The analysis
is applied to Mexico, a less-developed, mixed, open
economy with important oil reserves.

In 1980, Mexican oil reserves represented about 6 percent of total world reserves, i.e. a per capita level
equivalent to that of Venezuela or Iran. An accelerated
pace in the discovery of oil deposits and rapidly increasing oil output are recent phenomena; in 1980 oil
reserves were six times larger and oil output twice
as large as in 1976. The increase in oil exports has
been even more impressive. In the first half of the
1970s, oil exports were almost nonexistent. In 1980
they attained ten times the volume of 1976. Oil exports
then represented about two-thirds of total exports.

As shown in Chapter 2, the Mexican oil boom appears to
have been a structural consequence of the 1976 economic
slowdown, which originated mainly in the external sector. The Mexican pattern of development - the so-called
'import substitution strategy' - which had succeeded
in high rates of overall and industrial growth since
the 1950s, seems to have reached a point of exhaustion
by the mid-1970s. The balance of payments represented
an increasingly severe restriction on growth. The oil
boom may then have been a structural, long-run complement to the stabilization policies agreed on with

the International Monetary Fund in that year in order
to alleviate the problem of the external sector.

The 'oil-led' development strategy is not without
problems, as the experience of those countries which
have followed such a pattern over a longer period has
shown. Oil-led development seems to be particularly
detrimental to agriculture, which is typically the
sector where underdevelopment problems are the most
serious. The results are increased rural poverty,
migration and urban un- and underemployment. Increased
food prices and inflation provoke tendencies towards
income concentration. Traditionally food-exporting, or
self-sufficient, countries become increasingly dependent on imports of staple-foods.

Mexican agriculture has stagnated since the mid-1960s.
Output growth has been slower than population and demand growth; increasing agricultural imports have
followed. The causes are to be found in the dualistic
structure of Mexican agriculture. A modern capitalist sector concentrates capital endowments and technology and produces a larger share of output, whereas
the dry-land,peasant agriculture, which comprises most
of the rural population, produces at very low (labor)
productivity levels. Low productivity, poverty and underemployment affect a large part of the rural population. Several approaches to reforming agricultural
policies and institutions, aimed at increasing agricultural efficiency and reducing skewness in resource endowments and income distribution,have been proposed.

Conditions in the agricultural sector explain a large
part of the poverty and income concentration in Mexico.
But poverty and income concentration are also considerable in the urban economy. By international standards, the overall level of income inequality is high

in Mexico. The relative standard of the lowest income
groups, and presumably also their real incomes, have
deteriorated in recent years. The tax system has mainly played a regressive redistributional role, in spite
of recent reforms. The ratio of fiscal revenues to
GNP has been low, although it has increased somewhat
since 1976 due to the growth in oil revenues. On the
expenditure side, current expenditures have been restricted and public investment, which accounts for a
major part - about 45 percent - of total investment,
has been aimed at promoting private profitability.

The Mexican pattern of industrialization has not brought
about the absorption of un- and underemployment. The
output elasticity of employment has decreased; the
supply of labor has increased at a higher rate than
employment. Agricultural stagnation has implied increased rural underemployment. The results have been
increased migration (to the cities and the United
States) and lower labor-force participation rates.

Chapter 3 deals with the alternatives which appear to
be open to Mexican development; the aims of the study
and the methodological approach adopted are specified.
The theoretical origins of our approach are surveyed.
The approach is compared with that of other models of
the Mexican economy.

In the presence of large oil reserves, 'oil-intensive
development' may be seen as an appealing strategy. The
expansion of oil production may increase the state's
revenues in terms of taxes and profits from the nationalized oil industry. It may be a relatively facile
way to increase the government's capacity to undertake
more ambitious development policies.

Furthermore, oil exports may appear to allow for
abundant external resources. A typical restriction on
accelerating growth in a developing economy might thus
be removed. Industrial development may be given new
impetus through an increased capacity for importing
investment goods and industrial inputs.

An oil-intensive strategy may imply some risks, however. If - as in recent years - 'petrolization' leads
to a concentration of public resources in the oil sector, at the expense of agriculture and other food-
producing sectors, then continued agricultural stagnation and increasing imports of food may follow. The
oil sector has relatively low labor requirements per
unit of output. Oil-intensive growth therefore has a
comparatively low impact on employment.

A basic change in the development pattern could also
be conceived, that is, a strategy which shifted the
flow of public resources from oil production to agriculture and other sectors which produce essential goods
and services.[1] Extensive agricultural reforms could
be introduced in order to increase efficiency and redistribute incomes. The shift on the supply side would
thus be consistent with a policy aimed at reducing
income inequalities, thereby increasing the demand for
basic goods and services. The income distribution
policy inherent in this strategy would imply the incorporation of social groups which have not benefited
from the past pattern of growth, viz. landless rural
workers, poor peasants and the urban poor, into the
process of economic and social development. The progressivity of the tax system would be increased, as
would the level of direct taxes.

---

[1] The terms 'essential' or 'basic' goods, or 'necessities',
refer in this study to those goods which constitute a major
part of the consumption of the lower income groups.

As suggested by this description of development alternatives, our notion of development strategy singles
out two policy elements: a public investment policy,
or the shares of the public investment fund allocated
to the different sectors; and an income distribution
policy, or the income shares accruing to the different
income classes.

Our aim is to explore the effects of adopting different
development strategies, in the case of Mexico, over
the period 1980-1990.

We concentrate on the effects on three indicators of
the performance of the economy. The first is the sectoral trade variable. The agricultural balance of trade
reflects the degree of agricultural self-sufficiency,
which is a highly valued policy objective in Mexico.
Oil exports indicate the level of 'petrolization' which
results from the application of the strategy. Limited
petrolization is also an important policy aim in
Mexico.

The second indicator of the state of the economy is
the level of employment associated with the development strategy, also a highly valued policy objective
in Mexico.

The third is the level of economic welfare. Real national income is a widely used indicator of welfare,
but it does not take the distribution of income into
account. Other measures of welfare which reflect both
the level of income and its distribution are also included.

Three types of development strategies are studied.
The first is the Mexican 'Global Plan' strategy. Two

different interpretations - 'optimistic' and 'pessimistic' - of the agricultural and income distribution
policies of the Plan are made. They are constrasted
with the public investment policy of the Plan and
serve to assess the ceteris paribus effects of income
redistribution and agricultural reform.

The second strategy is intended to simulate oil-intensive development. In this 'status-quo-plus-oil' scenario,
public investment continues to be concentrated, as in
recent years, in the oil sector. Agriculture and other
essential goods-producing sectors are allocated relatively low shares. It is also assumed that there are
no changes in income distribution, so that the income
shares of the different socio-economic groups remain
constant. This implies, in particular, that no significant changes in present agricultural policies and
institutions are assumed.

Finally, a 'new development strategy' is simulated.
Its aim is to change the pattern of development, in
the sense of higher equity in income distribution and
a consistent increase in the output of essential goods.
The structure of income distribution changes in favor
of those socio-economic groups which did not benefit
from past growth. The progressivity and level of direct
taxes are increased. Public investment is reoriented
from the oil-producing sector to agriculture and other
basic goods-producing sectors. Sweeping reforms are
assumed to be introduced in the agricultural sector,
which result in higher effectiveness of sectoral investment and a decrease in inequality.

The analysis of alternative strategies is conducted
by means of a multisectoral, dynamic input-output
type model, which is described in Chapter 4. The

model's variables and equations are listed in Appendix A.

The model is constructed within the consistency framework of a social accounting matrix (SAM), which gives an integrated and consistent picture of the economy. Both the supply and the demand side of the (real) economy are represented in detail; financial and monetary markets are not included. The growth of sectoral output is determined by sectoral investment, for given capital output ratios. Investment has a private and a public component. Private investment behaves according to a modified version of the acceleration principle, in which past growth and capital output ratios govern the sectoral distribution of investment. The sectoral distribution of public investment is a policy variable. The sequence of shares of the public investment fund allocated to the different sectors within the planning horizon constitutes a public investment policy.

The demand side includes consumption and investment demands, at the sectoral level. Intermediate consumption demands depend on sectoral gross outputs, given known technical coefficients. Final consumption demands depend on (disposable) income levels and their distribution among socio-economic groups. Consumption and saving propensities differ among income classes. An exogenously determined rate of foreign saving is included. Incomes are linked to output via value added coefficients that distribute sectoral income among income classes. Value added coefficients are assumed to reflect the effect of policy instruments which influence income distribution (i.e. taxes and subsidies). An income distribution policy is a sequence of coefficients of incomes accruing to the different socio-economic groups within the planning horizon.

Investment demands (sector of origin) are obtained from sectoral investment (sector of destination), given known sector-of-origin ratios for sectoral investment. Noncompetitive imports and exogenous exports complement internal supply and demand.

Fixed prices are assumed. Mexico is assumed to be a relatively small, open economy, where exogenous, constant world prices prevail. All sectors are assumed to produce internationally tradeable goods or services. In this context, whenever there is a difference between sectoral supplies and demands, the difference is internationally traded. That is, excess demands are traded; they are net exports when positive and net imports when negative.

Employment is a function of sectoral output. The function consists of coefficients, specific to each sector, of labor utilization per unit of output. Welfare depends on income levels by income class.

As the dynamic Leontief model, our model may be conceived of as a disaggregated Harrod-Domar model. At the macro level, it is assumed that there are no effective demand problems, so that saving equals investment. The growth trend is then determined by the rate of savings, for a given (average) output capital ratio. But our model differs from the dynamic Leontief model in several respects. The dynamic Leontief model is an 'equilibrium' model, which states sectorally balanced supplies and demands - or, in the terms of our model, zero sectoral trade balances. Also, sectoral investment is totally endogenous; there is no public investment which acts as a policy instrument as in our case.

The solution of Leontief's dynamic model finds a growth
path for the system at which sectoral outputs remain
in fixed proportions and growth at equal, constant
rates. This type of solution may also be found in our
model, if the conditions of the Leontief model are
added. The differences would be the specification of
income distribution and the inclusion of external saving.

Our model admits other types of solutions. For instance,
it can be treated as a system under control. Public
investment can be used as a control variable for
achieving a certain desired structure of the sectoral
balance of trade (e.g. 'agricultural self-sufficiency',
'restricted petrolization', etc.), for a given income
redistribution policy over time. Or, both policies
may be used to maximize some expression of welfare
and/or employment. The maximization might also include
some restriction on the structure of the sectoral
balance of trade. The control process might include pe-
riodic updating and revision of parameters and policies,
as new information is produced (rolling planning, or
learning). There are, of course, many other possibilities.

As mentioned above, the aim of this study is to explore
the effects of some relevant development strategies.
The simulation approach is adopted; no analytical solution or control mechanism is tried. Different public investment and income distribution policies are
stipulated and the model is solved (recursively forward in time) for these data, given the behavioral
parameters and initial conditions of the Mexican
economy.

Chapter 5 deals with estimation of the model using
Mexican data. The estimated version includes a 45-
sector classification, which is the one used for

Mexican national accounts. Seven different socio-
economic groups are distinguished: four urban ('high
bourgeoisie', 'middle classes', 'marginal population',
'workers') and three rural ('rich' and 'middle-poor
peasants' and 'landless workers'). This degree of
detail results in a rather large system, with 772
equations.

Theoretically, all behavioral coefficients in the model
may change over time. In the specification adopted for
the estimation with Mexican data, most coefficients are
assumed to be constant. The exceptions are: the subsistence consumption parameters, exogenous trade and
sectoral labor requirements ratios, which are assumed
to vary over time according to their trend.

In all cases, estimation of the coefficients of the
model implied a certain amount of processing, i.e. an
addition to existing data. The technical coefficients
matrix of 1970, for instance, is aggregated from 72
to 45 sectors and updated (by the RAS method) to 1978.
The income distribution and personal consumption coefficients of the model were estimated from original
data of the household income and expenditure survey
of 1977. Sectoral incremental capital output ratios,
labor requirements coefficients and their rates of
change were also computed for the first time for this
study. An overview of the estimation is presented in
Appendix B. The estimated coefficients appear in
Appendix C.

The results of the simulations with the model are discussed in Chapter 6. The first simulation is historical
and aimed at assessing the validity of the model. The
model is solved for the actual, past values of the policy variables. The solution is then compared with ac-

tual development. The result of the comparison is
rather satisfactory, given the fact that - with one exception - only statistically estimated coefficients
were used and no 'calibration' was tried. The solution
of the model for the years 1975-1979, when the policy
parameters are given their actual values, traces quite
well the actual evolution of the Mexican economy, particularly in aggregated terms. Most sectoral production
results also agree quite well, in that they reflect
the changes in the output structure which occur in the
period; oil output grows at a high rate, while agriculture stagnates, as do other sectors which produce
essential goods. For a few 'small' sectors, which
produce a very low share of total output, the adjustment is not good, which would suggest that some sectors
of the 45-sector classification of Mexican national
accounts should be aggregated for this type of study.

From 1980 to 1990, the policy parameters in this experiment take values that correspond to the historical
trend. The results of this 'basic' simulation, which
may be regarded as a trend projection of Mexican development, agree quite well with the aggregate results
of other 'basic' projections (those of the Industrial
Development Plan and the Mexican Wharton model). For
some important sectors (agriculture and oil in particular), the model gives seemingly more realistic results than other projections.

The following four policy experiments refer to the
Mexican Global Plan 1980-82. The Global Plan aims at
changes in the pattern of development. Among its highest
policy objectives are an increase in employment, pro-
vision for welfare minima, supplying primarily essential goods and services, and improvement in income
distribution. It aims at attaining agricultural self-
sufficiency in the medium term. The public investment

policy of the Global Plan reflects an increased emphasis
on the basic goods-producing sectors and some diminution of concentration in the oil sector. The investment policy of the Global Plan is contrasted with two
different assumptions about income distribution and
agricultural efficiency, thus estimating potential
ceteris paribus effects of policy changes.

The results of the basic interpretation of the Global
Plan agree quite well with the macroeconomic targets
of the Plan. There are some discrepancies, however,
at the sectoral level. An interesting discrepancy
occurs in the oil sector; oil production might increase
at a much higher rate than expected if investment in
the oil sector follows its planned pattern. The Global
Plan might then imply higher 'petrolization' than expected. (The macroeconometric model of the Plan does
not reflect these effects, as it does not specify sectoral investments and their impact on growth.)

Next, the separate effects of (an exogenously stipulated) income redistribution and agricultural reform
are analyzed. A reform program, the Mexican Food System, is specified; its implementation is assumed to
increase investment effectiveness. The (overall) growth
impact of redistribution and improved agricultural
performance is similarly slight, i.e. they have a
weak effect on total output - in opposite ways. The
agricultural trade balance is negatively affected by
redistribution - higher consumption of necessities -
and positively affected by increased agricultural efficiency. Without increases in efficiency, the agricultural trade deficit continues to deteriorate, under
the assumed ('Global Plan') investment policy. A well-
functioning agricultural sector is also highly important for employment; agriculture is relatively
labor intensive. Welfare, as measured by an indicator

which includes efficiency and equity effects, is positively affected by redistribution and increased
agricultural efficiency.

Next, a 'status-quo-plus-oil' scenario, aimed at simu-
lating an oil-intensive development strategy, is introduced. This 'petrolization' strategy assumes that
the high rate of concentration of public investment
in the oil sector attained in 1979 is maintained, and
that the shares of agriculture and other sectors which
produce essential goods remain at their (low) 1979
levels. The neglect of the agricultural sector implied
by the oil-intensive development strategy is also
reflected in this simulation by the assumption that
sectoral investment maintains its present low level
of effectiveness. No significant changes in agricultural policies and institutions are introduced. The
income distribution policy of this strategy is then
such that income distribution does not change, thus
maintaining its present high level of concentration.

The status-quo-plus-oil strategy implies high rates of
GNP growth for 1980-1990 (9 percent per year). Quite
naturally, the oil-producing sector is the most dynamic
sector (it grows by 22 percent). Agriculture and other
essential goods-producing sectors grow less than the
average. The consumption of these goods grows faster
than output. The agricultural trade deficit then de-
teriorates steadily (by 10 percent). By 1990, almost
60 percent of private consumption is supplied by imports.

Total employment increases at a higher rate (5.5 percent) than that of labor supply (3.3 percent). Unemployment diminishes constantly, but still exists in
1990 (10 percent of the economically active population).

The workers in the oil sector receive a higher share
of private incomes than in other production sectors.
In the status-quo-plus-oil strategy, the oil sector
produces a growing share of total output. This makes
the incomes of the workers grow at the fastest rate.
The average incomes of high-income classes, both urban and rural, and the urban middle classes increase.
The urban and rural poor receive more or less unchanged
average incomes.

The last policy experiment assumes important changes
in the development pattern. The 'new development strategy' aims at basic changes in income distribution and
output composition. An advanced income redistribution
policy is assumed. Income redistribution is the result
of an increase in tax progressivity and the introduction of agricultural reforms. Direct taxes - which are
very low and unequally distributed - are assumed to be
doubled. The sectoral allocation of public investment
is reoriented. Concentration in the oil sector is rapidly reduced; investment is instead directed towards
agriculture and other basic goods-producing sectors.
After 1985, the share of capital goods-producing sectors is increased, at the expense of service-producing
sectors.

The 'new development strategy' shows a high growth performance (10.6 percent annually in 1980-1990). Income
redistribution supplemented by increased public revenues (direct taxes), is a savings-increasing redistribution which positively affects growth, as the saving
propensity of the government (assumed to remain unchanged) is comparatively high.

The agricultural balance of trade deficit diminishes
constantly and disappears in 1986. This result depends
on the assumption of efficiency-increasing reforms in

agriculture. If the present (low) level of effectiveness were assumed for increased public investments,
the deficit would disappear later, after the simulation horizon.

Output growth in the oil sector shows a declining pattern; the average growth rate, however, is high (10.9
percent). Oil exports increase somewhat until 1985,
after which they decrease slightly; this pattern con-
forms to the official aim of restricting 'petrolization'.

The 'new development strategy' has a rather impressive
impact on employment; it increases by 10 percent per
year in 1980-1990. High agricultural output growth due
to increased flows of public resources and augmented
efficiency gives rise to rapid growth in labor demand.
Unemployment is absorbed in 1986, if labor participation rates are maintained at their present (low) level,
or in 1989, if they increase to their 'normal' level.

Welfare increases are also high, due to high growth in
total income and increased equality.

CHAPTER 2. OIL AND DEVELOPMENT: THE MEXICAN BACKGROUND

1. Some General Features of Oil-led Development

The evolution of countries which exhibited an oil-
intensive pattern of growth during a relatively long
period shows that some characteristic problems of the
underdeveloped economy remain unsolved, or have even
become aggravated.[1]

Underdevelopment problems are typically concentrated
in the agricultural sector. Low productivity is a source
of extensive poverty in the countryside. Output stagnation is a frequent constraint on overall growth and
income redistribution. Migration to the cities from
rural areas exceeds the absorption capacity of the
urban economy.

The impact of an oil-intensive development strategy
on agriculture seems to be mostly negative. According
to Katouzian (1979) - whose study serves as a basis
for the following description - 'the most direct and
destructive result (of an oil-intensive strategy) has
been its devastating effect on the agricultural
sector' (p. 4).[2] The agricultural sector has been in-
capable of meeting the rapid rise in demand, due partly

---

[1] This refers to the 'nondesert' oil-exporting countries. 'Desert
countries' deserve a separate analysis. 'Desert countries' are
oil-exporting countries with very high per capita oil reserves
and production (Katouzian, 1979, p. 5). They are Abu Dhabi,
Kuwait, Qatar, and the United Arab Emirats. The World Bank (1981,
p. 88) distinguishes between 'capital-deficit' and 'capital-surplus'
oil exporters. The capital-surplus oil exporters are the above-
mentioned desert countries, plus Iraq and Libya.

[2] See also Katouzian (1978), that concentrates on the case of
Iran. For the case of Nigerian agriculture, see World Bank (1982,
p. 46).

to technical and institutional constraints, and partly
to the deliberate neglect of agriculture which has
characterized this strategy, as reflected in, among other
things, a low - and often falling - share in the allocation of public resources.[1] The resulting urban food
shortage has been met by rising imports - which were
possible only because of increasing oil export revenues.

In spite of the increased supply of imported goods, inflationary pressures have persisted because of physical
limitations on the volume of imports and their distribution (i.e. inadequate supply of ports, roads, storage
and transport facilities) or because of consumers' preferences for home products.

Inflation has produced negative distribution effects.
Increases in food prices have hit the urban labor force
the hardest. Increasing demand (growing migration from
the countryside, speculative investment in real estate)
provoked increases in housing prices with the same distributive effects. On the other hand, food price subsidies, utilized to correct income distribution, have
been most effective in urban areas; they have seldom
benefited landless rural laborers and poor peasants
who are usually not reached by the subsidized marketing
system.

The possibility of negative distributional effects
resulting from continuing devaluations has presumably
been an economic policy argument against neutralizing
the effect of internal inflation on the real exchange
rate (relative to the dollar).[2] The overvalued curren-

---

[1] The World Bank (1981) also points out the frequent neglect of
agriculture (p. 89), and the problem of achieving fundamental
structural changes - particularly in agriculture - before oil
reserves have been exhausted (p. 88).

[2] Singh (1981, pp. 143-145) for instance, argues that a scenario
of continuing devaluations is infeasible, due to 'real wage re-
sistance', i.e. the ability of trade unions to resist the reductions in real wages which in the short run normally accompany a
devaluation.

cy has provoked large increases in imports, often
higher than the growth in exports - even after the
oil-price boom of 1974.[1] It has also had an adverse
effect on nonfuel exports. Some oil-exporting countries have since experienced trade deficits.[2]

The crisis in the agricultural economy has aggravated
employment problems. Low incomes and decreasing employment opportunities in the countryside, plus the illu-
sion of a share in the oil bonanza, have resulted in
high rates of rural-urban migration. The growth in
urban employment has not sufficed to absorb rural mi-
grants; open and disguised unemployment have increased.

The oil boom has also been paralleled by a 'state boom'.
Public revenues and spending have increased, also in
relation to national income. The expenditure pattern
of the government has become a decisive factor in influencing the pattern of development.

Since 1976, oil production and exports have been rapidly increasing in Mexico. Traditionally an agricultural
exporter, Mexico is becoming an 'oil-exporting country'.[3]

---

[1] The real exchange rate relative to the dollar (the nominal
rate adjusted for the country's rate of inflation relative to
that in the US) appreciated between 1972 and 1977 - for example,
in Nigeria (50 percent), Indonesia (70 percent), Gabon (40 percent) and Ecuador (25 percent) (World Bank, 1981, p. 89). In developed oil-(and gas-)exporting countries, 'de-industrialization' is thought to be the result of this process, the so-called
'Dutch disease' (see Kaldor, 1981, and other contributions to
the same work; for an analysis within standard international
trade theory, see Corden and Neary, 1982).

[2] Argelia and Venezuela in 1977-78, Nigeria in 1978 (IMF, 1981).
Payments deficits were more frequent.

[3] Oil exports were 400 million barrels in 1981, about two-thirds
of total exports (see Table 2.2). According to the classification of the International Monetary Fund, 'oil-exporting countries'
are those where oil exports amount to more than two-thirds of
total exports, and more than 100 million barrels a year as an
average of the last three years (see e.g. IMF, 1981, p. 8).

Some of the typical symptoms of the oil-led pattern
of growth are appearing in the Mexican economy.

In the remainder of this chapter, we discuss the origins of the present oil boom and survey some of the
main problems of the Mexican economy. The alternatives
which we think are open to Mexican economic development are presented in the next chapter. In later
chapters, these alternatives are specified, quantified
and assessed.

2. The 1976 Crisis and the Oil Boom in Mexico

In 1976,Mexico - a country long characterized by high
and steady economic growth and political stability -
underwent a severe economic crisis. The general production level stagnated and production capacities were
largely underutilized. The most critical symptoms of
the crisis, however, appeared in the external sector
of the economy. In 1975 the deficit of external
(current account) payments reached 3.7 billion dollars,
4.7 percent of GNP.[1] The external public debt reached
20 billion dollars in 1976, five times the amount in
1970. This was the lowest point of a rapid and constant
deterioration of the external trade deficit during the
1970s. Such accelerated deterioration marked the increasing difficulties inherent in the pattern of capital accumulation followed by the country since the
Second World War, the so-called import-substitution
development strategy.

Until the mid-1970s import-substitution growth had
succeeded in producing high GNP growth rates (7-8 percent over the period 1950-70). It consisted of promoting

---

[1] When not specified, the source of the figures quoted in this
chapter is Banco de México (Mexico, 1969, 1980a and 1981).

industrialization by means of protective policies - the
main one being a system of import licenses for almost
all industrial products.

Although effective in increasing industrial output (by
about 8 percent yearly in 1950-70), import-substitution did not succeed in substituting imports of industrial goods. A study on the causes of the 1976
crisis, made by CIDE (1980), shows how the industrial
trade deficit, as a percentage of manufacturing output,
was more or less constant during 1961-1975 (Table 2.1).[1]

Table 2.1: Sources of finance for the industrial trade
deficit, 1961-1975 (as a percentage of the
industrial deficit)

	1961-65	1966-70	1971	1972	1973	1974	1975
Industrial deficit (in % of manu- facturing output)[a]	12	11	10	10	11	11	13
Agricultural surplus[b]	49	38	29	29	19	3	2
Services surplus[c]	43	36	42	40	48	43	29
Oil surplus[d]	1	0	-3	-4	-9	-8	3
Foreign indebtedness	7	26	32	35	42	62	66
	100	100	100	100	100	100	100

a) The industrial deficit is comprised of exports of
manufacturing and minerals and imports of nonagricul-
tural consumer goods, intermediate and capital goods;
b) trade balance in agriculture, livestock, forestry
and fisheries; c) comprises tourism, border transactions, value added by in-bond industries, transport
and other services; d) comprises net exports of oil
and petro-chemical products.

Source: Official sources in CIDE (1980, p. 178).

---

[1] The industrial trade deficit tripled between 1965 and 1975,
from 1.2 to 3.9 billion dollars. The implied growth rate is
11.8 percent.

Quite typically, the import-substitution process concentrated on the consumption goods-producing industries,
while the intermediate goods and capital goods industries lagged behind.[1] Moreover, in the consumption
goods industries, industrial development was led by
wholly new lines of production, mainly consumer durables. Extremely unequal income distribution fostered
rapid growth in these new sectors, while inhibiting
that of the 'old' industries. The high import content
of the new production lines counterbalanced the effects
of the import-substitution process in the old consumer
industries on the industrial trade deficit (CIDE, 1980,
p. 178).

The agricultural trade balance, on the other hand,
underwent accelerated deterioration. As shown in
Table 2.1, the agricultural trade surplus, which
financed almost half of the industrial trade deficit
in 1961-1965, had almost disappeared as a source of
finance for this deficit. As shown below, this evolution is explained by long-run agricultural stagnation and growth of internal consumption - at about the
same rate as population growth.

As a result of the widening trade gap, foreign borrowing began to play an increasing role, as shown in
Table 2.1. The increase in the external debt in turn
provoked a heavy burden in terms of interests paid
abroad (50 percent of the deficit on current account
in 1974-77).

By 1975-1976 the import-substitution strategy was
nearing exhaustion. Additional factors, particularly
the acceleration of inflation and some political in-

---

[1] In 1975, the ratios of imports to total supply in consumption,
intermediate and capital goods industries were 4.2, 20.0 and
34.2 percent, respectively (CIDE, 1980, p. 179).

stability, combined with massive speculation against
the peso, precipitated the 1976 crisis. The remedy
applied to the crisis was a stabilization policy package
with the usual ingredients (devaluation of the peso,
wage restraint, reduction of the government deficit,
reduction of industrial protectionism, control of the
money supply, limits on the growth of the external debt)
agreed on with the International Monetary Fund in order
to re-establish confidence in the financial solidity of
the country.[1]

The stabilization policy was relatively sucessful in
reducing some of the symptoms of the crisis: the rate
of inflation fell from 30 percent in 1977 to 20 percent in 1978; the deficit on current account was reduced by 50 percent. Output growth also recovered and
began to approach its long-term rate.[2]

A more strategic and structural element was added to
this short-run stabilization policy. Oil appeared to
be a potential source for removing the external payments limits to growth, and in general, all structural
limits to Mexican development. The share of public investment allocated to the (nationalized) oil industry
suddenly grew from about 12 percent in 1970-1976 to
23 percent in 1977; it more than tripled in absolute
(real) terms between 1976 and 1977 and continued to
grow in 1978 and 1979 (44 and 5 percent, respectively).

The oil-intensive investment policy immediately produced some expected results. One highly publicized
result was the huge increase in oil reserves. From
11.2 billion barrels of proved reserves in 1976, they

---

[1] For details on the adoption of the stabilization program, see
e.g. Tello (1979, Ch. 4), or Whitehead (1980).

[2] The annual rate of growth of GNP was 6.4 percent in 1960-1975,
about 1.0 percent in 1975 and 1976 and 7.3 in 1977.

increased to 16.8 billion one year later, 40.2 billion
in 1979 and 60.1 billion in 1980 (Díaz Serrano, 1980;
Pemex, 1981). Gross output growth in the oil sector
accelerated from 6.8 percent annually in 1970-76 -
about the same rate as total output - to 13 percent
in 1977 and a record 17.5 percent in 1980. Oil production (extraction), passed from 910 thousand barrels/day
in 1976 to 1 936 thousand in 1980 (19 percent growth
per year).[1] The 'production platform' of 2 250
thousand barrels/day initially fixed as an objective
for 1982 and later advanced to 1980 was almost ful-
filled in October 1980, with 2 182 barrels/day. Moreover the initial interpretation of the 'oil platform'
as a production ceiling (Mexico, 1979c, p. 39), seemed
to evolve towards that of a production floor, since
the production objective for 1981 is 2 750 thousand
barrels/day.

The traditional resource-conserving Mexican oil policy,
aimed primarily at satisfying internal demand, was thus
abandoned.[2] Oil exports exhibited an explosive growth.
Prior to 1974, exports of oil were almost nonexistent
(see Table 2.2). They grew significantly in 1974-76,
although they were still low. In 1976-81 the growth of
oil exports accelerated quickly; their value multiplied
24 times - a growth rate of 63 percent per year. The
effect was a rapid and deep change in the composition
of exports. Oil accounted for more than two-thirds of
Mexican exports in 1981; during the first half of the
1970s oil export averaged about 3 percent.

[1] The output of the oil sector consists of crude oil and other
products. This explains the differences between the rates of
growth; data on oil extraction from Díaz Serrano (1980) and
Pemex (1981).

[2] In 1968, the oil policy was to 'limit exports and constantly
substitute imports'. Ten years later, the old conservationism
was denounced as 'irrational avarice and technical primitivism'.
(Both quotations from the annual reports of the president of
Pemex, taken from Solís, 1980, p. 64).

Oil thus seems to have superseded agriculture as the
source of financing for Mexican development. Growth no
longer appears constrained by the external sector. The
increasing 'petrolization' of the Mexican economy may
be regarded as a major structural component of the
short-run policy adopted in 1976 as a result of the
crisis.

Table 2.2: Oil exports: volume, value and share of
            total export, 1970-81

Year	Millions of barrels	Millions of dollars	Share of total exports (%)
1970	22.4	40.3	3.1
1971	17.3	34.6	2.5
1972	9.4	25.9	1.5
1973	8.7	35.9	1.7
1974	6.5	133.5	4.7
1975	36.9	468.9	16.4
1976	35.7	560.2	13.1
1977	75.4	1 874.5	24.8
1978	133.9	3 220.7	31.5
1979	194.0	3 764.6	42.8
1980	303.0	9 429.6	61.6
1981	400.8	13 305.3	68.7

Source: Official sources given in Gutiérrez (1979) for
        1970-78; and in Departamento de Planeación
        (1981, 1982) for 1979-81.

The petrolization of the Mexican economy should put an
end to the most serious symptom of the import-substitution growth strategy. There is a risk, however, that
some fundamental problems in the Mexican development,
associated with the past growth pattern, will remain
unsolved. Rural stagnation, income concentration and
unemployment, which have been deteriorating for the
last two decades, could even become aggravated.

3. The Agricultural Crisis

Mexican agricultural development since the consolidation of the land reform in 1935-40 may be clearly divided into two periods. The first period, from 1940 to 1965, was characterized by rapid expansion. During this period, agricultural production grew at a rate of 6 percent per year, about the same as GNP.

The second period, from 1965 to 1979, was a period of stagnation. In 1965-79 the growth rate was one per cent, which implies a yearly decrease of 2 percent in _per capita_ terms.[1] GNP growth continued at the same rate as in the preceding period.

The successful performance of Mexican agriculture in 1940-65 is often attributed to the land reform - starting with the agrarian laws of 1915 - which attained its most radical intensity in 1935-40 during the Cárdenas administration (see e.g. Dovring,1970;Solís,1970,Ch.IV).

As reported by Dovring (1970), the Mexican land reform consisted mainly of distributing large parcels of land to communal institutions called _ejido_. In the _ejido_, the members (and their descendants) have the right to use the land alloted to them, but not to sell it. Although ownership is collective, each _ejidatario_ works his land individually; cooperative production arrangements are infrequent (2 percent of 1.6 million _ejidatarios_ were organized in such cooperatives in 1960). Other forms of cooperation, for credit, procurement of inputs and marketing of output, are more widespread. Individual units in the _ejido_ are quite small, 7 ha on the average, and their distribution is rather even. In addition to the _ejido_ land-tenure system, there is private ownership. Privatly-owned land represented

---

[1] Agricultural product growth was 7 percent in 1980, but it is still difficult to interpret this as a change in the long-run tendency.

67% of the cultivated area. A portion of the smallest
privatly-owned estates (minifundios) are also the
result of the land reform.

The distribution of private estates is very concentrated.
As shown in Table 2.3, 80.9 percent of the estates had
less than 10 ha and represented 16.6 percent of the cultivated private land, while 2 percent of the farmers
- those who had estates of more than 100 ha - owned
40.5 percent of the land.

Table 2.3:   Distribution of cultivated area of private
             estates, 1970

Size	Estates		Area	
(ha)	Number	Percent	Thousands of ha	Percent
Less than 5	567	68.8	954	9.2
5 to 10	100	12.1	767	7.4
10 to 25	80	9.7	1 340	12.9
25 to 50	38	4.6	1 382	13.3
50 to 100	23	2.8	1 735	16.7
100 to 200	11	1.3	1 592	15.3
200 to 400	4	0.5	1 164	11.2
More than 400	2	0.2	1 452	14.0
Total	825	100.0	10 386	100.0

Source: Mexico (1975), quoted by Tello (1979, p. 26).

Uneven distribution of land is one of the features of
the so-called dualism or polarization of the Mexican
agrarian structure. The concentration of all other
resource endowments and output is even more extreme.

In a study based on 1960 census data, Reyes Osorio and
Eckstein (1971) compared the productive performance

and resource endowments of agricultural units, both private and ejidos. The results are summarized in Table 2.4.

The study classified all agricultural units into five different categories, according to their gross output. The first and second categories correspond to estates with output levels which yield net incomes under the subsistence minimum ('undersubsistence' and 'subfamily' estates, respectively). Poor or middle peasants (campesinos) are the tenants of these estates. About 60 percent of them are ejidatarios, the remainder are owners.

The peasant economy is defined by the tenancy of small estates worked without the use of hired labor, at low levels of productivity. Hence, self-consumption is the main destination of the output and production for the market is secondary. In order to supplement their incomes, peasants often migrate temporarily to work as day-laborers in the modern agricultural sector or as nonskilled workers in the cities (see Stavenhagen, 1977, pp. 53-56).

The Mexican peasants are also frequently defined by their ethnicity. As most Latin American peasants, they belong to one of the many indigenous communities or ethnic groups. They have long traditions of communal cooperation, which constituted an important element in the Mexican revolution, and in the establishment of the ejido as the main institution of the land reform (see e.g., Esteva, 1978; Vío Grossi, 1980).

The third category is comprised of the richer peasants (the 'family' units). Hired work and production for the market are usual in this category. It constitutes a transitional productive form between the peasant and the following two groups.

Table 2.4: Distribution of the value of production, production variation and resources by estate size, 1960

Size (Thousands of 1960 pesos)	Ejidatarios (Thousands)	Private (Thousands)	Estates Total (Thousands)	(%)	Output	Output Variation (1950-60)	Cultivated Area	Agricultural Equipment	Irrigated Area	Land/Output Ratio	Equipment/Output Ratio	Irrigation/Output Ratio
Less than 1	670	571	1 241	50.3	4.2	-1.0	13.6	1.3	-	3.2	0.3	-
1 to 5	530	291	821	33.8	17.1	10.0	24.5	6.5	3.9	1.4	0.4	0.2
5 to 25	200	107	307	12.6	24.4	11.0	19.2	17.0	27.0	0.8	0.7	1.1
25 to 100	35	32	67	2.8	22.0	35.0	14.4	31.5	31.5	0.6	1.4	1.4
More than 100	-	12	12	0.5	32.3	45.0	28.3	43.7	37.6	0.9	1.4	1.2
	1 345	1 013	2 448	100.0	100.0	100.0	100.0	100.0	100.0			

Source: Tables 2-4 in Reyes Osorio and Eckstein (1971).

The last two categories include the capitalist type of farms, also called 'modern' or 'commercial'. They represent only 3.3 percent of the total number of estates, but produce more than half of total output.

Table 2.4 shows the marked polarization or dualism of Mexican agriculture. At one extreme, poor peasants, representing half of the total production units, produce only 4 percent of total agricultural output.[1] At the other, 0.5 percent of the farms produce almost one-third of total output.

The dualism is even more marked if the distribution of invested resources is taken into account. Both mechanization and irrigation are very concentrated in the capitalist type of farms.

Table 2.4 also shows that output growth between 1950 and 1960 was explained mainly by production increases in capitalist agriculture (80 percent of the total increase).[2] During this period the effects of the green revolution can be detected by the rapid increase in the returns of the land, which almost came to an end in 1965· (Gómez Oliver, 1978, p. 724). As is well known, large-scale agriculture is especially - or even exclusively - successful in incorporating the innovations of the

---

[1] The relative situation of poor peasants seems to have deteriorated further. According to Gómez Oliver (1978, p. 723), the share produced by poor peasants decreased to 2 percent in 1970. Absolute levels are not shown, but in the increasingly stagnating environment of the 1960s, they have probably also deteriorated. Other categories do not show significant changes.

[2] From 1960 to 1970, virtually the entire increase in output occurred in the largest 5 percent of the parcels, while the smallest 90 percent reported a decline in value of production in real terms (Bergsman, 1980, p. 37). Bergsman's statement is based on 1960 and 1970 agricultural censuses and does not include data on resource endowments. We therefore base our comments on the earlier - but more detailed - study by Reyes Osorio and Eckstein (1971).

green revolution, owing to their capital-intensive character.[1]

Both the ejido and private agriculture can be said to have contributed to the expansion of agricultural output until the mid-1960s, although in different ways. The distribution of land through the ejido system was effective in extending the area under cultivation. The area cultivated by the ejidos increased five times between 1930 and 1960, while privately-owned cultivated land remained almost constant (Dovring, 1970, p. 35). The expansion of cultivated land ceased in 1965 (see Gómez Oliver, 1978, p. 725).

Capitalist agriculture, on the other hand, seems to have been more effective in increasing returns. However, an important part of this success may be attributed to the fact that this sector was almost alone in benefiting from the large public investments in irrigation works and from the credit and agricultural input subsidization policies implemented (Brailovsky, 1981, p. 83). In spite of increased public investment efforts during the 1960s, the commercial sector's output began stagnating by the mid-1960s when produce per hectare seems to have attained an upper limit.[2]

By the mid-1960s then, the process of extensive growth in the peasant sector and technological change in the capitalist segment of Mexican agriculture appears to have reached the point of exhaustion, within the limits of the existent agrarian institutions.

---

[1] Most of these innovations, for example, have irrigation as a necessary complement. See e.g. Griffin (1974, Ch. 3).

[2] Public (real) investment in agriculture more than quadrupled from 1960 to 1970. Its share of total public investment rose from 6.9 to 12.9 percent.

The growing severity of the rural crisis in recent
years has been confirmed by the foreign trade performance of the agricultural sector. Agricultural exports
have stagnated during the 1970s, and their share of
total exports has diminished, especially after 1975, as
oil exports began to expand rapidly. On the other hand,
imports of agricultural products - mainly cereals and
other staple foodstuffs - which were almost nonexistent
in the 1960s, have increased in both absolute and relative terms. In 1980, they represented 10 percent of
total imports. In that year Mexico's agricultural trade
balance was negative for the first time (see Table 2.5).
Agricultural self-sufficiency, a high policy objective
in Mexico, seems to have become more and more difficult
to attain.

Table 2.5:   Total and agricultural exports, imports
             and balance of trade, 1960-1981
             (millions of dollars)

Year	Exports			Imports			Balance of trade	
	Total (1)	Agricul-ture (2)	(2)/ /(1)	Total (3)	Agricul-ture (4)	(4)/ /(3)	Total (5)	Agricul-ture (6)
1960	738.7	352.2	47.8	1 186.4	68.8	5.0	-447.7	294.4
1965	1 113.9	539.6	48.4	. 115.6	5.6	0.4	-445.7	534.0
1970	1 281.3	479.0	37.4	2 326.8	30.3	0.1	-1 045.5	448.7
1975	2 858.6	726.3	25.4	6 580.2	620.8	9.4	-3 721.6	105.5
1976	3 315.8	901.5	27.2	6 029.6	253.2	4.2	-2 713.8	648.3
1977	4 418.4	1 078.4	24.4	5 889.8	511.0	8.7	-1 471.4	567.4
1978	6 217.3	1 159.9	18.7	8 143.7	625.7	7.7	-1 507.3	534.2
1979	8 913.9	1 397.9	15.7	12 097.2	672.7	5.6	-3 183.9	725.2
1980	15 307.5	1 390.7	9.1	18.486.2	2 184.1	11.8	-3 178.7	-793.4
1981	19 379.0	1 329.1	6.9	23 104.4	2 294.5	9.9	-3 725.4	-965.4

Source: Banco de México, in Sección Nacional (1980b).
        For 1980-81, official sources given in Departa-
        mento de Planeación (1982).

Despite this, government attention to the rural problem, as reflected by the amount of public investment funds allocated to agriculture, seems to have declined. Since 1976, the share of public investment directed towards agriculture decreased, while that of the oil sector increased abruptly.

As the crisis deepened and its structural origin became clear, the question of changing agricultural institutions and policies gained in importance. Three types of approaches to agricultural reform can be distinguished. One approach is the so-called 'capitalist way' of agricultural development.[1] According to this approach, modern, capitalist entrepreneurship should take over the exploitation of areas under - supposedly inefficient - cultivation by the peasants. This would require the establishment of unrestricted property rights, i.e. a sort of land counterreform which would relieve the peasants of the communal burdens of the ejido system. Competition would then determine the selection process whereby the more capable farmers would prevail and overall production would increase. At the macro level, a new import-substitution era would be opened, this time for the industrialization of agriculture, allowing for substitution of increasing agricultural imports. The financial source of this new import-substitution process would be the oil sector (Warman, 1979, p. 400).

This approach seems to disregard the fact, pointed out by Warman (1979, pp. 400-402), that capitalist agriculture has operated according to perfectly capitalist (property) rules of the game in more than 60 percent of

---

[1] Representative of the 'capitalist way' is e.g. Yates (1978). Some of his main conclusions and recommendations also appear in Yates (1981).

the cultivated area.[1] It has also benefited almost
exclusively from public investment and subsidized
inputs and credit. In spite of this, stagnation has
prevailed since the mid-1960s. In other words, this
strategy would only serve to legitimatize the existing
agricultural structure and prolong the present situation. It is difficult to conceive how it would imply
any significant change in agricultural performance.

The 'capitalist way' could also produce a negative
impact on agricultural employment. If the production
methods prevalent in modern agriculture were applied
to the peasant, labor-intensive segment of Mexican
agriculture, large unemployment would result.[2] This,
in turn, could cause a further deterioration in income
concentration and poverty, which are prevalent throughout the Mexican economy, particularly in the agricultural sector.

A second approach is the 'peasant model' of rural development, according to which the peasants should be
the beneficiaries of and the agents in a new agricultural expansion which would extend the green revolution
to peasant agriculture.[3] The flow of public resources
should be reoriented from the seemingly saturated
large-scale farming segment towards low capital density, peasant agriculture. The low capital density
areas, which represent about 40 percent of total cul-

---

[1] The area effectively under cultivation by the capitalist sector
is more than the 61.9 percent (corresponding to the total area
cultivated by farms whose production exceeds 5 thousand 1960 pesos)
indicated in Table 2.4, as (illegal) land rent is quite frequent
among ejidatarios (Múgica Vélez, 1979, p. 407). Thus, a limited
spontaneous 'land counterreform' is already under way.
[2] Reyes Osorio and Eckstein (1971, p. 30) estimate that more than
3 million people in agriculture would become unemployed. A more
recent estimate by Warman (1979, p. 402) is 6.5 million, about
9 percent of the total population.
[3] Representative of the peasant way are e.g. Esteva (1978),
Reyes Osorio and Eckstein (1971), and Warman (1979).

tivated land, have not benefited to any large extent
from public investment and agricultural programs.
Peasant agriculture is much more efficient in the use
of scarce capital resources (cf. the equipment and
irrigation output ratios in Table 2.4).[1] Consequently,
much lower capital output ratios - i.e. much more effective output response to investment - may be expected.
A strategy which effectively shifted the focus of agricultural development policy from modern to peasant
agriculture would increase efficiency both statically
- better use of given resources - and dynamically -
increased growth capacity.

But the peasant model of rural development is a difficult way, as its supporters admit. It is not easy to
see to it that public incentives and support reach the
peasants, submerged as they often are by a chain of in-
termediaries-usurers (caciques) and corrupted officials
(Warman, 1979, p. 403; Esteva, 1978, p. 704). Without
supplementary measures, a mere shift in the orientation
of the flow of public investment and other support instruments might run the risk of neglecting to ensure
that these resources do not dissipate on their way to
the peasants.

In an attempt to overcome this limitation of the peasant
model, a third approach to agricultural change places
the problem of the peasant economy within a broader
framework. The MFS (Mexican Food System, Sistema Ali-

---

[1] Efficiency in land use, however, is lower (see Table 2.4). In
the more recent and statistically elaborated - but less comprehensive - study by Nguyen and Martínez Zaldívar (1979) based on
the 1970 Census, an indicator of overall efficiency is compared,
i.e. the ratio of monetary yield to total expenditure (average
return per peso spent on farm inputs). Ejido farms - which are
all peasant farms according to our classification - are clearly
superior to private farms of more than 5 ha (p. 628). The study
does not include private farms of less than 5 ha. Its results
are therefore not directly applicable to our discussion.

mentario Mexicano) is an exponent of this type of approach.[1] It is a large research program, which involves a great number of universities and research centers, as well as public institutions concerned with the food issue, aimed at the detailed design of a policy package oriented towards increasing the consumption levels of staple foods and the level of self-sufficiency in the supply of these goods.

According to MFS documents, the food consumption of about 50 percent of the Mexican population fails to meet minimum nutritional standards (2 750 calories and 80 grams of protein per day). This is the MFS' 'target population'. About 70 percent of the target population lives in rural peasant areas, the remainder in the cities.

The MFS shares the view of the peasant approach in that the peasant sector is regarded as having the greatest potential productive response, and that the focus of government support should be shifted to it. Increased resources should be allocated to the priority areas and target population groups. In addition, economic and institutional policies are conceived for all levels of the economic process (production-distribution-consumption) in order to increase the incomes and productive capacity of the peasants and other low-income groups.[2]

Thus, according to the MFS strategy, the problem of reducing malnutrition, poverty and income concentration on the one hand, and the problem of increasing agricul-

---

[1] See Sección Nacional (1980a); for an English summary see Anonymous (1981); also, Montes de Oca and Rello (1982).

[2] It is conceivable to dissociate the aspect of augmenting output in the peasant sector from the aspect of increasing peasant incomes, e.g. by taxation of additional incomes. But it should be recalled that most peasant farms yield incomes under the subsistence level, i.e. far below the minimum taxable income level. It should also be kept in mind that literacy rates are very low among the peasants, i.e. conventional forms of direct taxation would be very difficult to implement.

tural efficiency on the other, are one and the same.
That is, a policy intended to increase agricultural
output growth has to reduce the concentration of income;
a policy which aims at redistributing incomes has to
solve the crisis of the peasant economy.[1]

4. Income Distribution and Fiscal Policy

By international standards, Mexico's income distribution is more unequal than 'normal'. Income concentration, for instance, is higher than that 'predicted'
according to Mexico's per capita GNP, when the hypothetical relationship between income concentration and
economic development - the Kuznets (1955) U-shaped
curve - is taken into account.[2]

The international comparison score is also low if
the income share of the poorest 20 percent of households is considered. Among the 21 less-developed
countries with income distribution data recorded by the
World Bank (1981, Table 25), Mexico is the fourth from
the bottom. Similarly, the ratio of the share of the
highest 20 percent to the lowest 20 percent is higher
than in most other countries.

Income distribution data has been compiled in Mexico
since 1950, from population censuses (1950, 1970) and
family income surveys (1958, 1963, 1968, 1975 and 1977).
Some selected distributional indicators for those years
are presented in Table 2.6. These data show that, al-

---

[1] The MFS' policies are described in Chapter 6, Section 3, where
they are assumed to be implemented as a part of some of the simulated development strategies.

[2] On the basis of a cross section for 1971, Lydall (1977), reported
in van Ginneken (1980, p. 20), calculated the level of GNP per
capita at which income inequality is likely to diminish. The
maximum concentration is reached when GNP per capita at 1971
prices is $ 243, while Mexico's figure was $ 684, and income inequality should be decreasing. As shown later on, this was not
the case. Bergsman (1980, p. 17) made similar findings, with a
somewhat different data base.

though per capita incomes have been growing at a relatively high rate from 1950 to 1977 (by 2.5 percent
per year), the overall pattern of income distribution,
as indicated by the Gini-index, has not changed significantly, if the questionable figures for 1975 are dis-
regarded.[1]

Table 2.6: Selected income distribution indicators,
1950-1977

Indicator	1950	1958	1963	1968	1970	1975	1977	Annual growth rate (1950-77)
Percent of Disposable Household Income Received by:								
Lowest 10 percent	2.4	2.3	1.7	1.2	1.4	0.3	1.1	-2.7
Lowest 20 percent	5.6	5.5	3.7	3.4	3.8	1.7	3.3	-1.9
Lowest 40 percent	13.0	14.6	10.5	10.7	11.8	7.8	10.9	-0.6
41-80 percent	35.0	41.6	38.3	38.5	40.4	38.1	41.6	6.4
Top 20 percent	59.4	52.9	58.0	58.1	55.8	60.2	55.1	-2.8
Ratio Top 20 percent to Lowest 20 percent	10.6	9.6	15.7	17.1	14.7	35.4	16.7	
Gini-index[a]	0.516	0.450	0.527	0.526	0.496	0.570	0.496	

a) The Gini coefficient of inequality varies between
0 (equal distribution) and 1 (total concentration);
see Chapter 4, Section 11, eq. (82).

Source: Own calculations based on official sources in
Kalifa (1976) and Hernández Laos and Córdoba
Chávez (1979).

The relative standard of the poorest 20 percent of the
families, however, seems to have deteriorated. The
share of the poorest 10 percent of the families shows

[1] According to Bergsman (1980, p. 17), the 1975 survey was of
somewhat lower quality and reflects short-run effects of the
1975 crisis (drop in agricultural production, high inflation).

a more clear-cut decline, from 2.4 percent of total
income in 1950 to 1.1 percent in 1977.

The deterioration of the income share of the poorest
categories has widened the gap between high and low-
income families, as reflected by the ratio of the share
of the highest 20 percent to the lowest 20 percent of
families. The share of the middle-income families shows
a certain increase, while that of the high-income families does not exhibit any clear trend.

Table 2.6 may also provide a rough picture of the evolution of real incomes by income levels during the
period 1950-1970. Real incomes of the poorest 10 percent of the families do not seem to have changed during
the period, thus indicating long-term stagnation for
the very poor, as per capita GNP grew at 2.6 percent
per year, i.e. at about the same rate at which the
income share has decreased. The real incomes of the
poorest 20 percent of the families, on the other hand,
show a slight annual improvement of 0.7 percent. Middle-
income families benefited the most, by 9 percent per
year. It is more difficult to assess the case of the
highest 20 percent, due to the erratic nature of the
variations in the income share of this category.[1]

Bergsman (1980) analyzed Mexican poverty on the basis
of the 1975 family income survey, where the 'poor'
are defined as those households with incomes of less
than half the national mean. According to this definition, 45 percent, or 4.6 million families were poor
in 1975. Bergsman (1980, p. 20) found that the core
of Mexican poverty lies in rural areas. The largest

_____

[1] If e.g. 1958 were taken as the starting year instead of 1950,
the (1958-1977) growth rate of the top 20 percent share would be
2.1 percent, indicating an annual increase of 4.7 percent in the
real incomes of the richest category. The 1950-77 rate shown in
Table 2.6 indicated more or less constant real incomes.

number of poor families - 52 percent - was occupied
in the agricultural sector, 33 percent were small
peasants (ejidatarios and small proprietors) and 18.5
percent were landless day-workers. Our own estimations
for 1975, based on 1970 Census and 1977 household income survey data, show that small peasants receive
incomes of about one-third of the national average,
and landless rural workers earn less than a quarter
of the mean income.[1] These two groups amount to about
3.3 million families, representing 95 percent of the
rural population, and 28 percent of all families in
Mexico (see Table D.1.10 in the Appendix).

Another important group of Mexican poor is found in
urban areas, particularly in the service sectors.
Around 20 percent of the poor families earn incomes
from the service sectors, both as self-employed and
salaried employees. Manufacturing and construction
occupy 14 percent of the heads of the households
(Bergsman, 1980, p. 21). These urban poor are sometimes called the 'underemployed' or the 'marginal
population', occupied in the 'informal' or 'traditional'
sectors of the urban economy. According to our estimations, the average income of this group is 60 percent
of the national mean, and represents 26 percent of the
total employed population, i.e., 3.2 million families.[2]

Income concentration and poverty in the urban areas
seem to be related to concentration and dualism in
the productive structure, as is the case for agriculture. In the manufacturing sector, for instance, almost

---

[1] The method of estimation is described in Chapter 5, Section 3.
The results are presented in Table D.1.12 in the Appendix.

[2] The urban poor group thus defined is then somewhat larger than
that of the 1975 survey (incomes less than half of the national
mean).

two-thirds of the output is produced by the 1 percent
of the establishments which are the largest, as shown
in Table 2.7. Only 6 percent of the total value of
production may be attributed to the 92 percent of the
establishments which are the smallest. The earnings of
persons occupied in this last type of establishment
- presumably both salaried employees and self-employed -
are approximately one-third of the average earnings in
manufacturing (20.9 thousand 1970 pesos). Although
there is no corresponding information for the service
sectors, the structure is possibly more concentrated
there, as 'informal' production is typically widespread
in tertiary activities.

As concluded with respect to the agricultural sector,
it seems that a great deal can be done to diminish
income inequality and increase employment by promoting
the development of small-scale activities. If fixed
assets are accepted as indicative of capital endowments,
Table 2.7 shows that the efficiency of capital is about
the same for all types of establishments, while the
capital/labor ratio is much lower in the smaller establishments (cf. the fixed assets output ratios and values of fixed assets per occupied person). This suggests
inefficiency in resource allocation in manufacturing,
and that it may be diminished by reorienting investment. Of course, the cost of increased employment by
promoting investment in small-scale activities would
be a reduction in labor productivity (value added per
occupied person), although not a reduction in capital
productivity. But this would not be a problem when
there is extensive unemployment (as shown in the next
section).

Let us now look at the main features of Mexican fiscal
policy to see how it has influenced income distribution in the recent past.

Table 2.7: Distribution of establishments, labor force, fixed assets and value of production; value added and earnings per worker by type of establishment in manufacturing, 1970

Type of establishment (by value of 1970 production in thousands of pesos)	Number of establish-ments (percent)	Occupied persons (percent)	Fixed assets (percent)	Value of production (percent)	Value added per occupied person (thousands of 1970 pesos)	Earnings per occupied person (thousands of 1970 pesos)	Fixed assets/ output ratio	Fixed assets per occupied person (millions of pesos)
0 to 1 500	91.9	24.7	5.2	5.9	15.3	7.5	0.4	13.4
1 500 to 10 000	5.3	20.2	11.3	12.1	35.0	17.1	0.4	35.7
10 000 to 35 000	1.8	19.7	16.5	19.0	49.9	22.3	0.4	53.6
35 000 to 150 000	.8	22.7	33.8	29.7	69.2	28.1	0.5	95.1
More than 150 000	.2	12.7	33.2	33.3	123.9	39.3	0.5	166.6

Source: Calculated from IX Censo Industrial, 1971, in Tello (1979, p. 22).

Kaldor (1964, p. 265) has pointed out the major def-
fects of the Mexican tax system. They are, first, that
tax revenues are insufficient to meet the needs of a
community which is undergoing rapid growth, both economic and demographic. Tax revenues as a percentage of
GNP in Mexico are among the lowest in the world. The
second reason is political. The increasing economic inequality among the different classes, combined with
the regressive character of the present tax system,
threatens the prospects of peaceful social evolution.

According to Kaldor, the effective tax rate on high
incomes appears to be very low, due to both legislative
measures and administrative defects. The only exception are taxes on high salaries. The system is unjust
because it favors income from capital in relation to
income from labor, due to a multitude of omissions and
exceptions without parallel in countries with social
and economic objectives similar to those of Mexico.[1]

Although some reforms were introduced into the tax
system in 1965 and 1973, Kaldor's diagnosis still seems
to be valid. The ratio of government revenue to GNP is
still 'abnormally' low.

According to Aceituno (1980, p. 166), the fiscal revenues GNP ratio in 1976 was one-third less than what
is 'normal', given Mexico's level of economic development.[2] Also, the direct tax structure seems to

---

[1] The basic problem of the income tax system is that revenues from
different sources are not consolidated; tax rates on labor incomes
are progressive, while taxes levied on interest and dividends are
a fixed percentage. Moreover, it is impossible to ascertain capital gains, as the tenure of securities and stocks is anonymous
(see e.g. Solís, 1977, Chapters I and III).

[2] The Mexican ratio was 11.3 percent, while the 'normal' ratio
according to Mexico's per capita GNP would be 17.1 percent. The
regression was based on a sample of 20 countries in 1976.

favor capital in relation to labor since 1960 (Aceituno, 1980, pp. 167-170). And, as noted above, the
size distribution of income remained more or less unchanged, in spite of the reforms.

Since 1975, however, there has been a tendency towards
an increase in the public revenues GNP ratio, mainly
due to the rapid increase in oil revenues, which rose
from 1 percent of GNP on the average in 1970/74, to
3.5 percent in 1978 (Aceituno, 1980, Cuadro 1). The
expansion of oil production thus also seems to have
served as a means for strengthening the state economy,
without solving the cronic weaknesses of the tax system
(see Solís, 1980, Ch. IV).

The official reason for this reluctancy towards tax
reform has been the aim of not impairing savings and
capital formation by the private sector (Ortiz Mena,
1966, p. 49).

On the expenditure side, similar reasons have made the
promotion of private investment a principal policy
objective ever since the 1960s. Current expenditures
were restricted, and public investment was a major
part - around 45 percent - of the overall investment
effort. More than half of government investments were
made in infrastructure, while only 6 percent went to
social welfare sectors (education, health, dwellings,
etc.). One-third was destined for input (energy and
steel) production by public enterprises, which was
often sold at subsidized prices (Ortiz Mena, 1970,
quoted by Barkin, 1971, pp. 191-2).

5. The Employment Problem

Open unemployment is high in Mexico; in 1977-78 it
amounted to 7-8 percent of the economically active
population (Mexico, 1979d., p. 18). More recent official
estimates of open unemployment are not available. Our
employment estimates (see Table D. 1.9 in the Appendix),
however, suggest a slight decrease, since the rate of
increase in employment in 1975-80 (4.2 percent) was
higher than the rate of increase in the working population (3.3 percent).

But high, open unemployment reflects only a small part
of the overall employment problem. Unemployment in-
surance is practically nonexistent in Mexico. The
labor slack is revealed less in terms of open unemployment than in: 1) declining earnings of the low-income
classes, 2) falling labor-force participation rates, i.e.
decreasing shares of the economically active in the total
population, 3) increased underemployment, 4) increased
rural migration to the cities (urban informal sector),
and 5) increased migration to the United States (see
Reynolds, 1979).

The relative - and presumably absolute - deterioration
in the incomes of the poorest people in Mexico has already been commented on.

The labor participation rate in Mexico fell from 32.1
to 27.4 percent between 1950 and 1970.

The underemployment problem is extensive, and has also
grown worse. The visible variety of underemployment is
particularly widespread in rural areas.[1] The average

---

[1] A distinction is usually made between visible and invisible underemployment. The former refers to an involuntary reduction in
labor time under the normal level. This also applies to part-
time work and seasonal unemployment. Invisible underemployment
(also called 'disguised unemployment') implies occupation at very
low productivity levels (see e.g., ILO, 1966).

number of days worked in agriculture in 1960 was very
low: 40 days per year for the peasant owners who farmed
less than 5 ha, 186 days for the ejidatarios and 100
days for landless workers. In 1950 the number of days
worked by agricultural laborers was 194. The situation
for the peasants did not change noticeably between
1950 and 1960 (CIA, 1974, p. 368). Comparable figures
are not available for 1970, but other estimates suggest
that the 1970 average was even lower than that of
1960.[1]

Invisible underemployment signifies occupation at very
low income levels. In other words, invisible underemployment and poverty are synonymous. As we have seen, 45 percent of all Mexican families were under the poverty
line in 1975, 52 percent of these in agriculture - mostly small peasants and landless workers - and the remainder in the informal urban sector. Although there
are no comparable data for previous years, the figures
in Table 2.6 suggest that absolute poverty, or invisible underemployment, has been alleviated. The real
incomes of the poorest 40 percent increased in 1950-77,
as their share of total income diminished at a lower
rate than per capita GNP increased (2.6 percent).
The seemingly unchanged poverty of the poorest 10
percent still remains.

Needless to say, visible and invisible underemployment
largely intersect, especially in agriculture among
small peasants and seasonally unemployed landless
workers. In the informal urban sector, visible underemployment is possibly less extensive, and is included
in urban poverty.

---

[1] Hewitt de Alcántara (1976, p. 133) estimates that 84 percent
of the landless workers worked less than half of the number of
days available in 1970.

Widespread unemployment and underemployment in the
rural areas have contributed to high migration rates
to the cities and the United States.

The share of the Mexican population living in urban
areas increased from 51 to 67 percent between 1960 and
1980; the average annual growth rate of the urban
population was 4.5 percent during the same period,
while the total population growth rate was 3.3 percent
(World Bank, 1981, Table 20). This implies that about
10 million people have migrated from rural to urban
areas between 1960 and 1980.

There are presently about four million Mexicans (one-
fifth of the Mexican labor force) working in the United
States during some part of the year and the number was
growing by about 900 000 a year in 1975, as against
600 000 in 1970 (Reynolds, 1979, Table 1).

The decline in the capacity of the Mexican economy to
create employment has been associated with the polarized
pattern of development. In agriculture, the concentration of growth in large-scale, capital-intensive production since the 1960s has provoked a fall in the
rate of increase in the demand for labor. The economically active and remunerated population in agriculture increased by 1.3 percent in the 1950s, and 0.4
percent in the 1960s (Altimir, 1974, p. 81).[1] The
output elasticity of employment fell from 0.3 to 0.1.

In industry, similar factors determined a fall in the
output elasticity of employment from 0.6 in the 1950s
to 0.5 in the 1960s. However, employment and output

[1] Using a somewhat different approach (labor requirements coefficients), Rendón (1976) estimated that the demand for labor in
agriculture grew 3.1 percent a year during 1940-1960. For 1960-
1973, the annual labor-requirement growth rate fell to 1.4 percent.

continued to increase at a high rate, 3.0 and 6.3 percent, respectively, in the 1950s, 4.7 and 8.9 in the
1960s (Altimir, 1974, p. 81).

Altimir's results for the overall economy indicate that
during 1950-1960, the rate of growth in the labor supply
increased more or less at the same rate as the employed
population (2.7-2.8 percent). The 1960s, on the other
hand, have been characterized by a lower rate of increase in employment (2.3 percent) and a higher rate
of increase in the supply of labor (2.6 percent), resulting in higher unemployment and lower participation
rates.

Although a similar analysis cannot be performed for
the 1970s, as the 1980 population census figures are
not yet available, the high open unemployment and
emigration rates in the mid-1970s may suggest that unemployment and underemployment are still inherent
features of the Mexican pattern of development.

CHAPTER 3. DEVELOPMENT ALTERNATIVES AND STRATEGIES

1. Development Alternatives

Mexico's development problems were discussed in Chapter 2. As we have seen, in recent years, and as a result of the 1976 crisis, an oil-intensive pattern of economic development has been adhered to. Since 1976, public investment in Mexico - which constitutes a substantial part (an average of about 45 percent) of total investment - has been concentrated in the oil-producing sector, while the share allocated to agriculture and other basic goods-producing sectors has stagnated or diminished. Oil production and exports grew at increasing rates, while food production stagnated. Oil exports, which were almost nonexistent in the first half of the 1970s reached two-thirds of total exports in 1981. Imports of agricultural products rose rapidly, while agricultural exports stagnated. Agricultural foreign trade, the traditional external financing source of Mexican industrialization, showed a deficit for the first time in 1980.

Agricultural stagnation has not implied any improvement for the low-income groups in the countryside, i.e. landless workers and poor peasants. Nor has urban poverty been alleviated. In spite of high GNP growth rates since the 1950s, income concentration remained more or less constant, at a high level.

The distributive effects of the tax system have been regressive, and the tax revenues GNP ratio has been low by international standards.

The symptoms of employment problems in Mexico have been

underemployment and emigration rather than open unemployment, which is high, however. Open unemployment
has presumably diminished slightly in recent years,
but underemployment has possibly worsened.

In the presence of large and rapidly increasing oil
reserves, the expansion of oil production and exports
may be regarded as an appealing strategy, aimed at
solving Mexico's development problems. Oil exports
could contribute to removing the external payments
constraint on sustained growth, and even to super-
seding the agricultural sector as the financial source
for continued (import-substituting) industrialization.
'Petrolization' would present the additional advantage
of increased government revenues and hence, the possibility of strengthening the public sector and its capacity for undertaking more active development policies.
Moreover, the growth of industrial employment could
compensate urban population growth and emigration
from the countryside.

However, as the experience of some oil-exporting
countries has shown (see Chapter 2, Section 1), a
growth strategy based on oil production could leave
unsolved, or even aggravate, some of the above-mentioned
problems. A unilateral, oil-intensive growth pattern,
which concentrated public resources in the oil sector
while neglecting agriculture and other essential goods-
producing sectors, may prolong the present agricultural
stagnation. Increases in demand for foodstuffs resulting
from growing incomes would tend to be met by growing
imports.

This 'scenario' assumes that the growth in food demand
has not been reduced by price increases, or through increases in taxes on foodstuffs. Price increases may
result, e.g., from restrictions in import capacity or

the transport system. Food price increases could
trigger an inflationary process (Sunkel, 1960;
Chichilnisky and Taylor, 1980). Inflation may result
in increased income concentration.[1]

Oil-intensive development is, of course, not the only
conceivable development strategy. The Industrial
Development Plan 1979-82 (Mexico, 1979d) and the
Global Plan 1980-82 (Mexico 1980b) set a ceiling on
oil production and aim at a diversified and balanced
production and export structure. Improvement of income
distribution and an increase in the supply of essential goods and services are high policy objectives of
the Global Plan. However, these policies do not seem
to have been explicitly taken into account in the
macroeconomic projections of the Plan.

A new strategy of development, aimed at a basic change
in the past pattern of growth, might also be conceived.
It would differ in that social groups excluded from
the past pattern of development by unemployment and poverty would be incorporated in it. The new development
strategy would redistribute incomes in favor of the
low-income classes, located mainly - but not exlusively -
in rural areas. Institutional reforms in agriculture
and an increase in the amount of public resources
channelled into the agricultural sector, particularly
into the peasant segment, would result in income re-

---

[1] Kalecki (1970), originally published in 1963, is apparently the
first study of the relationships existing between income distribution and sectoral growth in economic development. For a closed
economy, the rate of overall growth is limited by the rate of increase in the production of necessities, if negative redistribution
is excluded. Therefore, the key to 'financing' a more rapid growth
under such conditions is the removal of obstacles to the expansion
of agriculture. When the import capacity is not a constraint (e.g.
in the oil-producing countries), the attainable growth rate is
higher; however, beyond a certain point, overall growth is im-
paired by the decreasing capacity to import investment goods.

distribution and increased agricultural efficiency.
The share of public investment funds directed towards
agriculture and other sectors which produce essential
goods and services would thus be increased, at the
expense of the share of the oil sector. Public investment in agriculture would also be reoriented, shifting
it from commercial, large-scale farming to small-scale,
peasant agriculture. The rate of direct taxes and tax
progressivity would be raised so as to promote equity
in distribution and the revenues of the public sector.

2. Aims of the Study

It follows from the above description of development
alternatives that two aspects which characterize a
development strategy are of particular importance, i.e.
the sectoral composition of output - in particular,
the share of oil, or essential goods - and the composition of demand associated with different income
distributions.

For the purposes of this study, a development strategy
is therefore defined as the combination of a public
investment policy and an income distribution policy.

A public investment policy is defined by the shares of
the public investment fund allocated (over time) to
the different sectors.[1] Public investment is traditionally an important policy instrument in Mexico,
owing to both its level and its scope, as it reaches
all sectors of economic activity. It is therefore an
effective instrument for influencing the composition
of output.

---

[1] A public investment policy could also include different types
of selective incentives to private investment, or long-run policies of a more qualitative character (e.g. technological policies). But we retain the restricted sense of the text. This and
all of the other concepts used in our analysis are formally
(mathematically) defined in the next chapter.

The structure of income distribution influences the
composition of demand with respect to commodities,
institutions (households, firms, government), and
final uses (consumption, investment). It is assumed
that different policy instruments (e.g. taxes and subsidies) can be used to influence income distribution
in a desired way. Hence, an <u>income distribution policy</u>
is given by the shares of disposable incomes accruing
in each period to the different income classes and
the public sector. Income classes are defined by level
of income and by position in the social structure, i.e.
income classes are also social classes, or socio-
economic groups. Thus, income distribution policy also
reflects the social context of the development strategy.

Different development strategies will produce different
effects over time. The desirability of a development
strategy will depend on its implications (over time)
for the state of the economy, as reflected by certain
relevant indicators or state variables.

As stated above, different development strategies will
lead to different patterns of sectoral supply and demand. In the context of a small open economy, this in
turn implies different patterns of sectoral trade. For
instance, oil-intensive investment policies will tend
to produce, for given sectoral patterns of domestic
demand, higher levels of oil exports. Conversely, for
given sectoral patterns of domestic supply, egalitarian
income distribution policies will imply higher demand
for staple-foods and will tend to produce higher levels
of imports of agricultural goods. In general, sectoral
foreign trade will reflect the combined effects of the
development strategy on both sectoral supplies and
demands.

Now, increased agricultural self-sufficiency is a high

economic policy objective in Mexico (see e.g. Mexico,
1980b, pp. 154-155). The level of oil exports, or the
degree of 'petrolization' associated with the strategy,
is another important indicator. Oil production and
exports are to be maintained within certain limits
(p. 149). That is, in the Mexican context, the foreign
trade performance of these sectors is an important indicator of the state of the economy. Hence, sectoral
trade is a relevant state variable, which has to be
represented in a model of the Mexican economy.

Different development strategies, implying different
output patterns, will generally produce varying levels
(and composition) of employment, if there are sectoral
differences in the relative use of labor. Un- and
underemployment are extensive in Mexico. Increased
employment is a high-priority objective of development
policy, both internationally (see e.g. ILO 1973, 1978a),
and in Mexico (Mexico, 1979d, 1980b). Employment is
included as a state variable in our analysis.

'Welfare' is a concept intended to summarize the overall state of the economy. The most widely used indicator of welfare is real national income, which we
include. National income, however, is a very rough
measure, since it disregards the distribution of incomes. Therefore, other measures of welfare have to
be added, which take both the level of national income
and its distribution into account.

Our study is aimed at quantifying the possible impli-
'cations for the Mexican economy - over the period
1980-1990 - of different development strategies. The
concept of development strategy, as defined here,
refers to a combination of different public investment
and income distribution policies, specified over time,
within the planning horizon. We propose to estimate

the effects of different development strategies on:

a)   sectoral trade, in particular imports of agricul-
     tural goods and exports of oil;

b)   the level and composition of employment; and

c)   the level of economic welfare.

Three types of development strategies are simulated.
First, four alternative interpretations of the strategy
of the Global Plan (Mexico, 1980b) are simulated. The
Global Plan is aimed at changing the pattern of development towards increased satisfaction of the basic needs
of the population, with limited petrolization. The public investment policy of the Global Plan is combined
with two different interpretations of income distribution policy, which has not, however, been explicitly
stated in the Plan. Also, two different hypotheses are
made about the future performance of the agricultural
sector. Unchanged or duplicated response to investment
reflects failure or success in introducing far-reaching
MFS reforms in agriculture.[1]

Second, a 'status-quo-plus-oil' strategy is simulated,
aimed at representing oil-intensive development. As in
recent years, public investment is concentrated in the
oil sector; agriculture and other basic goods-producing
sectors are neglected. No equity- and efficiency-
increasing reforms are introduced in agriculture.
Agricultural investment retains its present low level
of effectiveness. There no attempt to change income
distribution, which is reflected by unchanged income
shares.

Third, a more fundamental change in the development
pattern is assumed. A 'new development strategy' is

---

[1] The MFS (Mexican Food System) program is described in Chapter
6, Section 3.

simulated, in which public investment is shifted from
the oil-producing sector to agriculture and other
basic goods-producing sectors. The MFS reforms are introduced in agriculture, thereby increasing the effectiveness of agricultural investment. Concomitantly,
there are changes in income distribution which considerably reduce concentration. This strategy implies
incorporation into the development process of social
groups which have not benefited from the past pattern
of growth.

To summarize, our aim is to explore how the Mexican
economy is influenced by alternative development strategies which imply different public investment and income
distribution policies over time with respect to:
a) sectoral trade, b) the level and composition of
employment, and c) welfare (the level and distribution
of income). Three types of strategies are simulated
for the period 1980-1990: the Mexican Global Plan,
'status-quo-plus-oil', and a 'new development strategy'.

3. Theoretical Background

Our study of strategical alternatives is carried out
by means of a multisectoral, dynamic input-output type
model, in which income distribution, public investment
and sectoral foreign trade are given specific treatment. The model is constructed within the consistency
framework of a social accounting matrix (SAM).

The static model of Leontief (see Leontief, 1951, Part
IV) is the first mathematically elaborated and most
widely known work in input-output theory. It is based
on the hypothesis of fixed proportional relationships
in production between inputs and outputs. Given certain
exogenous sectoral final demands, it allows for the
determination of consistent sectoral gross outputs.
In its original form, the model does not consider the

generation of incomes in production, nor their distribution.

Leontief's (1953) dynamic model determines different
paths of equi-proportional and sectorally-balanced
growth, i.e. where sectoral gross outputs equal sectoral intermediate and final demands. Consistency between savings from incomes generated in production and
investment, and between consumption demands and supplies
is not considered.

Lange (1957) is apparently the first formal input-
output analysis of the relationships between 'vertical'
equilibrium (i.e. among intermediate inputs and value
added) and 'horizontal' equilibrium (i.e. among sectoral
supplies and demands) through the functions which link
incomes with consumption and savings/investment. Lange
thus introduced the Keynesian consumption function into
the disaggregated input-output framework.

Lange's multisectoral analysis, however, does not treat
the links between income distribution and the composition of final demand. Kalecki (1954, Ch. 5) and Kaldor
(1956) have extended the Keynesian framework to include
income distribution between two income classes ('workers'
and 'capitalists'), although maintaining a single aggregated production sector.

Miyasawa and Masegi (1963) incorporated the process of
income distribution and expenditure into the input-
output static system, thereby obtaining a generalized
and disaggregated Keynesian (Kaleckian) multiplier
(see also Miyasawa, 1976, Ch. 1).

Pyatt et al. (1973) is to our knowledge the first empirical study where a static Leontief model, including
explicit treatment of income distribution and utiliza-

tion, is estimated in order to analyze potential effects
of redistribution policies (for a summary, see Clark,
1975, pp. 138-147). The approach to model building
adopted in Pyatt et al. starts with a presentation of
the variables and consistency relationships within the
economy's social accounting matrix at some base date,
as in the tradition of the Cambridge Growth Project
(see Cambridge, Department of Applied Economics,
1962-74).

Paukert, Maton and Skolka (1976) is the first of a
series of case studies by the World Employment Programme
of the International Labour Organization, where a model
similar to that of Pyatt et al. is used. The aim of
these studies is to determine the effects of exogenous
income redistribution on employment, the balance of
payments and the rate of savings.

4. Method and Scope

In accordance with the latter three input-output models
of income distribution, this study includes a ('closed-
loop') specification of income generation, distribution and utilization. The approach differs in that it
is dynamic, in the sense that the investment and growth
processes are included in the model of the economy.
The consistency framework of the SAM, within which the
model is constructed, is thus enlarged so as to include
dynamically relevant aspects, i.e. sectoral investments
and their composition by sector of origin. Savings generated in the economy are invested through two channels:
by the private sector, where they are allocated according to an endogenous (accelerator-type) mechanism and
by the government, which allocates the public saving/
investment fund among sectors according to certain
proportions, which define a public investment policy.

The dynamic core of the model resembles a Leontief dynamic model, in which the allocation of a share of investment - public investment - is not endogenously determined, but is a policy variable. A further difference is that the rate of savings and the level and composition of consumption are explicitly dependent on income distribution, which is the other policy variable. Our model also differs from the Leontief dynamic model in that it includes (exogenously determined) foreign saving flows of planned or foreseen balance-of-payments imbalances.

Another differential feature of the approach lies in the treatment of sectoral foreign trade. Whereas standard input-output theory states the equality of sectoral supplies and demands, the model developed in this study is similar to recent 'temporary general equilibrium' models (see e.g. Grandmont, 1977) in that it allows for sectoral 'disequilibria'. A small open economy is assumed, where (temporarily fixed) world prices prevail. Sectoral excess demands are then assumed to be internationally traded.

Thus, the model adds some further assumptions to those which are conventional in input-output analysis. The usual limitations of this theory, which include the rigidity of fixed proportions in all behavioral relationships, the absence of a treatment of the monetary economy, the hypotheses of fixed prices, uniform gestation lags,constant utilization of production capacities, etc., have to be augmented by some new restrictions.

Some assumptions in our model are especially strong. For instance, the assumption of an efficient relative (fixed) price structure does not, of course, exactly reflect reality. There are distortions in relative prices - e.g. a low domestic oil price - and several

import restrictions and export subsidies. Also, some
of the sectors of the Mexican economy produce non-
tradeables.

Another type of limitation is due to exclusion of
important elements of the problem from our representation of the economic system. The fact that the model
does not include monetary variables precludes incorporation of the inflationary effects of oil-intensive
development, the possibility of endogenous negative redistribution, and payments deficits due to currency
overvaluation.

Further restrictions are those inherent in the statistical estimation of the model. As is typically the
case in less-developed countries, the statistical base
is weak in Mexico. Estimation methods have their own
additional limitations.

The above limitations imply that the results of the
model simulations should be interpreted as indicating
the probable direction and intensity of the effects
of different planned changes in the structure of the
economy, or policy scenarios. They are, at best, conditional forecasts, but they should not be taken as
exact predictions. These projections become less and
less accurate over time. However, the validity of the
model - which turned out to be rather high - and the
accuracy of the projections might be improved by adopting the approach of permanently updated and revised,
flexible (rolling) plans, thus explicitly taking into
consideration the existence of uncertainty and the
possibility of learning (see Chapter 4, Section 12).

5. <u>Models of the Mexican Economy</u>

The history of economy-wide models in Mexico is relatively short; the first attempts date from the 1970s.
But this history is rich in the sense that several
large models have been constructed which describe the
Mexican economy in great detail. The type of questions
that these models were aimed at investigating varied
a great deal. The type of theoretical approach adopted
in their construction also differed. Let us briefly
review them, in order to set the model developed in
this study in relation to these earlier models.

The first attempt was very ambitious. It was a multi-
period, multilevel, multisector planning model for
1968-1989 (Goreux and Manne, 1973). The levels are:
1) multisector (15 sectors), 2) sectoral, including only two sectors, energy and agriculture, and
3) local, including two projects.

The multisector model in this study (DINAMICO) is a
linear programming model, which maximizes consumption
in a gradualistic way. Employment is specified in
detail, including different skill categories and up-
grading (educational) activities. The specification
of income flows is very simple and does not include
income distribution. Only a few macroeconomic variables
are considered. The sectoral and project models are
also very detailed linear programming models. There
is some interaction between the three levels.

PREALC (1975), see also Vossenaar (1977), is one of
the studies made in the context of ILO's World Employment Program. It supplements the above-mentioned Pyatt
model by a representation of the ('formal-informal')
technological dualism in the Mexican economy. The
effects of exogenous changes in the technological
composition of sectoral output ('technological poli-

cies') on income distribution and employment are
determined, along with the effects of income redistribution.[1]

A multisectoral dynamic model was used in the preparation of the Mexican Industrial Development Plan 1979-82
(Mexico, 1979c). It is one of the latest members of a
family of dynamic models developed within the Cambridge
Growth Project and combines an aggregate time-series
econometric model with an input-output model (Barker
et al., 1980). The published results indicate a very
detailed structure, which covers most relevant macroeconomic variables, but not income distribution. The
studies related to the elaboration of the Industrial
Plan started with the construction of a SAM for 1975
(Mexico, 1978a).

There is also a Mexican version of the Wharton model.[2]
An important feature in the Mexican context is that
the exchange rate has been made endogenous. While the
influence of income distribution on macroeconomic activity was a subject of study in an initial stage, the
present version of the Wharton model does not seem to
have a specification of income distribution.

---

[1] Cline's (1972) model is a major attempt to measure the potential
effects of income redistribution on economic growth in several
Latin American countries, including Mexico. It focuses on the
effects on average savings and potential growth, and on intermediate import requirements. Stewart (1978) improved Cline's
method, by using sectoral incremental capital output ratios,
instead of an average. There is, however, no general macroeconomic consistency framework; partial models are used. Although
an important antecedent, Cline's model is not strictly an economy-
wide model.

[2] The Wharton model is a macroeconometric model, based on the
Keynesian theory of income determination and supplemented by
wage-price adjustment equations. It is used for short-run forecasting and policy simulation analysis. See, for example, Evans
and Klein (1968). The Mexican version is based on Beltrán del
Río (1973).

A macroeconometric model was used to establish the targets of the Global Development Plan 1980-1982 (Mexico
1980b, Anexo 2). It shares many features with the
Wharton model. Its aim was to model the behavior of
economic aggregates. However, it includes an input-
output block, in which the final demands obtained from
the macroeconometric model are disaggregated, after
which consistent sectoral outputs are determined, as
described by Preston (1975). As in the static Leontief
model, inconsistency may arise between total investment, determined by a macroeconometric function, and
the sectoral investments implied by the sectoral outputs already obtained. That is, there is no sectoral
specification of investment and production growth. The
policy variables are the standard macro-policy instruments (government expenditure, discount rate, reserve
ratio, tax rate). Oil export is an exogenous variable.
There is no specification of income distribution.

In the framework of the World Employment Programme,
van Ginneken (1980) studied the effects of income redistribution among socio-economic groups. He incorporated technologically different subsectors within the
main sectors. He used a static linear-programming framework to simulate different class alliances - by maxi-
mizing incomes accruing to the groups which form the
coalition. The estimation of a complete consistency
framework (SAM) was outside the scope of this work.

The model developed in our study is a multisectoral,
dynamic input-output type model. It is constructed
within the consistency framework of a SAM. Sectoral
investments and income distribution are specified in
detail. The sectoral destination of public investment

and the distribution of incomes among socio-economic
groups are the policy variables. The model is used to
simulate some relevant development strategies.
Special treatment is given to foreign trade, in order
to determine the effects of the strategies on sectoral
trade.

The closest Mexican structural antecedent of our model
is the static input-output model of income distribution
and technological policies by PREALC (1975). Our study
enlarges this type of framework by adding a representation of the (sectoral) investment and growth process,
within the accounting system of a SAM. It differs
from the 'equilibrium' structure of standard input-
output models, in that it allows for sectoral excess
demands. Another difference is that the sectoral allocation of public investment is singled out as an important policy instrument in the Mexican context for
influencing the output structure.

Our model is also related to the industrial model of
Mexico (Mexico, 1979c), a Cambridge-type, multisectoral
dynamic model (Barker et al., 1980). The Cambridge model is
an income-expenditure model with investment endogenous
and includes an input-output framework for the explanation of interindustry flows. It is a 'disequilibrium'
model in the sense that several elements of demand
(e.g. consumers' expenditure or stockbuilding) may be
out of balance. The model is not intended to represent
income distribution in detail.

In Chapter 6, Section 2, the results of the basic projection of our study are compared with the 'basic trajectory' of the industrial model of Mexico and the
Wharton Mexican model forecasts. In Section 3 of the
same chapter, our Global Plan simulation is compared
with the projections of the Global Plan model.

CHAPTER 4. THE MODEL

1. Social-accounting Matrices: A Consistency Framework for Model Building

The use of a social-accounting framework in the construction of economic models ensures a consistency check of any system of macroeconomic relationships. It also allows for systematic exposition and explanations. Social accounting has a long history in both statistical and theoretical approaches. A widely-used result of this evolution is the United Nations (1968) System of National Accounts that encompasses most of the theory and practice in the field.

A simple scheme for a basic social-accounting matrix (SAM) is illustrated in Table 4.1.

The structure of the table is such that i) for every row there is a corresponding column, ii) row and column totals are equal, and iii) row entries are receipts and columns entries are expenditures.

Column 1, for instance, depicts how production activities acquire inputs, either domestically produced (intersection with row 1), or imported (row 5). The remaining production costs appear as value added paid to the factors of production, in the form of wages, profits, and rents (row 2).

Row 3 provides interesting information for income distribution analysis or policy. It shows the incomes received by the different institutions which supply factors of production. Factor incomes are mapped into

Table 4.1: A basic social-accounting matrix*

Receipts / Expenditures	Production accounts		Institutional accounts		Rest of the world	Total
	Production activities 1	Factors of production 2	Current 3	Capital 4	5	6
Production accounts						
1 Production	Interindustry transactions	0	Consumption expenditures	Investment expenditures	Exports	Aggregate demand = gross outputs
2 Factors of production	Value added	0	0	0	Net factor income received from abroad	Incomes of the factors of production
Institutional accounts						
3 Current	0	Allocation of factorial incomes to institutions	Current domestic transfers	0	Net non-factor income from abroad	Incomes of domestic institutions after foreign transfers
4 Capital	0	0	Savings	Capital domestic transfers (flow of funds)	Net capital received from abroad	Aggregate savings
5 Rest of the world	Imports of intermediate goods	0	Imports of consumer goods	Imports of capital goods	0	Imports
6 Total	Total costs = gross output	Incomes of the factors of production	Incomes of domestic institutions after foreign transfers	Aggregate investment	Total foreign exchange receipts	

* Adapted from Tables 3.1 and 3.6, Pyatt and Roe (1977).

the different institutions. Institutions are usually
divided into three categories: households, companies,
and the government. The further disaggregation of institutions - households in particular - is of crucial
importance in the analysis of income distribution and
redistribution policies. Households are usually sub-
divided into income categories, that is, quantiles in
the size distribution of incomes. This information is
required in order to determine measures of the degree
of inequality in the size distribution of income. However, it might be insufficient for redistribution policy analysis, and possibly for taxation policy, where
some differentiation may exist between income classes
and regions.

Additional differentiation may be permitted by the
rural/urban dichotomy. This takes into account differences in policy instruments and measures available
for redistribution purposes in rural and urban areas.
By means of sociological insight into the conditions
in the country, some approach to the concept of 'social
class' could be adopted. This refers to sections of
the population which not only have homogeneous relationships in production and distribution, but also
culturally and politically. Such an extension allows
for the inclusion of an important dimension of the
socio-economic dynamics of development.

Although defined outside the framework of social-
accounting matrices and planning or simulation models,
the concept of 'target group' (Bell and Duloy, 1974)
is a related idea. It refers to homogeneous social
groups with a homogeneous response to policy instruments. 'Socio-economic group' and 'income class' are
other related concepts.

The cost of the additional wealth of insight permitted
by this type of classification is close to zero; the
usual sources for the size distribution of income are
income and demand surveys which already contain the information needed for further disaggregation of the
household sector.

The differences in the behavior of locally-owned and
foreign-owned (transnational) companies and small-scale
('informal') and medium and large-scale firms are often
discussed in underdeveloped countries and in the development literature. They could add a very interesting
aspect to the company's institutional sector of the
SAM framework, from which they are still absent.[1] This
limitation of the SAM is maintained in this study.

Analysis of the effects of investment is an important
objective of growth and development theory. It is also
one of the principal instruments for designing the development strategies generated in the context of this
study. The SAM includes entries for investment expenditure by sector of origin, or producing sectors (row
1, column 4). However, in a dynamic framework, knowledge about the destination of investment and its impact on production is also necessary. This aspect
should be included in the SAM structure, in the form
of an interindustry capital goods transactions matrix
of the same dimensions as for intermediate goods (row
1, column 1), where investment originated in each
sector is distributed among the sectors of destination.

In spite of the comprehensiveness of the SAM representation of the economic system, its monetary character

---

[1] The differentiation between scales of production has been included in a simulation model (PREALC, 1975), although in a conventional input-output context (row and column 1 in Table 4.1).

precludes information in physical terms. Employment-
unemployment statistics cannot be introduced into Table
4.1 and have to be presented in an additional table.[1]
Classifications which distinguish between production
sectors and income classes would be consistent with the
structure of the SAM.

Let us once again present the SAM table, with some notational additions, but without the elements omitted
from this study due to scarcity of information in the
Mexican case or lack of relevance to the aim of this
study.

The entries in Table 4.2 now appear as a letter representing transactions. The structure is simplified considerably, with one exception. Transactions in investment goods are disaggregated as suggested above in
terms of a distinction between origin and destination
of investment. Some of the blocks in Table 4.1 have
been eliminated.

Let us compare both tables, row by row, and explain
the notations.

Row 1 in Table 4.1 appears in Table 4.2 without omissions. The corresponding rows in Table 4.2 are the
first n rows, reflecting the sectoral classification
of production accounts. They depict the commodity balance between sectoral supplies and demands.

On the demand side, intermediate demands (x_{ij}) are

---

[1] If the table were given in (homogeneous) labor-time units, then
the column totals in row 2, column 1 ('value added') would represent total labor employed in the different production sectors. Even though it has been theoretically shown to be a good
aggregation device (Morishima, 1973, Ch. 8), the labor theory
of value has not been used to any large extent for accounting
and empirical purposes.

Table 4.2: Framework of accounts in the simplified SAM of the model*

Note: entries shown as ⟨ ⟩ are circled in the original (exports q_i and imports m_i).

EXPENDITURES	Sectors 1	2	⋯	n	Households 1	2	⋯	k	Govt.	Exports	Σ	Savings Private 1	2	⋯	n	Government 1	2	⋯	n	Foreign	Σ
Sectors 1	$x_{1,1}$	$x_{1,2}$	$\cdots$	$x_{1,n}$	$c_{1,1}^p$	$c_{1,2}^p$	$\cdots$	$c_{1,k}^p$	c_1^g	⟨q_1⟩	c_1	$f_{1,1}^p$	$f_{1,2}^p$	$\cdots$	$f_{1,n}^p$	$f_{1,1}^g$	$f_{1,2}^g$	$\cdots$	$f_{1,n}^g$	b_1	x_1
2	$x_{2,1}$	$x_{2,2}$	$\cdots$	$x_{2,n}$	$c_{2,1}^p$	$c_{2,2}^p$	$\cdots$	$c_{2,k}^p$	c_2^g	⟨q_2⟩	c_2	$f_{2,1}^p$	$f_{2,2}^p$	$\cdots$	$f_{2,n}^p$	$f_{2,1}^g$	$f_{2,2}^g$	$\cdots$	$f_{2,n}^g$	b_2	x_2
⋯	$\cdots$	$\cdots$	$\ddots$	$\cdots$	$\cdots$	$\cdots$	$\ddots$	$\cdots$	$\cdots$	$\cdots$	$\cdots$	$\cdots$	$\cdots$	$\ddots$	$\cdots$	$\cdots$	$\cdots$	$\ddots$	$\cdots$	$\cdots$	$\cdots$
n	$x_{n,1}$	$x_{n,2}$	$\cdots$	$x_{n,n}$	$c_{n,1}^p$	$c_{n,2}^p$	$\cdots$	$c_{n,k}^p$	c_n^g	⟨q_n⟩	c_n	$f_{n,1}^p$	$f_{n,2}^p$	$\cdots$	$f_{n,n}^p$	$f_{n,1}^g$	$f_{n,2}^g$	$\cdots$	$f_{n,n}^g$	b_n	x_n
House-holds 1	$y_{1,1}^p$	$y_{1,2}^p$	$\cdots$	$y_{1,n}^p$																	y_1^p
2	$y_{2,1}^p$	$y_{2,2}^p$	$\cdots$	$y_{2,n}^p$																	y_2^p
⋯	$\cdots$	$\cdots$	$\ddots$	$\cdots$																	$\cdots$
k	$y_{k,1}^p$	$y_{k,2}^p$	$\cdots$	$y_{k,n}^p$																	y_k^p
Government	y_1^g	y_2^g	$\cdots$	y_n^g																	y^g
Σ	x_1	x_2	$\cdots$	x_n	y_1^p	y_2^p	$\cdots$	y_k^p	y^g	φ	GNP	d_1^p	d_2^p	$\cdots$	d_n^p	d_1^g	d_2^g	$\cdots$	d_n^g	Σb_i	
Imports	⟨m_1⟩	⟨m_2⟩	$\cdots$	⟨m_n⟩							Σm_i										Σm
Savings Private					s_1^p	s_2^p	$\cdots$	s_k^p			Σs^p	$a\varphi$				$(1-a)\varphi$					s^{p*}
Govt.									s^g		s^g	$-a\varphi$				$-(1-a)\varphi$					s^{g*}
Foreign																					
Σ	x_1	x_2	$\cdots$	x_n	y_1^p	y_2^p	$\cdots$	y_k^p	y^g	φ	GNP	d_1^p	d_2^p	$\cdots$	d_n^p	d_1^g	d_2^g	$\cdots$	d_n^g	Σb_i	

* Adapted from Table 1, Clark (1975), in turn based on Table II.1, Pyatt et al. (1973).

listed first, followed by private consumption demands
(c_{ij}^p), disaggregated among k socio-economic groups,
government demands for consumption goods and services
(c_i^g), and export demands (q_i).

Investment demands - private (f_{ij}^p) and public (f_{ij}^g) -
are disaggregated by sector of destination. The element
f_{ij}^p represents expenditures in investment goods originating in sector i destined to (invested in) sector
j. Thus, row sums in this submatrix are total private
investments originating in sector i, and column sums
are total investments destined to sector j.

Sectoral trade balances appear in the next column. When
positive, they represent net exports, adding to internal demand. When negative, they represent net imports,
adding to internal supply. Then, sectoral exports -
and imports - should not be added, but taken as zero
in order to avoid double accounting. These variables
are encircled in Table 4.2. (Foreign trade is dealt
with in more detail in Section 8 of this chapter.)

Some simplifications are now introduced. Rows 2 and 3
of Table 4.1 are consolidated in Table 4.2. The specification of income distribution in the model is quite
simple and does not take into account differences in
the factoral sources of incomes among household categories. Such distinctions entail high statistical requirements and are outside the scope of our study. This
simplification implies, of course, a rather rough
approximation of the process of income generation and
accordingly, that tax policy analysis will be approximative.

In Table 4.2 then, as in Pyatt et al.(1973), sectoral
value added is 'paid' directly to households.

Hence, the y_{ij}^p denote the disposable income (net of direct taxes) received by the i'th income class in the j'th activity sector. The y_{ij}^p include factor incomes paid to households by the government. The y_j^g denote the part of government receipts not allotted to the payment of wages, interest and rents - that is, the part devoted to investment and public consumption of goods and services.

The fact that the simplified SAM of the model in this study excludes income transfers between institutions and international income flows is reflected by the absence of transactions in the remaining blocks of the households accounts.

The last three rows in Table 4.2 show the savings accounts. External savings (φ) - or the foreign trade deficit - are distributed between private and public investment in proportion to their share of total internal savings (a and (1-a) in the table). This assumption about the investment behavior of external savings is made in order to simplify the model structure. It is based on the hypothesis of proportionality between savings and external indebtedness capacity by institution.

The flow of capital funds between institutions (row 4, column 4 in Table 4.1) has been omitted from Table 4.2 because our model does not contain a financial sector.

The main components of the model are shown in Table 4.2. The following sections are devoted to a description of the functions through which these elements are interrelated. Time is introduced. Each variable is defined as a flow during time period t.

In the next section, we introduce a general picture
of the model's structure and main assumptions. The
different blocks of the model are then presented in
the following order: determination of the level and
distribution of incomes (Sections 3-4); consumption
behavior (Section 5); savings and investment (Sections
6-7); foreign trade (Section 8); output determination
and growth (Section 9); level and composition of employment (Section 10); and welfare indicators (Section 11).

A systems-type scheme of the functioning of the model
concludes this chapter (Section 12). It represents a
concise review of the variables and functions of the
entire model.[1]

2. The Economic System: Principal Features and Assump-
tions

We begin by describing the principal characteristics
of our representation of the economic system. As a
graphic and general introduction to the model, the
main assumptions about interrelationships in the economy are presented by means of key diagrams. The general features are elaborated mathematically in subse-
quent sections.

Our representation of the economic system is confined
to the product and labor markets. There is no monetary
or financial subsystem, and no general price level
associated with it. The general price level is assumed
to remain constant, which might be implied by the
hypothesis of a neutral or passive monetary policy.

---

[1]A list of the model's variables and equations is included in
Appendix A.

A relatively small, open economy is assumed, in which exogenous world prices prevail.[1] World prices are assumed to be constant.

As in the case of all other parameters in the model, world prices may also be assumed to be time dependent, i.e. changing over time at some exogenous rate.[2] But there does not seem to exist enough theoretical or empirical evidence so as to support the existence of definite patterns of change.[3]

Economic agents are thus assumed to be price-takers. On the supply side, technological choices and comparative advantages are assumed to have been solved efficiently. On the demand side, choices are assumed to be efficient. This hypothesis may be illustrated by the market situation where there is no rationing and consumers can buy their preferred consumption baskets at given constant prices.

Capital accumulation is the source of growth in the

---

[1] This assumption precludes the possibility of analyzing the distributional implications of changes in relative prices. In the case of Korea, for instance, increases in the agricultural terms of trade have been shown to have a strongly positive distributional impact (Adelman and Robinson, 1978, pp. 191-192). In an open economy, it could be argued whether the gains in equity via increased agricultural prices compensate the losses in efficiency that may result due to departures from world prices. For a cross-country analysis of agricultural price distortions, see Bale and Lutz (1981).

[2] The assumptions about the behavior of the model's coefficients over time are discussed in Chapter 5.

[3] In the case of the oil price, which is particularly relevant to our study, there is support for the thesis of both its increase (at a rate equal to the rate of interest; the Hotelling (1931) rule), and its decrease (in the oligopolistic case, with limit-pricing equilibrium, in which the cartel controlling the resource sets prices so as to keep the substitute 'backstop technology' out of the market (Dasgupta and Heal, 1979, Ch. 11)). The oil price could also follow a cyclical pattern, if discovery followed a Poisson process (Arrow and Chang, 1978). The observed time profile of the oil price in the long run is U-shaped.

system. Expansion of productive capacities in the different sectors allows for production increases. Output in successive periods is linked by investment in the growth process.

Savings are connected with gross output levels via incomes generated in production. Total savings equal total investments. That is, growth is assumed to be free from the cyclical fluctuations which originate in effective demand problems. Figure 4.1 shows the basic (Harrod-Domar) principle of growth in the system.

Figure 4.1

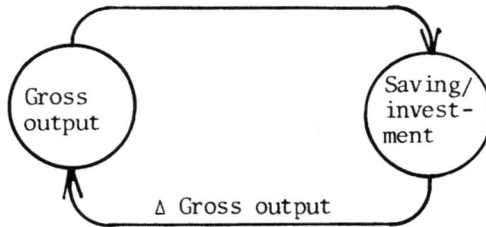

The transformations which link production and saving /investment are shown in more detail in Figure 4.2. The policy functions are represented in the boxes with double lines. In the upper part of Figure 4.2, income distribution parameters represent the share of value added in production accruing as (disposable) income to the different income classes or socio-economic groups and the government in different sectors. The government is assumed to be able to modify these parameters, via taxes and subsidies. Stipulation of a sequence of such proportions within a certain planning horizon constitutes an income distribution policy.

The lower part of the figure contains the parameters
which determine the shares of the available public
saving/investment fund allocated to the different
sectors. A sequence of such parameters constitutes a
public investment policy. A given combination of an
income distribution policy and a public investment
policy constitutes a development strategy.

Savings - private and public - are related to incomes
by known saving propensities, specific to each income
class and the government (the right-hand side of
Figure 4.2). The saving propensity of the public sector could also be assumed to be a policy parameter.
Our constancy assumption is a simplification that may
also reflect a realistic feature of rigidity in the
savings behavior of the government.

Figure 4.2

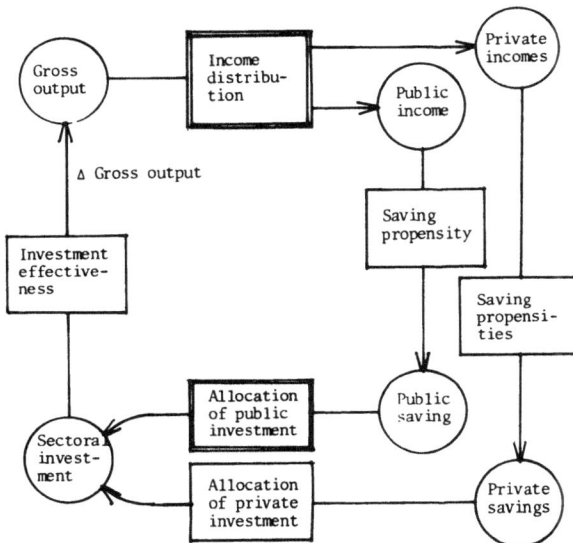

As already noted, public savings are allocated sectorally according to an investment policy. Private
investments, on the other hand, are allocated sectorally by an endogenous mechanism. Sectoral private investment is proportional to past growth in the sector
(the proportionality factor is the sector's capital
output ratio).

The loop is closed by the determination of growth in
gross outputs. Production capacities are increased by
sectoral investment. Additional production capacity,
which are assumed to be always employed at a constant
rate, depend on known capital output ratios.

Let us now expand the core of the system shown in
Figure 4.2 by adding foreign savings and the variables
which reflect the behavior of the economic system under different strategies: the sectoral balance of trade,
the employment level and welfare.

In the lower right-hand corner of Figure 4.3, a hexagon indicates an exogenously determined amount of
foreign savings, which is added proportionally to
private and public savings. The external debt grows
by the addition of foreign savings (or what amounts
to the same thing, the balance-of-payments deficit)
in each period, and by the accumulation of interest
on the debt.

Foreign trade is assumed to be the mechanism which
equilibrates supplies and demands. Imbalances between
internal supplies and demands are absorbed by foreign
trade. The sectoral balance of trade is then assumed
to be equal to sectoral excess demand. That is, when
sectoral demand is in excess of (less than) sectoral
supply, the difference is imported (exported).

Figure 4.3

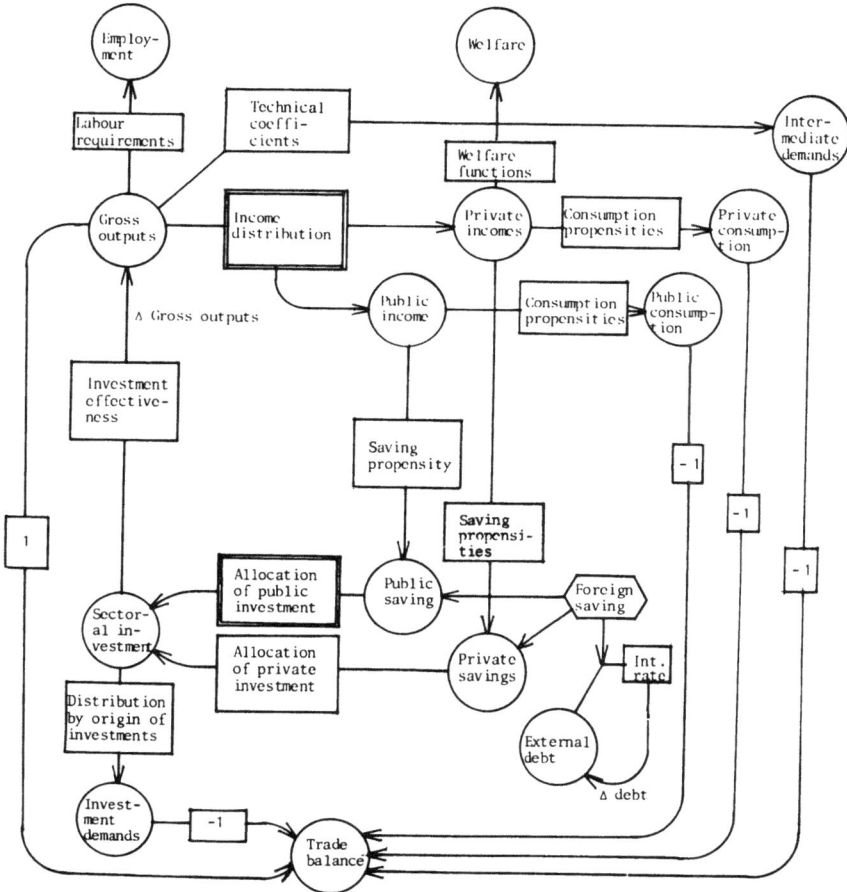

As stated at the outset, prices are assumed to be exogenously given and constant. It also has to be assumed
in relation to this behavior of foreign trade that
all sectors in the economy produce tradeable goods or
services. Then, as shown in the lower part of Figure
4.3, the sectoral balance of trade is the difference
between gross outputs minus sectoral investment demands
(now distributed by sector of origin), consumption
demands (private and public), and intermediate demands.

Employment depends on the level and composition of
output, given known coefficients of sectoral labor requirements per produced unit. This is shown in the
upper left-hand corner of the figure.

Social welfare is a function - which may be assigned
different specifications - of the income levels of the
different income categories. That is, it is a function
of income levels and their distribution.

3. Income Generation and Distribution

The most simple type of multisectoral model is the
open (-loop) Leontief model.[1] The central assumption
in Leontief's input-output framework is that intermediate flows (x_{ij}) are proportional to gross outputs.
That is, there exists a (n × n) matrix $A_t = (a_{ij,t})$

---

[1] The concept of 'open and closed loops', was first introduced
in systems engineering (Allen, 1957, Ch. 9). The distinction is
useful because it avoids the confusion between 'closed' as quali-
fying a model where international trade is not included and
'closed' (closed-loop) in the sense of a model where labor is
treated as a producing sector, or where there is an explicit
connection between incomes generated in production and final
demand. The classical cases of the closed-loop-type of model are
Leontief's 'closed' model and von Neumann's.

of current interindustry inputs required in period t
from sector of origin i per unit of output in sector
j. The time subscript will henceforth be omitted from
the A matrix, in order to simplify the notations.[1]
The basic commodity or material balance relations,
which equate total sectoral supply with all categories
of sectoral demand, can then be written:

$$x_t = A x_t + c_t + f_t + q_t - m_t \qquad (1)$$

where small letters are n-dimensional column vectors
of gross output (x_t), intermediate demands ($A x_t$),
consumption (c_t), investment (f_t), exports (q_t) and
imports (m_t).

If it is assumed that the elements of final demand are
exogenously determined, the gross output consistent
with that vector of final demands, is given by

$$x_t = (I-A)^{-1} (c_t + f_t + q_t - m_t). \qquad (2)$$

In this simple version of the Leontief model, however,
it is not known whether consistency exists between incomes generated in production as factor payments and
final demands. By implication, a consistency check
between sectoral and/or institutional consumption and
investment behavior, and total and sectoral consumption
and investment cannot be carried out.

Eq. (2) expresses only partial, i.e. 'horizontal',
consistency between production and uses in the sense
that it only includes row 1 in Table 4.1. There is no
explicit connection between incomes generated in production - column 1 in the same table - and final demands.

[1] The time subscripts are reintroduced whenever a matrix is explicitly assumed to change over time.

The relationship between income generation and final demand has been recognized for a long time. Keynesian aggregate analysis is a decisive bench mark in the long evolution which began at least as far back as the discussion of 'underconsumption' and 'overproduction'.

A natural extension of Keynesian analysis is the distinction between income classes with different savings-consumption behavior - e.g. capitalists and workers (Kalecki, 1954, Ch. 5; Kaldor, 1956). Miyasawa and Masegi (1963) introduced this approach in the Leontief model (also, Miyasawa, 1976, Ch. 1). They treated consumption demand as an endogenous variable and introduced the Keynesian consumption function on a disaggregated level, with respect to both income classes and production sectors.

Pyatt et al. (1973) is apparently the first empirical study where these ideas are included explicitly at the disaggregated level in a consistency framework of the SAM type.[1] In accordance with these ideas, it is assumed that a known relationship exists between sectoral output and (disposable) incomes accruing to each income class and the government, given by

$$y_t = V\, x_t \qquad\qquad (3)$$

in which y_t is a k+1-dimensional vector of disposable income of the k different socio-economic groups and the government. V is a $(k+1) \times n$ matrix of income distribution parameters, where each element denotes income accruing to class i per unit of output in sector j.

---

[1] Many others, however, have used value added distribution coefficients without a consistency or closed-loop multisectoral framework. (For a review see e.g. Cline, 1975.)

In our study the coefficients in the V matrix are treated as exogenous policy parameters. It is assumed that the government can influence income distribution in a desired way, through taxes, subsidies and other redistribution policies.

It should be noted that the V matrix may change over time, thus including the possibility of different rates of redistribution. In this more general case, income distribution parameters are stipulated over time, as a <u>sequence</u> V_t of income distribution matrices, which includes of course the constant case (maintainance of the existing distribution).

Such a sequence of income distribution matrices constitutes an <u>income distribution policy</u>. An income distribution policy combined with a public investment policy is a <u>development strategy</u>, in the context of this model.

The V matrix can also be seen as a partitioned matrix

$$V = \left[-\frac{V^p}{V^g}- \right] \qquad (4)$$

in which the first k rows form the V^p matrix of coefficients of disposable income accruing to the k different socio-economic classes. The last row V^g characterizes the government's income. Private disposable income by socio-economic class is then:

$$y_t^p = V^p x_t. \qquad (5)$$

We also add a condition for 'vertical' consistency in the model. Production costs have to be totally distributed between costs of intermediate inputs and value added:

$$\iota'A + \iota'V = \iota' \tag{6}$$

where ι' is a summing vector $(1, 1, \ldots, 1)$ of appropriate dimension.

4. Government Income and Fiscal Revenues

The government is assumed to have three sources of revenue: i) direct taxes, ii) indirect taxes, and iii) surplus from exploitation of nationalized enterprises.

Simple proportional functions are assumed for all sources of fiscal revenue, although a more elaborate nonlinear form for direct taxes would, of course, be more appropriate. Indirect taxes are aggregated with the surpluses (or deficits) from exploitation of nationalized enterprises. Among the latter, the profits accruing to the oil-producing sector are particularly relevant.

The total fiscal revenue is then

$$g_t = (V^d + V^i)\, x_t \tag{7}$$

where V^d and V^i are n-dimensional row vectors. V^d is the vector of coefficients of direct taxes, and V^i is the vector of indirect taxes plus surpluses from exploitation of nationalized enterprises.

A given portion χ of total revenue is assumed to be expended in wages and salaries. This part is accounted

for as private income, and is deducted from fiscal
revenues in order to avoid double accounting of incomes. The remainder, the part of fiscal revenues not
allotted to wage payments, is the government's income:

$$y_t^g = (1 - x)\ g_t \tag{8}$$

or, substituting for g_t in eq. (7);

$$y_t^g = (1 - x)(V^d + V^i)\ x_t. \tag{9}$$

If the following equivalence is adopted

$$V^g = (1 - x)(V^d + V^i), \tag{10}$$

then eq. (9) is simplified by substituting this expression to obtain:

$$y_t^g = V^g\ x_t \tag{11}$$

which is the lower part of the partitioned matrix in
eq. (4).

5. Consumption Behavior

As stated above, relative prices are assumed to be
constant throughout the period in which the effects of
alternative development strategies are explored. Markets for consumer goods, however, are assumed to exist.
Consumers are able to buy goods according to their
preferences, which are also stationary. At the given
(constant) relative prices, consumer and all other demands are always met by supply, either domestic or external (as shown later on in Section 7).

Now that consumer choices based on relative prices may

84

be assumed to be solved, disposable income is adopted
as the variable for explaining consumption behavior.

This type of assumption is standard in planning models.
In the simplest versions, Engel elasticities of consumption of particular goods with respect to total consumption are used. Total consumption is usually obtained from Keynesian macrofunctions. (See e.g. Taylor,
1975, Ch. 2.4.)

Models which attempt to trace the effects of income
redistribution in a multisectoral consistency framework, in the tradition begun by Pyatt et al. (1973),
include a disaggregation by income class.

If, instead of constant Engel elasticities, constant
marginal propensities to consume out of disposable income for each income class are assumed, the following
expression describes consumption behavior:

$$c_t = \theta \iota + \Gamma y_t \qquad (12)$$

where c_t denotes the n-dimensional vector of total
consumption expenditures in each good, θ is an
$n \times (k + 1)$ matrix and Γ is an $n \times (k + 1)$ matrix of constant parameters.[1]

In the literature on the linear expenditure system
(Stone, 1954), elements in the θ matrix are often
interpreted as representing basic needs, committed consumption or subsistence quantities of each good for
the different classes.

---

[1] If the ι summing vector in eq. (12) is omitted from the
first term on the r.h.s. and y_t is diagonalized, c_t becomes a
$n \times (k+1)$ matrix of sectoral consumption expenditures by socio-
economic class, thus allowing for the determination of the c_{ij}
in Table 4.2. They are omitted here in order to simplify the
notations.

The coefficients in matrix Γ represent the marginal propensities to consume good i out of disposable income by the j'th income class.[1] The linear system (12) resembles the <u>extended</u> linear expenditure system (Lluch, 1973 ; Lluch et al., 1977) in which the independent variables are disposable incomes. (Expression (12), however, assumes fixed prices, while the linear expenditure system allows for price effects.) In the linear expenditure system, consumption is instead a function of total <u>expenditure</u>, and the coefficients in the corresponding matrix represent marginal budget shares. The difference is then that the extended system allows for simultaneous determination of saving propensities by socio-economic class, or endogenous determination of total consumption expenditure.

Income elasticities for a particular good i and a particular consumer group j are:

$$e_{ij} = \frac{\partial c_{ij}}{\partial y_j} \frac{y_j}{c_{ij}}$$

or, using a linear relationship as in eq. (12) and substituting:

$$e_{ij} = \Gamma_{ij} \frac{y_j}{\theta_{ij} + \Gamma_{ij} y_j}$$

$$(12')$$

$$= \frac{\Gamma_{ij}}{\theta_{ij}/y_j + \Gamma_{ij}}$$

which shows that as income increases, income elasticities tend towards one.

As pointed out by Deaton (1975, pp. 28-29), this pro-

---

[1] $\frac{\partial c_{ij}}{\partial y_j} = \Gamma_{ij}$.

86

perty of the linear expenditure system 'poses difficulties for detailed disaggregation since it has often
been noted in the analysis of specific commodities
that the income elasticity tends to follow a general
pattern which would preclude the relationship [(12')]'.
The general life-cycle pattern of specific goods is
from high to low and even zero or negative income elasticities, as they become more commonplace. For broader
categories of wants, however, the tendency of unitary
elasticity could be accepted.

Private consumption

Using a notation with partitioned matrices as in the
definition of income in eq.(5), matrix Γ of marginal
propensities to consume by socio-economic class may
be written:

$$\Gamma = \left[\Gamma^p \; \vdots \; \Gamma^g \right] \tag{13}$$

where Γ^p is the $(n \times k)$ matrix of marginal coefficients of consumption for k classes of households, and
Γ^g is the $k+1$'th n-vector of marginal consumption
propensities by the government.

Total private consumption is then

$$c_t^p = \theta^p \, \iota + \Gamma^p \, y_t^p \tag{14}$$

where θ^p is an $n \times k$ matrix in the partitioned
$n \times (k+1)$ θ matrix:

$$\theta = \left[\theta^p \; \vdots \; \theta^g \right] \tag{15}$$

or, using eq. (5)

$$c_t^p = \theta^p \, \iota + \Gamma^p \, V^p x_t . \tag{16}$$

Government's consumption of goods and services

Government's income was defined as that part of fiscal revenues not allotted to wage payments which are registered as private income.

Government expenditures in consumption goods are also assumed to be a linear function of income:

$$c_t^g = \theta^g + \Gamma^g \, y_t^g \tag{17}$$

where θ^g is the k+1'th column in the θ matrix, Γ^g is the row defined in eq. (13) and y_t^g is the previously defined scalar of government's income.

Using eq. (11), eq. (17) can also be written

$$c_t^g = \theta^g + \Gamma^g \, V^g \, x_t. \tag{18}$$

Consumption and income distribution

Once income generated in the input-output system has been related to consumption out of income, the consistency framework of eq. (2) can be enlarged. Consumption demands are now endogenous and no longer included in an aggregate vector of final demands. This is a further step towards 'closing' the Leontief system, by augmenting its endogenous elements. In the basic commodity balance of eq. (1), c_t is thus substituted by its function, eq. (12) (for simplicity, the independent term θ is omitted):

$$x_t = A \, x_t + \Gamma \, y_t + f_t + q_t - m_t. \tag{19}$$

This expression is supplemented by the function which determines incomes, eq. (13), to form the system:

$$(I-A) \ x_t = \Gamma \ y_t + f_t + q_t - m_t \tag{20}$$

$$V \ x_t = y_t$$

or, written in partitioned matrices and operating:

$$\begin{bmatrix} x_t \\ ---- \\ y_t \end{bmatrix} = \begin{bmatrix} I-A & \vdots & \Gamma \\ -----+----- \\ -V & \vdots & I \end{bmatrix}^{-1} \begin{bmatrix} (f_t + q_t - m_t) \\ -------------- \\ 0 \end{bmatrix}. \tag{21}$$

This model, a simplified version of Pyatt's (Pyatt et al., 1973), produces output and income vectors that are mutually consistent because they have been calculated in a fully determined system. The closed loop is generated in this specification by an endogenous expenditure system (Γ, in the north-east partitioned matrix) functionally related to income distribution (V, in the lower part of the matrix).

In system (21), investments and foreign trade are exogenously given final demands. Inconsistency could still arise if exogenously determined investments are not consistent with endogenously generated savings. The analysis of consistency between the sectoral output generated by eq. (21), where investment by origin as a part of final demand is exogenously projected, and sectoral output generated by this same investment, but sectorally allocated (by destination), is also outside the scope of the model. This is a typically dynamic problem and one which our model is aimed at solving.

6.   Savings

In order to define savings by income class, let us first write the expression for total consumption <u>by income class</u> (it should be noted that the $n \times 1$ vector c_t defined in eq. (12) represents total <u>sectoral</u> consumption):

$$c_t^* = \theta' \iota + \hat{\iota' \Gamma} \, y_t. \tag{22}$$

This expression is obtained by simple operations (transposition ('), sum (ι) and diagonalization ($\hat{}$)) in eq. (12). Now, c_t^* is a $(k+1) \times 1$ vector and the first term on the r.h.s. is interpreted as total committed or subsistence consumption by income class. The coefficients multiplying incomes in the second term are (total) marginal propensities to consume. This expression is similar to the Keynesian consumption function, although it is disaggregated among income classes. The Keynesian absolute income hypothesis is qualified here in the sense that different (total) consumption functions for different income classes are assumed. The fact that saving rates differ among income classes, which later theories on aggregated consumption have tried to incorporate, is thus allowed for in eq. (22). Keynesian consumption functions have been tested with positive results for Latin American and other underdeveloped countries (Mikesell and Zinser, 1973; Snyder, 1974).

Income can be either consumed or saved. Or, saving is the nonconsumed part of income. Savings by income class are then:

$$s_t = y_t - c_t^* \tag{23}$$

or, substituting:

$$s_t = y_t - \theta'\iota - \iota'\hat{\Gamma}\, y_t$$

$$= -\theta'\iota + (I - \iota'\hat{\Gamma})\, y_t \qquad\qquad (24)$$

where I is the identity matrix. The expression in parenthesis on the r.h.s. of eq. (24) is the (k+1) diagonal matrix of marginal propensities to save by income class.

Private and government savings can easily be derived using the notations with partitioned matrices from equations (5) and (13).

Private savings by income class are then:

$$s_t^p = -\theta^p{}'\iota + (I - \iota'\hat{\Gamma}^p)\, y_t^p. \qquad\qquad (25)$$

Total private (internal) saving is the sum over income classes $\iota's_t^p$.

Public savings are:

$$s_t^g = -\theta^g{}'\iota + (1 - \iota'\Gamma^g)\, y_t^g. \qquad\qquad (26)$$

While the most plausible assumption about private marginal propensities to consume (Γ^p) in eq. (25) is that they are given and fixed, it could be maintained that this should not be the case for the government's propensities $(\Gamma^g$ in eq. (26)). The government's consumption level and pattern could be regarded as policy instruments. In our policy simulation experiments, the coefficients in eq. (26) are fixed. Public saving may change, however, as a result of changes in the coefficients of income accruing to the government (V^g).

Foreign Savings

In the overall balance of an open economy, total domestic savings are increased (diminished) by the balance-of-payments deficit (surplus). External payments
deficits are covered by different forms of external
financing, which contribute to the potential flow of
savings within the economy. The counterpart of external payments deficits is foreign borrowing.

Foreign saving (φ_t) is assumed to be an exogenously
determined share of the national income:

$$\varphi_t = \omega_t \iota' y_t \qquad (27)$$

where ω_t is the rate of foreign saving and $\iota' y_t$ is
national income or gross national product. The rate of
foreign saving is treated in this study as an exogenously given parameter. Another approach might be to
consider it a policy variable, thereby reflecting policies which influence the balance of payments, e.g.
exchange rate policy.

External debt

In each period, the external debt (E_t) is increased
by foreign saving. Foreign indebtedness has a cost,
i.e. interest is paid on the debt at a rate i. The
external debt in the initial period is known:

$$E_{t+1} = E_t (1 + i) + \varphi_t. \qquad (27')$$

It should be noted that if the interest rate effect
is excluded, E_t is (the sum over time of) an exogenously determined variable, and therefore has a rather
artificial character. It may be helpful, however, to
summarize the effects of different time paths of the
external debt on the whole planning period, thus re-

flecting the degree of self-relience or self-determination associated with different strategies.

7. Investment Behavior

Total investment in this model equals total (domestic plus foreign) savings. It is assumed that there are no absorptive capacity constraints on investment, and that all savings available find their way to accumulation in the producing sectors. The ex post identity between savings and investment is also assumed to hold as ex ante equality. The equality between savings and investment is then an equilibrium condition for balanced growth, in the sense that it is free from short-term fluctuations.

The equality between savings and investments also holds for the private and public sectors taken separately. It is assumed that there is no 'crowding out'. Although detailed, official flow-of-funds statistics are unavailable, there is some evidence that this assumption is a rough portrayal of reality (see FitzGerald, 1977, pp. 27-29). The flow of external savings is assumed to be channelled through the private and government sectors; private and public savings are increased by foreign savings in equal proportions. This assumption is necessitated by a lack of information about the distribution of foreign financing between direct investment and loans to the private sector and the government in Mexico.

Investment behavior differs among institutions. No policy instruments are assumed to exist which can directly modify allocational behavior with respect to private investment. The allocation of public investment funds - combined with income distribution - are

singled out as the policy instruments. Private investments are then totally endogenous, while public investments are endogenous in level, but exogenous in
composition.

A dynamic multisectoral framework requires a distinction between origin and destination of investment.
When analyzing the material balance between supplies
and demands, investment demands by origin need to be
specified. Sectoral growth possibilities cannot be
determined unless the allocation of investments among
different sectors is known. Let us now see how these
features are incorporated into the analytical framework.

<u>Private investment by destination</u>

Total savings available for investment by the private
sector are private savings, plus a portion of external
savings which are assumed to be channelled through
the domestic private sector. As information about the
distribution of external savings is not available,
we assume that they are allocated between the private
and public sectors proportionally to their share of
total savings.

That is,

$$s_t^{p*} = \iota's_t^p(1 + u_t) \qquad (28)$$

where s_t^{p*} denotes total private savings and

$$u_t = \frac{\varphi_t}{\iota's_t^p + s_t^g} . \qquad (29)$$

An accelerator-type function describes private sectoral
investment by destination (d_t^p):

$$d_t^p = z_t^p \, s_t^{p*} \tag{30}$$

where

$$z_t^p = \frac{\hat{\alpha}(x_t - x_{t-1})}{\iota' \hat{\alpha}(x_t - x_{t-1})} \tag{31}$$

in which $\hat{\alpha}$ is an $n \times n$ diagonal matrix of known sectoral incremental capital output ratios. As can be seen, z_t^p is a distribution vector $(\iota' z_t^p = 1)$, ensuring equality between private saving and investment $(\iota' d_t^p = s_t^{p*})$. Eq. (31) shows how private investments are distributed according to the acceleration principle. Relatively more investment is directed towards sectors with higher capital output ratios and/or higher output growth.

Eq. (30) is a modified version of the acceleration principle. Here, it determines the distribution of a certain level of investment. In its original form (see e.g. Junankar, 1972, pp. 28-32), investment (in aggregated terms) is given by an expression of the form of eq. (31), where the normalizing term in the denominator does not appear. It means that the level of investments is determined by output growth only, given the capital output ratios. This may be the case when the rate of saving is assumed to remain unchanged.

However, when the investigation focuses on the potential effects of alternative income distributions, the constancy of the saving rate is no longer a valid assumption. For given levels of sectoral output and given saving propensities for different income classes, the overall saving rate is determined by income distribution. If, for example, profit earners have a higher saving propensity than wage earners, then redistribution from the latter towards the former increases the saving rate. The effect of the rate of profit on the

level of investment is then clear. In the context of
the model, the same effect may be obtained by any redistribution from lower to higher saving-propensity
classes. (However, if only progressive redistributions
are considered, the class of redistributions which increase the saving rate is reduced considerably.)

In other words, an accelerator function of the original
type will in general infringe on the equilibrium assumption about the private sector stated above, that is
$\iota' d_t^p = s_t^{p*}$. In the modified version of eq. (30),
equality between total private savings and total private investment is ensured. Available private saving/
investment funds - which can be influenced by the rate
of profit - are then allocated sectorally according to
the acceleration principle. This means that the accelerator proposed here contains features from both accelerator and profit types of investment theory.

Public investment by destination

Total public savings available for government investment are the public savings defined in eq. (26) plus
that part of foreign savings which is assumed to be
channelled through the public sector. That is,

$$s_t^{g*} = s_t^g (1 + u_t).$$
(32)

This means that total investment funds for the government are endogenously generated. It should be recalled
that constant marginal expenditure shares are assumed
for the government, for both consumption in goods and
services, and wage payments. Total government savings
are influenced by V^g, the exogenously given income
coefficients for the government, which are in turn
determined by the sectoral (direct and indirect) tax
rates. Via changes in tax rates, i.e. as a part of income distribution policy, public savings may be modified.

While an endogenous mechanism describes allocational
behavior with respect to private sectoral investment,
the allocation of public investment funds among sectors
is a policy instrument. A public investment policy
is defined by a distribution (n-dimensional) vector,
z^g, which sums up to one. An exogenously given sequence z^g_t of such vectors is a <u>public investment po-
licy</u>. Public investment by sector of destination is
then

$$d^g_t = z^g_t \, s^{g^*}_t . \tag{33}$$

We can now show the equality between total (private
plus government) investment by destination, d_t, and
total (domestic plus foreign) savings. Total investment is by definition:

$$d_t = d^p_t + d^g_t . \tag{34}$$

Adding vertically, and replacing d^p_t and d^g_t by their
expressions in eqs. (30) and (33):

$$\imath' d_t = s^{p^*}_t + s^{g^*}_t \tag{35}$$

and, from eqs. (28), (29) and (32):

$$\imath' d_t = \imath' s^p_t + s^g_t + \varphi_t . \tag{36}$$

Investments by origin

The sectoral allocation of investment is of fundamental
interest in the analysis of the growth effects of redistribution and/or investment policies. The importance
of adding this type of information to the SAM framework
has already been stressed. However, within a consistency context, where the balance between sectoral supply
and demand is stated, investment as a source of (final)

demand for the producing sectors also has to be taken into account. In this way, investment is considered from the point of view of its sectoral origin.

As in the dynamic Leontief model (Leontief, 1953), investment in the different sectors of destination is assumed to have a known composition of goods from the n sectors of origin. The assumption is made that there exists an (n × n) distribution matrix B which in its j'th column denotes the breakdown of the basket of goods demanded for investment by sector j from producing sectors. That is, it denotes the quantities of goods from producing sector i demanded for a unit investment by sector j.

Investment demands by origin (f_t) are then related to demands by destination according to the following relationship:

$$f_t = B \, d_t \tag{37}$$

where

$$\imath'B = \imath' \tag{38}$$

and therefore

$$\imath'f_t = \imath'd_t. \tag{39}$$

Investment demands by origin may be disaggregated by institutional sector:

$$f_t^p = B \, d_t^p \tag{40}$$

and

$$f_t^g = B\ d_t^g \qquad\qquad\qquad (41)$$

with self-evident notations.

The preceding specification of investment demands
serves to (partially) 'endogenize' a further component
of final demand, thereby increasing the degree of
'closedness' of the system. The level of investment
is endogenous, but the government is still able to
stipulate alternative allocations. When specifying
private investment behavior, dynamic and nonlinear relationships, eqs. (30) and (31), have been introduced.
Thus there is no longer any possibility of utilizing
a static framework as in eq. (21). As shown later on,
we do not try to find a general solution of the system. A simulation approach is used instead.

8. Foreign Trade

When studying Mexican development alternatives, sectoral
trade has to be incorporated into the analytical model.
Agricultural self-sufficiency is a high objective of
development policy in Mexico. Restricted petrolization
is also an important policy goal.

Different development strategies - defined as the combination of income distribution and public investment
policies - generally have different implications for
sectoral trade. Strategies which combine more equal (or
even constant) distribution with concentration of public investment in the oil sector, at the expense of
the sectors which produce necessities, may imply stagnation and growing imports of the latter. This type
of strategy also tends to produce accelerated growth
in oil production and exports.

On the other hand, a strategy which gives priority to
income distribution considerations, but imposes restrictions on the structure of the trade balance, e.g. a
certain level, or rate of diminution, of the agricultural trade deficit, implies a defined pattern of
agricultural output resulting from a specific public
investment policy.

These effects of development strategy on sectoral
foreign trade have to be reflected by the analytical
framework. They are explained below.

Excess demands and foreign trade

As has already been commented on, the model is aimed
at depicting an open, relatively small economy. This
feature seems to be a good basis for the hypothesis of
exogenous - and for analytical purposes, fixed - relative prices. It was also assumed that existent allocations were efficient and that they could be expanded
without increasing average costs. This implies, in
particular, that production costs for the n (aggregated) goods being produced are comparable - except
for transport, transaction, and other similar costs -
to world prices. When, for some commodity, internal
supply is in excess (lower than) of internal demand,
there is a tendency for the internal price to fall
(increase) and the excess to be exported (imported).
A simple interpretation of this behavior is that excess
demands are traded:

$$\delta_t = x_t - Ax_t - c_t - f_t - \bar{q}_t + \tilde{m}_t$$

$$\delta_t = (I - A)x_t - c_t - f_t - \bar{q}_t + \tilde{m}_t$$

(42)

where δ_t is the vector of excess demands, with positive (negative) elements denoting net exports (imports). The first four terms on the r.h.s. describe

the balance between domestic production, intermediate and final demands. $\bar{q}_t$ denotes exogenous exports, i.e. exports which take place anyway, regardless of the excess demand in the sector. The reason we include them is that, even when n is very large, for very disaggregated specifications, composite goods still exist. The fact that Mexico could, for example, become a massive importer of corn, should not exclude the possibility of still being an exporter of melon or coffee. Since 'agriculture' is usually treated as an aggregated sector, an exogenously determined amount of exports must be fixed for those commodities which originate principally in the primary sectors and whose special comparative advantages are not accounted for because of aggregation. The last term in eq. (42) represents noncompetitive or complementary imports, i.e. imports of commodities which cannot be produced in the country (see e.g. United Nations, 1970).

The simplest approach to noncompetitive imports is to distribute them among producing sectors according to their destination, treated as a row of inputs. A natural extension is to allow for the determination of imports of intermediate inputs by sector of origin (m_t^a), assuming the following relationship:

$$m_t^a = M \hat{n} x_t \tag{43}$$

where M is a distribution matrix ($\iota'M = \iota'$) which describes the composition of imports of intermediate inputs by sector of origin and $\hat{n}$ is a diagonal matrix of input import coefficients by sector of destination. The transposition $x_t'\hat{n}$ of $\hat{n} x_t$ is then the row of input imports by sector of destination utilized in the first approach.

Among the components of final demand, only investment

demands are treated as having a noncompetitive proportional import content, due to lack of information
about other components. Given content of imported
goods in investment by sector of destination is
assumed. The imported investment goods have a known
composition by sector of origin. Imports of investment
goods by sector of origin are then:

$$f_t^m = N \; \hat{\sigma} \; d_t \qquad\qquad (44)$$

where N is a distribution matrix of imports of investment goods and $\hat{\sigma}$ is a diagonal matrix of import
content coefficients in investment demands by sector
of destination (d_t).

As in the case of exports, aggregation may not allow
for e.g. imports of special qualities of oil in an
oil-exporting country if the oil sector is - as usual -
aggregated. Hence, a nonproportional exogenous noncompetitive imports vector for consumption demands $(\bar{m}_t)$
is also included. Then, total noncompetitive import
demands by sector of origin are:

$$\tilde{m}_t = m_t^a + f_t^m + \bar{m}_t. \qquad\qquad (45)$$

Eq. (42) assumes that all sectors produce tradeable
goods or services. This is not the case in reality.
For the sectors which produce nontraded goods, we
assume that imbalances between supply and demand are
accumulated or disaccumulated from existing stocks. In
the case of the service-producing sectors, we assume
that imbalances are dissipated (when positive), or that
there is rationing (when negative).

This treatment of sectoral imbalances resembles that of
the 'almost consistent' linear programming model of
Bergsman and Manne (1966), where external trade acts

as a 'shock absorber' for the traded goods sectors and there are demand restrictions in the case of the non-traded goods sectors (see also Taylor, 1975, pp. 57-58).

Sectoral exports and imports

Eq. (42) gives δ_t, the sectoral excess demand, assumed to be imports when negative or exports when positive. Noncompetitive imports and exogenous exports have to be taken into account so as to obtain total sectoral exports and imports.

In order to define total exports (q_t), the positive elements in the δ_t vector are added to exogenous exports in the corresponding sector. Total imports (m_t) are the negative elements in the δ_t vector plus the corresponding noncompetitive imports. That is:

for $i = 1, 2, \ldots, n$ $\qquad \delta_{it} \geq 0$ $\qquad$ then

$$q_{it} = \bar{q}_{it} + \delta_{it} \tag{46}$$

and

$$m_{it} = \tilde{m}_{it} \tag{47}$$

If $\delta_{it} < 0$ then

$$q_{it} = \bar{q}_{it} \tag{48}$$

and

$$m_{it} = \tilde{m}_{it} - \delta_{it} \tag{49}$$

$$q_t = \begin{bmatrix} q_{1t} \\ q_{2t} \\ \vdots \\ q_{nt} \end{bmatrix} \; ; \; m_t = \begin{bmatrix} m_{1t} \\ m_{2t} \\ \vdots \\ m_{nt} \end{bmatrix}$$

Balance of trade

The sectoral balance of trade (b_t) is the difference between total exports and imports. That is:

$$b_t = q_t - m_t . \tag{50}$$

Or, according to eqs. (46) and (47), or (48) and (49):

$$b_t = \bar{q}_t - \tilde{m}_t + \delta_t . \tag{51}$$

And, using eq. (42):

$$b_t = (I - A)x_t - c_t - f_t . \tag{52}$$

The overall balance of trade, or simply trade balance, is the sum of the sectoral trade balances ($\imath'b_t$). It can be shown that this definition of the balance of trade is consistent with that of foreign savings in eq. (27).[1]

---

[1] The proof amounts to showing the identity between the balance of payments as defined in eq. (52) and (minus) foreign savings.

Let us write the expression of the overall trade balance, by adding vertically in eq. (52):

$$\imath'b_t = \imath'\left[(I - A)x_t - c_t - f_t\right]. \tag{53}$$

Using eqs. (36) and (39), total investment demand equals total (domestic plus foreign, exogenous) savings:

$$\imath'f_t = \imath's_t + \varphi_t . \tag{54}$$

Adding $\imath'c_t$ to both sides of eq. (54), and recalling that according to eq. (23), internal incomes are distributed exhaustively between consumption and saving:

$$\imath'c_t + \imath'f_t = \imath'y_t + \varphi_t . \tag{55}$$

Substituting in eq. (53):

$$\imath'b_t = \imath'(I - A)x_t - \imath'y_t - \varphi_t . \tag{56}$$

On the other hand, production costs are distributed exhaustively between intermediate inputs and value added (eq. (4)):

$$\imath'Ax_t + \imath'Vx_t = \imath'x_t . \tag{57}$$

Cont. on page 104

9. Growth: The Dynamic Link

In the model, the accumulation of capital is the source of output growth, for a given technology. The increase in investment goods available in each sector permits an increase in sectoral outputs. The outputs of successive periods are linked by investment in the growth process.

In the following expression

$$x_{t+1} = \hat{a}^{-1} d_t + x_t \tag{60}$$

the production capacities added in each sector, i.e. investment by sector of destination, give rise to an increment in output proportional to the (reciprocal of) incremental capital output ratios, or output capital ratios. This is the acceleration principle mentioned previously. It amounts to assuming, among other things, equal (one-year) construction periods and constant capacity utilization of capital equipment.[1]

---

[1] Technological change may appear as a source of growth in the model, if the capital output ratios were allowed to change over time. Changes over time in the A matrix of technical coefficients - so as to increase (decrease) the share of value added (intermediate inputs) in output - would also increase the growth (savings) potential.

Footnote 1, p.103, cont.

And, according to the equality between value added and income stated in eq. (3):

$$\iota'Ax_t + \iota'y_t = \iota'x_t. \tag{58}$$

Substituting in eq. (56), we get:

$$\iota'b_t = - \varphi_t. \tag{59}$$

It should be noted, however, that the consistency shown here holds in the case where all goods are tradeable, i.e. when all excess demands can be assumed to be traded. When this is not the case, i.e. when there are some nontraded goods, excess demands appearing in those sectors cannot be interpreted as equivalent to foreign savings. When there are nontraded goods, the model becomes 'almost consistent'.

Eq. (60) can be conceived of as a disaggregated version of the growth models elaborated by Harrod (1936)
and Domar (1946).[1] In the Harrod-Domar model, the
following equation describes the process of growth:

Growth rate = output capital ratio × saving ratio

or, multiplying by output:

Increment of output = output capital ratio × savings.

If a vector of distribution of investment by destination z_t^*, which adds to one, is defined and the identity of total investment with total savings is recalled, eq. (36), then eq. (60) can be written as:

$$x_{t+1} - x_t = \hat{a}^{-1} z_t^* s_t^* \tag{61}$$

where

$$z_t^* s_t^* = d_t. \tag{62}$$

Or, adding:

$$\imath'(x_{t+1} - x_t) = \imath'(\hat{a}^{-1} z_t^*) s_t^* \tag{63}$$

where the term in parentheses on the r.h.s. can be interpreted as the average output capital ratio, since
$\imath' z_t^* = 1$. As in the Harrod-Domar model, eq. (63) shows
how increments in total output are determined by the
(average) output capital ratio multiplied by total
savings.

Eq. (60) is the dynamic principle of the model which determines the behavior of the economy over time. It can
be seen as a version of the closed-loop dynamic input-

---

[1] A less known original formulation is that of Lundberg (1937,
Ch. IX) (Hansen, 1966, p. 126).

output system (Leontief, 1953), which has also been interpreted (Lange, 1957; Bródy, 1970) as a multi-sector Harrod-Domar model. Johansen (1973) extended the analysis to the open-loop version of Leontief's dynamic model.

In Leontief's closed-loop dynamic model, total production of individual sectors has to cover intermediate consumption plus the investments required to increase production:

$$x_t = A\, x_t + H(x_{t+1} - x_t) \qquad (64)$$

where H is the product matrix $B\hat{a}$ (Taylor, 1975, p. 53). H is a stock-flow matrix, showing the stock of the i'th commodity required for production of one unit of the j'th.

Eq. (64) can also be written as:

$$x_{t+1} = H^{-1}(I - A)x_t + x_t. \qquad (65)$$

If certain conditions with respect to the coefficients in the matrices are satisfied (see e.g. Chakravarty, 1969, pp. 158-169; Jorgenson, 1961) a nonnegative, nonzero solution exists with the following exponential matrix form:

$$x_t = e^{H^{-1}(I-A)t}\, x_o. \qquad (66)$$

The behavior of this solution depends on the characteristic values of the matrix $H^{-1}(I-A)$. One of these corresponds to a proportionate or steady-growth path for the system, along which the elements of vector x_t stay in fixed proportions and grow at equal, constant rates. The sense of the solution tried is to choose the highest proportionate growth rate (characteristic

value) compatible with positive values of x_t, i.e.,
where demands for intermediate use and investment consistent with these growth rates are satisfied by outputs.

Proportional growth in all sectors and fixed output
proportions - most probably different from those prevalent in the initial period of analysis - may have
interesting implications for the long-run growth capa-
bilities of the economy or the 'dynamic efficiency'
of a system when the 'turnpike' path is compared with
actual growth (see, e.g., Tsukui, 1968; also Tsukui
and Murakami, 1979).

When analyzing development alternatives in the medium
to long run, a more flexible approach seems necessary.
There is no logical reason to impose the condition of
equal rates in all sectors. In a sense, this is the
approach followed here. The distribution of (public)
investment is kept as an policy instrument (a part
of the d_t vector in eq. (60)). Then, the sectoral
growth rates will in general differ, and the composition of output will vary accordingly. The problem of
the possible imbalances between supplies and demands
is solved here by foreign trade, and thus the possibility that outputs will not cover demand requirements
is allowed for. However, there is no clearcut general
analytical solution to the model, and the simulation
or numerical experiment approach has to be followed.

It is easier to compare eq. (60) and the closed-loop
dynamic input-output model in eq. (65) if d_t in eq.
(60) is written as an explicit function of x_t. Substituting backwards in eqs. (34), (33), (32), (31),
(30), (28), (24), (23), (11) and (6) we get:

$$x_{t+1} = \hat{a}^{-1}\left[\frac{\hat{a}(x_t - x_{t-1})}{\imath'\hat{a}(x_t - x_{t-1})} \imath'\left[-\theta^{p'}\imath + (I - \imath'\hat{\Gamma}^p)V^p x_t\right] + z_t^g\left[-\theta^{g'}\imath + (1 - \imath'\Gamma^g)V^g x_t\right]\right](1+u_t) + x_t .\tag{67}$$

In this difference-equation system, the term in brackets multiplying $\hat{a}^{-1}$ on the r.h.s. is similar to the $(I-A)$ term in the Leontief dynamic eq. (65) in that it reflects the surplus or saving capacity of the economy. The term in brackets in eq. (67) is not a linear expression which has the elegant simplicity found in Leontief's equation. But the difference system of eq. (67) does permit detailed exploration of alternative strategies aimed at changing the distribution of income (the V matrices) and the composition of output, by means of public investment policy (the z_t^g vector). It also includes the effects of foreign savings (represented by the exogenous variable u_t).

Given the values of the behavioral parameters ($\hat{a}$, θ, Γ) and the policy parameters (V, z_t^g and u_t), eq. (67) can be solved recursively forward, for known values of x_t and x_{t-1}. Such a solution is called a simulation or numerical experiment.

Once the values of x_t are determined in this way during the simulation or planning period ($t = 0, 1 \ldots \tau$), their growth rates can be obtained. These growth rates of sectoral output are in general not constant over time nor equal for all sectors. Thus, when analyzing in detail the output growth implications of different strategies, cumulative rates of growth are defined for sector i:

$$\mu_{it_0 t_1} = \left[\frac{x_{it_1}}{x_{it_0}}\right]^{\frac{1}{t_1-t_0}} - 1 \quad \text{for} \quad 0 \leq t_0 < t_1 \leq \tau \quad (68)$$
$$i = 1,2,\ldots,n$$

When time is given in years, this general expression
is valid for the annual rate, the simulation period
rate, and for any subperiod.

It may be noted that eq. (67) still pertains to the
class of dynamic models criticized by Georgescu-Roegen
(1974) for being 'mechanico-descriptive', where the
simple formula 'Save-Invest-Grow' is the open sesame
of a merely quantitative growth process. However, the
incorporation of income distribution as an explicit
component, aimed at characterizing the style or quality
of growth, hopefully invokes some features of the more
illustrious class of 'analytico-physiological' models.

10. Employment

The scope of the underemployment and unemployment
problem in developing countries is well known. A great
deal of international effort is devoted to analyzing
the employment problem and its possible solutions (see
e.g. International Labour Office, 1973 and 1976). Employment is in fact as important a quality aspect of
the growth process as income distribution. Employment
repercussions should be included when analyzing alternative development strategies.

The most simple and usual assumption about employment
in an input-output framework is that labor use is proportional to sectoral production.[1] A translation of
this hypothesis into the context of this model, where
different income classes are defined and different
types of employment are represented, is the following

[1] A large variety of multisectoral models aimed at analyzing the
employment effects of income redistribution use this type of
specification. For a survey, see Morawetz (1974). His conclusion
is that although they are highly imperfect, these types of models provide the only currently available means of investigating
the distribution-employment question (p. 505).

equation for labor requirements by income class:

$$\ell_t = \Lambda_t \, x_t \tag{69}$$

where ℓ_t is a (k-dimensional) vector of labor use by
socio-economic class, and Λ_t is a (k × n) matrix of
labor productivity ratios representing the quantity
of employment of the different types required per
unit of gross output in each sector. Λ_t is a function of time, indicating changes in labor productivity
over time.

The specification in eq. (69) implies 'unlimited
supply of labor' or extended underemployment and unemployment during the period of analysis. The equation
will not be supplemented with more complicated - and
speculative - interactions. For instance, feedback
from expenditure in education and health services,
with the effect of diminishing the coefficients in the
Λ and B matrices, would have an impact on growth and
employment (Clark, 1975, pp.133-4). The source of growth
in the model is capital accumulation, and no mechanism
for 'speeding up' technical change is introduced. The ·
assumption here is that different development strategies as defined in this study are 'technologically
neutral', in the sense that they do not affect the rate
of technical progress. Or, technical progress is the
same regardless of what the development strategy may
be. If, as is often maintained, education, health and
/or nutrition have a positive effect on labor productivity, the treatment of technical progress in this
model puts a handicap on redistributive (or 'basic
needs') strategies.

Sectoral disaggregation is usually applied to employment. By simple transformations in eq. (69), an expression for total employment requirements by producing

sector can be obtained:

$$\lambda_t = \hat{\Lambda}_t' \iota \, x_t \qquad \qquad (70)$$

where λ_t is the (n-dimensional) vector of sectoral employment, and Λ_t has been transformed into an (n × n) diagonal matrix by transposition and summation, and then diagonalization. The elements in this diagonal matrix are the total employment output ratios by producing sector.

Growth rates for sectoral employment, similar to those of output growth, eq. (68), are defined as:

$$\rho_{it_0 t_1} = \left[\frac{\lambda_{it_1}}{\lambda_{it_0}} \right]^{\frac{1}{t_0 - t_1}} - 1 \qquad \begin{array}{l} 0 \le t_0 < t_1 \le \tau \\ i = 1,2,\ldots,n \end{array} \qquad (71)$$

In view of eq. (60), it can be argued intuitively about the possible trade-offs between employment and growth. The greatest effect on growth is reached if investment is concentrated in the sector with the highest output capital ratio. On the other hand, the greatest impact on employment is reached if investment is allocated to the sector with the highest employment output ratio. If these sectors do not coincide, then a choice is available between less employment and more growth now, but more employment in the future, once the growth effect has more than compensated the employment effect. As Lange (1957) has shown, it is possible to determine how far in the future the 'growth-intensive' strategy surpasses the 'employment-intensive' strategy. But a problem neglected in Lange's formal discussion is the large sectoral imbalances that this kind of extreme strategies may imply. These trade-offs can be explored by the type of model approach adopted here.

However, economic development means something more
than growth and/or employment. Equity in the distribution of economic resources may be the kind of concept that indicates the quality of the economic growth
process. It could also be understood as reflecting
noneconomic values, e.g. political democracy, and
the prevalence in culture of solidarity and unselfish-
ness.

11. Welfare: National Income and Income Distribution

Gross national product or national income has been
widely critized as a measure of economic welfare. In
measuring economic welfare, it has been asserted (see,
e.g., Nordhaus and Tobin, 1972) that GNP should exclude
external effects (pollution, congestion, etc.) and 're-
grettable necessities' (such as defense expenditures),
while estimates of the value of leisure and the services of consumer durables should be added.

This type of adjustment, however, does not take the
problem of distribution into account. The national
income measure does not fulfill the weakly stringent
Pareto distribution criterion for ordering socio-
economic states. According to the Pareto criterion,
there is an improvement in welfare when at least one
person is better off and no one else becomes worse off.
The national income measure, on the other hand, may
increase even when someone's income has decreased (i.e.
it increases when the sum of the changes in individual
incomes is positive). The national income measure expresses Pareto-sanctioned welfare increases only when
there are no reductions in income for any individual.
Hence, national income is not a well-behaved indicator
of Pareto-sanctioned welfare increases.

If national income is taken as a measure of welfare,

then welfare is an additive function of individual incomes. Or, if it is assumed that income classes are comprised of homogeneous individuals, national income may be expressed as the sum of the income of all classes:

$$W_1 = \iota' y_t^p \tag{73}$$

where y_t^p is the vector of private incomes defined in eq. (6): $y_t^p = V^p x_t$.

Now, the (instantaneous) rate of growth of a sum such as eq. (73) may - by taking logarithmic derivatives - be expressed as a weighted average of the growth rate of the components (see e.g. Chiang, 1974, Ch. 10). Thus:

$$G_1 = w_1 \epsilon_1 + w_2 \epsilon_2 + \ldots + w_k \epsilon_k \tag{74}$$

where G_1 is the rate of growth of national income, w_i is the income share of the i'th income class, i.e.

$$w_i = \frac{y_i^p}{\iota' y^p} \tag{75}$$

and ϵ_i is the rate of income growth.

The growth rates of classes of incomes associated with each solution are:

$$\epsilon_{i t_0 t_1} = \left[\frac{y_{i t_1}^p}{y_{i t_0}^p} \right]^{\frac{1}{t_0 - t_1}} - 1 \qquad \begin{matrix} 0 \le t_0 < t_1 \le \tau \\ i = 1, 2, \ldots, k \end{matrix} \tag{76}$$

As revealed by eq. (74), national income growth as a measure of welfare growth provides only a partial picture. When income is concentrated in, for example, group one, G_1 measures essentially the income growth of this group. Eq. (74) gives a higher social value to percentage income increments accruing to higher income classes. Or, a unitary increase in income creates the same additional social welfare regardless of the income level of the recipient.

When comparing alternative development strategies, this distributional bias may be a serious shortcoming.

It seems more equitable to assign the same social value to a one percent increase in income for any income class. Thus the weights in eq. (74) should be proportional to the number of people in each group, that is, equal weights when there are equal populations in the different groups:[1]

$$G_2 = \epsilon_1 + \epsilon_2 + \ldots + \epsilon_k. \qquad (77)$$

A multiplicative type of welfare function underlies this formulation:

$$W_2 = (y_1 \cdot y_2 \cdot \ldots \cdot y_k)^{1/k}. \qquad (78)$$

This function has been referred to as the 'democratic criterion' (Pyatt and Thorbecke, 1976, p. 11).

When there is extensive poverty and income is very concentrated, a natural policy objective may be to assign a higher social value to relative increases in income accruing to the lower-income groups. This is the sense of the 'poverty weighted' index introduced by Ahluwalia and Chenery (1974):

$$G_3 = v_1 \epsilon_1 + v_2 \epsilon_2 + \ldots + v_k \epsilon_k \qquad (79)$$

---

[1] The assumption of equal percentile income groups is maintained throughout this section. It is removed when the model is estimated in Chapter 5.

where $y_i > y_j$ implies $v_i < v_j$, and $\iota'v_i = 1$. The social welfare function from which this expression is derived is of the form:

$$W_3 = y_1^{v_1} \cdot y_2^{v_2} \cdot \ldots \cdot y_k^{v_k}. \tag{80}$$

Several authors (see Sen, 1979) have proposed the standard real income index corrected by the value of (one minus) the Gini coefficient of inequality as a welfare indicator:

$$W_4 = W_1 (1 - \text{Gini}) \tag{81}$$

in which

$$\text{Gini} = 1 + \frac{1}{k} - \frac{2}{k\iota'y^p} (y_1 + 2y_2 + \ldots + ky_k) \tag{82}$$

$$\text{for } y_1 \geq y_2 \geq \cdots \geq y_k.$$

The distributional value judgement implicit in the welfare interpretation of the Gini coefficient is the 'rank-order weighting'. As shown by Blackorby and Donaldson (1978), the Gini social welfare function is:

$$W_5 = \frac{1}{k^2} (y_1 + 3y_2 + \ldots + (2k - 1) y_k) \tag{83}$$

$$y_1 \geq y_2 \geq \cdots \geq y_2.$$

In this expression, the weighting coefficients are determined by the rank order of the income recipient, and not given exogenously as in eq. (79).

The social welfare index in eq. (81) has been interpreted (Graaff, 1977) as a combination of a measure of 'efficiency', reflected by national income, and a measure of 'equity', given by the Gini coefficient. We therefore call it the 'efficiency-equity' index.

12. Overview: Structure and Operation

Structural diagram

Let us now present the block diagram of the model in order to give an overall view of its structure and comment on its main features.

The basic dynamic principle of the model is given, as in the Harrod-Domar model, by the addition of productive capacity through the accumulation of savings.

In Figure 4.4, variables are encircled, including x (the sectoral outputs) and s* total (private plus government plus foreign) savings. The boxes - which will shortly be given explicit contents - represent functions or transformations which specify the determination of the variable to which an arrow leads by the variable from which an arrow originates. The upper box contains the functions which determine savings from outputs through incomes. The lower box contains the functions which determine output growth from savings through investment.

Figure 4.4

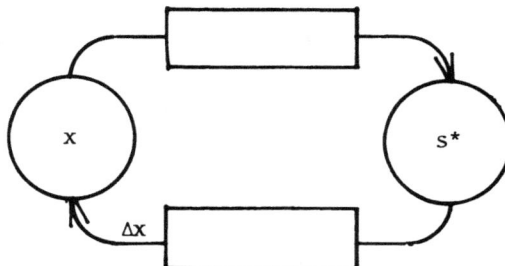

Figure 4.5

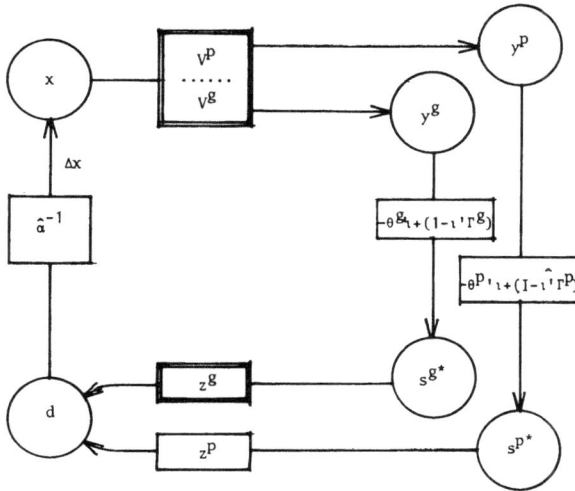

Let us now see what the boxes in Figure 4.4 contain.
Eqs. (6) and (11) for (private and government) income
determination from outputs are represented in the upper part of Figure 4.5. The double lines in the boxes
mean that the coefficients of the functions are policy
parameters.

The right-hand side of Figure 4.5 represents the
determination of private and public savings from incomes. The corresponding equations are eqs. (25)
and (26). In the lower part, government savings are
transformed into sectoral investments by a policy
function of distribution, describing the stipulated
public investment policy (eq. (33)). Private savings,
on the other hand, are transformed into sectoral investments via an endogenous distribution function of
the accelerator type (eq. (30)).

The last transformation in the system, on the left-
hand side of Figure 4.5, is the function describing

the growth effect of sectoral investment. The corresponding equation is eq. (60).

The direction of all of the arrows in Figure 4.5 is one way, indicating unilateral relations between variables. This type of configuration characterizes recursive models - as opposed to interdependent models - and is advocated because of its simple causal interpretation (see e.g. Fox and Thorbecke, 1965).

Another way of looking at recursiveness is to show that by substitution, the system can be expressed in terms of only one (endogenous) variable. Such an expression was presented in eq. (67), obtained by backward substitution from eq. (60).

Figure 4.5 shows the dynamic core of the model. The performance of the system or, in the present case, the effects of the development strategies, cannot be observed directly in the figure. State or 'peripheral' variables, without feedback in the system, have been defined; they indicate the performance of the economic system under alternative development strategies. They are the (sectoral and class) employment vectors, the sectoral trade-balance vector, and the welfare indicators. These are incorporated in Figure 4.6.

Figure 4.6 also contains φ, exogenously determined foreign savings, represented by a hexagon on the lower right-hand side. On the one hand, foreign savings add to the saving capacity of the economy, eqs. (28) and (32). On the other hand, they increase foreign indebtedness, eq. (27').

Employment is represented in the upper left-hand corner of Figure 4.6. It is a 'peripheral' variable and does not have any feedback in the central circuit of the

Figure 4.6

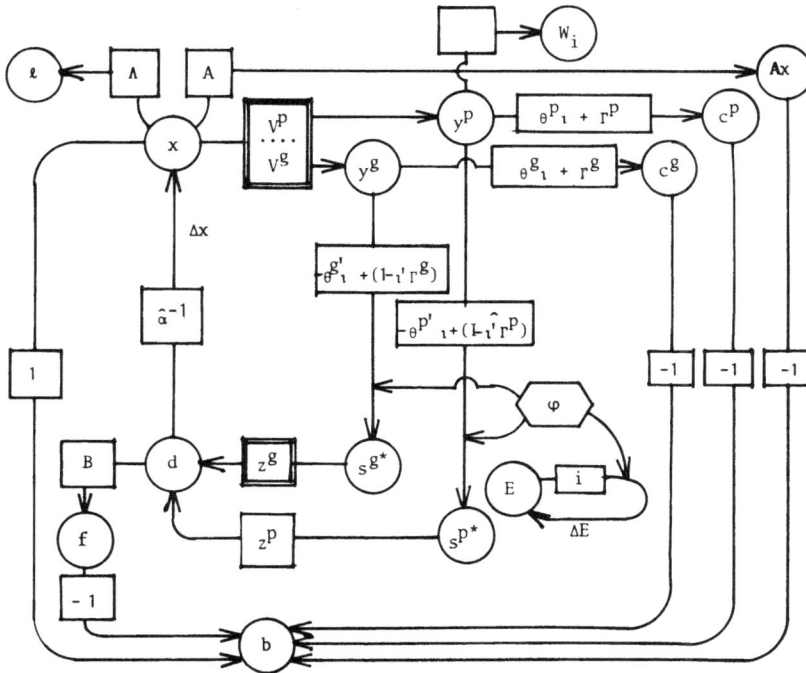

system. (There is no arrow originating from either
ℓ, W_i or b.) Corresponding to each level and structure of output, there is an associated vector of employment by socio-economic class, given in eq. (69),
in each period. For simplicity, a similar expression
which relates output with labor requirements by producing sector, eq. (70), has not been included in
Figure 4.6.

An arrow from the private incomes vector, y^p, in the
center of the upper part of the diagram, represents
the relationships which determine welfare. Several
different expressions of welfare have been defined
(eqs. (73), (78), (80), (81), (83)). For simplicity, an
empty box indicates different transformations.

Figure 4.7

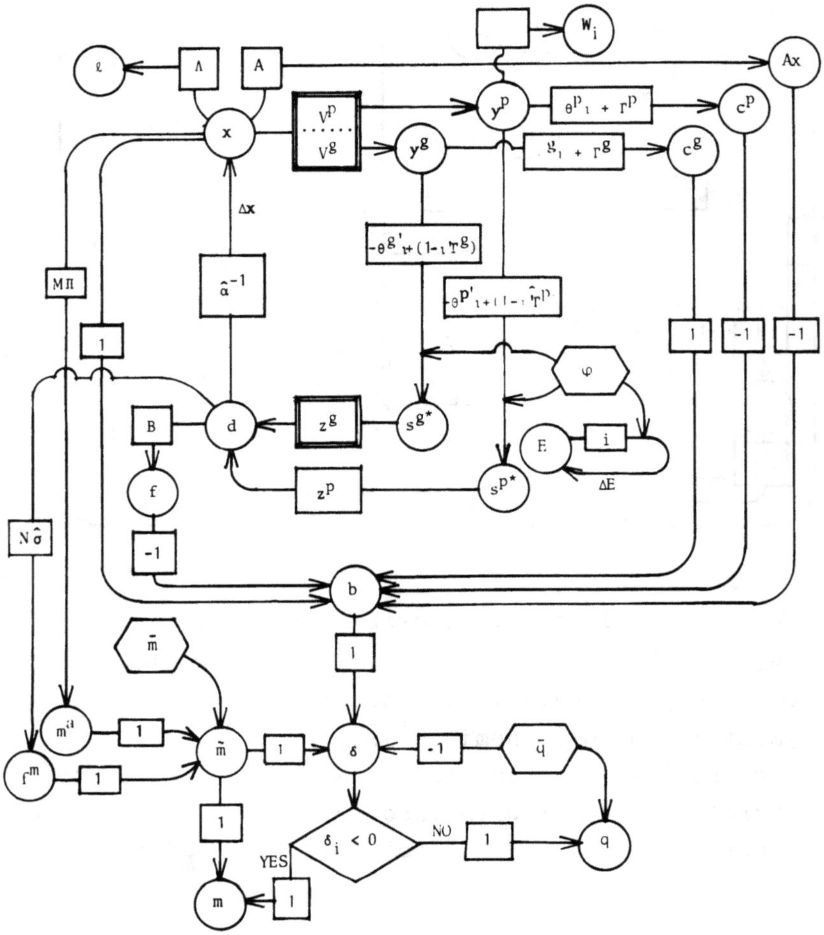

The sectoral balance-of-trade variable (b), defined
in eq. (52), is shown in the lower part of Figure
4.6. The sectoral balance of trade has been proved
to be equal to domestic production, less domestic
demand, eqs. (50) to (52). Then, intermediate demands Ax (in the upper part of the figure), consumption demands, eqs. (14) and (17) in the upper
right-hand corner, and investment demands by origin,
eq. (37) in the lower left-hand corner, are sub-
tracted from total production.

Figure 4.6 includes b, the vector of trade balances,
a synthetic expression of the foreign trade performance of the system. It does not include imports and
exports taken separately. They are shown in the lower
part of Figure 4.7, where the entire model is presented.

Eqs. (43) to (45), which determine total (noncompetitive plus exogenous) imports, are represented in the
lower left-hand part of Figure 4.7. Exogenous exports
are shown on the right-hand side. The vector of excess
demands is represented in the center as the sum of
trade balances plus total imports minus exogenous exports, eq. (42).

The lower part shows how imports and exports are determined separately. On the left, negative imbalances
between total supply and demand are added to (already
determined) imports, giving the vector of imports,
eq. (48). On the right, total exports add excess
supplies to exogenous exports, eq. (46).

It has been shown in eq. (59) that φ, exogenously determined foreign savings, or the trade deficit, equals
(minus) the sum of the sectoral balance-of-trade vector (b). The interesting feature of the b vector,
however, is not the level of its sum, which is an exo-

genously determined variable, but its structure. A
zero overall trade deficit is compatible, for example,
with a situation where large agricultural net imports
and large oil exports cancel each other. If trade
balances have to be kept within certain limits, income distribution policy has to be associated with a
consistent investment policy. Unilateral investment
policies will tend to produce large imbalances, if
equally unilateral income distribution policies are
undesirable.

Modes of operation

When income redistribution is a central objective, development strategies may be considered as follows. A
certain path for income redistribution over time is
stipulated exogenously, i.e. annual changes in the V
matrices, after which the z^g vector of distribution
of public investment is found which, in each period,
is consistent with the desired structure of the balance-of-trade vector (b), for an exogenously given
overall trade balance.

This type of analysis is related to the regulation of
a controlled system. A function may be introduced which
couples the balance of trade vector with the public
investment vector, so as to eliminate deviations from
the required values. This type of function could be
called a regulator or servomechanism by analogy with
the device used in engineering (see e.g. Lange, 1970,
Ch. 1). The distribution of public investment would
thus become an endogenous vector, with a role similar
to that of prices in a Walrasian model, that is, the
role of equating supplies and demands.

In Mexico, another type of regulation is seemingly being adopted in practice. Most often, the allocation of
public investment appears to be decided exogenously,

according to some criteria (growth, for instance) or
as a result of an administrative bargaining process -
which reflects, of course, the configuration of social
forces outside the administration. Thus, resources have
been concentrated in the oil sector. Sectors which
produce staple goods have stagnated. The (spontaneous)
regulating mechanism has been the negative redistribution provoked by inflation, which was set off by rising
agricultural prices, as the growth in demand could not
be totally met by imports.[1] It should be possible to
dispell explicitly the (negative) redistribution policy
consistent with an oil intensive development for given
accepted levels of imports of necessities, that is,
without excessive inflationary pressures. Then, a
coupling from b to V could be introduced, thereby
determining distribution endogenously for a given
public investment policy.

Sectoral balance of trade effects are an important aspect
of development strategies in the Mexican case. Employment and 'welfare' - in the sense of some indicator
of income growth and distribution - are also important
aspects that should be included.

Different expressions for employment and welfare have
already been defined in eqs. (69) to (83). These could
be used as criteria to be maximized, thus transforming
the problem into one of optimal control. Or a mixed
approach could be chosen, combining optimization with
the elimination of trade disturbances (complex control).

The analysis could be elaborated further by the explicit
consideration of uncertainty with respect to various
elements of the problem (stochastic control). Functions
and policies are allowed to change over time as new information about the system is produced, thus including

[1] This type of process, the so-called structuralist inflation
model, was first described by Sunkel (1960).

the possibility of learning.[1] This specification of
the policy problem resemble the notion of <u>strategy</u> in
the sense of a <u>decision rule</u> which states how policy
should be determined in each period on the basis of
information available at the beginning of that period
(see Johansen, 1978, Ch. 8). Out of the entire sequence
of instrument values for the whole planning period, only
those corresponding to the first period are implemented.
The values for future periods are then recalculated,
once actual values of variables have been produced.
Flexible or rolling plans are the results of this type
of approach.

In this study, no attempt is made to introduce self-
regulating control mechanisms into the system. A simulation approach is adopted. Different relevant development strategies are stipulated. They consist of a set
of V and z^g values and an assumed rate of external
savings, ω, all in a given period of time. Given the
initial values of outputs, the model is solved recursively forward in time for known values of the behavioral parameters. The endogenous variables can thus
be calculated over time to represent the effects of the
strategy.

---

[1] See e.g. Kendrick (1981). Svennilson's (1938, see also, 1965)
'alternative planning' scheme is a remarkable early discussion of
this type of approach.

CHAPTER 5. ESTIMATION OF THE MODEL

1. Introduction

A basic SAM was presented in Chapter 4, Section 1 as a consistency framework for model building. Estimation of the system of accounts in the SAM for a given country in a given year is a task which requires the efforts of large groups and a mass of information. An estimation of good statistical standard would, at a minimum, re- quire economic and population censuses and household surveys on income distribution and demand for the year in question.

This is why the yearly estimation of a complete SAM is beyond the capability of most - even developed - countries. For less developed countries, the choice is usually between a total lack of data and partial, approximative - and often outdated - information. When the second alternative is chosen, many ad hoc assump- tions, indirect estimations, and 'guesstimates' have to be made.[1]

The approach adopted in this study does not involve the estimation of the SAM for Mexico for a given year.[2] The SAM approach has been adopted as a consistency framework for model construction. That is, as a result of application of the SAM framework, a number of be-

---

[1] For an account of the experience in three countries, see Pyatt and Round (1977).

[2] A SAM was estimated for Mexico for 1975 (Mexico, 1978a), as an input in the preparation of the industrial development plan 1979-1982 (Mexico,1979c). The blocks corresponding to factor and institutional accounts related to income distribution, were not calculated.

havioral matrices have been defined. It is not the
flows in the SAM for a given year that have to be estimated, but the structural relationships assumed to
exist between them. The flows for a particular year
constitute the solution of the model for the exogenous
variables to which values are assigned for that year.
A good approximation of the model solution to the SAM
flows estimated directly indicates that the model is
a good simulator of the real economy, or that it has
been validated.

The methods and sources used for the estimation of the
matrices in the model are presented in this chapter.
They are introduced in the order they appear in the
description of the model in Chapter 4. The corresponding tables are compiled in Appendix C. A synoptic
table including sources, methods and authors of the
estimations may be found in Appendix B.

2. Current Interindustry Input Requirements Matrix

Mexico (1978a) estimates a (45 × 45) A matrix for 1975
using a transaction matrix for 1960 and census and
other official information. By the time it was published,
a more disaggregated matrix of 72 sectors was under
construction for 1970, with UN technical support (Mexico, n.d.a). The methods of estimation of the latter
matrix were more detailed and direct.

The less recent, but more direct, estimation was chosen.
The 1970 matrix in Mexico (n.d.a) was updated by the
RAS method for the years 1975 (A_{1975}) and 1978 (A_{1978}).[1]

---

[1] The RAS method is one of the procedures available for updating
input-output matrices. It produces intermediate flow values mi-
nimizing the changes in entries needed for consistency, along
with more recent values of total intermediate demands and total
inputs. This information is produced yearly and with short de-
lays. (See e.g. Bacharach, 1970, Ch. 9.) The computer program of
the RAS used appears in Slater (1972, Ch. 4).

It was then aggregated into the 45-sector classification used in Mexican national accounts. The key for
aggregating the 72-sector classification is presented
in Mexico (1980b, Anexo 2.7).

The A_{1975} matrix served for the validation experiment,
in which the solution of the model for the years
1975-1979 is compared with published statistics. The
A_{1978} matrix was used for all policy simulations. When
the estimations were made (February-May 1980), 1978
was the last year for which the necessary data were
available.

This implies that the A matrix was assumed to be constant - in itself, of course, a strong assumption. A
more elaborated treatment, in which future changes in
A were a function of past changes (as in e.g. Carter,
1970) was unfortunately excluded. Such projections
would deserve a separate study in their own right. Anyway, as changes in technical coefficients are rather
slow, it can be said that they do not seriously affect
the results for, say, the first 5-10 years of the simulation period. A_{1975} and A_{1978} are presented in Tables
C.I and C.II, respectively.

3. Income Distribution Matrix

As we have seen in Chapter 4, Section 3, the model
assumes the existence of a matrix of sectoral income
coefficients which distribute income generated in the
producing sectors among different socio-economic
groups. The following relationship was stated in eq.
(3):

$$y_t = V x_t.$$

It is assumed that economic policy can influence the
V matrix. Although not exactly a policy instrument,
the V matrix is assumed to reflect the effects of other
policy instruments such as taxes and subsidies. The
coefficients in the V matrix are then regarded as
policy parameters.

It should be recalled that a development strategy was
defined as the combination of an income distribution
and a public investment policy, i.e. the stipulation
(of a sequence) of V_t matrices and z_t^g vectors.

A variety of simulated development strategies assumes
an unchanged V_t matrix, so that the prevailing income
distribution becomes the desired one. The current distribution of sectoral incomes then has to be estimated,
for both private and government incomes. But let us
first present a condition used to render the V_t
matrix consistent with the rest of the model.

In eq. (4), a 'vertical consistency' condition, by
which total inputs plus total value added equal sectoral gross output, was imposed:

$$\iota'A + \iota'V = \iota'.$$

That is, column sums have to be equal to one. This condition was utilized in the estimation procedure. First,
a V* distribution matrix whose columns sum to one
($\iota' V^* = \iota'$) was estimated. Then, this matrix was
transformed into a matrix satisfying eq. (4) for the
known values of A (A_{1975} and A_{1978}), by multiplying
it by the diagonal matrix of complements to one of the
columns in the A matrix ($\hat{\iota' - \iota'A}$). Or, in more intuitive
terms, first percentages of total sectoral income ac-

cruing to each class were determined; they were then
multiplied by the percentage of total sectoral income
(total value added) in sectoral output.

It should be noted that since A_t is assumed fixed
for the values A_{1975} and A_{1978}, the condition of eq.
(4) implies that the ratio of total value added to
total output remains constant over time. Technical
change of this kind is then assumed not to exist.

Private income distribution matrix

The data used to estimate the private income distribution matrix are drawn from the household income and
expenditure survey of 1977. The sample consisted of
11,273 households. It was a nationwide survey, covering
both urban and rural areas.[1]

It is usually difficult to obtain acceptably reliable
data on income distribution. The problem is even greater
when, as in Mexico, a significant part of the population is only occasionally connected to the market (the
so-called informal, or traditional, rural sector).
Additional errors may be introduced when expanding the
sample's results to the whole economy, as is done in
this study.[2] On the other hand, in the context of the
type of study carried out here, a survey which gathers
information on income and consumption demand simultaneously has the advantage of consistency over more
exhaustive estimations that only cover the income side
(e.g. population censuses). But the most probable signi-
ficance of the biases introduced when using survey
results in Latin America is known. As concluded by
Altimir (1977, pp. 89-91), due to over and underreport-
ing at both ends of the distribution, there is a high

[1] For a full description of the survey, see Mexico (n.d.b).

[2] This and other problems of income distribution estimates in
Latin America are thoroughly discussed by Altimir (1977).

likelihood that the survey results understate inequalities in income distribution. This should be kept in mind when discussing different development strategies; the estimated V^p matrix is most probably less unequal than the actual V^p.

It should also be noted that a V^{p*} matrix for 1977 (V^{p*}_{1977}) was estimated. When running the model from 1975, or from 1978, it has to be assumed that income distribution did not change between 1977 and 1975 or 1978.

The concept of socio-economic class, rather than income levels, is used for defining a criterion for the partition of the data set. The Mexican sample distinguishes five main types of occupations.[1] This information is combined with the position in the size distribution of income to form the basis for the definition of socio-economic classes. The classes adopted, the sample size and the corresponding deciles in the size distribution of incomes are grouped in Table 5.1.

Seven different socio-economic classes were thus defined. The first four are urban and cover about 2/3 of the total sample. The last three classes are rural. They are assumed to have a homogeneous economic, social and political behavior. Class 1 corresponds to the concept of 'high bourgeoisie' in sociology. Class 2 comprises the 'middle classes' or 'petty bourgeoisie'. Class 3 consists of the urban underemployed, sometimes called the 'marginal population'. The remaining classes have an immediate sociological signification.

van Ginneken (1980, Ch. 3) uses a similar classifica-

---

[1] The correspondence with the classes defined in this study is given in Table 5.5.

Table 5.1:   Sample size and income level of socio-
             economic classes, 1977

	Sample size	Decile
1. Entrepreneurs, employees, professionals (high)	722	8 - 10
2. Entrepreneurs, employees, professionals (middle)	2 109	4 - 7
3. Entrepreneurs, employees, professionals (low)	3 038	1 - 3
4. Workers	2 186	1 - 10
5. Peasants (high-middle)	370	2 - 10
6. Peasants (low)	1 245	1
7. Landless workers	1 553	1 - 10

Source: Based on original data obtained in joint re-
        search with the Coordinación del Sistema Na-
        cional de Información, Secretaría de Programa-
        ción y Presupuesto, Mexico.

tion. He distinguishes between: 1) medium and large-
scale employers, 2) salaried employees, 3) regular wage
earners, 4) small-scale employers (rural and urban),
and 5) day laborers. Another, similar class division
may be found in Solís (1977, Ch. V).

In their study on consumption and saving behavior in
Mexico, Lluch, Powell and Williams (1977, Ch. 6) distinguished three socio-economic classes: workers, en-
trepreneurs and technocrats. They disaggregated households into rural-urban categories, young and old,
large and small. Households were thus classified into
36 groups.

This degree of disaggregation could not be applied
here; the number of observations in each class has
to be large enough to allow the estimation of consump-

tion functions for 45 different types of goods. (Lluch, Powell and Williams divided consumption into only five commodity groups: food, clothing, housing, durables and other.) But it may also be said that from a macro-economic or macro-sociological point of view, highly de-tailed classifications are not necessary (or even de-sirable).

As indicated in the preceding section, there are 45 sectors of economic activity. The household income and expenditure survey of 1977 distinguishes 90 sectors of economic activity, the same as the 1970 population census (Mexico, 1971). They were aggregated into the 45 sectors defined for the A matrix. Households were attributed to the sector of economic activity and socio-economic class of the principal income recipient in the household.

The dimension of the V^{p^*} matrix retained here is then 7×45. Once each household is attributed to one of the 7×45 groups in the matrix, its construction is immediate. First, annual disposable incomes are accumulated for each category (cell) in the 7×45 matrix, after which column totals are formed. Totals in each cell are then divided by column totals. The $V^{p^*}_{1977}$ distribution matrix is thus obtained, for which $\iota' V^{p^*}_{1977} = \iota'$, that is, column totals add up to one (see Table C.III).

Government income matrix

Let us recall the relevant equations related to gov-ernment income. According to eq. (11), the income of the government is:

$$y_t^g = V_t^g \, x_t$$

where (eq. (10))

$$V_t^g = (1 - x_t)(V_t^d + V_t^i).$$

In the latter expression, x_t is the part of the government's revenues devoted to wage payments. V_t^d and V_t^i are (row) matrices of sectoral direct and indirect tax (plus exploitation surplues) coefficients, respectively.

V_t^g is a matrix of policy parameters. However, only one element which determines V_t^g, viz. V_t^d, the matrix of direct tax coefficients, is used as a policy instrument. x_t and V_t^i are fixed in all of the simulations, either at their 1975 or 1978 levels. In some simulations, the direct tax parameters are also assumed to be fixed at their 1975 or 1978 levels, i.e. no changes in tax policy are assumed. Then, all parameters which determine V_t^g, i.e. x, V^d and V^i, have to be estimated for 1975 and 1978.

Let us take x first. The data and sources utilized for its estimation are presented in Table 5.2.

There are no official Mexican estimates on direct taxes paid in different sectors. As a result, the simple assumption was made that the totals in Table 5.2 are distributed proportionally to sectoral value added. After estimating sectoral direct taxes in this way, the V_{1975}^d coefficients could be determined (sectoral direct taxes/sectoral gross output). The changes in direct taxes between 1975 and 1978 were small. Therefore we simply assumed $V_{1975}^d = V_{1978}^d$. Table C.IV contains V_{1975}^d.

Table 5.2:   Government revenues. Expenditures in wages,
             1975 and 1978 (billions of 1975 pesos)

	1975	1978
1. Direct taxes	52 900	72 400
2. Indirect taxes	75 166	79 232
3. Surplus of exploitation	10 376	23 446
4. Total government revenues	138 442	175 078
5. Wages paid by the government	68 700	80 178
6. χ (= 5. $\div$ 4.)	.4962	.4580

Sources: 1) Estimated by Aceituno (1980) from official
         sources; 2) Mexican National Accounts (Mexico
         1979a); 3) author's estimation from the 1970
         input-output tables (Mexico, no date a); only
         the nationalized oil sector is taken into
         account; it is assumed that the growth in the
         share of value added in total costs is due to
         increased exploitation surpluses (increased
         oil-price effect), that is, the share of wages
         and taxes is left constant; 5) value added of
         the government as estimated in Mexico (1978 a).

As in input to the 1975 Mexican SAM (Mexico 1978a),
although not included in the publication itself, sectoral indirect taxes and subsidies were computed for
1975. The total given by Mexico (1978a), however, differs from that of Banco de México (Mexico, 1979a),
which is the standard and consistent source on national
accounts. The coefficients calculated according to the
former sectoral estimation were then scaled by 1.1608
for consistency with Banco de Mexico's total figures.

The V_t^i matrix defined also includes the surplus of
exploitation of the nationalized oil industries, the
only sector for which surpluses are really considerable
and easy to estimate. As explained in the notes to
Table 5.2, all variations in the share of total inputs
in gross output of the oil sector are attributed to
changes in the share of the surplus of exploitation;
the shares of other components of value added are

assumed constant. In other words, it is assumed that
the increased value added in the oil sector - due to
the oil price increases - is absorbed by increases in
profits, while the share of labor and taxes is constant. This surplus - shown in Table 5.2 - is then
expressed as a coefficient and added to the indirect
tax less subsidies coefficient of the oil sector.
For reasons similar to those for V_t^d , the V_t^i coefficients are left constant between 1975 and 1978, with
the exception of the oil sector, which increases by
about one-third - from .305854 to .409392 - due to the
assumed increases in exploitation surpluses. V_{1975}^i
appears in Table C.IV. V_{1978}^i is identical to
V_{1975}^i, except for the coefficient of the oil sector.

After having estimated x_t, V_t^d and V_t^i for 1975 and
1978, the simple transformations of eq. (10) give the
V_t^g matrix.

4. Private Consumption Function

The data used for the estimation were drawn from the
household income and expenditure survey from 1977
(see Mexico, n.d.b). The consumption items in the
survey were attributed to the corresponding producing
sectors. There is no private consumption from sectors
which do not produce consumer goods or services.

The private consumption behavior assumed in the model
was given in eq. (14):

$$c_t^p = \theta_t^p \iota + \Gamma_t^p \, y_t^p$$

where c_t^p is an $n \times 1$ vector of consumption from the
different producing sectors; θ^p is an $n \times k$ matrix
of parameters (often called 'subsistence consumption'
parameters); and Γ^p is an $n \times k$ matrix of marginal

consumption coefficients (or marginal consumption propensities). Given the dimensions adopted for the estimation of output and incomes, the dimension of θ^p and Γ^p is 45×7. Keeping in mind that 1977 is the year of estimation, the time subscripts are temporarily dropped. The p superscript will also be dropped for notational simplicity.

Eq. (14) actually summarizes (by addition) the consumption behavior of k different socio-economic classes. The estimation procedure requires the determination of 7 different consumption vectors. For any class it holds that:[1]

$$c_j = \theta_j + \Gamma_j \, y_j \qquad j = 1,2,\ldots,7. \qquad (5.1)$$

In this expression c_j is a 45×1 vector of consumption expenditures by the j'th class; θ_j and Γ_j are the corresponding columns in the θ and Γ matrices; and y_j is the j'th element in the y vector, i.e. the income of the j'th class.

We are thus confronted with the problem of estimating the coefficients of the following regression equations:

$$c_j^h = \theta_j + \Gamma_j \, y_j^h + \epsilon_j^h \qquad \begin{array}{l} j = 1,2\ldots,7 \\ h = 1,2,\ldots N_j \end{array} \qquad (5.2)$$

where c_j^h is a $45 \times N_j$ matrix of the N_j sample values of the dependent variable, θ_j and Γ_j are 45×1 vectors of regression coefficients, y_j^h is a $45 \times N_j$ matrix of the sample values of the explanatory variable, and ϵ_j^h is a $45 \times N_j$ matrix of the sample values of the disturbances.[2]

---

[1] The following description of the estimation draws largely on an unpublished paper by Sabau (1980) where the demand system of the model is discussed and the estimation procedure is designed.

[2] The N_j, i.e. the sample sizes for the different socio-economic classes, are given in Table 5.1.

This type of system is called a system of <u>seemingly unrelated regression equations</u> (see e.g. Kmenta, 1971, Ch. 12). The <u>two-stage Zellner-Aitken</u> estimator is a consistent and asymptotically efficient estimator of its coefficients.

The Zellner-Aitken estimators of the Θ and Γ of the 1977 Mexican sample are presented in Tables C.V and C.VI. The quality of the estimation was good; most coefficients are significantly different from zero. It may be noted that some Θ values are negative, which contradicts the intuitive meaning of 'subsistence consumption'.[1] Possibly, the 'subsistence' interpretation of the Θ coefficients is only valid when time series are used in the estimation. When cross-section data are utilized, a good local adjustment around the mean income of the class may imply negative consumption when a zero income level is assumed. In any case, this affects the interpretation of the model, but not its performance. On the other hand, the converse problem of the prevalence of <u>positive</u> Θ values causes perverse long-term behavior of the model, i.e. an increase in the overall growth rate over time. The reason is that for positive Θ's, the <u>average</u> consumption (saving) propensity decreases (increases) as income rises. Paradoxically, it would seem that the long-term realism of the model - i.e. the tendency of growth to decay in the long run, as economic maturity approaches - would require the prevalence of negative Θ values (increasing average consumption propensity). This is quite a counterintuitive assumption in the short run.

The most natural way of avoiding these problems would be to assume constant average consumption propensities,

---

[1] In most cases, however, negative θ_i's are not significantly different from zero (at the 5 percent level). See Table C.V.

i.e. homogeneous functions without the θ terms.
Another possibility - the one tried in this study -
is to assume autonomous growth of subsistence consumption, sufficient to avoid an acceleration of growth.
A plausible ad hoc explanation is that some kind of
'demonstration effect' or natural increase in aspira-
tions is at work. Several runs of the model showed
that the annual growth rate of total sectoral subsistence consumption (θι), consistent with an unchanged
growth rate of total output throughout the simulation
period, is one percent. In order to avoid (the growth
of) negative θ's, the x-axes were displaced to the
highest negative value of θι (sector 45). The final
specification of private consumption behavior is then:

$$c_t^p = (\theta_{0}\iota + 18100)(1 + .01)^t - 18100 + r^p\, y_t^p$$

$$(5.3)$$

where 18100 is to be read as a vector (18100, 18100,...,
18100).

5. Government's Consumption Function

Government expenditures for goods and services were
assumed to be a linear function of government income
(eq. (17)). There are only two recent estimations of
government's consumption by sector of origin: Mexico
(n.d.a) and (1978a). Thus, a statistical method cannot
be used to estimate eq. (17). The θ^g vector is
assumed to be zero, and the r^g become fixed proportions of sectoral consumption by the government out of
government revenues. Government sectoral consumption
expenditures for 1975 - as given by the most recent
estimation in Mexico (1978a, p. 114-5) - are then divided by total revenues for the same period. Total government revenues were given in Table 5.2. The r^g
(column) matrix for 1975 is thus obtained. It is as-

sumed to remain constant over time for all simulations.
The estimated r^g is shown in Table C.VII.

6. Incremental Capital Output Ratios

The incremental capital output ratios ($\hat{a}$) play an important role in the model. First, along with past output growth, they determine the distribution of available private investment funds among producing sectors,
eqs. (30) and (31). Second, and more important, given
the amounts of sectoral investment, they determine
sectoral output growth, connecting outputs in successive periods as dynamic links in the system, eq. (60).

The α's may be regarded as the slope of a linear
function which relates sectoral capital stocks (κ_i)
to sectoral outputs (x_i):

$$\kappa_i = a_i + \alpha_i x_i \qquad i = 1,2,\ldots,n. \qquad (5.4)$$

This specification does not include a time variable,
i.e. it assumes that the capital output ratios remain
constant over the simulation period. This kind of technical change is thus assumed not to exist.

In this expression,

$$\frac{d\kappa_i}{dx_i} = \alpha_i$$

that is, α_i are the incremental capital output
ratios.

It is assumed that there is no correlation between the
disturbances of the n different sectoral regression
equations, i.e., the classical normal regression model
applies. Hence, least-squares estimators are used to

estimate:

$$\kappa_i^t = a_i + \alpha_i x_i^t + \epsilon_i^t \qquad \begin{array}{l} i = 1,2,\ldots,n \\ t = 0,1,\ldots,T \end{array} \qquad (5.5)$$

where a new dimension is added for the T sample values over time, and the disturbances ϵ_i^t are included.

The most recent source for sectoral capital stocks is Mexico (1978c). This study includes capital estimates from 1960 to 1975. Unfortunately, it is not complete; it does not include agriculture and other sectors (sectors number 1-4, 14, 15, 18, 19 and 42). But an older study (Mexico, 1969) does cover thoroughly all sectors for the period 1950-1967. It then becomes tempting to assume that the effectiveness of investment in those sectors without information for the period 1960-75 was the same as in 1950-67, i.e. an unchanged output response to investment.

In the case of agriculture, this assumption is most probably not valid. One indication is that in spite of continued public investment efforts - there is no recent information about private investment, but the relative shares were probably more or less constant - Mexican agricultural output has stagnated since the mid-1960s. By contrast, the period 1950-67 exhibited rapid agricultural expansion; output doubled between 1950 and 1965. Total investment flows in agriculture also doubled in that period (see Mexico, 1969, Cuadro 149). The corresponding $\alpha_{agriculture}$ was 2.119297.

This coefficient cannot, of course, reflect adequately the stagnant behavior of the latter period. The model simulation approach was used instead to determine the $\alpha_{agriculture}$ which matched the behavior of the agricultural sector to the real-world development. A co-

efficient twice that of the former period adjusted
the actual performance of agriculture from 1975 to
1978 quite well. Nevertheless, the fact that agricultural investment has recently been much less effective
than in the early 1960s should not be interpreted as
the result of an irreversible change in purely economic and technical conditions. It would be misleading
to regard this fact as the result of, for instance, an
overall and homogeneous capital deepening process con-
comitant with agricultural development.

On the contrary, more detailed and qualitative analysis
has stressed the problem of duality in Mexican agriculture (see Chapter 2, Section 3). There are large
disparities between modern, capitalist, large-scale
agriculture and traditional, peasant, small-scale
farming. Investment - both public and private - has
been concentrated in the modern sector which seems to
have reached saturation, while the traditional sector
produces with very low capital density. Capital resources
are apparently not being allocated efficiently within
the agricultural sector. A reallocation, which would
imply changes in the institutional framework for ca-
nalizing investment funds and other structural changes,
seems necessary. The Mexican Food System is a programme
for income redistribution and agricultural reform which
specifies this type of changes.[1]

Such changes are assumed in some simulations, where
the development strategy includes thorough reforms in
the rural economy. These reforms are assumed to increase the efficacy of investment, so as to reach the
αagriculture prevalent in 1952-1967.

The crucial importance of the rural economy in a developing economy makes this kind of 'structural para-
metrization' of the agricultural sector not only in-

---

[1] The Mexican Food System is described in Chapter 6, Section 3.

teresting, but necessary. This does not apply to the
other sectors for which recent data do not exist.
With respect to these sectors, no important changes
in behavior are assumed to have occurred.

These and other specific assumptions and relevant information are documented in Table C.VII, where the
estimated incremental capital output ratios are presented.

It should be recalled that eq. (31), the distribution
of private investment funds among sectors of destination, states:

$$z_t^p = \frac{\hat{a}(x_t - x_{t-1})}{\iota' \hat{a}(x_t - x_{t-1})} \quad .$$

When simulated using real data, this expression turned
out to be overly sensitive to yearly output fluctuations. If the changes in output in the last year do
not represent long-term performance, eq. (31) does not
provide an adequate picture of investment behavior.
The two starting years of the simulations, 1975 and
1978, exhibited negative growth for several sectors.
But this was not the result of a permanent tendency;
it occurred only for that year for most sectors. Hence,
a less rigid response than that of the naive accelerator in eq. (31) is necessary. The assumption of lags
in the adjustment process has to be introduced. A
flexible accelerator type of function is then utilized,
where the effect of output changes on investment is
distributed over time (see e.g. Junankar, 1972, Ch. 3).
It is assumed that investment at time t is dependent
on the output levels of the preceding three years. The
following coefficients match the performance of the
model to real behavior quite well:

$$z_t^p = \frac{\hat{a}(x_t - .5x_{t-1} - .3x_{t-2} - .2x_{t-3})}{\iota'\hat{a}(x_t - .5x_{t-1} - .3x_{t-2} - .2x_{t-3})}. \quad (5.6)$$

7. Capital Coefficients Matrix

The capital coefficient matrix traces the sectoral
origin or composition of investment. Given investment
by sector of destination, and its pattern of composition, the sectoral origin of investment can be obtained. This was stated by eq. (37) as:

$$f_t = B_t \ d_t$$

where f_t denotes investments by sector of origin, B_t
the distribution matrix for investments (the t subscript is reintroduced), and d_t investments by
sector of destination. Since B_t is a distribution
matrix, $\iota'B_t = \iota'$ holds.

The survey on capital stocks, Mexico (1978c), is a
recent source for the estimation of B. Unfortunately,
several primary sectors are not included in the survey. The composition of capital stocks by sector of
origin is determined for those sectors which appear in
Mexico (1978c). The classification in Mexico (1978c)
is equivalent to the capital-goods producing sectors
of the national accounts, except for Machinery and
Operation Equipment. This sector was disaggregated into
sectors 31 and 32, in proportion to output (42.7 and
57.3 percent, respectively).

The 54-sector classification used in Mexico (1978c)
was aggregated into the 45-sector classification of the
national accounts. As mentioned above, some sectors
(1-4, 14, 15, 18, 19 and 42) are missing. The estimations of Franchet, Inman and Manne (1973, pp. 100-103)

(FIM) were used for these sectors, updated from 1968, the date of the original estimation, to 1975. The row correction factor method proposed by FIM, so as to allow for the annual rates of change in the capital coefficients, was applied. The elements of the diagonal of B_t, which provide for self-construction and do not appear in Mexico (1978c), were all taken from FIM.

The B_{1975} capital coefficients matrix estimated in this way is assumed to remain stationary. Although this is a strong assumption, there is no data base for stating more plausible hypotheses. The correction method by exogenous row factors used by FIM to project the B_t matrix was considered to require too much computation without adding much realism, given the quality of the data. The B_{1975} matrix is presented in Table C.IX.

8. Foreign Trade Coefficients

Foreign trade is assumed to have three main components: a 'competitive', a 'noncompetitive' and an exogenous part. The competitive component is determined by the sectoral commodity balances between domestic production and demand, i.e. the sectoral excess demand. This part of the trade behavior is explained by means of the functions describing domestic production, consumption and investment, eq. (52). Their estimates have already been presented.

The noncompetitive component of imports is comprised of imports which cannot be produced internally. Two types are distinguished: imports of intermediate inputs and imports of capital goods. They are assumed to be proportional to sectoral outputs and sectoral investments, respectively. The corresponding matrices are presented in the following two sections.

When commodities are aggregated into broad sectors,
an exogenous category of trade becomes necessary.
Exogenous imports and exports are estimated in the
last term.

The foreign sector includes an equation for determining
the foreign debt, eq. (27'), as a function of the debt
in the preceding period, the rate of interest and the
balance of trade. The rate of interest on the external
debt adopted is 10 percent (i = .10). It is a 'guess-
timate', as no official source produces such information.

Matrices of imports of intermediate inputs

Eq. (43) stated that the imports of intermediate inputs
by sector of origin (m_t^a) are proportional to sectoral
output:

$$m_t^a = M_t \; \hat{\Pi}_t \; x_t$$

where   M   is a distribution matrix ($\iota'M = \iota'$) tracing
the sectoral origin of imports in different sectors,
and $\hat{\Pi}$ is a diagonal matrix of coefficients of intermediate imports by sector of destination. (The   t   coefficients are reintroduced in order to date the
matrices.)

The source for the estimation of   M   is Mexico (n.d. a),
dating from 1970. First, the input-output matrix is
deduced from the total transactions matrix. The
(72×72) difference matrix shows imports from sector   i
being utilized in sector   j. Second, this matrix is
aggregated into the 45-sector classification of the
national accounts, using the conversions presented in
Mexico (1980b, Anexo 2.7). Third, the 45×45 matrix is
normalized by dividing each element by its respective
column total. The resulting matrix is then a distri-

bution matrix of sectoral origin of imports of intermediate inputs. M_{1970} is assumed to be stationary.
It is shown in Table C.X.

Mexico (n.d.a) also gives data on intermediate imports by sector of destination $(\hat{n})$. These data correspond to 1970. They were updated to 1975 and 1978 by
the RAS method. $\hat{n}_{1975}$ and $\hat{n}_{1978}$ are shown in
Table C.XI. They are assumed to be constant.

Matrices of imports of capital goods

Imports of capital goods (f_t^m) were assumed to be proportional to sectoral investment by sector of destination, d_t, eq. (44):

$$f_t^m = N_t \; \hat{\sigma}_t \; d_t$$

where N_t is a distribution matrix $(\iota'N = \iota')$ of imports of capital goods by sector of origin, and $\hat{\sigma}$ is
a diagonal matrix of import content coefficients in
investment demands.

The source for the estimation of N_t is Mexico (1978a)
dating from 1975. The more direct investigation of
Mexico (n.d.a) does not include estimates of the sectoral distribution of capital goods imports.

Table IX.2 in Mexico (1978a, pp. 168-169) is a matrix
of flows. It was transformed into a distribution
matrix by normalization. The result, matrix N_{1975},
appears in Table C.XII.

The data available for the estimation of $\hat{\sigma}_t$ is in-
complete. The following indirect estimation was made.
Mexico (n.d.a) estimates total imports of capital
goods for 1970, but not their distribution by destination. They represent .16811 of total investment for

that year. Imports of capital goods are assumed to be
sectorally distributed in proportion to $\hat{n}_t$, the diagonal matrix of imports of intermediate inputs; that
is, imports of capital goods and of intermediate inputs have a similar distribution. The proportionality
factor is such that $\iota'\hat{n}_t x_t$ - intermediate inputs -
represent .16811 of total output $(\iota'x_t)$. As
$\iota'\hat{n}_t x_t/\iota'x_t$ equals .03226 in 1975 and .03121 in 1978,
the proportionality factors are $(.16811/.03226=)$ 5.2111
for 1975 and $(.16811/.03121=)$ 5.3864 for 1978. Then,
the resulting matrices are:

$$\hat{\sigma}_{1975} = 5.2111 \; \hat{n}_{1975}$$

$$\hat{\sigma}_{1978} = 5.3864 \; \hat{n}_{1978}$$

They are assumed to remain constant during the simulation periods starting in the years indicated.

Exogenous imports

Exogenous exports and imports are included in the model
in order to allow for the ('noncompetitive') trade of
commodities whose special comparative advantages or
disadvantages are not accounted for because of aggregation.

In the case of imports, only imports of consumption
goods are exogenously determined. Noncompetitive imports of intermediate inputs and capital goods are (endogenously) determined by functions which have been
estimated in the previous subsections.

Thus, exogenous imports $(\bar{m}_t)$, eq. (45), are included
to allow for imports of consumption goods appearing
in sectors which are potential net exporters. Some
qualities of fuel, for instance, are imported regardless of the exports of the oil sector.

On the other hand, some consumption goods are not pro-

duced in the country, and most probably cannot be produced in the near future at competitive prices. Examples
are watches, cameras, and specially-equipped cars.

Of course, these kinds of considerations have an ar-
bitrary element and are affected in the present case
by the author's limited knowledge of such matters.

Exogenous imports are given in Table 5.3. After 1978,
the last year for which information is available, exogenous imports are assumed to grow at an annual rate
of 5 percent. That is:

$$\bar{m}_{1978+t} = \bar{m}_{1978} (1.05)^t \qquad t = 1, 2, \ldots, \tau$$

Table 5.3: Exogenous imports, 1975-1978 (millions of 1975 pesos)*

Sector	1975	1976	1977	1978
2. Livestock[a]	127.07	187.48	120.52	177.00
7. Petroleum[b]	1 819.12	2 196.68	673.38	764.59
8. Slaughter of live-stock and poultry[c]	349.56	506.50	400.39	397.72
17. Paper and paper products[d]	1 265.97	1.648.09	1.263.29	726.53
18. Printing,publishing[e]	648.24	748.27	503.34	775.85
20. Rubber products[f]	453.40	820.18	407.50	995.65
21. Basic chemicals[g]	4 718.76	5 543.19	4 493.44	5 026.64
28. Nonmetal mineral products[h]	1 182.80	975.00	495.79	987.71
29. Metallic industries[i]	720.35	742.10	511.36	672.58
32. Electrical machinery[j]	4 521.34	7 468.07	4 878.24	4 448.12
34. Motor vehicles[k]	1 830.16	1 946.07	947.54	1 411.75
35. Other manufacturing[l]	669.69	889.04	535.62	724.62

* After 1978, exogenous imports grow by 5 percent per year.

a) Corresponds to the following items of the foreign trade statistics: II.A.c.2 (wool products), b) II.A.b.1-6 (various petroleum
products), c) I.6 (powdered milk), d) II.A.d.1 (paper and card-
board rolls), e) I.2 (graphic products), f) II.A.h.5 (rubber products), g) II.A.e.8 (organic chemical products), h) II.A.h.3 (as-
bestos and other products), i) II.A.g.1 (metallic products),
j) II.B.a.2 (electrical products), k) II.B.c.3 (specially-equipped
cars), l) II.A.h.7 (photographic products).

Source: Mexico (1977, Cuadro IV-5 and 1979b, Cuadro IV-4).

Exogenous exports

Exogenous exports $(\bar{q}_t)$ are included in the model to allow for exports made on the basis of special comparative advantages, which apply to particular commodities in aggregated sectors. Such exports may be assumed to take place regardless of the excess demand in the sector. If the model were estimated for as many sectors as there are goods and services in the economy – or, at least, in the foreign trade classifications – this problem would not arise, and exogenous exports could be excluded. In that case, only (negative) excess demands could be correctly assumed to be exported. But in the present case where agriculture is an aggregated sector, large imports of corn and beans may coexist with exports of products which can be produced with comparative advantages, e.g. coffee, tomatoes or melons. This latter type of exports is regarded as exogenous. These exports appear in several sectors, although they are concentrated in agriculture (see Table 5.4). After 1978, they are assumed to grow by 5 percent per year:

$$\bar{q}_{1978+t} = \bar{q}_{1978}(1.05)^t \qquad t = 1,2,\ldots,\tau$$

Table 5.4: Exogenous exports, 1975-1978 (millions
of 1975 pesos)*

Sector	1975	1976	1977	1978
1. Agriculture[a]	7 721.76	13 357.51	12 597.70	12 706.99
2. Livestock[b]	746.52	1 725.36	1 946.14	2 783.99
4. Fishing[c]	1 716.90	2 053.28	2 156.73	1 797.33
5. Mining[d]	30.45	92.75	6.12	30.18
6. Quarrying[e]	1 160.46	1 279.97	1 107.86	1 046.45
10. Other processed food[f]	2 303.07	1 291.79	1 520.29	1 365.90
11. Beverages[g]	182.79	227.66	173.36	217.18
14. Other textiles[h]	390.89	514.97	423.52	386.26
15. Wearing apparel and footwear[i]	950.02	1 221.10	787.13	765.05
25. Drugs and medicines[j]	177.07	223.95	276.30	314.63
29. Metallic industries[k]	1 627.07	1 955.73	990.54	1 561.45

*After 1978, exogenous imports grow by 5 percent per
year.

a) Corresponds to the following items of the foreign
trade statistics: I.1, 4, 5, 7, 9, 12, 14, 16, 18
(agricultural products), b) II.1, 3, 4 (meat products),
c) II.2 (shellfish), d) III.a.8 (lead), e) III.a.1, 5
(mineral products), f) IV.a.1 to 6 (food products),
g) IV.a.7 (tequila), h) IV.b.4, 7 (textiles), i) IV.b.1,
6 (shoes, clothes), j) IV.c.12 (pharmaceutical products),
k) III.a.7, 11, 12 (processed metals).

Source: Mexico (1977, Cuadro IV-4 and 1979b, Cuadro
IV-5).

9. Employment Matrices

Eq. (69) posed a proportional relationship between
labor requirements by socio-economic class (ℓ_t) and
sectoral outputs (x_t):

$$\ell_t = \Lambda_t \, x_t$$

where Λ_t is a $k \times n$ matrix of sectoral labor productivity ratios by socio-economic class. Contrary to

the behavioral matrices estimated so far, the Λ_t matrix is not assumed to be constant over time. There are strong indications that this is the case, and a quite plausible and easily computable assumption can be made about its evolution over time. It is assumed that, for all socio-economic classes, labor productivity grows at constant exponential rates, which are speci- fic to each producing sector. That is, disembodied labor-saving technical change occurs, at known sectoral rates. Thus:

$$\Lambda_t = \Lambda_o \, e^{-\hat{r}t} \qquad\qquad\qquad (5.7)$$

where $e^{-\hat{r}t}$ is a (diagonal) matrix exponential func- tion, and $\hat{r}$ are the sectoral rates of labor produc- tivity change. The Λ_o matrix corresponding to the base year is then corrected yearly by sectoral factors representing rates of change in productivity.

The most recent source for the estimation of Λ_o is the Mexican population census of 1970 with data on em- ployment in 1969 (Mexico, 1971, Cuadro 44). It contains a 5×90 table of sectoral employment by type of occupa- tion. This table is first transformed into a 5×45 table by aggregation into the 45-sector classification of the national accounts. Then, sectoral productivity ratios are obtained, using the 1969 sectoral output figures for Mexico (1979a), at 1975 prices. The (5×45) matrix estimated in this way is tranformed into the (7×45) Λ_{1969} matrix by multiplication by the (7×5) matrix presented in Table 5.5. The matrix distributed the types of occupations in the population census among the seven socio-economic classes already defined.

152

Table 5.5:   Distribution of the types of occupations
in the 1970 Mexican census

Socio-economic class	Type of occupation				
	Employers	Workers or employees	Agricultural workers	Self-employed	Peasants
1. Entrepreneurs,employees, professionals (high)	.26606	.09883	0	.06908	0
2. Entrepreneurs,employees, professionals (middle)	.37615	.25082	0	.30139	0
3. Entrepreneurs,employees, professionals (low)	.35779	.25246	0	.62953	0
4. Workers	0	.39789	0	0	0
5. Peasants (high-middle)	0	0	0	0	.22910
6. Peasants (low)	0	0	0	0	.77090
7. Landless workers	0	0	1	0	0

Source: Based on original data obtained from the income
and expenditure survey of 1977, in joint research with the Coordinación General del
Sistema Nacional de Información, Secretaría de
Programación y Presupuesto, Mexico.

The resulting Λ_{1969} matrix is presented in Table
C.XIII.

Sectoral (exponential) rates of productivity change
($\hat{r}$) are calculated between two years: 1969 and 1978.
The source for 1969 is the previously mentioned population census. Sectoral employment estimations made for
the National Employment Program (Mexico, 1979d) are
used for 1978. The resulting $\hat{r}$ matrix is presented
in Table C.XIV.

10. Welfare Indicators

Three different indicators of the increase in social
welfare were defined in Chapter 4, Section 11.

A widely used - and also widely criticized - measure
of social welfare is the national income indicator.
It is simply the sum of incomes, eq. (71). Its growth
rate is obtained with respect to each simulated solution by a formula equivalent to eq. (76), for the simulation period and for different periods within it.

The bias of the national income measure in favor of
high income recipients is diminished if percentage
increases in income of all individuals are assigned the
same social value, or, when the population is partitioned into homogenous income classes, if the weights
attributed to income growth for each class are proportional to the population in each class. This means
equal weights when the population is classified by income size into percentile groups, eq. (77).

The populations in the seven different socio-economic
classes defined above are listed in Table 5.1. Their
share of the total population are the coefficients of
the following 'equal-weights' index adopted for social
welfare growth:

$$G_2 = .068 \; \epsilon_1 + .187 \; \epsilon_2 + .269 \; \epsilon_3 + .194 \; \epsilon_4 +$$

$$+ .034 \; \epsilon_5 + .110 \; \epsilon_6 + .138 \; \epsilon_7 \qquad (5.8)$$

where the ϵ_i are the rates of income growth in each
class. They are obtained for each simulated strategy,
and for different periods, according to the formula in
eq. (76).

An ethically more appealing measure of social welfare
increases may be obtained by augmenting the value
assigned to income growth in low-income groups. Such a
'poverty-weighted' index was written in eq. (79). The
coefficients adopted for the poverty-weighted measure

are as follows:

$$G_3 = 0.0\ \epsilon_1 + .1\ \epsilon_2 + .2\ \epsilon_3 + .3\ \epsilon_4 + 0.0\ \epsilon_5$$
$$+ .2\ \epsilon_6 + .2\ \epsilon_7 \qquad (5.9)$$

Finally, the Gini coefficient is introduced to compute
eq. (81), the 'efficiency-equity' welfare indicator.
Eq. (82) defined the Gini coefficient when income
classes are given in percentile groups. In the present
case, the populations of the income classes differ.
Hence, the average incomes of the different classes are
used instead (the time subscripts are incorporated):

$$\text{Gini}_t = 1 + \frac{1}{7} - \frac{2}{7\ \iota'\bar{y}_t^p}\ (\bar{y}_{t,1}^p + 2\bar{y}_{t,2}^p + \ldots + 7\bar{y}_{t,7}^p)$$
$$(5.10)$$

where the average incomes are:

$$\bar{y}_t^p = \hat{\iota}_t^{-1}\ y_t^p \qquad (5.11)$$

and where: $\bar{y}_{t,1}^p \geq \bar{y}_{t,2}^p \geq \ldots \geq \bar{y}_{t,7}^p$

that is, the components of the $\bar{y}_t^p$ vector are ranked.

It should be noted that the Gini coefficient obtained
in this way reflects distributional inequality among
socio-economic classes, as defined in this study. It
can be seen from Table 5.1 that there is some overlap-
ping when the socio-economic classes are ordered
by income size. However, average incomes are quite
representative of the income of the class in most cases,
as income is rather concentrated around the average
levels. Thus, the Gini coefficient estimated according
to eq. (5.10) reflects quite well the overall degree
of income inequality.

CHAPTER 6. POLICY EXPERIMENTS

1. Introduction

In this chapter we study the behavior of the Mexican
economy over time under different assumptions about
the values assigned to policy variables, i.e. under
different development strategies. 'The Mexican economy'
refers, strictly speaking, to a model of the Mexican
economy, or an analytical structure based on certain
assumptions about relevant causal relationships in the
actual economy, and about their specific, quantitative
form over time. That is, the model described in Chapter
4 and estimated in Chapter 5 is now numerically solved
(recursively forward) over a period of time, for different assumed parameter values.[1]

First of all, an attempt is made to check the validity
of our model of the economy. A historical simulation
starting in 1975 is performed, where parameters are
given their actual values, and the solution compared
with the actual evolution of the Mexican economy. From
1980 to 1990, the parameters are assigned values which
correspond to the historical trend, thus constituting
a sort of trend projection of Mexican development. This
projection is compared with those made using the Mexican
Industrial and Wharton models.

---

[1] The numerical solution of a mathematical model which describes
the behavior of a complex system over time is called simulation
(see, e.g., Naylor, 1971, Ch. 1). Numerical solutions may also
be interesting for quantitative economic policy analysis, regardless of the complexity of the model. In this context, the terms
'exploration' or 'numerical experimentation' have been suggested
(see Taylor, 1975, pp. 101-102).

The model is then used to analyze the separate effects
of income redistribution and institutional reforms in
the agricultural sector, in the context of the Global
Development Plan. The investment policy and the expected
rate of foreign saving of the Global Plan are combined
with two different income distribution policies (with
and without redistribution), under two different assumptions about the behavior of the agricultural sector.
Four policy experiments are then referred to the Global
Plan. The results of the 'basic' experiment are compared with the macroeconometric projections of the
Global Plan model.

An oil-intensive type of development strategy is then
assumed. In this 'status-quo-plus-oil' scenario, public
investment remains concentrated in the oil sector.
The share of agriculture continues to be low. There
are no policies aimed at reducing income concentration;
income distribution remains constant. This implies,
in particular, that no significant changes in agricultural policies and institutions are introduced; present
inefficiencies in the use of capital and other resources
are assumed to prevail. The rate of foreign saving is
maintained at its trend level.

The last simulation is intended to explore the consequences of basic changes in the pattern of development,
with respect to both the structure of income distribution and the composition of output. A 'new development strategy' is simulated, where an advanced income
redistribution policy is assumed, along with changes
in the sectoral destination of public investment, which
reduce concentration in the oil sector and shift the
focus towards agriculture and other basic goods-producing sectors. Within the agricultural sector, increased resources and institutional reforms succeed in
reorienting all forms of support towards the peasant
segment, thus simultaneously redistributing agricultural

incomes and increasing efficiency. The balance of payments is assumed to be in equilibrium, so that the external debt increases only by interest accumulation.

The 'realism' of the different policy changes assumed is, of course, debatable. In a restricted sense, any conceivable configuration of policy parameters is 'possible' or 'admissible', as it gives logically consistent results within the formal context of the model.[1] (But nothing is implied, of course, about the viability of any policy configuration.) The set of all policy vectors generates a set of 'feasible' states of the economy.

However, only a bounded subset within the larger set of all conceivable strategies is politically permissible, or permitted.[2] The constraints on the set of conceivable policies are very difficult to establish a priori, and depend on which political philosophy is held. From a strictly laisser-faire point of view, for instance, the set of permissible policies should be empty.[3] In terms of an economic planning type of insight, on the other hand, the set of possible policies should not be politically restricted, so as to allow for the unconstrained optimization of a social welfare function.[4]

---

[1] It should be recalled that in our model, policy parameters are distribution coefficients, i.e. they vary between 0 and 1, adding up to one. Concerning income distribution parameters, 'any' should be qualified in the sense of 'any above some subsistence minimum'.

[2] Hansen (1967, p. 6). Johansen (1977, pp. 55-56) refers to this subset as the 'set of all possible policies'. In the context of our model, an interesting related subset is the set of all Pareto-sanctioned strategies, i.e. the set of strategies which assume redistribution of income increases.

[3] An ancient and rigorous statement of laisser-faire philosophy is given in the classical chinese Lao Tzu (1963): 'Do that which consists in taking no action, and order will prevail' (p. 59). Or: 'The empire is a sacred vessel and nothing should be done to it' (p. 87).

[4] Frisch (1965), for instance, suggested comparing free optimization with institutionally constrained maximization, so as to visualize the penalty which has to be paid for restricting the list of politically permissible means of implementation.

We do not know whether all of the scenarios simulated
in this chapter belong to the set of permissible policies, although it can be said that those which assume
increased equality correspond better to official policy
objectives. In any case, the specification and exploration of alternatives which are beneficial to a large
majority may increase their 'permissibility', in the
sense that they may be perceived more clearly and more
distinctly as possible and permissible by increasing
numbers of people. Initially unpermissible changes may
thus eventually become accepted and obvious policies, if
the political system is more or less flexible and democratic.

The assumptions and results of the different simulations are first discussed separately. The strategies
are compared in a concluding section. The detailed
results of the simulations appear in Appendix D.

2. Reference Run. Model Validation and Basic Projec-
    tion

The aim of the reference run is to assess the plausibility of the model. In this simulation, the model is
solved for actual values of the parameters between
1975 and 1979. For 1980-1990, the values of the parameters correspond to their trend. The solution values
for 1975-1979 are compared with actual values, thereby
providing an idea of the precision of the model as a
representation of the functioning of the Mexican economy
in that period, i.e. of the model's explicative power.
The solution for 1980-1990 constitutes a 'basic' projection, in the sense that assumed changes in parameters
are small and adhere to their historical pattern. The
results of the basic projection are compared with those
made using two different macroeconometric models, viz.
the Industrial Model of Mexico and the Mexican version

of the Wharton model. The comparison serves to assess
the plausibility of the model as an instrument for
macroeconomic forecasting.

Table 6.1 lists the assumed income distribution parameters of the reference run. They are assumed to be
fixed. There are no other estimations for 1975-1979,
but as suggested in Chapter 2, Section 4, income distribution was more or less constant, or deteriorated
slightly during that period. For 1980-1990, the assumption of a fixed income distribution structure reflects
the 'basic' character of the projection. The A and
$\hat{\Pi}$ (behavioral) parameters, which have been estimated
for both 1975 and 1978, take their 1975 values in the
reference simulation and are also assumed to be constant. In all of the other simulations they take their
1978 values.

Table 6.1:   Reference Run: Assumed Parameter Values

Definition	Notation	Estimation Year
Technical coefficients	A	1975
Income distribution (private)	V^{p*}	1977
Input imports	$\hat{\Pi}$	1975

The actual distribution coefficients for public investment, the actual rate of foreign savings between 1975-
1979 and their assumed patterns for 1980-1990 are presented in Table 6.2.

The initial (1972-1975) values of gross outputs and the
external (public) debt (1975) are given in Mexico
(1979a) and Mexico (1980c), respectively. The results
of the reference run are presented in Appendix D.1.

Table 6.2: Distribution of public investment and rate of foreign saving 1975-1990. Reference run.

	1975	1976	1977	1978	1979	1980	1981	1982	1983	1984-90
Distribution of public investment [1][2]										
1 Agriculture	.073	.073	.057	.046	.073	.073	.046	.057	.073	.073
2 Livestock	.010	.010	.007	.006	.010	.010	.006	.007	.010	.010
3 Forestry	.006	.005	.005	.005	.008	.008	.005	.005	.005	.006
4 Fishing	.009	.008	.007	.008	.005	.005	.008	.007	.008	.009
5 Mining	.003	.003	.010	.010	.010	.010	.010	.010	.003	.003
6 Quarrying	.003	.003	.010	.010	.010	.010	.010	.010	.003	.003
7 Petroleum	.129	.139	.231	.288	.331	.331	.288	.231	.139	.129
23 Fertilizers	.042	.047	.081	.028	.025	.025	.028	.081	.047	.042
29 Basic metallic ind.	.080	.067	.026	.011	.011	.011	.011	.026	.067	.080
33 Transport equipment	.002	.003	.004	.002	.002	.002	.002	.004	.003	.002
34 Motor vehicles	.011	.013	.021	.007	.007	.007	.007	.021	.013	.011
36 Construction	.133	.123	.075	.111	.101	.101	.111	.075	.123	.133
37 Electricity	.103	.113	.132	.126	.110	.110	.126	.132	.113	.103
39 Transport	.078	.072	.061	.032	.030	.030	.032	.061	.072	.078
40 Communications	.135	.136	.120	.108	.100	.100	.108	.120	.136	.135
45 Other services	.096	.098	.066	.115	.080	.080	.115	.066	.098	.096
Rate of foreign saving [3]	.032	.016	.013	.016	.016	.016	.016	.016	.016	.016

[1] Actual values are given for 1975-1979, with the exception of sector 1 - see note 2. The assumption about the evolution for 1980-1990 is that after the peak attained in 1979, concentration in the oil sector gradually decreases, thereby reproducing the profile for 1975-1979 (i.e.

$z_{1980}^g = z_{1979}^g$, $z_{1981}^g = z_{1978}^g$, etc.). The pattern is unchanged for 1984-1990.

[2] The highly aggregated data presented by Mexico (1979a) only include the sectors which appear in the table. However, it is well known that the Mexican State has some kind of activity in nearly all sectors (see, for instance, Fajnzylber and Tarragó, 1976, p. 154, Cuadro 2). In addition, the figure corresponding to agriculture is too high, given the stagnation in agricultural performance. These two aspects are reflected in Table 6.2 by the assumption that half of agricultural investments are dispersed over all of the sectors which do not appear in the table. That is, agriculture has one-half of the 'actual' coefficient, and all sectors not covered by the table are attributed a .003 coefficient.

[3] Actual values for 1975-1978. After 1978, the rate is assumed to remain unchanged.

Source: Mexico (1979a).

Validation of the model

The purpose of the validation run is to assess the performance of the model when the policy parameters and
the exogenous variable take their actual values. If
the solution for these values coincides with past development acceptably well, then some confidence may be
attributed to its (conditional) predictions. The question as to how much confidence can be ascribed to the
model and how much discrepancy with reality is accept-
able may be elaborated by means of statistical methods,
but cannot be decided in an ultimate way. Although
stable in the past, structural parameters (and structures) may change in the future. In any event, if the
causal relationships posed by the model are considered
relevant and true, then the model could be accepted as
a good instrument for exploring the response of a
complex structure to different interventions. The model
would then be useful, regardless of its (ex post) pre-
dictive power.[1]

---

[1]Cf. the following view of Leif Johansen (1977, p. 342): 'The
forecasting viewpoint is too narrow when there is in fact some
planning and conscious economic policy taking place. The planning
models can only be judged and compared in a broader context,
according to the contributions they make to good planning and
policy. In such a context the ability of a model to span a large
set of alternatives as a basis for choice is of great importance.
...No comparison between planned and realized figures as if we
were only concerned with forecasting can provide a basis for
judging about the performance of a model in this crucial function.' This kind of conditional determinism is a widespread
attitude even in modern natural sciences. 'The future is not included in the past. Even in physics, as in sociology, only various
possible 'scenarios' can be predicted. But it is for this very
reason that we are participating in a fascinating adventure in
which, in the words of Niels Bohr, we are 'both spectators and
actors'.' (Prigogine, 1980, p. xvii.) That is, there is always
some kind of interaction between observer and observed, both are
'merging and interpenetrating aspects of one whole reality' (Bohm,
1980, p. 9). (Cf. the problem of the 'publication effect' in
economic forecasting (Frisch, 1962).) 'Pure science', on the other
hand, may be understood (Weil, 1950, p. 24) as 'a contemplation
of the world order as a necessity.'

Table 6.3 shows the growth rates of the economic variables which are currently produced in the national
accounts statistics and the corresponding values of the
reference experiment using the model. The performance
of the model seems to be rather satisfactory when
aggregate variables are compared. Most sectoral production results also agree quite well. Some sectoral
rates, however, show rather large discrepancies. The
sectors with the largest errors (sectors 4, 14, 16,
19, 23, 24, 26 and 27) are relatively 'small' sectors,
with a very low share of total output. Slight errors
in the estimation of the investment parameters (incremental capital output ratios and/or public investment allocation shares) might then have had considerable
impact on growth rates. This result would suggest the
convenience of avoiding excessively detailed disaggre-
gations and of adopting sectoral classifications which
imply homogeneous output shares.

Table 6.3: Comparison of model and actual values. Growth rates of selected variables, 1975-79 and 1979-90.

Variables	Model 1975-79	Actual[1] 1975-79	Actual[1] 1976-79	Model 1979-90
GNP	6.9	5.0	. 6.0	7.7
Total consumption	6.8	3.7	4.8	7.2
Private consumption	6.8	3.2	4.5	7.1
Government consumption	8.3	6.6	6.5	9.0
Total investment	5.5	5.0	7.6	9.6
Total exports	6.1	11.3	13.0	12.9
Total imports	6.6	3.5	7.8	7.7
Total output	8.0	5.2	6.3	8.5
Sectoral output				
1 Agriculture	3.0	2.2	2.6	4.5
2 Livestock	3.1	2.9	2.8	3.0
3 Forestry	7.8	5.0	5.8	10.6
4 Fishing	22.9	6.4	6.5	17.3
5 Mining	-.1	4.4	2.9	3.0
6 Quarrying	7.2	.8	2.2	8.6
7 Petroleum	15.9	11.4	12.9	13.5
8 Slaughter of livestock and poultry	7.9	5.0	4.4	11.0
9 Milling	6.3	4.3	5.4	6.9
10 Other processed food	4.2	2.9	2.3	3.7
11 Beverages	7.7	8.0	12.8	3.0
12 Tobacco	10.6	4.7	6.4	12.9
13 Soft fiber textiles	4.6	4.9	5.7	3.1
14 Other textiles	17.6	-3.3	-2.8	20.0
15 Wearing apparel and footwear	4.2	5.6	6.0	3.5
16 Wood and cork	17.2	6.2	6.0	14.5
17 Paper and paper products	2.5	8.8	7.0	5.0
18 Printing, publishing	7.3	5.0	4.4	7.1
19 Leather	19.4	-.3	-.8	16.8
20 Rubber products	9.1	4.9	2.5	7.0
21 Basic chemicals	2.9	1.2	0.0	5.6
22 Synthetic fibers	8.6	10.2	9.9	5.5
23 Fertilizers	36.4	1.3	1.8	18.0
24 Soaps and detergents	19.7	6.7	6.7	15.1
25 Drugs and medicines	2.0	-4.7	-6.4	6.8
26 Perfumes, cosmetics	19.2	-1.1	-2.2	15.0
27 Other chemical industries	14.5	6.3	6.1	14.3
28 Nonmetallic mineral products	6.6	6.7	7.4	3.7
29 Masic metallic industries	13.9	9.2	10.9	14.0
30 Metal products	6.4	7.3	10.0	6.3
31 Machinery	10.1	8.1	10.8	6.3
32 Electrical machinery	4.9	10.1	9.0	6.0
33 Transport equipment	8.6	4.4	5.9	7.1
34 Motor vehicles	12.4	6.9	12.9	9.4
35 Other manufacturing industries	2.4	9.6	12.9	12.0
36 Construction	18.2	5.4	7.9	15.3
37 Electricity	15.1	6.4	8.5	12.3
38 Cinema	4.7	2.7	2.9	7.0
39 Transport	7.6	6.7	7.5	5.6
40 Communications	23.6	7.3	9.7	15.7
41 Trade	3.2	3.4	4.9	1.0
42 Dwellings	2.0	1.5	2.0	.6
43 Hotels and restaurants	3.9	5.9	6.6	3.3
44 Credit and insurance	6.0	4.1	5.5	6.0
45 Other services	7.3	2.6	3.5	8.9

[1] The 1975-79 rates are affected by the fact that 1975 was a year of stagnation. It therefore seems more appropriate to compare the model results with the actual rates for 1976-79. Sources: Appendix D.1 and Mexico (1980a).

Basic projection results

Let us now turn to the basic simulation results for
1979-1990, as given in Table 6.3. Under the assumptions
of the basic run, the Mexican growth rate remains high.
GNP grows at an annual rate of 7.7 percent during the
period.[1] Sectoral output growth, however, is not proportional. While agricultural output grows slowly (4.5
percent), as do most basic goods-producing sectors,[2]
the petroleum sector and some manufacturing sectors exhibit high growth rates. Oil production and related
industries (sector 7) grow at an average of 13.5 percent, although at a decreasing annual rate.

The 'basic trajectory' projections of the Mexican industrial plan (Mexico, 1979c) produced comparable
results.[3] According to this projection, the growth
rate of output is 6.5 percent in 1980-1990. Agricultural
output grows by 2 percent. This more realistic result
for the evolution of agriculture under 'conservative'
assumptions was reached by imposing the trend growth
rate exogenously. On the other hand, for 1980-1990, the
'basic trajectory' projections assume a less plausible
growth rate for the oil sector (5.7 percent on the
average, below GNP growth).

The Mexican version of the Wharton Econometric Model,
used to forecast the long-run effects of two different
stabilization policies, showed similar results (see
Beltrán del Río, 1980). The solutions of the Wharton
model implied growth rates above 8 percent per year

---

[1] All rates can be transformed into per-capita terms on the basis
of an average population growth of 3.3 percent during the 1970s.
However, the rate of population growth is expected to decrease
about one percentage point in the 1980s.

[2] The basic ('socially necessary') goods-producing sectors are
those numbered 8-15, 17-19, 24, 25 and 35 (Mexico, 1980b, Anexo
2.7.2).

[3] A brief description of the Industrial Plan and Wharton models
was given in Chapter 3, Section 5.

for the first half of the 1980s. Fluctuations, and
some decay afterwards, reduce the growth rate for
1979-1990 to 6.9 percent.

Total private consumption grows by 7.2 percent in
1979-1990. Private consumption of agricultural goods
grows by 5.2 percent, i.e. more rapidly than agricultural output. The average rate of the 'basic trajectory' is 5.6 percent.

Government consumption of goods and services grows by
9 percent. (The 'basic trajectory' projections show a
9.5 percent rate.) As a result of the linear homogeneous functions assumed for public consumption, there
is equiproportional growth in the consumption of all
goods and services.

Public investment by sector of destination (see Appendix D.1.4) reflects the investment policy assumed in
the basic run. In 1980, it attains its highest concentration in the oil sector (33.1 percent), and decreases thereafter until 1984, when it becomes stable.
Average growth of total public investment is 8.8 percent for 1979-1990. This result differs from both the
'basic trajectory' and the Wharton model forecasts
(15.0 and 11.4 percent, respectively). Although a less
realistic forecast, the basic run solution is 'more
basic' in the sense that fewer changes are assumed in
the behavior of the government, whereas the other
projections assume increases in the government's
activity parameters.

Private investment by sector of destination (Table D.1.5)
shows negative investment values in some sectors in
the initial years. This is a result of the acceleration
principle that governs the allocation of private investments. When capital equipment is assumed to be spe-

cific to each sector, or when it has a low mobility, such behavior seems difficult to accept. Total private investment grows slightly faster than public investment (10.6 percent). There are no large differences with the 'basic trajectory' or Wharton projections (8.4 and 8.5 percent, respectively).

The foreign trade accounts (Table D.1.7) show a permanent deterioration in the agricultural trade deficit (7.5 percent). In 1990, imports cover nearly two-thirds of the final consumption of agricultural goods.[1]

Other basic goods and capital goods-producing sectors also show increasing trade deficits. The oil sector does not begin to produce a positive surplus until 1980, after which oil exports grow by 16.0 percent. The Wharton model assumes a rate of 16.3 percent.[2] The 'basic trajectory' assumes that oil exports have attained a maximum in 1982. This latter assumption, which seems out-dated today, produces a very low rate of growth in oil exports for 1979-1990 (3.1 percent).

The public sector accounts (Table D.1.8) indicate the 'basic' character of the assumptions related to the behavior of the government sector. Tax pressure is rather low and stable. The government's share of total investment does not increase. The Wharton model shows important increases for both indicators (from 18.8 to 28.4, and from 44.1 to 52.5 percent, respectively).

The effects of the basic projection on sectoral employ-

---

[1] Agricultural imports increase by 6.8 percent. The 'basic trajectory' result is 8.4. Sectoral balances of trade are not calculated. The Wharton model, an aggregated model, does not produce sectoral results.

[2] Assumptions about probable future values of exogenous and policy variables were worked out by a consulting group, where experts from the private and public sectors participated (Beltrán del Río 1980, p. 563).

ment are shown in Table D.1.9. Total employment increases by 5.5 percent (as compared to 3.9 and 3.5
percent in the 'basic trajectory' and Wharton Forecasts, respectively). Agricultural employment decreases
in relation to total employment, although it increases
by an average of 3 percent in absolute terms. Employment in the construction and some manufacturing sectors
increase at more rapid rates.

Rural social classes decrease their share of total employment (Table D.1.10), due to the decline in the
relative importance of agriculture.[1] The same reason
explains the slight decrease in the income shares of
rural social classes (Table D.1.11). Total private
incomes increase by 7.9 percent.[2] Total average incomes - as defined in this study, i.e., disposable
income per employed person - increase by 1.9 percent
(Table D.1.12). The inequality Gini index maintains
a stable (high) level over the period. This is due to
the assumption of a constant income distribution
structure, combined with an investment policy which
does not change output composition to any large extent.
There are no relevant differences between different indicators of welfare growth; they vary between 1.5
(for the 'equal weights' index) and 2 percent (for the
efficiency-equity index).

---

[1] The Industrial Plan and the Wharton model do not produce comparable indicators for this and the following indicators.

[2] Per capita incomes would then increase by 4.4 percent, assuming
an unchanged rate of demographic growth (3.3 percent).

3. Global Plan Simulations

The aim of the Mexican Global Development Plan 1980-
1982 (Mexico, 1980b) is to change the quality of growth.
The main economic objectives of the new development
strategy are to:

- increase Mexico's self-reliance
- increase employment
- provide for welfare minima, primarily meeting the
  needs for food, education, health care and housing
- promote high, efficient and sustained economic
  growth
- reduce the skewness in income distribution, among persons, regions, and factors of production (p. 6).

These main objectives are disaggregated further into
22 more specific policies or guidelines. The following
are particularly relevant to our study:

- reorient the productive structure; increase the
  production of basic goods (p. 8)
- accelerate development in the agricultural sector;
  attain agricultural self-sufficiency in the medium
  term (p. 8, pp. 154-155).

There are no other specific indications regarding income distribution policies; the guidelines only state
the general purpose of adequate distribution of increased productivity (p. 8).

The Global Plan specifies measures and guidelines for
economic and social policy of a qualitative and indicative character. The principal instrument of quantitative economic policy is the state budget. Public investment will be given a new impetus (its planned
growth is 14 percent per year in 1978-1982). This possibility is opened up by increased revenues from the
oil-exploiting sector. The growing emphasis on basic

goods is reflected in the reorientation of public investment. Additional weight is given to basic goods-
producing sectors. Investment in agriculture and related sectors will grow by 22 percent, and in other
basic goods-producing industrial sectors by 17 percent.
Investment in the production of social services is
planned to grow by 21 percent. Investment in the transport and communications sectors will grow by 18 percent (pp. 86-87).

The effects of this policy are estimated by means of a
macroeconometric model (see Mexico, 1980b, Anexo 2).[1]
They are the quantitative macroeconomic targets of the
Global Plan.

In the following subsections, our model is used to
analyze the effects of the Global Plan policies. First,
the effects of a 'basic' interpretation of the strategy
represented in the Plan are compared with the macroeconometric projections of the Global Plan model. This
allows for further assessment of the plausibility of
our model and discussion of possible implications of
the Global Plan strategy.

Then, the model is used to analyze the partial effects
of income redistribution and agricultural reform, under
the assumption of the Global Plan investment policy (see
Table D.2.4) and its expected rate of foreign savings
(1 percent of GNP). Two different assumptions about
the performance of the agricultural sector are considered. The first is 'optimistic', where agricultural investment is assumed to recover its prestagnation level
of effectiveness as a result of the introduction of a
reform program; the second is 'pessimistic', where no
significant changes occur and agriculture maintains
its present low level of efficiency.

---

[1] For a short description of the model, see Chapter 3, Section 5.

Case One simulation

Case One is a 'conservative' projection, based on the assumption of no changes in income distribution and agricultural efficiency. It may also be considered 'basic', as it is perhaps possible that income re-distribution and agricultural reform policies - even if consistently devised and implemented - may take more than the three years of the Global Plan to produce their effects. There is also the previously mentioned fact that the Global Plan does not specify income redistribution policies, and that the macro-econometric projections of the Plan do not seem to have assumed changes in income distribution.

Income distribution is thus kept unchanged in this simulation, i.e. sectoral income shares by income class and government's income parameters are fixed throughout the simulation period (see Table 6.6 in the next sub-section).

Table 6.4 shows the macroeconomic targets of the Global Plan and the corresponding Case One simulation values. Most of the growth rates of the variables agree quite well.

Table 6.4: Global Plan - Case One comparison. Growth rates of economic aggregates, 1979-82

Variable	Global Plan	Case One Simulation
GNP	8.0	8.1
Total consumption	7.7	6.4
Private consumption	7.7	6.4
Public consumption	7.5	10.3
Total investment	13.5	11.5
Private investment	13.0	12.7
Public investment	14.0	10.0
Imports	20.8	7.2
Exports	14.4	11.0

Sources: Mexico (1980b, p. 83) and Appendix D.2.

However, the Case One simulation does not exactly reflect the planned change in the behavior of the public sector. As mentioned above, the simulation does not assume any changes in the behavior of the government, whereas the Global Plan assumes an increased public investment effort.

The projections of total imports also reflect large differences. The high import elasticities experienced in Mexico in recent years determined this result in the econometric imports function of the Global Plan model.[1] The optimistic result of the Case One simulation depends on our proportionality assumptions for imports.

The Global Plan set production targets at a disaggregated level.[2] The level of disaggregation is 14 sectors, instead of the 45-sector classification of the national accounts. The projected growth rates are shown in Table 6.5, and compared with the Case One simulation results (aggregated to 14 sectors).

Table 6.5 shows considerable discrepancies for the forestry and fishing sectors. The planned increases in public investment directed towards these sectors are reflected in growth rates which are higher than those estimated by the macroeconometric model of the Global Plan, whose structure does not include this type of effects.

---

[1] The income elasticity of demand for imports has increased considerably since 1976, presumably due to the liberalization of protective policies initiated in that year (Brailovsky, 1981, pp. 92-96).

[2] Aggregate demand obtained from a macroeconometric function is disaggregated by an input-output block, as in Preston (1975). See Chapter 3, Section 5.

Table 6.5: Global Plan - Case One comparison. Sectoral
            growth rates, 1979-1982

	Global Plan	Case One
1. Agriculture and livestock[a]	4.0	3.8
2. Forestry	5.6	11.8
3. Fishing	9.4	18.2
4. Mining[b]	6.8	7.1
5. Petroleum	14.0	‹22.8
6. Manufactured basic goods[c]	8.0	6.3
7. Chemical industries[d]	9.7	13.3
8. Durable and capital goods[e]	13.5	7.3
9. Construction and inputs[f]	11.1	16.2
10. Electricity	10.7	15.0
11. Trade	6.7	2.6
12. Transport and communications[g]	9.5	8.0
13. Tourism and recreation[h]	7.8	3.3
14. Other services[i]	6.0	4.6

a) Corresponds to sectors 1 and 2 of the 45-sector
classification; b) sectors 5 and 6; c) sectors 8 to 15,
17 to 19, 24, 25 and 35; d) sectors 20 to 23, 26 and
27; e) sectors 29 to 34; f) sectors 16, 28 and 36;
g) sectors 39 and 40; h) sectors 43 and 38; i) sectors
42, 44 and 45. Other sectors are the same as in the
45-sector classification (Mexico, 1980b, pp. 81-82).

Sources: Mexico (1980b, p. 154) and Appendix D.2.1.

The differences in the growth estimates of the oil sector are more interesting. The implementation of the
investment policy of the Global Plan may have a stronger
impact on oil production than expected. If investment
in the oil sector follows its planned path, oil production and exports might increase at a much higher rate
than planned, thus implying an unexpectedly high degree
of 'petrolization'.

According to the Case One simulation, the manufactured
basic goods-producing sectors grow less than the average.

The same applies to agriculture and livestock. In the
case of the former, the Global Plan projections show
a slightly more optimistic estimate, thus possibly un-
derrating inflationary or sectoral import pressures
and negative distribution effects.

The projections of private consumption (Table D.2.2)
seem to confirm this possibility, as the consumption
of basic goods in most cases grows faster than output.
Hence, the corresponding sectoral trade balances
(Table D.2.7) deteriorate rapidly. In the case of the
agricultural sector, for instance, the trade deficit
increases by 8.0 percent per year in 1979-1982. This
result contradicts the stated objective of increased
self-sufficiency for the sector.

Now, large agricultural trade deficits such as those
predicted in the Case One simulation may turn out to
be impossible - e.g. due to lack of transport or storage capacity. Or they may become inadmissible - e.g.
because of inconsistency with the highly valued objective of agricultural self-sufficiency. In both cases,
the result would be excess demands, which would increase agricultural prices. Inflationary pressures may
then increase. The hypothesis of unchanged distribution
adopted in the Case One simulation may appear to be
optimistic under these circumstances.

One of the aims of the Global Plan is to create 2.2
million new jobs, i.e. an average annual increase of
4.2 percent. The Case One simulation agrees; 2.1 million
more people are employed in 1982. Employment increases
at a rate of 4.7 percent, 1.4 percent more than labor
supply growth (Table D.2.9).

Income redistribution and agricultural reform: Case
Two-Four simulations

We now turn to an analysis of the effects of income
redistribution policy and efficiency-increasing reforms
in the agricultural sector. Two new hypotheses about
income distribution policy and agricultural reform are
introduced and combined with the investment policy
of the Global Plan 1980-82 and its expected rate of
foreign saving. Between 1982 and 1990, the Plan's investment policy is assumed to remain unchanged. Strictly speaking, only the first three years of these simulations apply to the Global Plan, as 1982 is its last
year.

The alternative assumption about income distribution
policy is that there is an initial once and for all
income redistribution. As shown in Table 6.6, Cases
Three and Four assume that the income share of the
highest class is reduced by 30 percent, the following four are unchanged, poor peasants receive 50 percent more, and landless workers double their income
share. This implies a 16 percent increase in income
equality (as measured by the Gini coefficient). That
is, an exogenous change in the structure of income.
distribution is stipulated, which can be assumed to
reflect an increase in tax progressivity and the
establishment of a subsidies system. The very simple
specification of income distribution adopted in our
model, where value added is directly 'paid' to households, does not allow for a more elaborated specification of the tax policy.[1] The subsidies side is
represented by the public investment policy variable.
In the sectors where there is no significant

---

[1] For a (static) general equilibrium study of taxation in Mexico,
see Serra Puche (1979). For a survey of this type of empirical
general equilibrium models of taxation and fiscal reform, see
Fullerton et al. (1981).

Table 6.6:   Global Plan runs: assumed parameter values [a]

Simulation	Income distribution (private)		Incremental capital output ratio in agriculture
Case One		V^{p*}_{1977}	4.2
Case Two		V^{p*}_{1977}	2.1
Case Three	(0.7 1.0 $\hat{1.0}$ 1.0 1.0 1.5 2.0)	V^{p*}_{1977}	4.2
Case Four	(0.7 1.0 $\hat{1.0}$ 1.0 1.0 1.5 2.0)	V^{p*}_{1977}	2.1

[a] Parameters not appearing in the table take the same values in all Global Plan simulations.

public ownership - as in agriculture - public investment is understood to be a form of subsidization. One of the effects of institutional reforms in the agricultural sector would be to shift public investment from the saturated, modern farming to the low capital density, poor, peasant segment (see Chapter 2, Section 3). This would contribute to a simultaneous redistribution of agricultural incomes and increase investment effectiveness.

The MFS (Mexican Food System, Sistema Alimentario Mexicano) represents this type of approach to agricultural reform. The MFS is a large official research program - it includes 20 research projects - aimed at the detailed design of a policy oriented towards increasing the consumption levels of staple-foods and the level of self-sufficiency in the supply of these goods. This, of course, implies a considerable growth effort in the agricultural sector.

The MFS program began in 1979. Up until now it has

produced several studies and two preliminary surveys.[1]

As seen in Chapter 2, Section 3, the MFS studies con-
clude that income redistribution is necessary for increasing output. Or, in other words, it is not possible
to augment agricultural effectiveness without increasing the earning capacity of the peasant sector.

The basic policy is to shift the focus of all forms of
state support - public investment, credit, agricultural
extension, seeds, fertilizers - from the saturated and
highly concentrated 'modern' - often irrigated - sector,
towards the peasant, 'traditional', dry-land sector.
Thus, by introducing new resources and knowledge, large
idle productive capacities could be mobilized.[2]

The aspects of self-organization and cooperation among
poor peasants and rural workers are stressed in order
to increase their capacity for adopting new technolo-
gies and their bargaining power, incomes and accumulation possibilities. Different forms of cooperation,
with state support, are proposed for the development
of the 'agri-business' or agricultural industries.
Peasants and landless workers would be associated with
the state - and possibly private capital - in large-
scale, but labor-intensive, agro-industrial projects.
The organizational principle would be as little state
administration and as much peasant self-management as
possible.

---

[1] They are summarized in Sección Nacional (1980a); for a summary
in English see Anonymous (1981). See also Montes de Oca and Rello
(1982).

[2] MFS agronomic studies quoted by Montes de Oca and Rello (1982,
p. 175) indicate the possibility of doubling yields per hectare
in peasant areas, by simple investments such as small irrigation
works and fertilization.

The implementation of the measures suggested by the
MFS is to be performed on a decentralized basis. This
requires profound reforms in the bureaucratic institutions and practices prevalent today in government
agencies which deal with the agricultural sector, so
as to 'radically change the old paternalistic and
authoritarian conception' (Montes de Oca and Rello,
1982, p. 176). A prerequisite for institutional change
is an increase in the level of organization of the
peasants and their capacity to influence policy-making
effectively. The peasants would have to participate in
the design and implementation of policies and projects
at the local level. The local governments and the
ejido - the collective local organizations of the
Mexican peasants - would enter into contracts on
planned production levels. They would also be respon-
sible for control and evaluation of the agreed production targets.

As shown in Table 6.6, the Case Two and Case Four simulations assume that agricultural investment recovers
its pre-stagnation level of efficiency, i.e. that the
incremental capital output ratio takes the value adjusted for the period 1952-1967 (see Chapter 5, Section 6). It is assumed then that the shift in the resource flow towards the peasant sector reaches the
1952-1967 level of effectiveness, at negligible (re-
organization and other) costs. In cases One and Three,
the incremental capital output ratio maintains its 'actual' value.

Income redistribution and increased agricultural efficiency, as in Case Four, can be interpreted as a result
of the successful implementation of the MFS reforms

which, as we have seen, aim at reducing inequality and
increasing agricultural output growth. Case Two, where
constant income distribution is assumed along with increased agricultural efficiency, may be regarded as
'unrealistic', as it does not seem possible to increase
investment effectiveness without increasing the earning capacity of the peasants, and thereby changing income distribution (see Chapter 2, Section 3). It may
also seem unrealistic that, as in Case Three, incomes
could be redistributed, without simultaneously increasing agricultural efficiency. As stated in the preceding
subsection, the high and increasing agricultural imports that would result in such a situation may become
impossible in the sense that food price increases, inflation, (endogenous) income concentration and reduced
consumption could occur. But the purpose of the simulations in this section is to assess the partial effects
of policy parameter changes, and not to suggest realistic scenarios.

Let us now present and compare the result of the Case
One-Four simulations.[1] Figure 6.1 shows the time
pattern of total gross output results for the four
assumed cases of the Global Plan for 1980-1990. The
figure illustrates the savings-reducing effect of the
assumed redistribution, which affects output growth negatively (cf. cases One and Three). However, the effect
is rather weak (it represents a decrease of .7 in the
growth rate; see Table 6.7). The ceteris paribus effect
of the assumed recovery in agricultural investment effectiveness on total output growth is weaker (cf.
cases One and Two); it implies a .3 increase in the
growth rate (see Table 6.7). In Case Four, then, the
savings-reducing effect dominates over the acceleration of growth in agricultural output (cf. cases One
and Four).

---

[1] Tables corresponding to Case Two to Case Four simulations are
not included in the Appendix. They can be obtained from the
author on request.

Figure 6.1: Global Plan Cases. Total output, 1980-1990

10^{12} 1978 pesos

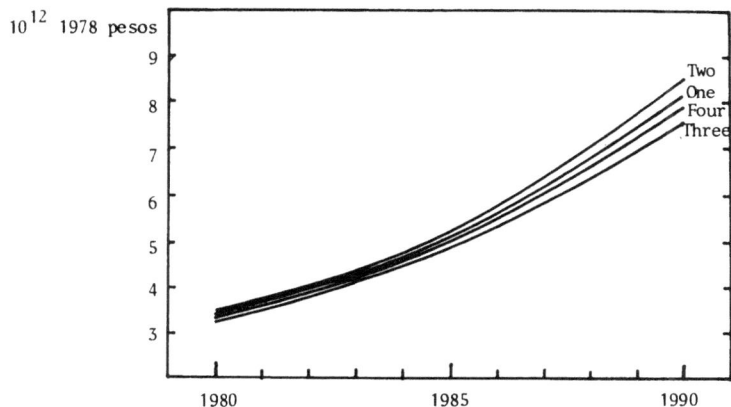

Low output response of agricultural investment has
significant consequences for the evolution of the agricultural balance of trade, as shown in Figure 6.2.
There is a permanent deterioration in the balance of
trade, as demand grows faster than domestic output.
When incomes are redistributed (Case Three), there is
a higher level of consumption of agricultural products
and the trade deficit is slightly larger than when
there is no income redistribution (Case One). The rate
of deterioration is the same in both cases.

Figure 6.2: Global Plan Cases. Agricultural balance of trade,
             1980-1990

10^9 1978 pesos

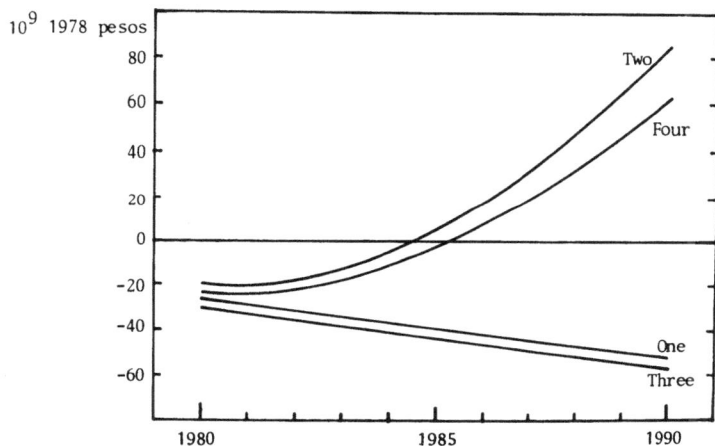

When the investment response of agricultural output is increased, the agricultural balance of trade improves at a high rate. Depending on whether or not there is redistribution, trade equilibrates in 1985 or 1984, respectively.

When, as in Case Two, agriculture responds effectively and incomes are not redistributed, employment increases the most (see Figure 6.3). This is due to the high employment output ratio of agriculture and to the positive relationship between employment and output on one hand, and between output growth and income concentration on the other. (Case Two also has the best growth performance.)

Figure 6.3: Global Plan Cases. Total employment, 1980-1990

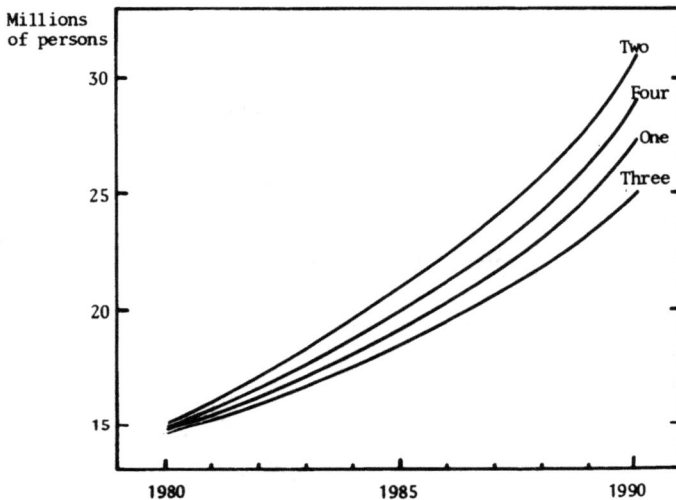

Redistribution, when combined with stagnating agriculture (Case Three), gives the lowest improvement in employment. (It also gave the worst growth results.)

However, redistribution combined with efficient agriculture (Case Four) has a better employment performance than no redistribution with inefficient agriculture (Case One). The result is the converse with respect to growth.

In short, the existence of a well-functioning agricultural sector is most important for employment, while a high savings rate - no redistribution - is most important for growth.

The inclusion of a social preference function modifies the order given by the output or the national income indicators. Figure 6.4 shows the results for the efficiency-equity social welfare function, i.e. national income corrected by (one minus) the Gini coefficient of inequality (see Chapter 3, Section 9).

Figure 6.4: Global Plan Cases. Efficiency-equity social welfare index, 1980-1990

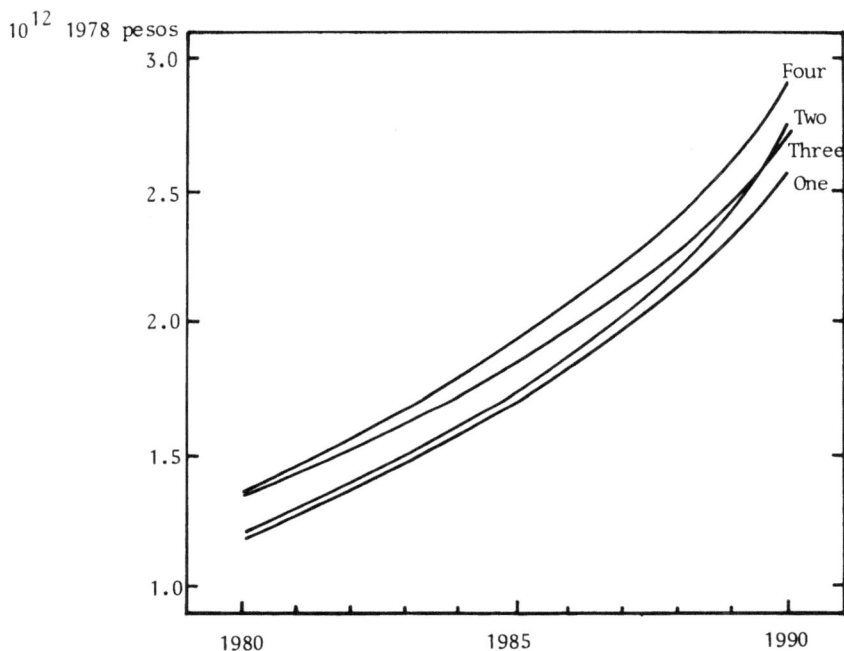

The income redistribution assumed in cases Three and
Four increases equality - one minus the Gini coefficient - by about 16 percent. Welfare performance in
cases Three and Four is therefore about 16 percent
higher than in the corresponding cases without redistribution.

The redistributive cases have higher welfare performance
throughout most of the simulation period. Towards 1989,
however, the higher (dynamic) 'efficiency' of the case
without redistribution where growth is fastest (Case
Two), more than compensates the higher 'equity' of
Case Three, which has the lowest growth performance.

The adoption of other welfare functions (i.e. 'equal
weights' and 'poverty weighted' functions) yields results similar to those of the efficiency-equity function; the relative position of the different cases is
the same.

The results are summarized in Table 6.7.

Table 6.7: Global Plan Cases. Growth rates of selected
            state variables, 1980-1990

	Output	Agricultural balance of trade	Employment	Welfare [a]
Case One	8.8	-.7	6.0	7.8
Case Two	9.1	11.6	7.4	8.3
Case Three	8.1	-.6	5.3	8.3
Case Four	8.5	11.4	6.7	9.0

[a] Efficiency-equity welfare index.

4. Status-Quo-Plus-Oil Scenario

The purpose of the Status-quo-plus-oil run is to simulate oil-intensive development, or 'petrolization'.
As we have seen in our description of the characteristic features of oil-led development in 'nondesert'
countries (Chapter 2, Section 1), this type of strategy concentrates public resources in the oil-producing
sector. The agricultural sector, on the other hand, is
neglected, in the sense that it is allocated a low
- and often falling - share of public expenditure and
that no significant changes in agricultural policies
and institutions are introduced in order to remove
existent obstacles to growth and equity. The oil-intensive strategy has accelerated inflation and produced
tendencies towards negative redistribution. Economic
policy, however, has tried to compensate some of the
negative redistributive effects.

The Status-quo-plus-oil scenario interprets the above
features of the oil-intensive development strategy as
follows. Public investment policy is assumed to remain
constant during the period 1979-1990. That is, the
distribution of public investment maintains the high
level of concentration in the oil sector attained in
1979 (33 percent), while the share of agriculture
remains at its relatively low level in that year (see
Table D.3.4).

No significant agricultural reforms are assumed to be
introduced. Agricultural investment is assumed to
retain its present (low) level of effectiveness. The
absence of agricultural reforms also implies that the
present skewness in income distribution is not reduced.[1]

---

[1] Alternative hypotheses about the value of the agricultural effectiveness parameter might, of course, be made. For instance, it could
be assumed that this parameter increases as in Case Two above. A
Status-quo scenario with doubled agricultural effectiveness (and no
redistribution) would be similar to Case Two. They would differ only
in their rates of foreign saving (.010 in Case Two, .016 in Status-
quo), and in the higher oil intensity (and lower agriculture intensity) of the Status-quo public investment policy (cf. tables

Cont. on next page

The income distribution policy of the Status-quo-plus-oil scenario assumes that the structure of income distribution remains constant, which is intended to reflect the fact that negative distributive effects are compensated by policy measures.

The rate of external trade deficit is assumed to maintain the 1978 level (see Table 6.8).

Table 6.8: Status-quo-plus-oil scenario: assumed parameter values[a]

Rate of foreign saving	Income distribution		Incremental capital output ratio in agriculture
	Private	Government	
0.016	v^{p*}_{1977}	v^d	4.2

[a] Parameters which do not appear in the table take the same values in all simulations, except for public investment distribution coefficients.

Let us now briefly comment on the results of the Status-quo-plus-oil simulation.

In the Status-quo-plus-oil strategy, oil production is among the most dynamic sectors, as could be expected given its high rate of investment (Table D.3.1). The long-run rate of growth is about 22 percent, while the economy as a whole grows at about 9 percent. Agriculture and other food-producing sectors grow less than the average. Private consumption of these goods grows faster than production (Table D.3.2).

Cont. of note from page 183.

D.2.4 and D.3.4 in the Appendix). However, such a scenario may seem 'unrealistic', for the reasons discussed in relation to Case Two (necessary link between increased effectiveness and reduced incomes concentration). An estimate of the effects of this type of scenario on the growth rates of the state variables is presented in the concluding section (Table 6.11).

The agricultural trade deficit (Table D.3.7) then
shows permanent deterioration (it increases annually
by 10 percent). In 1990, almost 60 percent of private
consumption is supplied by imports.

Investments, both private and public, increase at a
high rate in 1979-1990 (13.5 and 11.5 percent, respectively; see Tables D.3.4 and D.3.5). The slightly higher
growth rate of private investment reduces the share of
public investment in total investment (Table D.3.8)
from 48.1 to 42.5 percent. Another indicator of the
public sector's dimension, viz. the tax burden, expands
from 16.8 to 23.8 percent. This is due to the rising
weight of the oil sector in total output, which increases the profits accruing to the government.

Total employment increases by 5.5 percent (Table D.3.9).
Agricultural employment grows less (3.3 percent), and
employment in the oil sector more (14.7 percent), than
the average. There is a relative increase in urban
social groups, due to low agricultural growth (Table
D.3.10).

Total incomes grow at 7.9 percent. Workers, as a class,
benefit from more rapid increases in income, due to
the special income distribution structure of the oil
sector, which tends to dominate in the Status-quo-plus-
oil strategy (Table D.3.11). The average income of the
workers (Table D.3.12) increases at the fastest rate
(4.5 percent). Other classes which benefit are the
high bourgeoisie, both urban and rural, and the urban
middle classes. Urban and rural poor receive more or
less unchanged average incomes during the simulation
period.

The social welfare growth indicators do not exhibit
any significant differences. The slightly higher value

186

in the 'poverty-weighted' index (2 percent) is due to
the increase in the income share of the workers. The
'equal-weights' and 'efficiency-equity' indicators
grow by 1.6 and 1.7 percent, respectively.

5. Towards a New Development Strategy

At first glance, the model described in Chapter 4
seems to correspond to the 'incomes' approach, for
which it is essential to reduce income concentration.[1]
Models constructed in this tradition are aimed at
tracing the effects of (exogenous) income redistribution on consumption demands, and then exploring the
effects of these changes in demands on, e.g., imports,
employment and saving.

'Income redistribution models' determine output structures that are consistent with the demands generated
by alternative income distributions. But, as pointed
out in Chapter 4, Section 5, the resulting changes in
the composition of output may be infeasible, or in-
consistent with saving and investment behavior in the
economy.

The 'basic needs' approach, on the other hand, stresses
the supply aspects (see e.g. Streeten, 1979). For
this approach, it is essential to produce and supply
basic goods and services for the poor. It calls for
changing the composition of output, to provide appropriate products. Investment projects and aid for meeting basic needs should be given the highest priority.

However, a problem could arise in connection with this
approach if, given the existent income distribution,

[1] A classical exponent of this approach is Chenery et al. (1974).

there is no consistent demand for essential goods and services; if 'supply (of these goods does not) create(s) its own demand'. Another problem is that meeting basic needs could be rendered consistent with increasing inequality, thus presenting the ethical risk of allowing for charitable-manipulative specifications.[1]

Similar to the 'income redistribution models', the model presented in this study stipulates a certain income redistribution - or income distribution policy. The effects on demands are then traced. The model also retains the emphasis on the supply side found in the basic needs approach. Given constraints on sectoral trade, policies aimed at redistributing incomes have to be consistent with policies aimed at increasing the production of basic goods. Public investment policy has the function of stimulating production in those sectors where undesired imbalances may exist (see Chapter 4, Section 8).

The new development strategy (NDS) described in this section implies both income redistribution and changes in the composition of output which increase the relative supply of essential goods.

On the production side, the NDS assumes important changes in the sectoral allocation of public invest-ment. Concentration in the oil sector is rapidly re-duced (e.g. faster than in the Global Plan public in-vestment policy). Investment is instead directed to-wards agriculture - which more than doubles its share of total public investment - and other basic goods-producing sectors. After 1985, capital goods-producing sectors increase their share, at the expense of the service-producing sectors (see Table D.4.4).

---

[1] It should be emphasized that this type of approach usually stresses the importance of reducing inequality and reforming in-stitutions (see e.g.Griffin, 1978, Ch. 7; ILO, 1976; Myrdal, 1981).

The NDS assumes that external payments are in balance throughout the simulation period. That is, it assumes that the existing high level of external indebtedness will not be increased by additional foreign savings. The external debt then increases only by the accumulation of interests.

On the income side, the NDS stipulates an advanced redistribution. It implies important improvements in the incomes of agricultural day laborers, poor peasants and the urban poor. The NDS also has a much greater impact on employment, which makes industrial workers and, in general, all wage earners potential beneficiaries of this strategy. The NDS thus incorporates these classes into the process of economic and social development, from which they have been excluded by the past pattern of growth.

Income shares are modified once and for all, as indicated in Table 6.9. This advanced income redistribution increases equality - one minus the Gini coefficient - by 26 percent (from .587 to .740).

Table 6.9:   New Development Strategy: assumed parameter values[a]

Rate of foreign saving	Income distribution		Incremental capital output ratio in agriculture
	Private	Government	
0.0	(.57 1.0 1.34 1.0 $\hat{.}$43 1.32 1.92) V^{p*}_{1977}	$2V^d$	2.1

[a] Parameters which do not appear in the table are the same in all simulations, with the exception of public investment distribution parameters.

The above income redistribution, as in the Global Plan (cases Three and Four) simulations, may be interpreted as an increase in tax progressivity. The NDS adds an important increase in the level of direct taxes. It is

assumed that direct taxes are doubled. This increases
the share of incomes accruing to the goverrment.

Income redistribution is also assumed to be the result
of far-reaching reforms in the agricultural sector. The
NDS assumes a thorough implementation of the MFS policies surveyed in Section 3 in this chapter, aimed at
improving the effectiveness of investment in agriculture
and reducing income concentration. Agricultural investment is assumed to recover its prestagnation level of
effectiveness.

Let us now comment on the results of the NDS scenario.

The NDS exhibits high growth performance. Total output
increases at a high rate, 10.6 percent in 1980-1990
(see the results in Appendix D.4.1). The NDS then implies a relatively high rate of savings. In the NDS,
redistribution does not imply a reduction in the overall
rate of savings, as it did in the redistributions simulated within the framework of the Global Plan (cases
Three and Four). In the NDS case, a rise in the rate
of direct taxes - which increases the share of incomes
channelled through the public sector - supplements the
redistribution of incomes among socio-economic groups.
The decline in private savings provoked by the reduction in income concentration is then compensated by
increased public saving. The public sector appears to
have a relatively high savings coefficient.[1]

Agricultural output reflects the assumed effects of the
MFS strategy in the countryside. The increase in both
the effectiveness and volume of agricultural investment
makes agricultural output grow faster than total output.

---

[1] It should be recalled that fixed consumption propensities are
assumed for the government in all simulations.

Most manufactured basic goods follow the same pattern.

The rate of output growth in the oil sector shows a
declining pattern, as a result of the reduction in the
share of public investment allocated to the sector.
The average rate of growth in 1980-1990 is high, however (10.9 percent), due to the high and increasing
overall investment level.

After 1985, the growth of the capital goods-producing
sectors accelerates as a consequence of an increased
investment rate.

Consumption of agricultural products grows less than
output. The level of consumption is high, however, as
a result of the once and for all redistribution operated
in the first year of the simulation. The same applies
to other goods with high budget shares in low income
groups. For this reason, there is a trade deficit in
the agricultural sector which diminishes constantly
and disappears towards 1987. After this, there is a
trade surplus. The trade balances of some manufactured
basic goods-producing sectors have the same evolution.
There are permanent surpluses or deficits in a few·
sectors. (Table D.4.7.)

The high rate of growth in the NDS implies a considerable investment effort. Imports represent a significant
share of the supply of investment goods throughout the
period, in spite of the increased share of public resources that capital goods-producing sectors receive
after 1985. Trade deficits appear in most of these sectors throughout the period.

The NDS assumed a doubling of the coefficients of direct
taxes. Direct taxes now represent one-half of total
fiscal revenues (Table D.4.8). The ratio of fiscal re-

venues to GNP is .22, higher than in preceding simulations, although not excessively high if compared with
other countries.[1] The share of public investment in
total investment is also high (70.7 percent in the
first year of the simulation). It declines continuously,
however.

Total employment increases by 10.5 percent in 1980-
1990; this rate is similar to that of total output
(Table D.4.9). Sectors such as agriculture, which have
high employment coefficients, grow faster than the average. The proportion of the labor force occupied in
agriculture increases slightly (to about 39 percent).

Total private incomes grow at high rates, 9.5 percent
in 1980-1990 (Table D.4.11). This growth rate is lower,
however, than that of total employment. Hence, average
income - as defined in this study - declines slightly
in 1980-1990, though not in all subperiods. Low-income
classes exhibit slightly increasing average income,
while there is a decline in that of high-income classes.

The Gini coefficient of the NDS (.26) is lower than that
of the actual income distribution (.41). This implies
a 26 percent increase in equality which is reflected
in the level of the efficiency-equity social welfare
index. Its rate of growth and the growth rates of the
other welfare indicators do not differ significantly
from the average incomes indicator. (Table D.4.12.)

---

[1] The 'normal' ratio, given Mexico's per capita GNP in 1976, was
.17 (Aceituno, 1980, p. 166); see Chapter 2, Section 4.

6. Comparison of the Strategies

Thus far, we have discussed the main results of the simulated development strategies separately. Let us now assemble them and compare the performance of relevant variables under the policy assumptions implied by the different strategies.

Four strategies will be compared: the Status-quo-plus-oil strategy, the NDS, and cases One and Four of the Global Plan.

The remaining two strategical scenarios (cases Two and Three of the Global Plan) will not be included in this comparison, since they cannot be considered consistent, or 'realistic', as argued in Section 3 of this chapter.[1] Income concentration and agricultural stagnation seem to be two aspects of the same problem, i.e. two symptoms of the structural segmentation of the agricultural sector (see Chapter 2, Section 3). Therefore, it does not seem possible to increase agricultural efficiency without simultaneously redistributing incomes, or vice versa. Cases Two and Three, designed in order to analyze the effects of isolated parameter changes, included this type of assumptions.

In this section, we do not intend to isolate the effects of changes in one type of parameter, but to assess the consequences of comprehensive policy packages, or strategies. We compare strategical scenarios which imply different assumptions about several policy variables and parameters simultaneously. As shown in Table 6.10, all scenarios differ in more than one assumption about parameters. An important difference is the assumption about the effects of agricultural reform on the performance of agricultural investment; Case Four and NDS assume increased effectiveness (and income redistribution), while

---

[1] But, of course, any of the cases of the Global Plan can be compared with other strategies by contrasting Figures 6.1-6.4 with Figures 6.5-6.9, or by combining Tables 6.7 and 6.11.

Case One and Status-quo assume constant effectiveness
(and no redistribution). The assumed behavioral (parameter) change, however well-founded, is the hypothetical
result of some reform policy. This difference between
these two pairs may be regarded as a difference in quality, which would prevent comparability. An alternative
view may be to consider the differences in potential effects as the 'cost' of not introducing the specified
reforms.

On the other hand, within each pair, there are quantitative differences in the policies assumed. These two
pairs of more closely related scenarios differ in their
rates of foreign indebtedness, or in the degree of redistribution (NDS is more advanced than Case Four and
includes an increase in direct tax coefficients). It
should be recalled that public investment policy is
the same in cases One and Four, and resembles that of
the NDS, which, however, is more 'basic goods intensive'.
Status-quo, on the other hand, is oil intensive. It
should also be kept in mind that cases One and Four represent different interpretations of the Global Plan
only during the first three years of the simulations.
We have assumed that the (1980-82) Global Plan strategy
is applied without changes also after 1982. Cases One
and Four should therefore be conceived of as an independent type of 'intermediate' scenario.

Table 6.10:   Development strategies: assumed parameter values [a]

Scenario	Rate of foreign saving	Income distribution		Incremental capital output ratio in agriculture
		Private	Government	
Case One	0.010		V_{1977}^{p*} V^d	4.2
Case Four	0.010	(.7 1.0 1.0 1.0 1.0 1.5 2.0)	V_{1977}^{p*} [b] V^d	2.1
Status-quo	0.016		V_{1977}^{p*} V^d	4.2
NDS	0.0	(.57 1.0 1.34 1.0 .43 1.32 1.92)	V_{1977}^{p*} [c] $2V^d$	2.1

a)Parameters which do not appear here, with the exception of public investment distribution parameters, are the same in all simulations; b) This redistribution implies a 16 percent increase in (the Gini coefficient of) equality; c) implies a 26 percent increase.

Let us now turn to the growth performance of the simulated strategies, presented in Figure 6.5.

Figure 6.5   Development strategies. Total output, 1980-1990

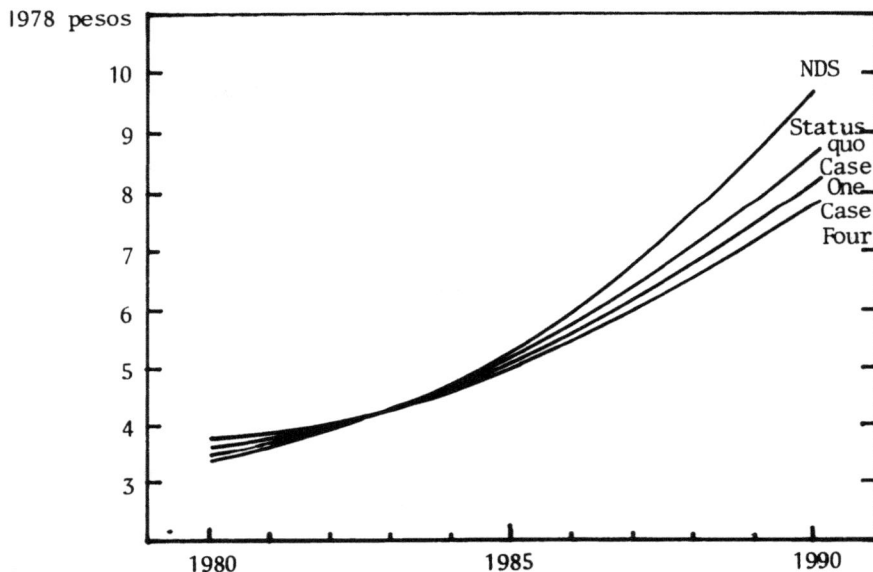

Gross output levels for the first years of the 1980s
are very similar for all strategies. The slight relative inferiority of the NDS at the beginning of the
period disappears after two years due to its slightly higher growth rates. The overall rate of saving/in-
vestment, the source of growth in the system, is then
slightly higher than that of the strategies with more
unequal distribution and higher rates of foreign saving.
The decrease in private savings provoked by income redistribution in the NDS is more than compensated by
the increase in public savings. The crucial assumption
here is that the (comparatively low) consumption propensities of the government are kept constant. The increase in the share of incomes accruing to the public
sector via increased direct taxes is then a savings-
increasing redistribution.

Direct taxes are one-half of total fiscal revenues in
the NDS, against one-third for the Status-quo and
'Global Plan' strategies. Total tax revenues are 22-24
percent of national income in 1980-1990, against 16-23
percent for the other strategies (see Appendix D). The
share of public investment in total investment is also
higher in the NDS, 70.7 percent in the first year of
the simulation, against 48.9 percent. This share decreases constantly, however, as a result of a faster
growth in private investment. It is 47.7 in 1990,
against 41-42 percent for the other strategies.

It is more difficult to assess the causes of the higher
growth performance of the Status-quo strategy in relation to cases One and Four. This is possibly due to
the higher rate of foreign indebtedness, but it may
also be that a more oil-intensive output structure
gives rise to higher public incomes and savings. Cases
One and Four exhibit rather similar growth performances.
The decrease in the growth potential which results from
redistribution is almost compensated by the assumed

increase in the output response of agricultural investment.[1]

The agricultural balance of trade reflects the combined
effects of output and demand growth. It is characteristic of the evolution of most basic-goods sectors (see
Figure 6.6).

Figure 6.6   Development strategies. Agricultural
             balance of trade, 1980-1990

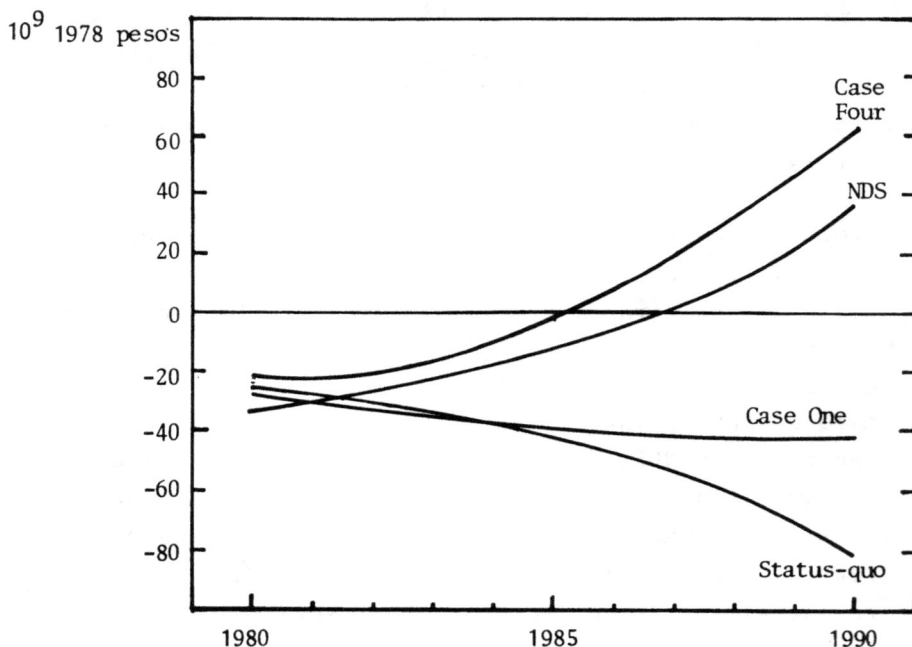

Both the Case One and Status-quo strategies show a
constantly deteriorating agricultural trade deficit.
The differences in the rate of deterioration are
explained by the differences in the respective public
investment policies. The investment policy of the

[1] It should be recalled that (ceteris paribus) neither redistribution nor increased agricultural efficiency produce significant
differences in growth performance (see the comments to Figure
6.1 in Section 3).

Case One strategy increases the share allocated to
agriculture. The Status-quo-plus-oil strategy, on the
other hand, assumed that the actual 1979 composition
is maintained. Hence the lower deficit in Case One.

These results are due to the hypothesis that agricultural output continues to exhibit a low response to
investment. If, instead of a continued stagnating
agricultural response, efficiency- (and equity-) increasing reforms are assumed, as in Case Four and NDS,
the trade deficit disappears in 1985 or 1986. The NDS
assumes a more advanced redistribution than Case Four;
higher domestic consumption and a slower decrease in
the trade deficit result. The higher concentration of
the NDS public investment policy in agriculture is
not enough to compensate for the redistribution
effect.[1] These results suggest that reforming agriculture is more important or more effective for reducing the agricultural trade deficit than increasing
public investment. But it should be possible, of
course, to find the sequence of agricultural shares
that produces a desired time pattern of trade for
the present level of effectiveness in agriculture;
e.g. the public investment policy which eliminates
the deficit in a predetermined number of years.

Figure 6.7 shows a rather impressive evolution of oil
exports for the Status-quo scenario. The evolution is
natural, however, given the oil-intensive hypothesis of
the Status-quo public investment policy. The 'Global
Plan' cases show a less expected rapid growth in oil
exports. The public investment policy of the Plan
produces higher growth rates in oil output for the
period 1979-1982 than those expected (see Section 3).

[1] The NDS assumes agricultural shares which are about twice those
of the Global Plan cases (see Tables D.4.4 and D.2.4).

The assumed maintainance of the 1982 public investment
structure throughout the remainder of the simulation
period also results in rather high rates of growth in
oil exports. The NDS, on the other hand, shows a much
lower growth until 1985, and then a slow and constant
decline. This type of pattern seems to reflect the
official aim of putting a ceiling on oil exports.

Figure 6.7   Development strategies. Oil exports,
              1980-1990

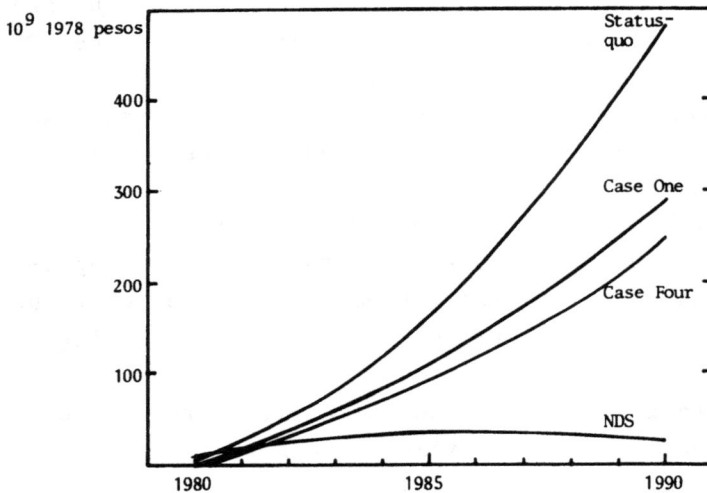

The employment performance of the different strategies
is shown in Figure 6.8. A projection of the total
labor force is also represented.[1] The Case One and
the Status-quo strategies have about the same impact
on employment. After 1983, Case One has a slightly
better performance, inverting the initial order. Both
scenarios assume unchanged low effectiveness of agricultural investment. The better employment performance
of Case One, which contrasts with its less favorable

[1]Projection of the economically active population in Table 3,
Reynolds (1979, p. 128). It is based on the hypothesis of a
constant (low) labor participation rate of 29 percent of the
total population.

growth performance (see Figure 6.5), is due to the
higher 'agriculture intensity' (and lower oil intensity)
of its output structure, as agriculture has a comparatively high employment coefficient. Neither
of them succeeds in eliminating un- and underemployment within the simulation period. However, the rate
of un- and underemployment (relative to active population) decreases from 25 to 10 percent in 1980-1990.

Figure 6.8   Development strategies. Total employment,
              1980-1990

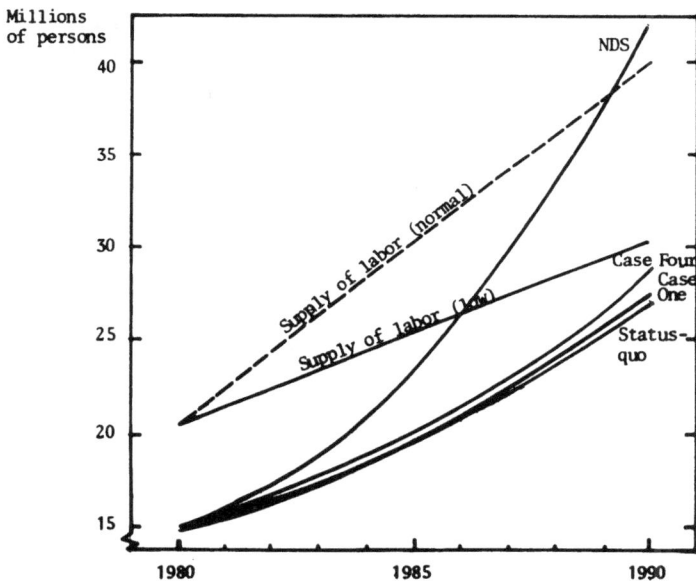

Case Four and the NDS assume doubled effectiveness of
agricultural investment. For this reason, Case Four
shows higher levels of employment than Case One, in
spite of its lower overall growth performance, since
employment is positively related to the share of agricultural output. Case Four employment growth, however,
is not sufficient to absorb unemployment completely

within the simulation period. In addition to increased agricultural efficiency, the NDS assumes that a larger proportion (about double) of public investment funds is allocated to agriculture. This accelerates the growth of agricultural output and employment. In 1986, the entire economically active population is employed, under the assumption of continued low labor participation rates.[1] After 1986, then, the 'unlimited supply of labor' assumption of this study would become less plausible, as would the hypothesis of constant distributive shares. The constant-technology assumption would no longer be valid either.

Social welfare, as defined by the efficiency-equity index, is shown in Figure 6.9. The time patterns of the different scenarios exhibit about the same shape as total outputs (cf. Figure 6.5). But the position of the curves is now modified. NDS and Case Four have a higher level in this case, due to the initial once and for all increase in equality (represented by a 26 and 16 percent increase in the Gini index, respectively).

---

[1] If, for instance, the labor participation rate increased monotonically from 29 percent in 1980 to the more 'normal' value of 40 percent in 1990, unemployment would instead disappear in 1989 under the NDS assumptions (see the broken line in Figure 6.8). In 1975, the average (world) participation rate was 41.5 percent; for the less developed regions, the rate was 39.7 percent (ILO, 1978, p. 16).

201

Figure 6.9   Development strategies. Efficiency-
equity social welfare index, 1980-1990

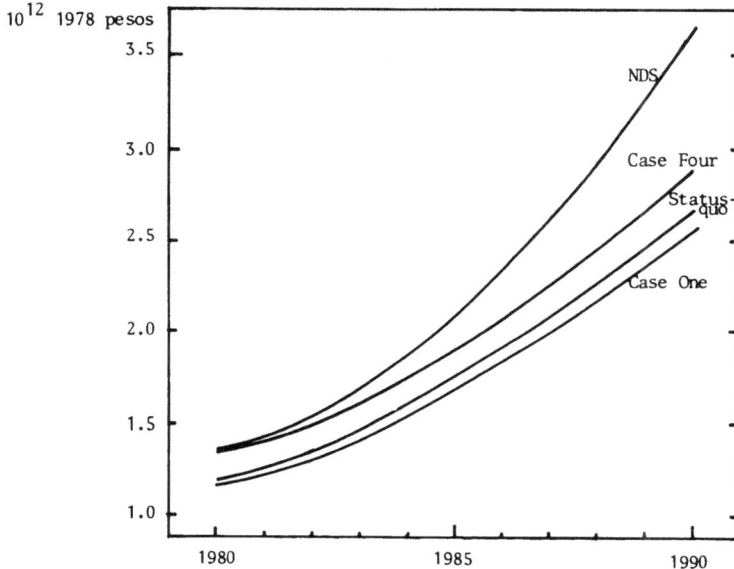

The results are summarized in Table 6.11. In addition
to the variables already presented, the rate of growth
of the external debt is included, which reflects the
assumed levels of foreign trade deficit and accumulated
interest. As mentioned in Chapter 4, Section 6, it may
be understood as an indicator of the degree of self-
reliance. Table 6.11 also includes (in parentheses)
estimates of the growth rates of the variables when
increased (doubled) agricultural investment effectiveness (with no redistribution) is assumed in the Status-
quo case.[1]

---

[1] They are based on the estimates of partial effects obtained in
Section 3 of this chapter.

Table 6.11:   Development strategies. Rates of growth of
              selected variables. 1980-1990

Scenario	Output	Agricultural balance of trade	External debt	Employment	Welfare[a]
Case One	8.8	- 7.0	11.6	6.0	7.8
Status-quo-plus-oil	9.2 (9.5)	-11.3 (7.5)	12.6 (12.7)	5.9 (7.6)	8.1 (8.4)
Case Four	8.5	11.4	11.5	6.7	9.0
New development strategy	10.6	7.5	9.5	10.5	11.2

Note: Estimates of assuming halved incremental capital
output ratios in agriculture in the Status-quo case are
given in parentheses.
a) Efficiency-equity welfare index.
Source: Appendix D.

Finally, it should be recalled that there is a qualitative difference between Case One and Status-quo on
the one hand, and Case Four and NDS on the other, in
that the latter assume agricultural reform and income
redistribution, while the former do not. It should also
be kept in mind that the scenarios represent the effects
of simultaneous changes in more than one policy parameter.

APPENDIX A: LIST OF PARAMETERS, VARIABLES AND EQUATIONS

General

k   denotes the number of socio-economic groups

n   denotes the number of producing sectors

^   above a vector transforms it into a diagonal matrix

'   denotes transposition

ι is the summing vector

I   is the unit matrix.

Policy Parameters

v^p (k × n) matrix of sectoral value added distribution co-efficients, private

v^d (1 × n) matrix of sectoral direct tax coefficients

v^i (1 × n) matrix of sectoral indirect tax plus exploitation surpluses of nationalized enterprises

v^g (1 × n) matrix of sectoral value added distribution co-efficients, government

$z^{g.}_t$ (n × 1) distribution vector of sectoral allocation of public investment.

Behavioral Parameters

χ (scalar) share of wages in total fiscal revenues

θ^p (n × k) matrix of subsistence consumption parameters, private

r^p (n × k) matrix of marginal propensities to consume, private

r^g (n × 1) matrix of marginal (= average) propensities to consume, government

$\hat{\alpha}$ (n × n) matrix of incremental capital output ratios

i   (scalar) rate of interest on the external debt

B $(n \times n)$ distribution matrix of investment demands

A $(n \times n)$ matrix of technical coefficients

M $(n \times n)$ distribution matrix for imports of inputs

$\hat{\Pi}$ $(n \times n)$ matrix of input import coefficients by sector of destination

N $(n \times n)$ distribution matrix of imports of investment goods

$\hat{\sigma}$ $(n \times n)$ matrix of import content coefficients of investment demands

Λ $(k \times n)$ matrix of labor productivity ratios

$\hat{r}$ $(n \times n)$ matrix of exponential rates of labor productivity change.

Weighting parameters

ν_i $(i=1,2,\ldots,k)$ 'poverty weights' of the social welfare function

Exogenous variables

ω_t (scalar) foreign saving (balance-of-payment deficit) as a proportion of national income

$\bar{q}_t$ $(n \times 1)$ vector of exogenous exports

$\bar{m}_t$ $(n \times 1)$ vector of exogenous imports

τ (scalar) length of the simulation period.

Endogenous output variables

x_t $(n \times 1)$ vector of gross outputs

y_t^p $(k \times 1)$ vector of private disposable incomes by socio-economic class

y_t^g (scalar) income of the government

c_t^p $(n \times 1)$ vector of consumption expenditures, private

c_t^g $(n \times 1)$ vector of consumption expenditures, government

c_t $(n \times 1)$ vector of consumption expenditures, total

s_t^p (k × 1) vector of savings by income class, private

s_t^g (scalar) government savings

φ_t (scalar) foreign saving

u_t (scalar) adds foreign savings to domestic, private and government savings

s_t^{p*} (scalar) total (domestic plus foreign) savings, private

d_t^p (n × 1) vector of investments by sector of destination, private

z_t^p (n × 1) distribution vector of sectoral allocation of investment, private

s_t^{g*} (scalar) total (domestic plus foreign) savings, government

d_t^g (n × 1) vector of public investments by sector of destination

d_t (n × 1) vector of total (private plus public) investment by sector of destination

f_t (n × 1) vector of investment demands by sector of origin

δ_t (n × 1) vector of excess demands

m_t^a (n × 1) vector of imports of intermediate inputs by sector of origin

f_t^m (n × 1) vector of imports of investment goods by sector of origin

m_t (n × 1) vector of total noncompetitive imports by sector of origin

q_t (n × 1) vector of total exports

m_t (n × 1) vector of total imports

$W_{t,1}$ (scalar) national income

w_t (k × 1) vector of income shares

$\bar{y}_t^p$ (k × 1) vector of average incomes

ϵ_{i,t_0t_1} (scalar) rate of growth of incomes of the i'th income class.

Endogenous state variables

E_t (scalar) external indebtedness

b_t $(n \times 1)$ vector of sectoral trade balances

ℓ_t $(k \times 1)$ vector of labor requirements by socio-economic class

λ_t $(n \times 1)$ vector of sectoral labor requirements

$G_{1,t_o t_1}$ (scalar) annual rate of growth of national income between t_o and t_1

$G_{2,t_o t_1}$ (scalar) annual rate of growth of 'equal weights' index of social welfare between t_o and t_1

$G_{3,t_o t_1}$ (scalar) annual rate of growth of the 'poverty weighted' index of social welfare between t_o and t_1

Gini   (scalar) coefficient of inequality

$W_{t,4}$ efficiency-equity index

ρ_t^1 (scalar) tax pressure

ρ_t^2 (scalar) share of public investments in total investment.

Dynamic core equations

Private incomes

$$y_t^p = V_t^p x_t \tag{6}$$

Government incomes

$$y_t^g = V_t^g x_t \tag{11}$$

Sectoral private consumption

$$c_t^p = \theta^p \iota + \Gamma^p y_t^p \tag{14}$$

Sectoral government consumption

$$c_t^g = \Gamma^g y_t^g \tag{17}$$

Private savings by income class

$$s_t^p = -\theta^{p'} \iota + (I - \iota' \hat{\Gamma}^p) y_t^p \tag{25}$$

Government savings

$$s_t^g = (1 - \iota' \Gamma^g) \, y_t^g \qquad (26)$$

External debt growth

$$E_{t+1} = E_t(1 + i) + \varphi_t \qquad (27 \text{ bis})$$

Total (domestic plus foreign) private savings

$$s_t^{p*} = \iota' s_t^p (1 + u_t) \qquad (28)$$

Total (domestic plus foreign) government savings

$$s_t^{g*} = s_t^g (1 + u_t) \qquad (32)$$

Private investment allocation vector[1]

$$z_t^p = \frac{\hat{\alpha}(x_t - x_{t-1})}{\iota' \hat{\alpha}(x_t - x_{t-1})} \qquad (31)$$

Private investments by sector of destination

$$d_t^p = z_t^p \, s_t^{p*} \qquad (30)$$

Public investments by sector of destination

$$d_t^g = z_t^g \, s_t^{g*} \qquad (33)$$

Total investments by sector of destination

$$d_t = d_t^p + d_t^g$$

Output growth

$$x_{t+1} = \hat{\alpha}^{-1} \, d_t + x_t \qquad (60)$$

---

[1] For simplicity in the notations the original eq. (31), and not the estimated expression, eq. (5.6), is written here. The estimated form is a flexible accelerator including outputs from year t to year t-3.

By backward substitution from eq. (60) to eq. (6), we obtain the following difference equation system:

$$x_{t+1} = \hat{\alpha}^{-1} \left[\frac{\hat{\alpha}\left[x_t - x_{t-1}\right]}{\imath'\hat{\alpha}\left[x_t - x_{t-1}\right]} \imath'\left[-\theta p' \imath + (I - \imath'\hat{\imath} r^p)\right] v^p x_t + \right.$$
$$\left. z_t^g (1 - \imath' r^g) v^g x_t \right] (1 + u_t) + x_t \qquad (67)$$

in which outputs in the following period appear as a function of the known current and past outputs, and the exogenous rate of foreign saving (u_t).

Identities and peripheral equations

Total fiscal revenues

$$g_t = (v^d + v^i)\, x_t \qquad (7)$$

Income of the government

$$y_t^g = (1 - x)\, g_t \qquad (8)$$

Value added distribution matrix of the government

$$v^g = (1 - x)(v^d + v^i) \qquad (10)$$

Foreign saving

$$\varphi_t = w_t\, \imath'\, y_t^p \qquad (27)$$

Rate of foreign saving

$$u_t = \frac{\varphi}{\imath'\, s_t^p + s_t^g} \qquad (29)$$

Total investments by sector of origin

$$f_t = B\, d_t \qquad (37)$$

Imports of intermediate inputs by sector of origin (noncompetitive)

$$m_t^a = M\, \hat{\pi}\, x_t \qquad (43)$$

Imports of investment goods by sector of origin (noncompetitive)

$$f_t^m = N \hat{\sigma} d_t \tag{44}$$

Total noncompetitive import demands by sector of origin

$$\tilde{m}_t = m_t^a + f_t^m + \bar{m}_t \tag{45}$$

Excess demands

$$\delta_t = x_t - Ax_t - c_t - f_t - \bar{q}_t + \tilde{m}_t \tag{42}$$

Total sectoral exports

$$q_t = \delta_t + \bar{q}_t \quad \text{(for } \delta_{i,t} \geq 0, \ i = 1,2,\ldots,n) \tag{46}$$

Total sectoral imports

$$m_t = -\delta_t + \tilde{m}_t \quad \text{(for } \delta_{i,t} < 0, \ i = 1,2,\ldots,n) \tag{48}$$

Sectoral balance of trade

$$b_t = x_t - Ax_t - c_t - f_t \tag{52}$$

Employment by socio-economic class

$$\ell_t = \Lambda_o \ e^{-\hat{r}t} \ x_t \tag{69}$$

Sectoral employment

$$\lambda_t = \Lambda_o^{\hat{i}\imath} \ e^{-\hat{r}t} \ x_t \tag{70}$$

National income

$$W_{t,1} = \imath' \ y_t^p \tag{73}$$

Rate of growth of national income

$$G_{1,t_o t_1} = w_{1,t_o} \ \epsilon_{1,t_o t_1} + w_{2,t_o} \ \epsilon_{2,t_o t_1} + \ldots + w_{k,t_o} \ \epsilon_{k,t_o t_1} \tag{74}$$

Income shares

$$w_t = \frac{y_t^p}{\imath' \, y_t^p} \qquad (75)$$

Rates of growth of income of the i'th socio-economic class

$$\epsilon_{i,t_o t_1} = \frac{\left[y_{t_1,i}^p \right]^{1/t_o - t_1}}{\left[y_{t_o,i}^p \right]} - 1 \qquad \begin{array}{l} i = 1,2\ldots,k \\[4pt] 0 \le t_o \le t_1 \le \tau \end{array} \qquad (76)$$

'Equal weights' index of social welfare growth

$$G_{2,t_o t_1} = \frac{\ell_{1,o}}{\imath' \, \ell_o} \, \epsilon_{1,t_o t_1} + \frac{\ell_{2,o}}{\imath' \, \ell_o} \, \epsilon_{2,t_o t_1} + \ldots + \frac{\ell_{4,o}}{\imath' \, \ell_o} \, \epsilon_{k,t_o t_1} \qquad \begin{array}{l}(77)+ \\ (5.8)\end{array}$$

$$0 \le t_o < t_1 \le \tau$$

'Poverty weighted' index of social welfare growth

$$G_{3,t_o t_1} = \nu_1 \, \epsilon_{1,t_o t_1} + \nu_2 \, \epsilon_{2,t_o t_1} + \ldots + \nu_k \, \epsilon_{k,t_o t_1} \qquad \begin{array}{l}(79)+ \\ (5.9)\end{array}$$

$$0 \le t_o < t_1 \le \tau$$

Efficiency-equity index

$$W_{t,4} = W_{t,1} \, (1 - Gini_t) \qquad (81)$$

Gini coefficient of inequality

$$Gini_t = 1 + \frac{1}{k} - \frac{2}{k \, \imath' \, y_t^p} \, (\bar{y}_{t,1}^p + 2\bar{y}_{t,2}^p + \ldots + k \, \bar{y}_{t,k}^p) \qquad \begin{array}{l}(82)+ \\ (5.10)\end{array}$$

Average incomes

$$\bar{y}_t^p = \hat{\ell}_t^{-1} \, y_t^p \qquad (5.11)$$

Tax pressure

$$\rho_t^1 = \frac{g_t}{\imath' \, y_t^p}$$

Public investment's share in total investment

$$\rho_t^2 = \frac{\iota' \, d_t^g}{\iota' \, d_t}$$

APPENDIX B: OVERVIEW OF THE ESTIMATION

Nota-tion	Definition	Table	Source	Procedure, method	Authors (institution)
A	Technical coefficients	C.I,C.II	Mexico (n.d.a)	Aggregation from 72 to 45 sectors. Up-dating from 1970 to 1975 and 1978 by the RAS method (Slater, 1972, Ch. 4)	J.A. Gaitán, E. Suárez. Supervision: V. Solís. Programming: A. Chacón. (DARE[a])
v^p	Income distribution co-efficients	C.III	Original data from the house-hold income and expenditure survey of 1977 (see Mexico, n.d.b)	Direct processing	H. Sabau (CIDE[b]-SCNI[c]-DARE)
x	Share of wages in total fiscal revenues	5.2	Aceituno (1980), Mexico (1978a, 1979a)		J. Buzaglo
v^d	Direct tax coefficients	C.IV	Aceituno (1980), Mexico (1979a)	Sectorally distributed propor-tional to value added	Idem
v^i	Indirect tax coefficients	C.IV	Original data from Mexico (1978a), Mexico (1979a)		Idem
θ^p, η^p	Consumption coefficients, private	C.V,C.VI	Original data from the house-hold income and expenditure survey of 1977 (see Mexico, n.d.b)	Two stage Zellner-Aitken estimator (Sabau, 1980)	H. Sabau (CIDE-CSNI-DARE)
r^g	Consumption coefficients, gvt.	C.VII	Mexico (1978a, 1979a)		J. Buzaglo
$\hat{\alpha}$	Incremental capital output ratios	C.VIII	Mexico (1978c)	Ordinary least squares, Cochrane-Orcutt, Hildreth-Lu	J.A. Gaitán, E. Suárez. Supervision: V. Solís. Programming: C. Ramirez (DARE)
B	Capital coefficients	C.IX	Mexico (1978c), Franchet et al. (1973)	Up-dating by row correction factor method (Franchet et al., 1973, pp. 100-103)	J.A. Gaitán, E. Suárez. Supervision: V. Solís Programming: A. Chacón (DARE)
M, $\hat{n}$	Input imports coefficients	C.X,C.XI	Mexico (n.d.a)	Aggregation, normalization, RAS	Idem
N, $\hat{\sigma}$	Coefficients of imports of investment goods	C.XII	Mexico .1978a)	Normalization	Idem
$\wedge$	Employment coefficients	C.XIII	Mexico (1971, 1979a)		R. Ramos, G. Rivera. Supervision: H. Sabau (CIDE)
$\hat{r}$	Rates of productivity change	C.XIV	Mexico (1971), Original data from Mexico (1979d)	Exponential rates between 1969 and 1978	Idem

a) Dirección de Análisis de Ramas Económicas. Secretaría de Programación y Presupuesto, b) Centro de Investigación y Docencia Económicas, c) Coordinación del Sistema Nacional de Información. Secretaría de Programación y Presupuesto.

APPENDIX C: ESTIMATED COEFFICIENTS

Table C.I Technical coefficients (1975)

	1	2	3	4	5	6	7	8	9	10	11	12	13	14	15	16	17	18	19	20
1 Agriculture	.0397	.2163						.0002	.2180	.2899	.0395	.1467	.0966	.0530			.0025			
2 Livestock	.0003	.0013						.5000	.0055	.0010	.0005		.0026	.0043	.0001	.1107	.0064		.0078	.0285
3 Forestry							.0016			.0033	.0007			.0094	.0002			.0014	.0005	.0015
4 Fishing					.0015					.0261										.0012
5 Mining	.0004	.0012			.2316	.0966	.0035	.0008	.0002	.0001	.0001		.0001	.0001	.0001	.0001	.0001	.0001	.0003	.0408
6 Quarrying	.0235	.0049	.0180	.0554	.0136	.0814	.2921	.0086	.0227	.0015	.0070	.0037	.0041	.0074	.0009	.0002	.0020	.0025	.0086	
7 Petroleum					.0199			.0037	.0037	.0089				.0004		.0110	.0150		.0245	
8 Slaughter of livest. and poultry								.0086	.0037	.0022	.0022									
9 Milling	.0090			.0144				.0003	.1795	.1314	.0998	.0029	.0038	.0002		.0003	.0064		.0090	
10 Other processed food	.1490							.0037	.0408		.0407					.0036		.0001		
11 Beverages	.0020											.0329								
12 Tobacco										.0254			.1258	.1075	.1821	.0331	.0012	.0035	.0144	.0260
13 Soft fibre textiles	.0020	.0005		.0033	.0003	.0055	.0001		.0001	.0006	.0001	.0008	.0003	.0604	.0030	.0033	.0038	.0002	.0021	.0007
14 Other textiles	.0001				.0004	.0005				.0002	.0004	.0001	.0002	.0008	.0309		.0003	.0010	.0004	.0006
15 Wearing apparel and footwear	.0030	.0001		.0008	.0008		.0005			.0001	.0013	.0001	.0002	.0007		.0806	.0105	.0001	.0002	.0020
16 Wood and cork	.0001	.0025	.0010		.0012	.0043	.0011	.0025	.0091	.0137	.0146	.0139	.0041	.0099	.0031	.0013	.3295	.1877	.0170	.0269
17 Paper and paper products				.0019	.0040		.0010	.0003	.0003	.0023	.0167	.0285	.0030	.0116	.0050	.0006	.0071	.0806	.0034	.0072
18 Printing, publishing			.0013										.0001	.0004	.0009	.0003				.1388
19 Leather								.0001					.0006							
20 Rubber products	.0020	.0005	.0039	.0004	.0013	.0015	.0003	.0002	.0004	.0020	.0011	.0001	.0006	.0072	.0021	.0025	.0015	.0013	.0060	.0126
21 Basic chemicals	.0004				.0197	.0119	.0145	.0028	.0006	.0081	.0078	.0015	.0229	.0259	.0018	.0035	.0239	.0010	.0300	.0071
22 Synthetic fibres			.0019	.0055		.0003				.0047		.0182	.0634	.0807	.0432	.0131	.0042	.0032	.0179	.1539
23 Fertilizers	.0283																			
24 Soaps and detergents	.0150						.0002	.0001		.0014	.0001			.0006				.0012		
25 Drug and medicines							.0002													
26 Perfumes, cosmetics															.0001					
27 Other chemical industries	.0092	.0006	.0023		.0054	.0053	.0044	.0002	.0001	.0037	.0005	.0053	.0012	.0040		.0129	.0109	.0131	.0187	.0201
28 Non-methallic mineral products	.0010	.0009		.0039	.0028	.0003	.0010	.0012		.0076	.0183		.0002	.0007		.0034	.0002		.0001	.0024
29 Basic methallic industries	.0012	.0013	.0016	.0003	.0043	.0020	.0074		.0002	.0010	.0005	.0089	.0008	.0044	.0001	.0071	.0022	.0032	.0008	.0028
30 Metal products	.0013	.0036	.0191	.0040	.0053	.0064	.0042	.0028	.0006	.0185	.0269	.0003	.0011	.0057	.0018	.0232	.0034	.0006	.0121	.0028
31 Machinery	.0010	.0004	.0125	.0185	.0012	.0010	.0202		.0005	.0008	.0016	.0044	.0004	.0003	.0005	.0003	.0005	.0011	.0008	.0003
32 Electrical machinery	.0002	.0010	.0023	.0025	.0020	.0029	.0018	.0001	.0003	.0015	.0007	.0001	.0019	.0016	.0002	.0011	.0016	.0005	.0007	.0008
33 Transport equipment	.0024			.1134			.0039													
34 Motor vehicles	.0005	.0005	.0012		.0010	.0016		.0002	.0002	.0008	.0004	.0001	.0003	.0004	.0001	.0005	.0006	.0001	.0002	.0003
35 Other manufacturing industries	.0001	.0020		.0005			.0029							.0006		.0010	.0010	.0051	.0117	.0017
36 Construction	.0058	.0010			.0178	.0144	.0060	.0010	.0118	.0085	.0042	.0023	.0099	.0132	.0024	.0074	.0172	.0047	.0067	.0123
37 Electricity								.0005	.0004	.0015	.0078	.0040	.0004	.0010	.0011	.0011	.0015	.0006	.0019	.0011
38 Cinema																				.0127
39 Transport	.0025	.0024	.0021	.0039	.0033	.0039	.0164	.0025	.0013	.0062	.0093	.0015	.0048	.0102	.0035	.0099	.0078	.0067	.0060	.0008
40 Communication				.0003	.0009	.0020	.0007	.0011	.0010	.0010	.0006	.0006	.0007	.0011	.0006	.0010	.0010	.0006	.0013	.1104
41 Trade	.0281	.0385	.0273	.0322	.1057	.0448	.0119	.0662	.0576	.0883	.0808	.0387	.0806	.1228	.0672	.1660	.0729	.0780	.1597	.1104
42 Dwellings					.0016	.0058	.0008	.0003	.0072	.0031	.0032	.0016	.0023	.0071	.0043	.0083	.0026	.0080	.0088	.0066
43 Hotels and restaurants	.0038	.0040	.0026	.0025	.0045	.0051	.0025		.0016	.0021	.0022	.0005	.0022	.0046	.0023	.0019	.0033			.0034
44 Credit and insurance				.0404	.0063	.0071	.0022	.0018	.0039	.0045	.0040	.0042	.0031	.0064	.0051	.0051	.0046	.0024	.0024	.0048
45 Other services	.0004	.0037	.0086	.0070	.0099	.0139	.0091	.0003	.0031	.0083	.0068	.0025	.0032	.0060	.0018	.0048	.0067	.0010	.0047	.0103

21	22	23	24	25	26	27	28	29	30	31	32	33	34	35	36	37	38	39	40	41	42	43	44	45
.0006		.0047	.0013	.0004	.0008	.0084	.0002							.0353		.0003								.0012
				.0002		.0001								.0009										.0011
			.0002	.0067	.0001	.0118	.0001					.0001				.0002								
	.0009					.0002							.0001	.0004						.0001				.0001
		.0202	.0001	.0001	.0001	.0091	.0038	.0686	.0100	.0079	.0100		.0027	.1474	.0111	.0011								
.0429	.0001	.0699	.0648	.0002	.0402	.0098	.1059	.0285	.0002	.0017	.0035		.0003	.0058	.0258	.0014	.0034	.0005	.0013	.0104	.0003		.0012
.0236	.0040	.2133	.0245	.0083	.0152	.1039	.0456	.0125	.0050	.0050	.0032	.0051	.0031	.0635		.1732	.0033	.1147			.0057	.0055	.0027	.0109
.0747	.3166			.0001	.0395	.0025								.0031		.0002								.0008
				.0002										.0002				.0003						.0011
	.0014		.0636	.0070		.0028						.0001	.0001				.0027	.0001						.0008
		.0053	.0005		.0004	.0004	.0006	.0003	.0008	.0001	.0003	.0064	.0004	.0037	.0003		.0001	.0002	.0003	.0001		.0006		.0002
.0006	.0017	.0009	.0006	.0007	.0004	.0003		.0001	.0002	.0010	.0005	.0006	.0024	.0028	.0008		.0036	.0015	.0015	.0012		.0026	.0004	.0004
	.0017				.0004	.0007	.0006	.0005	.0004	.0003	.0004		.0002	.0004	.0258	.0021	.0004	.0012		.0001	.0001	.0001		.0026
.0123	.0702	.0281	.0343	.0137	.0213	.0156	.0316	.0055	.0039	.0016	.0102	.0026	.0005	.0049	.0013	.0030	.0061	.0060	.0060	.0058	.0016	.0001	.0102	.0003
.0052	.0166	.0080	.0412	.0444	.0256	.0109	.0135	.0050	.0048	.0070	.0121	.0002	.0028	.0264	.0002	.0063	.0018	.0023	.0003	.0058	.0008	.0049	.0157	.0074
			.0001	.0001		.0048				.0031	.0041	.0021	.0039	.0173					.0002					.0040
												.0004		.0002										.0021
.0028	.0074	.0018	.0212	.0144	.0132	.0023	.0044	.0026	.0025	.0033	.0045	.0077	.0117	.0046	.0044	.0005	.0007	.0164	.0022	.0010	.0002	.0007	.0006	.0020
.1183	.0677	.1813	.0391	.1185	.0244	.1203	.0294	.0075	.0032	.0010	.0051	.0016	.0002	.0138	.0024	.0011	.0064	.0003						.0126
.0054	.0611	.0111	.0414	.0009	.0257	.0401	.0024	.0003	.0013	.0015	.0070	.0004	.0020	.0109	.0008	.0002				.0017				.0008
.0035		.0849	.0012		.0007	.0049																		
	.0002		.0132		.0082	.0005	.0003		.0001											.0004	.0009	.0016	.0006	.0014
	.0017		.0041		.0025	.0025								.0002		.0001	.0002	.0002			.0008	.0014		.0211
	.0002		.0132	.1549	.0082	.0005	.0002	.0001	.0001	.0016	.0038	.0029	.0032	.0109	.0170	.0001	.0002	.0002		.0003	.0018	.0022	.0006	.0013
.0443	.0193	.0079	.0143	.0028	.0089	.1163	.0044	.0026	.0089	.0013	.0135	.0005	.9087	.0050	.1257	.0006	.0006	.0011	.0016	.0001	.0001	.0004	.0015	.0058
.0021			.0002	.0180	.0516	.0055	.0411	.0001	.0018	.0963	.0661	.1048	.0295	.0260	.0762	.0016	.0017	.0012		.0001	.0013	.0006		.0043
.0607	.0009	.0014	.0204	.0002	.0043	.0043	.0056	.3088	.0371	.0211	.0176	.0473	.0109	.0161	.0450	.0029	.0010	.0034	.0030	.0018	.0001	.0096	.0003	.0010
.0080	.0027	.0043	.0204	.0160	.0126	.0235	.0070	.0377	.0073	.1180	.0068	.0260	.0191	.0020	.0119	.0095	.0032	.0041	.0095	.0029	.0012	.0026	.0017	.0066
.0016	.0004	.0006	.0025	.0004	.0003	.0003	.0032	.0012	.0020	.0197	.1823	.0120	.0145	.0046	.0046	.0174	.0005	.0012	.0016		.0004	.0008	.0002	.0023
.0014	.0012	.0020	.0003	.0004	.0002	.0004	.0026	.0029	.0016	.0003		.1393	.0002		.0003	.0242	.0037	.0040	.0086	.0001		.0016	.0006	.0158
								.0013		.0032	.0032	.0189	.4768	.0001	.0001	.0003		.0173						.0052
.0008	.0007	.0011	.0008	.0001	.0005	.0002	.0010	.0012	.0005	.0214	.0018	.0189	.0011	.0428	.0004	.0075	.0011	.0525	.0024	.0001	.0001	.0005	.0007	.0269
						.0005						.0002				.0033	.0049	.0012	.0003	.0009	.0009	.0015	.0066	.0080
.0258	.0177	.0201	.0039	.0035	.0024	.0077	.0311	.0227	.0073	.0065	.0070	.0057	.0061	.0055	.0038	.0012	.0212	.0025	.0042	.0090	.0062	.0097	.0057	.0045
.0002	.0202	.0174	.0079	.0007	.0049	.0007	.0010	.0007	.0007	.0092	.0023	.0005	.0009	.0007		.0009	.1655	.0006	.0097	.0025	.0001	.0120	.0065	.0004
.0069	.0010	.0107	.0067	.0136	.0067	.0129	.0149	.0085	.0007	.0092	.0092	.0034	.0058	.0056	.0214	.0011	.0062	.0193	.0097	.0019		.0021	.0070	.0051
.0008	.0804	.0012	.0009	.0009	.0005	.0014	.0007	.0008	.0008	.0008	.0009	.0008	.0058	.1211	.0009	.0037	.0131	.0044	.0003	.0039	.0010	.0108	.0171	.0031
.0804	.1416	.1147	.1536	.1256	.0953	.1886	.0861	.0096	.0907	.0921	.1330	.0661	.1391	.1221	.1091	.0277	.0148	.0621	.0217	.0183	.0103	.0191	.0104	.0498
.0058	.0021	.0014	.0029	.0035	.0018	.0042	.0046	.0012	.0061	.0054	.0053	.0031	.0019	.0063	.0011	.0034	.0404	.0056	.0107	.0222	.0257	.0106	.0179	.0171
	.0262	.0040	.0040	.0118	.0015	.0042	.0046	.0016	.0016	.0031	.0022	.0023	.0014	.0021	.0002		.0099			.0015	.0015	.0056	.0056	.0043
.0133	.0066	.0058	.0056	.0056	.0035	.0057	.0056	.0038	.0036	.0043	.0044	.0043	.0042	.0052	.0085	.0005	.0401	.0084	.0014	.0060	.0014	.0126	.0452	.1441
.0054	.0209	.0101	.0044	.0127	.0025	.0088	.0159	.0098	.0042	.0048	.0052	.0039	.0025	.0050	.0070	.0115	.0286	.0168	.0194	.0117	.0824	.0199	.0138	.0112

216

Table C.II Technical coefficients (1978)

	1	2	3	4	5	6	7	8	9	10	11	12	13	14	15	16	17	18	19	20
1 Agriculture	.0390	.1686						.0002	.2175	.2830	.0396	.1409	.0939	.0491			.0023			
2 Livestock	.0003	.0010						.4445	.0055	.0009	.0005									
3 Forestry					.0017				.0037						.0001	.1203	.0086		.0079	.0284
4 Fishing							.0008												.0006	.0006
5 Mining	.0000				.2069				.0013	.0001	.0001		.0001	.0001	.0001	.0001	.0001	.0012	.0002	.0013
6 Quarrying	.0003	.0008			.0132	.0074	.0019		.0002	.0013	.0000		.0023	.0001	.0002	.0002	.0018		.0002	.0011
7 Petroleum	.0383	.0046	.0181	.0464	.0224	.0845	.2155	.0009	.0277	.0106	.0085	.0043	.0048	.0084	.0011	.0130	.0171	.0029	.0104	.0464
8 Slaughter of livestock and poultry								.0062	.0041	.0025				.0004		.0000	.0000		.0148	
9 Milling		.0062						.0002	.1598	.0010	.0020					.0003	.0000			
10 Other processed food		.1149		.0098				.0032	.0402	.1270	.0989	.0027	.0036	.0002	.0000	.0034	.0059	.0000	.0087	.0000
11 Beverages		.0016								.0002	.0423					.0003		.0001		
12 Tobacco												.0351								
13 Soft fibre textiles	.0014			.0016	.0002	.0039	.0001	.0000	.0028	.0215	.0000	.0006	.1064	.0864	.1516	.0275	.0009	.0033	.0121	.0220
14 Other textiles	.0001	.0001			.0004	.0005		.0000	.0001	.0004	.0015	.0001	.0002	.0414	.0021	.0025	.0026	.0001	.0015	.0005
15 Wearing apparel and footwear	.0031			.0006	.0008			.0000	.0098	.0001	.0015	.0001	.0002	.0009	.0000	.0829	.0104	.0001	.0004	.0007
16 Wood and cork	.0001	.0021	.0009		.0014		.0007	.0023	.0003	.0144	.0159	.0144	.0043	.0100	.0033	.0014	.3309	.1925	.0182	.0290
17 Paper and paper products					.0043	.0040	.0006	.0002	.0003	.0024	.0178	.0291	.0031	.0114	.0051	.0007	.0071	.0838	.0036	.0076
18 Printing, publishing			.0016					.0000	.0000	.0000	.0000		.0005		.0012	.0004	.0000	.0000	.1784	.0000
19 Leather	.0019	.0000	.0031	.0003	.0013	.0013	.0002	.0001	.0004	.0019	.0012	.0001	.0008	.0066	.0020	.0024	.0014	.0013	.0058	.0125
20 Rubber products	.0004	.0004			.0210	.0111	.0091		.0006	.0046	.0081	.0014	.0230	.0251	.0019	.0036	.0235	.0010	.0309	.0072
21 Drugs and medicines			.0013		.0056	.0000	.0003	.0036	.0000	.0000	.0000	.0178	.0628	.0763	.0426	.0130	.0040	.0032	.0180	.1551
22 Basic chemicals	.0195																			
23 Synthetic fibres							.0001						.0000	.0005		.0000	.0000	.0010	.0000	
24 Fertilizers		.0101					.0001	.0001		.0011	.0001		.0000		.0000		.0000	.0000	.0000	.0000
25 Soaps and detergents	.0096	.0005	.0020		.0058	.0060	.0027	.0010	.0001	.0037	.0005	.0054	.0013	.0039	.0001	.0133	.0108	.0135	.0191	.0209
26 Perfumes, cosmetics	.0011	.0007			.0030	.0003	.0006	.0005	.0080	.0017	.0197	.0043	.0007	.0007		.0035	.0002	.0002	.0001	.0025
27 Other chemical industries	.0013	.0011	.0014		.0049	.0020	.0049	.0012	.0002	.0011	.0005	.0094	.0008	.0045	.0001	.0075	.0023	.0035	.0008	.0030
28 Non-metallic mineral products	.0014	.0029	.0164	.0029	.0057	.0060	.0026	.0007	.0007	.0830	.0280	.0003	.0011	.0055	.0018	.0234	.0033	.0006	.0124	.0029
29 Basic metallic industries	.0010	.0003	.0113	.0139	.0013	.0010	.0130	.0000	.0005	.0008	.0016	.0043	.0004	.0003	.0005	.0003	.0005	.0011	.0008	.0004
30 Metal products	.0003	.0009	.0021	.0019	.0023	.0029	.0011	.0001	.0003	.0017	.0008	.0001	.0019	.0016	.0002	.0012	.0016	.0005	.0008	.0009
31 Machinery	.0037			.0886			.0027									.0003				
32 Electrical machinery	.0001	.0006	.0014	.0004	.0015	.0020	.0018	.0000	.0002	.0011	.0005	.0001	.0004	.0005	.0001	.0007	.0008	.0005	.0003	.0004
33 Transport equipment	.0002	.0018												.0007		.0011	.0001	.0056	.0131	.0019
34 Motor vehicles	.0064	.0009			.0204	.0144	.0041	.0010	.0132	.0093	.0047	.0025	.0107	.0137	.0026	.0080	.0180	.0051	.0074	.0137
35 Other manufacturing industries							.0000	.0005	.0004	.0017	.0088	.0043	.0004	.0010	.0012	.0013	.0015	.0007	.0021	.0013
36 Construction	.0027	.0021	.0019	.0029	.0037	.0038	.0110	.0025	.0026	.0067	.0103	.0016	.0052	.0105	.0038	.0106	.0081	.0073	.0085	.0139
37 Electricity	.0000			.0002	.0011	.0005	.0005	.0012	.0015	.0012	.0009	.0007	.0009	.0012	.0007	.0012	.0011	.0006	.0015	.0009
38 Cinema	.0267	.0290	.0216	.0213	.1040	.0364	.0566	.0002	.0553	.0830	.0781	.0356	.0755	.1097	.0629	.1556	.0656	.0736	.1519	.1058
39 Transport					.0013	.0043	.0004	.0060	.0060	.0035	.0027	.0013	.0019	.0055	.0035	.0068	.0021	.0045	.0072	.0055
40 Communication				.0021	.0056	.0055	.0018	.0019	.0019	.0025	.0027	.0005	.0027	.0052	.0002	.0023	.0037			.0041
41 Trade	.0047	.0039	.0027	.0348	.0081	.0079	.0017	.0020	.0048	.0035	.0050	.0050	.0038	.0074	.0039	.0062	.0053	.0030	.0030	.0060
42 Dwellings	.0004	.0029	.0073	.0049	.0103	.0127	.0056	.0002	.0032	.0083	.0069	.0025	.0032	.0056	.0018	.0047	.0064	.0011	.0048	.0105

	21	22	23	24	25	26	27	28	29	30	31	32	33	34	35	36	37	38	39	40	41	42	43	44	45
	.0006		.0043	.0012	.0004	.0008	.0080	.0002							.0336		.0002								.0011
															.0009			.0032							.0010
					.0002		.0001	.0001																	.0000
							.0125										.0002								.0001
		.0010		.0002	.0075	.0001	.0002							.0001	.0004	.0000									.0000
	.0375	.0001	.0164	.0001	.0001	.0001	.0076	.0032	.0565	.0084	.0066	.0086		.0016	.1365	.0096	.0008		.0003		.0001				.0009
	.0207	.0034	.0560		.0002		.0084	.0866	.0236	.0002	.0014	.0033		.0002	.0054		.0010								.0115
	.0869	.3399	.3413	.0700	.0095	.0440	.1161	.0495	.0139	.0059	.0054	.0038	.0062	.0026	.0698	.0305	.0002	.0038	.1111	.0016	.0124	.0066	.0058	.0027	.0008
				.0229	.0002	.0144	.0027								.0030			.0025	.0003						.0009
					.0002														.0000						.0007
	.0013	.0013		.0564	.0071	.0355	.0027						.0000	.0000	.0000							.0002			.0000
		.0014					.0004	.0004	.0003	.0006	.0001	.0003	.0004	.0002	.0031	.0003	.0001	.0001	.0000	.0000		.0000	.0004		.0001
		.0016	.0034				.0003	.0000	.0001	.0001	.0009	.0005	.0004	.0011	.0022	.0008	.0001	.0037	.0001	.0016	.0007	.0000	.0025	.0005	.0002
	.0007	.0013	.0009	.0005	.0008	.0004	.0007	.0006	.0005	.0004	.0003	.0005		.0003	.0005	.0008	.0003	.0003	.0003	.0016	.0013	.0000	.0001		.0025
				.0008		.0004		.0015	.0005	.0039	.0015	.0106	.0027	.0004	.0049	.0265	.0004	.0004	.0010		.0001	.0001	.0001	.0004	.0003
	.0133	.0691	.0283	.0354	.0152	.0210	.0162	.0305	.0055	.0050	.0068	.0128	.0002	.0021	.0273	.0014	.0025	.0062	.0031	.0065	.0043	.0017	.0056	.0043	.0069
	.0055	.0168	.0078	.0392	.0484	.0247	.0111	.0391	.0048	.0049	.0030	.0043	.0022	.0028	.0176	.0002	.0051	.0018	.0020	.0003	.0060	.0008	.0045	.0140	.0037
	.0000	.0000	.0000	.0001	.0001		.0070	.0001	.0001	.0000			.0004	.0000	.0003		.0001	.0000	.0000	.0004	.0000		.0000	.0000	.0027
	.0028	.0070	.0017	.0187	.0145	.0117	.0022	.0039	.0024	.0024	.0029	.0043	.0078	.0078	.0043	.0042	.0004	.0000	.0000	.0022	.0010	.0002	.0006	.0005	.0017
	.1214	.0447	.1668	.0356	.1235	.0225	.1181	.0270	.0069	.0073	.1106	.0072	.0274	.0135	.0138	.0024	.0135	.0063	.0130	.0017	.0030		.0000		.0113
	.0055	.0564	.0820	.0377	.0009	.0237	.0390	.0022	.0003	.0018	.0184	.1882	.0124	.0106	.0047	.0050	.0192	.0040	.0035	.0096	.0001	.0005	.0015	.0006	.0007
	.0024			.0007			.0032				.0002		.1548			.0001	.0003		.0149						.0000
		.0002		.0116			.0005	.0002		.0001			.0021		.0000				.0501	.0000	.0004	.0008	.0013	.0005	.0012
		.0015		.0031	.1503	.0073	.0020						.0200	.4006		.0000	.0080	.0015	.0000	.0033	.0003	.0007			.0155
		.0003		.0113		.0070	.0004						.0002	.0007	.0001	.0004	.0027	.0050		.0004	.0010	.0010	.0015	.0063	.0010
	.0468	.0192	.0078	.0770	.0039	.0485	.1185	.0041	.0025	.0090	.0015	.0039	.0031	.0023	.0110	.0175	.0002	.0002	.0001	.0000	.0003	.0007	.0012	.0005	.0010
	.0021			.0138	.0198	.0086	.0056	.0391	.0001	.0019	.0012	.0137	.0006	.0062	.0050	.1313	.0013	.0017	.0010	.0017	.0001	.0018	.0004	.0013	.0052
	.0865	.0009	.0014	.0003	.0002	.0001	.0045	.0055	.0001	.0019	.0012	.0698	.1148	.0021	.0273	.0806	.0023	.0010	.0030	.0032	.0019	.0013	.0020	.0003	.0040
	.0082	.0037	.0042	.0190	.0170	.0119	.0234	.0065	.3086	.0370	.0932	.0178	.0487	.0077	.0160	.0455	.0075	.0031	.0034	.0098	.0030	.0001	.0023	.0006	.0058
	.0016	.0005	.0006	.0022	.0028	.0014	.0003	.0029	.0348	.0073	.1106	.0072	.0274	.0135	.0021	.0125	.0135	.0005	.0010	.0017	.0000	.0000	.0007	.0002	.0021
	.0016	.0013	.0021	.0003	.0004	.0002	.0004	.0025	.0030	.0018	.0184	.1882	.0124	.0106	.0047	.0050	.0192	.0040	.0035	.0096	.0001	.0005	.0015	.0006	.0150
								.0012		.0002		.1548												.0051
	.0011	.0009	.0014	.0010	.0002	.0006	.0003	.0012	.0016	.0007	.0236	.0011	.0200	.4006	.0002	.0001	.0080	.0015	.0501	.0033	.0001	.0001	.0006	.0008	.0309
							.0006	.0002		.0004		.0018	.0002	.0007	.0438	.0004	.0027	.0050	.0010	.0004	.0010	.0010	.0015	.0063	.0075
	.0380	.0180	.0209	.0039	.0040	.0024	.0083	.0311	.0232	.0079	.0065	.0078	.0083	.0046	.0059	.0042	.0009	.0223	.0022	.0047	.0098	.0066	.0093	.0054	.0043
	.0003			.0080	.0008	.0050	.0007	.0010		.007		.0025	.0006	.0007	.007		.0008	.1661	.0005	.0028		.0001	.0115	.0062	.0004
	.0077	.0314	.0178	.0106	.0154	.0087	.0137	.0146	.0097	.0090	.0091	.0100	.0037	.0043	.0059	.0231	.0010	.0064	.0166	.0107	.0020	.0012	.0020	.0065	.0049
	.0009	.0011	.0013	.0009	.0011	.0006	.0016	.0007	.0013	.0009	.0009	.0011	.0010	.0004	.0013	.0010	.0034	.0034	.0042	.0004	.0046	.0012	.0111	.0174	.0032
	.0774	.1306	.1024	.1323	.1239	.0833	.1736	.0739	.0889	.0838	.0790	.1252	.0828	.0905	.1123	.1024	.0203	.0134	.0479	.0208	.0172	.0094	.0157	.0085	.0413
	.0049	.0017	.0011	.0032	.0030	.0014	.0033	.0034	.0012	.0049	.0040	.0044	.0026	.0011	.0050	.0009	.0022	.0038	.0038	.0089	.0181		.0184	.0126	.0123
		.0304	.0046	.0044	.0146	.0027	.0047	.0043	.0007	.0032	.0034	.0027	.0037	.0011	.0025	.0003			.0097		.0017	.0017	.0110	.0057	.0045
	.0041	.0205	.0087	.0083	.0071	.0040	.0043	.0082	.0043	.0043	.0048	.0054	.0054	.0035	.0063	.0104	.0005	.0471	.0084	.0018	.0074	.0016	.0135	.0411	.1553
	.0056	.0205	.0095	.0041	.0133	.0023	.0086	.0144	.0091	.0041	.0044	.0052	.0040	.0017	.0048	.0070	.0090	.0275	.0137	.0197	.0117	.0805	.0174	.0119	.0099

Table C.III Income distribution coefficients

	1	2	3	4	5	6	7	8	9	10	11	12	13	14	15	16	17	18	19	20
1 Entrepreneurs, employees, professionals (high)	.0387	.1018				.5407	.2975	.2157	2157	.2157	.2240	.2240	.1618		.1901	.1104	.4589	.4228	.1951	.4021
2 Entrepreneurs, employees, professionals (middle)	.0438	.1062	.1174	.1327		.1322	.2912	.2469	.2469	.2469	.3360	.3360	.0840	.3110	.1833	.2360	.1836	.2373	.2558	.1996
3 Entrepreneurs, employees, professionals (low)	.0257	.0770	.1294			.0566	.0327	.1282	.1282	.1282	.1354	.1354	.1014	.1304	.1688	.0979	.0485	.0805	.1127	.0186
4 Workers	.0069	.0067	.0885			.2647	.3737	.3831	.3831	.3831	.2854	.2854	.6300	.5585	.4579	.5434	.3090	.2593	.4364	.3797
5 Peasants (high - middle)	.2736	.2327	.1342	.3344	1.0			.0071	.0071	.0071	.0131	.0131								
6 Peasants (low)	.2040	.0421	-.1193	.1422		.0057		.0023	.0023	.0023										
7 Landless workers	.4072	.4335	.4113	.3908			.0048	.0168	.0168	.0168	.0060	.0060	.0229			.0123				

Table C.IV Tax coefficients

	1	2	3	4	5	6	7	8	9	10	11	12	13	14	15	16	17	18	19	20
a Direct tax coefficients	.0478	.0544	.0765	.0397	.0422	.0426	.0106	.0265	.0242	.0185	.0237	.0144	.0195	.0777	.0144	.0582	.0248	.0264	.0742	.0769
b Indirect tax plus surpluses of exploitation coefficients	.0094	.0036	.0225	.0217	.0349	.0403	.3059	.0108	.0176	.0722	.1448	.4416	.0163	.0099	.0210	.0291	.0303	.0440	.0210	.0698

21	22	23	24	25	26	27	28	29	30	31	32	33	34	35	36	37	38	39	40	41	42	43	44	45
.4620	.2772	.4620	.2908	.3338	.2908	.4620	.1542	.2640	.1542	.3654	.3682		.1310	.4479	.1846	.2438	.1377	.2671	.3126	.2807	.4313	.1777	.4311	.4037
.1622	.2562	.1622	.2577	.3351	.2577	.1622	.2124	.1033	.1796	.1505	.2775	.1959	.2963	.1862	.1320	.2256	.3702	.4485	.4401	.4250	.2451	.4942	.4651	.3558
.0347	.1267	.0347	.1148	.1089	.1148	.0347	.0999	.0242	.0935	.0716	.1026	.0243	.0801	.0762	.1099	.0334	.3488	.1824	.0510	.2484	.2568	.2928	.0664	.1834
.3411	.3138	.3411	.3367	.2221	.3367	.3411	.5301	.6085	.5727	.4126	.2517	.7798	.4925	.2860	.5704	.4973	.1012	.1001	.1962	.0442	.0428	.0353	.0345	.0509
														.0037						.0009				
															.0030					.0003			.0011	.0001
							.0034										.0421	.0018		.0005	.0240		.0018	.0061
	.0261																							

21	22	23	24	25	26	27	28	29	30	31	32	33	34	35	36	37	38	39	40	41	42	43	44	45
.0166	.0769	.0246	.0174	.0354	.0174	.0248	.0317	.0205	.0285	.0262	.0379	.0063	.0168	.0249	.0230	.0348	.0826	.0692	.0407	.0366	.0841	.0537	.0407	.0967
.0399	.0528	.0487	.0291	.1402	.0171	.0273	.0206	.0273	.0542	.0713	.0601	.0412	.0268	.0588	.0096	.0117	.0999	.0151	.2668	.0650	.0111	.0338	.0253	.0133

Table C.V Subsistence consumption coefficients (private)

	1	2	3	4	5	6	7	Total
1 Agriculture	6181.7 (447.4)	3926.2 (356.6)	2319.1 (133.0)	3129.6 (146.7)	6994.5 (566.1)	2550.3 (246.3)	4312.7 (171.9)	29414.1
2 Livestock	1681.2 (150.1)	920.4 (105.2)	187.7 (35.8)	575.5 (37.4)	704.0 (97.8)	-26.0 (28.4)	102.7 (28.3)	4145.5
3 Forestry								
4 Fishing	376.4 (349.2)	2.6 (142.5)	-9.1 (29.2)	2.3 (35.0)	395.7 (115.8)	15.5 (27.5)	37.8 (25.5)	819.3
5 Mining								
6 Quarrying								
7 Petroleum	4196.8ᵃ(683.1)	-1953.9ᵃ(445.7)	-80.4ᵃ(61.1)	-602.8ᵃ(73.5)	-2134.1ᵃ(675.8)	143.3ᵃ(46.6)	-365.7ᵃ(50.5)	-796.9ᵃ
8 Slaughter of livest.and poultry	11540.4 (1345.4)	6143.7 (746.4)	559.9 (191.9)	2939.5 (223.8)	4968.7 (651.6)	311.3 (148.4)	451.3 (139.3)	26914.9
9 Milling	4463.7 (293.9)	3300.8 (257.9)	684.9 (86.1)	2222.9 (100.4)	1781.9 (255.4)	55.5 (76.0)	331.2 (81.0)	12864.9
10 Other processed food	7034.6 (630.9)	3882.2 (444.5)	1298.0 (126.6)	1930.2 (142.9)	5531.6 (571.5)	1053.9 (157.5)	1268.6 (129.1)	21999.1
11 Beverages	2992.3 (507.6)	1425.4 (528.0)	128.8 (75.1)	777.1 (106.9)	1761.2 (349.3)	140.2 (96.4)	207.6 (95.6)	7483.0
12 Tobacco	521.9 (152.3)	254.5 (87.4)	76.2 (24.2)	143.5 (35.5)	495.5 (76.7)	84.1 (22.8)	54.8 (23.7)	1630.5
13 Soft fibre textiles	429.9 (165.1)	-34.5 (82.5)	-41.0 (16.9)	-86.4 (35.1)	211.5 (82.0)	-5.9 (12.3)	-11.9 (16.8)	461.6
14 Other textiles								
15 Wearing apparel and footwear	9170.7 (1433.8)	-1650.0 (585.8)	-564.3 (105.9)	-941.1 (189.1)	2407.3 (508.5)	75.8 (101.6)	-191.0 (111.1)	8387.3
16 Wood and cork	750.7ᵃ(892.3)	423.3ᵃ(263.7)	-14.1ᵃ(69.3)	86.7ᵃ(88.6)	192.6ᵃ(175.0)	8.0ᵃ(29.1)	-53.2ᵃ(40.9)	1396.0ᵃ
17 Paper and paper products	531.5 (51.6)	207.3 (39.3)	-31.2 (10.1)	.8 (13.4)	46.1 (27.5)	-12.5 (5.9)	-34.8 (6.7)	687.3
18 Printing, publishing	525.5ᵃ(340.8)	-166.4ᵃ(137.0)	-76.8ᵃ(25.7)	-192.2ᵃ(36.1)	-187.0ᵃ(80.4)	-2.3ᵃ(14.4)	-101.2ᵃ(19.3)	-200.4ᵃ
19 Leather	125.7ᵃ(91.5)	-144.9ᵃ(31.5)	-8.2ᵃ(3.4)	-57.2ᵃ(7.9)	25.5ᵃ(21.7)	-.4ᵃ(3.3)	-11.6ᵃ(3.1)	-71.1ᵃ
20 Rubber products	571.8ᵃ(290.5)	-219.5ᵃ(94.8)	-17.9ᵃ(13.4)	-119.2ᵃ(21.7)	-71.2ᵃ(104.7)	-4.2ᵃ(6.3)	-33.4ᵃ(7.1)	106.4ᵃ
21 Basic chemicals	109.8ᵃ(29.0)	-14.7ᵃ(14.6)	-7.0ᵃ(3.2)	-29.2ᵃ(5.3)	-39.8ᵃ(14.6)	.5ᵃ(.8)	-11.2ᵃ(1.9)	8.1ᵃ
22 Synthetic fibres								
23 Fertilizers	-55.6ᵃ(43.0)	43.5ᵃ(14.0)	.5ᵃ(3.7)	-.6ᵃ(5.6)	-.8ᵃ(12.1)	-.2ᵃ(2.6)	-8.8ᵃ(3.4)	-21.9ᵃ
24 Soaps and detergents	978.4 (110.0)	978.7 (77.4)	255.1 (26.6)	638.8 (28.5)	1057.8 (89.1)	308.4 (25.4)	655.9 (23.2)	4473.1
25 Drugs and medicines	1233.9 (483.5)	338.4 (175.2)	131.7 (41.2)	134.5 (37.9)	634.4 (187.6)	26.1 (33.9)	140.9 (39.5)	2640.1
26 Perfumes, cosmetics	2300.6 (221.5)	384.4 (111.6)	-16.8 (23.2)	68.6 (32.5)	401.7 (97.3)	14.2 (15.7)	-23.0 (17.3)	3129.7
27 Other chemical industries	-62.0ᵃ(182.6)	-31.3ᵃ(28.7)	-1.1ᵃ(8.3)	-119.2ᵃ(8.5)	-7.4ᵃ(18.8)	-.6ᵃ(1.1)	-8.8ᵃ(2.7)	-146.8ᵃ
28 Non-metallic mineral products	369.1 (100.1)	125.2 (46.4)	-25.9 (12.7)	54.2 (17.4)	69.8 (41.9)	-.3 (7.5)	1.2 (9.9)	593.4
29 Basic metallic industries								
30 Metal products	401.0ᵃ(207.5)	213.8ᵃ(109.6)	-71.4ᵃ(27.0)	-13.1ᵃ(43.6)	-19.6ᵃ(107.9)	-19.2ᵃ(24.3)	-35.6ᵃ(23.4)	454.3ᵃ
31 Machinery	101.3ᵃ(57.3)	-17.1ᵃ(46.6)	-4.8ᵃ(2.3)	6.2ᵃ(13.0)	39.3ᵃ(50.4)	-10.4ᵃ(9.3)	-3.7ᵃ(1.4)	110.1ᵃ
32 Electrical machinery	1081.5ᵃ(648.3)	62.1ᵃ(330.8)	-262.9ᵃ(70.6)	-80.7ᵃ(109.1)	847.3ᵃ(296.6)	14.5ᵃ(44.9)	-161.1ᵃ(45.7)	1500.7ᵃ
33 Transport equipment	786.5ᵃ(456.3)	-730.5ᵃ(469.3)	-50.3ᵃ(26.3)	-253.6ᵃ(42.1)	-26.8ᵃ(278.5)	4.2ᵃ(18.8)	-247.1ᵃ(49.3)	-517.6ᵃ
34 Motor vehicles	-1747.2ᵃ(3498.1)	-4112.5ᵃ(1162.2)	-71.5ᵃ(40.0)	-2471.5ᵃ(301.0)	1694.7ᵃ(1051.7)	-2.0ᵃ(3.7)	-316.0ᵃ(97.7)	-1044.0ᵃ
35 Other manufacturing industries	-481.9ᵃ(611.9)	-189.9ᵃ(225.9)	-11.3ᵃ(32.5)	-239.1ᵃ(63.3)	180.9ᵃ(132.9)	78.8ᵃ(20.5)	-26.8ᵃ(36.0)	-689.4ᵃ
36 Construction								
37 Electricity	1388.8 (234.1)	1014.2 (114r.8)	167.3 (34.3)	254.5 (38.7)	226.9 (105.0)	-27.8 (21.3)	-167.1 (26.4)	2856.8
38 Cinema	-3796.4ᵃ(567.2)	-778.3ᵃ(241.3)	-129.1ᵃ(31.1)	-298.8ᵃ(57.6)	-457.6ᵃ(119.7)	-12.9ᵃ(13.9)	-221.9ᵃ(33.2)	-5695.1ᵃ
39 Transport	1400.1 (790.4)	1531.5 (343.9)	-45.2 (80.4)	266.9 (110.4)	1393.6 (257.3)	-20.3 (53.3)	-19.1 (54.9)	4507.4
40 Communications	-251.2ᵃ(287.3)	-639.4ᵃ(148.4)	-44.2ᵃ(23.1)	-239.0ᵃ(25.5)	-343.1ᵃ(83.6)	4.0ᵃ(4.7)	-31.0ᵃ(9.9)	-1543.9ᵃ
41 Trade	-902.4ᵃ(310.8)	-588.4ᵃ(129.6)	-7.1ᵃ(55.6)	-137.8ᵃ(38.3)	-12.7ᵃ(86.6)	-1.4 (15.1)	-38.7ᵃ(16.5)	-1691.5ᵃ
42 Dwellings	5069.0 (1114.5)	974.2 (510.9)	33.9 (101.7)	548.9 (125.7)	-269.6 (152.9)	-1.4 (15.1)	-128.2 (33.1)	6228.8
43 Hotels and restaurants	665.2ᵃ(294.4)	-200.9ᵃ(175.5)	-9.5ᵃ(37.1)	13.1ᵃ(53.8)	82.1ᵃ(78.0)	-6.6ᵃ(16.4)	-12.1ᵃ(16.6)	531.0ᵃ
44 Credit and insurance	-1102.0ᵃ(439.8)	-291.6ᵃ(110.6)	-11.2ᵃ(7.9)	-128.2ᵃ(22.0)	-32.3ᵃ(35.0)		-19.9 (7.6)	-1585.4
45 Other services	-14999.3ᵃ(2611.5)	-3118.3ᵃ(987.1)	14.1ᵃ(150.2)	-1236.6ᵃ(214.3)	1271.4ᵃ(641.2)	213.2ᵃ(98.4)	-232.1ᵃ(98.6)	-18087.1ᵃ

Note: standard errors are given in parentheses
a: the coefficient is not significantly different from zero at the 5 percent level

Table C.VI Marginal consumption propensities (private)

	Socio-economic group						
	1	2	3	4	5	6	7
1 Agriculture	.0115 (.0018)	.0255 (.0037)	.0493 (.0372)	.0387 (.0021)	.0124[a] (.0069)	.1461 (.0157)	.0374 (.0051)
2 Livestock	.0018 (.0006)	.0070 (.0011)	.0211 (.0010)	.0105 (.0005)	.0054 (.0012)	.0227 (.0018)	.0171 (.0008)
3 Forestry							
4 Fishing	.0038 (.0013)	.0067 (.0015)	.0070 (.0008)	.0049 (.0005)	-.0002[a] (.0014)	.0063 (.0018)	.0033 (.0008)
5 Mining							
6 Quarrying							
7 Petroleum	.0190 (.0026)	.0521 (.0047)	.0152 (.0017)	.0223 (.0010)	.0680 (.0082)	.0024[a] (.0030)	.0291 (.0015)
8 Slaughter of livest.and poultry	.0560 (.0051)	.1005 (.0078)	.1915 (.0054)	.1131 (.0032)	.0664 (.0079)	.1677 (.0095)	.1461 (.0041)
9 Milling	.001[a] (.0011)	.0087 (.0027)	.0607 (.0024)	.0272 (.0014)	.0149 (.0031)	.0539 (.0048)	.0541 (.0024)
10 Other processed food	.0089 (.0240)	.0275 (.0047)	.0657 (.0035)	.0478 (.0020)	.0195 (.0069)	.1249 (.0100)	.0868 (.0038)
11 Beverages	.0061 (.0019)	.0153 (.0055)	.0330 (.0021)	.0201 (.0015)	.0129 (.0042)	.0443 (.0061)	.0384 (.0028)
12 Tobacco	.0025 (.0006)	.0036 (.0009)	.0062 (.0007)	.0049 (.0005)	.0003[a] (.0009)	.0078 (.0014)	.0104 (.0007)
13 Soft fibre textiles	.0029 (.0006)	.0057 (.0009)	.0062 (.0005)	.0077 (.0005)	.0024 (.0010)	.0062 (.0008)	.0060 (.0005)
14 Other textiles							
15 Wearing apparel and footwear	.0574 (.0054)	.1158 (.0061)	.0970 (.0030)	.1098 (.0027)	.0677 (.0062)	.1216 (.0065)	.1096 (.0033)
16 Wood and cork	.0107 (.0034)	.0077 (.0028)	.0137 (.0019)	.0115 (.0013)	.0107 (.0021)	.0107 (.0019)	.0173 (.0012)
17 Paper and paper products	.0016 (.0002)	.0035 (.0004)	.0073 (.0003)	.0055 (.0002)	.0024 (.0003)	.0026 (.0004)	.0055 (.0002)
18 Printing, publishing	.0125 (.0013)	.0152 (.0014)	.0123 (.0007)	.0136 (.0010)	.0113 (.0010)	.0084 (.0009)	.0125 (.0006)
19 Leather	.0019 (.0003)	.0033 (.0003)	.0009 (.0001)	.0021 (.0001)	.0006 (.0003)	.0008 (.0002)	.0012 (.0001)
20 Rubber products	.0020 (.0009)	.0052[a] (.0010)	.0014 (.0004)	.0034 (.0003)	.0046 (.0013)	.0008[a] (.0004)	.0028 (.0005)
21 Basic chemicals	.0005[a] (.0001)	.0011[a] (.0002)	.0009 (.0001)	.0013 (.0001)	.0012 (.0002)	.0001[a] (.0001)	.0007 (.0001)
22 Synthetic fibres							
23 Fertilizers	.0009 (.0002)	.0004 (.0001)	.0010 (.0001)	.0010 (.0001)	.0008 (.0001)	.0008 (.0002)	.0012 (.0001)
24 Soaps and detergents	.0036 (.0004)	.0039 (.0008)	.0174 (.0007)	.0081 (.0004)	.0062 (.0011)	.0240 (.0016)	.0139 (.0007)
25 Drugs and medicines	.0021 (.0018)	.0058 (.0018)	.0086 (.0011)	.0057 (.0005)	.0050 (.0023)	.0176 (.0022)	.0102 (.0012)
26 Perfumes, cosmetics	.0071 (.0008)	.0169 (.0012)	.0225 (.0006)	.0190 (.0005)	.0114 (.0012)	.0172[a] (.0010)	.0188 (.0005)
27 Other chemical industries	.0018 (.0007)	.0010 (.0013)	.0006 (.0002)	.0011 (.0002)	.0006 (.0002)	.0001[a] (.0001)	.0006 (.0001)
28 Non-metallic mineral products	.0006[a] (.0004)	.0009[a] (.0005)	.0036 (.0004)	.0022 (.0002)	.0018 (.0005)	.0028 (.0005)	.0029 (.0003)
29 Basic metallic industries							
30 Metal products	.0016 (.0008)	.0014[a] (.0012)	.0063 (.0008)	.0052 (.0006)	.0054 (.0013)	.0062 (.0015)	.0061 (.0007)
31 Machinery	.0000 (.0001)	.0009 (.0005)	.0005 (.0005)	.0003 (.0002)	.0003 (.0006)	.0012 (.0006)	.0002 (.0006)
32 Electrical machinery	.0129 (.0025)	.0180 (.0035)	.0230 (.0020)	.0204 (.0015)	.0075 (.0036)	.0096[a] (.0029)	.0201 (.0014)
33 Transport equipment	.0061 (.0017)	.0159 (.0049)	.0039 (.0007)	.0077 (.0006)	.0106 (.0034)	.0016[a] (.0012)	.0141 (.0015)
34 Motor vehicles	.0075 (.0133)	.0670 (.0122)	.0043 (.0011)	.0556 (.0043)	.0518 (.0127)	.0003[a] (.0013)	.0194 (.0029)
35 Other manufacturing industries	.0242 (.0023)	.0206 (.0024)	.0137 (.0009)	.0211 (.0030)	.0097 (.0016)	.0103 (.0013)	.0155 (.0011)
36 Construction							
37 Electricity	.0101 (.0009)	.0120 (.0015)	.0252 (.0010)	.0172 (.0010)	.0144 (.0013)	.0143 (.0014)	.0232 (.0008)
38 Cinema	.0342 (.0022)	.0217 (.0025)	.0115 (.0009)	.0161 (.0008)	.0138 (.0014)	.0041 (.0009)	.0172 (.0010)
39 Transport	.0176 (.0030)	.0194 (.0036)	.0453 (.0022)	.0389 (.0016)	.0090 (.0031)	.0405 (.0034)	.0300 (.0016)
40 Communications	.0135 (.0011)	.0155 (.0016)	.0054 (.0006)	.068 (.0004)	.0087 (.0010)	.0002[a] (.0003)	.0021 (.0003)
41 Trade	.0131 (.0012)	.0120 (.0014)	.0038 (.0016)	.0060 (.0005)	.0035 (.0010)	.0009 (.0003)	.0030 (.0005)
42 Dwellings	.0125 (.0042)	.0323 (.0053)	.0459 (.0028)	.0239 (.0018)	.0106 (.0019)	.0047 (.0010)	.0150 (.0010)
43 Hotels and restaurants	.0035 (.0011)	.0102 (.0018)	.0070 (.0010)	.0073 (.0008)	.0034 (.0009)	.0041 (.0010)	.0041 (.0005)
44 Credit and insurance	.0135 (.0016)	.0052 (.0012)	.0007 (.0002)	.0029 (.0003)	.0011 (.0004)		.0010 (.0002)
45 Other services	.1942 (.0092)	.1170 (.0103)	.0562 (.0042)	.0728 (.0030)	.0452 (.0078)	.0347 (.0063)	.0526 (.0029)

Note: standard errors are given in parentheses
a: the coefficient is not significantly different from zero at the 5 percent level

Table C.VII Consumption propensities of the government

1 Agriculture	.0006
2 Livestock	
3 Forestry	
4 Fishing	
5 Mining	
6 Quarrying	
7 Petroleum	.0045
8 Slaughter of livest.and poultry	.0009
9 Milling	
10 Other processed food	.0009
11 Beverages	
12 Tobacco	
13 Soft fibre textiles	
14 Other textiles	
15 Wearing apparel and footwear	.0055
16 Wood and cork	.0002
17 Paper and paper products	.0003
18 Printing, publishing	.0076
19 Leather	.0001
20 Rubber products	
21 Basic chemicals	.0007
22 Synthetic fibres	
23 Fertilizers	
24 Soap and detergents	.0026
25 Drugs and medicines	.0175
26 Perfumed cosmetics	
27 Other chemical industries	.0011
28 Non-metallic mineral products	.0009
29 Basic metallic industries	.0085
30 Metal products	
31 Machinery	.0045
32 Electrical machinery	.0055
33 Transport equipment	.0008
34 Motor vehicles	.0003
35 Other manufacturing industries	.0059
36 Construction	.0045
37 Electricity	.0033
38 Cinema	.0002
39 Transport	.0044
40 Communications	.0033
41 Trade	.0137
42 Dwellings	.0100
43 Hotels and restaurants	.0038
44 Credit and insurance	.0059
45 Other services	.0085

Table C.VIII   Incremental capital output ratios

Sector	Sample 1952-67	1960-75	Estimation Method 1)2)	Standard error	T-statistic	R²	Durbin-Watson	â Estimated	Adopted
1 Agriculture	x		a	.06	32.75	.99	1.42	2.119297	2.119297 and 4.238594 3)
2 Livestock	x		a	.07	24.30	.98	1.55	1.683264	1.683264
3 Forestry			(4)					-	2.119297
4 Fishing	x		a	.09	9.70	.87	.64	.903384	.903384
5 Mining		x	a	.60	5.98	.72	1.19	3.583579	3.583579
6 Quarrying		x	a	.13	10.54	.89	1.11	1.376215	1.376215
7 Petroleum		x	a	.09	25.66	.98	2.10	2.414701	2.414701
8 Slaughter of livestock and poultry		x	b	.02	8.69	.97	1.47	.181945	.20000 5)
9 Milling		x	c	.03	1.34	.95	1.22	.035269	.20000
10 Other processed food		x	c	.02	14.52	.99	1.60	.310001	.310001
11 Beverages		x	a	.06	15.98	.95	1.32	.965369	.965369
12 Tobacco		x	a	.06	5.62	.69	.93	.356794	.356794
13 Soft fibre textiles		x	b	.03	30.05	.99	.71	.889711	.889711
14 Other textiles	x		c	.19	1.23	.93	1.02	.229864	.229864
15 Wearing apparel and footwear	x		a	.04	11.67	.91	1.08	.452318	.452318
16 Wood and cork		x	c	.10	1.14	.96	1.25	.108972	.200000
17 Paper and paper products		x	a	.04	18.76	.96	1.63	.811601	.811601
18 Printing, publishing	x		c	.34	1.84	.95	.81	.629934	.629934
19 Leather	x		b	.10	1.69	.84	1.32	.161608	.200000
20 Rubber products		x	a	.05	23.51	.98	1.31	1.071331	1.071331
21 Basic chemicals		x	a	.07	19.28	.96	1.93	1.355548	1.355548
22 Synthetic fibres		x	a	.03	46.45	.99	1.27	1.312126	1.312126
23 Fertilizers		x	c	.22	8.67	.96	2.07	1.930024	1.930024
24 Soaps and detergents		x	a	.01	12.64	.92	1.86	.132341	.200000
25 Drugs and medicines		x	a	.03	27.36	.98	1.44	.881763	.881763
26 Perfumes, cosmetics		x	a	.01	16.40	.95	1.84	.111321	.200000
27 Other chemical industries		x	b	.01	8.49	.97	1.80	.100042	.200000
28 Non-metallic mineral products		x	a	.03	28.52	.98	1.19	.896984	.896984
29 Basic metallic industries		x	b	.08	11.76	.98	1.60	.942930	.942930 6)
30 Metal products		x	c	.04	2.05	.98	.85	.092857	.412366 6)
31 Machinery		x	a	.03	21.45	.97	1.60	.672922	.672922
32 Electrical machinery		x	b	.06	8.69	.96	1.80	.562423	.562423
33 Transport equipment		x	b	.01	6.30	.96	2.30	.088697	.412366
34 Motor vehicles		x	a	.01	36.49	.99	1.16	.430227	.430227
35 Other manufacturing industries		x	b	.59	.60	.99	1.57	.353826	.412366
36 Construction		x	c	.04	11.20	.97	1.77	.412366	.412366
37 Electricity		x	b	.30	17.40	.99	1.22	5.233189	5.233189
38 Cinema		x	a	.13	7.30	.79	1.38	.964542	.964542
39 Transport		x	a	1.78	3.66	.69	2.42	6.528661	6.528661
40 Communication		x	a	.63	8.77	.92	.23	5.493044	5.493044
41 Trade		x	b	.04	6.92	.98	1.61	.275698	.275698
42 Dwellings	x		a	.06	136.99	1.00	1.39	7.645479	7.645479
43 Hotels and restaurants		x	c	.11	6.77	.94	1.56	.747470	.747470
44 Credit and insurance		x	c	.05	7.00	(7)	1.36	.369994	.369994
45 Other services		x	c	.35	7.41	.99	1.48	2.621852	2.621852

1) a: ordinary least squares; b: Cochrane-Orcutt iterative technique; c: Hildreth-Lu scanning technique.
2) For sectors numbers 39, 40 and 44 homogeneous functions have been estimated, the adjustment of the form in eq.(5.5) being bad.
3) Value that adjusts the model to actual behavior in 1975-78.
4) Insufficient data; the coefficient of agriculture was adopted.
5) The estimated coefficients of sectors 8, 9, 16, 19, 24, 26 and 27 were unrealistically low; a minimum value of .2 was adopted.
6) Sectors numbers 30, 33 and 35 are capital goods producing sectors. The estimated coefficients were too low, due to the inclusion of repair activities. The 'intermediate' value of the construction sector was assumed to apply to them.
7) Not determined, the result was an (impossible) negative value, due perhaps to the use by the Time-Series Processor of an approximation.

Table C.IX   Distribution of investment demands

	1	2	3	4	5	6	7	8	9	10	11	12	13	14	15	16	17	18	19	20
1 Agriculture	.3640																			
2 Livestock		.3640																		
3 Forestry			.3640																	
4 Fishing				.3640																
5 Mining					.0590															
6 Quarrying						.0780														
7 Petroleum							.0020													
8 Slaughter of livestock and poultry								.2460												
9 Milling									.4950											
10 Other processed food										.1450										
11 Beverages											.0560									
12 Tobacco												.1000								
13 Soft fibre textiles													.0610							
14 Other textiles														.0610						
15 Wearing apparel and footwear															.0610					
16 Wood and cork																.2790				
17 Paper and paper products																	.1400			
18 Printing, publishing																		.0920		
19 Leather																			.0610	
20 Rubber products																				.1140
21 Basic chemicals																				
22 Synthetic fibres																				
23 Fertilizers																				
24 Soaps and detergents																				
25 Drugs and medicines																				
26 Perfumes, cosmetics																				
27 Other chemical industries																				
28 Non-metallic mineral products																				
29 Basic metallic industries																				
30 Metal products																				
31 Machinery	.1250	.1250	.1250	.1250	.2400	.2580	.2010	.2310	.1310	.2660	.2590	.2310	.3370	.2550	.2550	.1990	.2720	.2440	.2550	.2760
32 Electrical machinery	.1250	.1250	.1250	.1250	.2950	.2580	.2240	.2280	.1520	.3370	.2840	.2690	.4370	.2550	.2550	.2210	.3520	.2440	.2550	.3440
33 Transport equipment	.1250	.1250	.1250	.1250	.0770	.0610	.0370	.0760	.0700	.0300	.0600	.0470	.0080	.2550	.2550	.0990	.0120	.2440	.2550	.0240
34 Motor vehicles																				
35 Other manufacturing industries																				
36 Construction	.3810	.2610	.2610	.2610	.3390	.3650	.5360	.2210	.1520	.2220	.3410	.3530	.1570	.1740	.1740	.2030	.2240	.1760	.1740	.2420
37 Electricity																				
38 Cinema																				
39 Transport																				
40 Communication																				
41 Trade																				
42 Dwellings																				
43 Hotels and restaurants																				
44 Credit and insurance																				
45 Other Services																				

21	22	23	24	25	26	27	28	29	30	31	32	33	34	35	36	37	38	39	40	41	42	43	44	45
.0740	.0690	.1140	.3370	.1270	.3370	.4870	.0840	.3730	.5130															
.3110	.3280	.3000	.1980	.1910	.1980	.1350	.2610	.2220	.1410	.3160	.3360	.2720	.1910	.2760	.3860	.1490	.2710	.1640	.1910	.0950	.1030	.0680	.1600	.1440
.3940	.4310	.3860	.1840	.1850	.1840	.1220	.3400	.2830	.1700	.3540	.3410	.2980	.2190	.3120	.4510	.1940	.2930	.2110	.2470	.0570	.1030	.0610	.0050	.0870
.0170	.0060	.0140	.0380	.0850	.0280	.0350	.0290	.0390	.0200	.0340	.0320	.0180	.0230	.0580	.1220	.0060	.0360	.0010	.0050	.0780	.1030	.0100	.0170	.1170
												.3570		.0300										
.2040	.1750	.1870	.2830	.4120	.2830	.2310	.3860	.1940	.1580	.2960	.2910	.4120	.2100	.3340	.0410	.5770	.2230	.5940	.5340	.3320	.6470	.6720	.5550	.5000
																.0740	.1770	.0300	.0230	.4380	.0440	.1890	.2630	.1520

Table C.X   Distribution of input imports

	1	2	3	4	5	6	7	8	9	10	11	12	13	14	15	16	17	18	19	20
1 Agriculture	.5136							.0131	.9515	.3934	.1248	.0032		.1816						
2 Livestock		.1955												.0156	.0167					
3 Forestry																.0764	.0146		.0895	.2396
4 Fishing																				
5 Mining					.0378					.0051	.0524	.0288								
6 Quarrying					.2625	.4346	.0024			.0013										
7 Petroleum					.3833	.5121	.0814			.0143							.0311		.0019	.1240
8 Slaughter of livestock and poultry							.7070		.0026	.0032			.0016							
9 Milling									.0017											
10 Other processed food		.6175					.0012		.0291	.3575	.0945									
11 Beverages										.0023	.2097									
12 Tobacco												.3227								
13 Soft fibre textiles	.0036								.0022	.0741			.5975	.3603	.8224			.0261		.0001
14 Other textiles							.0004		.0021			.0288	.0003	.2539	.0251				.0029	.0004
15 Wearing apparel and footwear																				
16 Wood and cork							.0004			.0028	.0059		.0022			.5927	.0016			.0010
17 Paper and paper products							.0171	.2096	.0001	.0512		.1022	.0003			.0782	.9294	.9106		
18 Printing, publishing							.0273							.0184				.0247		
19 Leather													.0003		.0345				.7354	
20 Rubber products			.0031		.0081		.0074	.0217	.0025	.0041	.0155	.0671	.0993			.0073	.0037	.0047	.0243	.5068
21 Basic chemicals	.1316				.0161	.0064	.1244	.0420					.2942			.0145	.0016	.0012		.0429
22 Synthetic fibres					.1892		.0020					.0607	.0267	.0355					.0078	.0397
23 Fertilizers	.0045																			
24 Soaps and detergents																				
25 Drugs and medicines		.1458																		
26 Perfumes, cosmetics																				
27 Other chemical industries	.0563				.0081	.0025	.1441	.0007		.0770	.0185		.0030		.0010	.0745	.0044	.0167	.1029	.0357
28 Non-metallic mineral products					.0765		.0129				.0547					.0273	.0056			.0059
29 Basic metallic industries						.0025	.0225				.3050									
30 Metal products		.0233					.0693	.0039		.0051			.0005	.0057	.0157	.1218		.0009	.0243	.0005
31 Machinery	.2904	.0047			.0185		.3302	.0020	.0081	.0086	.1189	.3866	.0111		.0721		.0022	.0098	.0081	.0006
32 Electrical machinery							.0697										.0075		.0046	.0007
33 Transport equipment							.0086	.0081					.0624	.0298	.0125			.0029		
34 Motor vehicles				1.0000																
35 Other manufacturing industries	.2458						.0784													
36 Construction	.1719																			
37 Electricity																				
38 Cinema																				
39 Transport																				
40 Communication																				
41 Trade																				
42 Dwellings																				
43 Hotels and restaurants																				
44 Credit and insurance																				
45 Other Services																			.0024	

	21	22	23	24	25	26	27	28	29	30	31	32	33	34	35	36	37	38	39	40	41	42	43	44	45
			.0005																						.0002
							.0018										.0059	.0016							
		.0003					.0009																		
				.0019	.0073	.0014	.0134																		
	.0021	.0013		.0444	.0173	.0441	.0142	.0408	.1899	.0002	.0096	.0181			.0024	.0208	.0065		.1150						
	.2590	.6433		.1702		.1708	.2291	.6290	.0852		.0022				.6195	.0161	.0072		.0063						.0109
				.1073		.1074	.0080		.0017						.1142		.0039		.0011						
															.0177										
		.0055			.0050		.0015								.0014	.0129			.0002						.0002
										.0361	.0004				.0073										.0002
	.0014	.1647			.0021			.0023		.0084	.0020	.0128		.0004	.0047	.1461	.0359		.0051					.0253	.0006
								.0138			.0022		.0037	.0068	.0041	.0189	.0046	.0037	.0003						.0120
																.0070			.0021						.0117
																			.0001						
	.6584	.0105	.8583	.2851	.4914	.2858	.4708	.0534	.0005	.0227	.0076	.0072	.0073		.0061	.0013	.0039		.0231				.1250	.0008	.0032
	.0854	.0854					.0469	.1470	.0864		.0076	.0122			.0022	.0123	.0020		.0005						.0041
	.0628	.0628						.0040			.0036	.0030				.0001	.0013								.0122
			.1412	.0114		.0110								.0004											
	.0017	.0017		.4465																					.0228
	.0348	.0348		.3397	.0081	.3416	.2087	.0118	.0062	.0027	.0092	.0045	.0024	.0134	.0010	.0017	.0026		.0007					.0020	.0378
				.0019	.0010	.0014	.0006	.0393	.0006	.0035	.1158	.0412	.1809	.0020	.0079	.0827	.0183	.0008	.0008				.5000		.0128
	.0444			.0006	.0087		.0030	.0118	.1728	.7489	.0627	.0911	.1112	.0030	.0010	.3362	.0437		.0113						.1860
	.0139			.0354	.0104	.0255	.0012	.0418	.4229	.0976	.5235	.0338	.3447	.0473	.0067	.2345	.0437		.0104					.0012	.0698
				.0005	.0005			.0150	.0054	.0785	.1218	.0033	.0053	.0290	.0014	.0879	.3585	.0004	.0033	1.0000				.0036	.1976
									.0010	.0014	.0026	.1381	.0076	.0143	.0120	.0206	.4042	.0007	.0261	.5311					.0002
									.0177	.0864		.7563		.2115	.8790	.1661	.0033	.0267	.1512	.0005			.3750		
												.0864			.0048		.0010	.0274	.0291						
																				.9652	.1109				.9671
	.0097																								

Table C.XI   Input import coefficients by sector of destination

	1975	1978
1 Agriculture	.0033	.0032
2 Livestock	.0062	.0049
3 Forestry		
4 Fishing	.0016	.0011
5 Mining	.0287	.0295
6 Quarrying	.0394	.0352
7 Petroleum	.0198	.0120
8 Slaughter of livestock and poultry	.0044	.0039
9 Milling	.0426	.0426
10 Other processed food	.0267	.0262
11 Beverages	.0110	.0111
12 Tobacco	.0113	.0109
13 Soft fiber textiles	.0225	.0220
14 Other textiles	.0281	.0261
15 Wearing apparel and footwear	.0065	.0064
16 Wood and cork	.0115	.0112
17 Paper and paper products	.0498	.0468
18 Printing, publishing	.1010	.0995
19 Leather	.0798	.0792
20 Rubber products	.1187	.1187
21 Basic chemicals	.0760	.0763
22 Synthetic fibers	.3039	.2926
23 Fertilizers	.1788	.1665
24 Soaps and detergents	.0930	.0836
25 Drugs and medicines	.2159	.2222
26 Perfumes, cosmetics	.0577	.0526
27 Other chemical industries	.1089	.1046
28 Nonmetallic mineral products	.0537	.0480
29 Basic metallic industries	.0745	.0684
30 Metal products	.0591	.0569
31 Machinery	.1040	.0930
32 Electrical machinery	.1476	.1451
33 Transport equipment	.0775	.0777
34 Motor vehicles	.2209	.1499
35 Other manufacturing industries	.1758	.1685
36 Construction	.0271	.0265
37 Electricity	.0431	.0330
38 Cinema	.0738	.0696
39 Transport	.0531	.0427
40 Communications	.0012	.0012
41 Trade		
42 Dwellings		
43 Hotels and restaurants	.0001	.0001
44 Credit and insurance	.0331	.0281
45 Other services	.0192	.0166

Table C.XII   Distribution of imports of investment goods

	1	2	3	4	5	6	7	8	9	10	11	12	13	14	15	16	17	18	19	20
1 Agriculture																				
2 Livestock		1.0000																		
3 Forestry			1.0000																	
4 Fishing																				
5 Mining																				
6 Quarrying																				
7 Petroleum																				
8 Slaughter of livestock and poultry																				
9 Milling																				
10 Other processed food																				
11 Beverages																				
12 Tobacco																				
13 Soft fibre textiles																				
14 Other textiles				.0627																
15 Wearing apparel and footwear																				
16 Wood and cork																				
17 Paper and paper products																				
18 Printing, publishing																				
19 Leather																				
20 Rubber products																				
21 Basic chemicals																				
22 Synthetic fibres																				
23 Fertilisers																				
24 Soaps and detergents																				
25 Drugs and medicines																				
26 Perfumes, cosmetics																				
27 Other chemical industries																				
28 Non-metallic mineral products																				
29 Basic metallic industries	.0009				.0266		.2017						.0007	.0030						
30 Metal products	.8803				.0952	.0614	.1322	.0255	.1545	.1144	.0436		.0023		.0305	.0215				.0915
31 Machinery					.3527	.5988	.0934		.0649	.0192	.0462				.6351		.0012			
32 Electrical machinery	.0052				.2233	.3399	.3338	.9745	.7805	.8664	.8757	1.0000	.9969	.9735	.3345	.9785	.9928			
33 Transport equipment	.1136			.9373	.3022		.1873							.0235				.7270	1.0000	.9085
34 Motor vehicles																	.0037	.0072		
35 Other manufacturing industries							.0515				.0345						.0023	.2658		
36 Construction																				
37 Electricity																				
38 Cinema																				
39 Transport																				
40 Communication																				
41 Trade																				
42 Dwellings																				
43 Hotels and restaurants																				
44 Credit and insurance																				
45 Other Services																				

21	22	23	24	25	26	27	28	29	30	31	32	33	34	35	36	37	38	39	40	41	42	43	44	45
																								.0092
																		.0323						
						.2176	.0162	.0879	.0027	.0056					.0042	.0697		.0012		.0226				.0046
						.1900	.0746	.2414	.1397	.1853	.0614	.0307	.0936	.2370	.0174	.1346		.0042		.2321				.0300
						.1727	.5980	.0461	.0527	.3656	.3998	.0991	.5726	.5757	.7898	.1411		.1841	.9843	.7453				.0755
						.4197	.3061	.5251	.7254	.3104	.3267	.7346	.2377		.1360	.6309		.0079				.6303		.6649
							.0051	.0813	.0132			.0590	.0960	.1873	.0165	.0044		.6990						.0021
								.0183	.0664	.1332	.2121	.0765			.0332			.0628						.0022
															.0028	.0193	1.0000	.0085	.0157			.3697	1.0000	.2116
.0696	.0148	.0250		.0486																				
	.0667	.0350																						
.8635	.8985	.9750	1.0000	.9514	1.0000																			
.0669																								

Table C.XIII Labor requirements ratios

	1	2	3	4	5	6	7	8	9	10	11	12	13	14	15	16	17	18	19	20
1 Entrepreneurs, employees, professionals (high)	1.496	.251	1.347	.552	.122	.841	.176	1.239	.500	.208	.337	.136	.455	.737	.624	2.542	.359	.673	.478	.473
2 Entrepreneurs, employees, professionals (middle)	5.050	.630	4.226	1.834	.296	2.065	.447	3.011	1.215	.504	.786	.318	1.131	1.866	1.614	6.790	.872	1.557	1.166	1.113
3 Entrepreneurs, employees, professionals (low)	9.293	.928	7.147	1.716	.322	2.361	.450	3.502	1.414	.587	.816	.331	1.247	2.314	2.067	9.295	.928	1.669	1.391	1.226
4 Workers	1.034	.305	1.795	1.111	.383	2.475	.710	3.399	1.372	.569	1.042	.422	1.497	1.946	1.606	5.847	1.183	1.907	1.245	1.331
5 Peasants (high - middle)	2.248	.027	.251	.019																
6 Peasants (high - middle)	7.565	.092	.843	.066																
7 Landless workers	25.949	2.184	5.329	.862	.181	1.717	.056	.793	.320	.133	.126	.051	.162	.247	.114	2.123	.105	.048	.185	.093

	21	22	23	24	25	26	27	28	29	30	31	32	33	34	35	36	37	38	39	40	41	42	43	44	45
1	.375	.292	.379	.130	.537	.231	.151	.592	.264	.889	.815	1.113	1.488	.279	2.937	.485	.492	1.543	1.645	.675	.497	.015	1.047	.699	1.749
2	.890	.692	.898	.310	1.236	.549	.346	1.487	.637	2.178	1.923	2.692	3.560	.653	7.124	1.217	1.139	4.008	3.995	1.553	1.269	.035	2.494	1.596	4.421
3	.941	.782	.950	.329	1.281	.583	.357	1.771	.655	2.501	2.221	3.048	4.243	.669	8.077	1.456	1.171	5.375	4.831	1.613	1.776	.040	3.015	1.655	5.840
4	1.172	.911	1.183	.409	1.604	.725	.446	1.695	.905	2.579	2.080	3.206	3.661	.916	8.499	1.366	1.514	3.472	4.088	2.005	.882	.039	2.442	2.084	4.926
5																									.002
6																									.008
7	.099	.077	.099	.019	.179	.034	.031	1.105	.071	.262	.311	.188	.525	.030	1.165	1.279	.167	.551	.780	.096	.134	.005	.314	.079	.237

Table C.XIV   Rates of productivity change

1	Agriculture	.014420
2	Livestock	.007410
3	Forestry	.018340
4	Fishing	.024070
5	Mining	.078860
6	Quarrying	.056380
7	Petroleum	.057500
8	Slaughter of livestock and poultry	.001510
9	Milling	.020240
10	Other processed food	.045560
11	Beverages	.046950
12	Tobacco	.037920
13	Soft fibre textiles	.079460
14	Other textiles	.014480
15	Wearing apparel and footwear	.066700
16	Wood and cork	.033900
17	Paper and paper products	.011340
18	Printing, publishing	.062230
19	Leather	.038150
20	Rubber procducts	.094770
21	Basic chemicals	.070300
22	Sinthetic fibres	.032710
23	Fertilizers	.008080
24	Soaps and detergents	.104920
25	Drugs and medicines	.028860
26	Perfumes, cosmetics	.055330
27	Other chemical industries	.035980
28	Non-metallic mineral products	.069090
29	Basic metallic industries	.037870
30	Metal products	.019860
31	Machinery	.017160
32	Electrical machinery	.013900
33	Transport equipment	.030500
34	Motor vehicles	.038940
35	Other manufacturing industries	—.036150
36	Construction	.026650
37	Electricity	.042790
38	Cinema	—.007630
39	Transport	.016400
40	Communication	.081580
41	Trade	.004170
42	Dwellings	—
43	Hotels and restaurants	.030080
44	Credit and insurance	—.006740
45	Other Services	.057930

APPENDIX D: SIMULATION RESULTS

D.1: Reference Run

Reference Run

Table D.1: Sectoral Gross output

Millions of 197? pesos

Sector	1975	1979	1980	1981	1982	1985	1990	79/78	80/79	81/80	82/81	80/75	85/80	90/85	90/79
1 Agriculture	83531.	94159.	97314.	100808.	104084.	117053.	152153.	2.8	3.4	3.6	3.3	3.1	3.8	5.4	4.5
2 Livestock	45885.	51507.	52887.	54321.	55615.	60326.	72617.	2.5	2.7	2.7	3.3	2.7	2.7	3.8	3.
3 Forestry	3549.	4862.	5410.	6062.	6689.	8909.	14725.	8.7	11.3	12.1	10.3	8.7	10.5	10.6	10.6
4 Fishing	2576.	6446.	7677.	8991.	10709.	17420.	37121.	24.8	19.1	17.1	19.1	24.4	17.8	16.3	17.3
5 Mining	10659.	10340.	10600.	10975.	11453.	12933.	15222.	1.4	2.5	3.5	4.4	-.1	4.1	3.3	3.
6 Quarrying	7421.	9888.	11006.	12326.	13845.	18220.	24557.	10.3	11.3	12.0	12.3	8.2	10.6	6.2	8.0
7 Petroleum	49366.	93304.	113557.	137684.	164029.	240088.	374412.	20.3	21.7	21.2	19.1	18.1	16.2	9.3	13.5
8 Slaughter of livestock	17733.	24287.	26840.	29752.	33034.	45308.	76544.	9.9	10.5	10.8	11.0	8.4	11.0	11.1	11.
9 Milling	39486.	50897.	54103.	57530.	61217.	74264.	106064.	6.3	6.3	6.3	6.4	6.5	7.4	7.4	6.9
10 Other processed food	65191.	77167.	79816.	82483.	85222.	94327.	115345.	3.6	3.4	3.3	3.3	4.2	3.4	4.1	3.7
11 Beverages	27887.	37898.	39565.	41865.	42451.	46342.	53796.	5.3	4.4	3.8	3.7	7.2	3.2	3.0	3.3
12 Tobacco	26482.	10387.	11809.	13435.	15269.	28439.	39641.	13.3	13.7	13.8	13.7	11.7	13.4	12.4	12.9
13 Soft fibre textiles	3328.	35676.	36835.	37950.	39051.	42503.	50029.	3.6	3.2	3.0	2.9	4.4	2.9	3.3	3.1
14 Other textiles	47983.	6732.	8649.	9311.	13610.	23927.	50843.	27.2	28.5	26.5	26.5	22.6	22.6	16.3	20.
15 Wearing apparel	7770.	56685.	58559.	60434.	62348.	86858.	83114.	3.5	3.3	3.2	3.2	4.1	3.2	3.9	3.8
16 Wood and cork	15442.	15356.	18053.	18411.	24450.	36893.	68254.	18.3	17.6	16.8	16.6	18.5	15.4	13.1	14.5
17 Paper	11755.	17094.	17707.	17915.	19210.	22215.	29890.	3.2	3.6	4.0	4.3	2.8	4.6	6.1	5.
18 Printing, publishing	5283.	15734.	16794.	16889.	19117.	23304.	33436.	6.9	6.7	6.7	6.7	4.6	6.8	7.5	5.7
19 Leather	5548.	11502.	14011.	20395.	20144.	32366.	63565.	22.8	21.8	20.5	19.3	21.5	18.2	14.5	16.8
20 Rubber products	8294.	11502.	8639.	9311.	10024.	12509.	18481.	8.3	8.0	7.8	7.7	9.3	7.7	8.1	7.7
21 Basic chemicals	8268.	9317.	9689.	10116.	10598.	12404.	17009.	3.6	4.0	4.4	4.8	3.2	5.1	4.5	5.6
22 Synthetic fibers	3206.	11679.	12381.	13072.	13767.	16009.	21041.	6.7	6.0	5.6	5.3	8.4	5.3	5.6	5.5
23 Fertilizers	6522.	13756.	17014.	20395.	24039.	44298.	91011.	29.8	23.7	19.9	17.9	39.6	21.1	15.4	18.
24 Soaps and detergents	9949.	14327.	17048.	20092.	23470.	35951.	67333.	20.2	19.0	17.9	16.9	21.2	16.1	7.9	15.1
25 Drugs and medicines	6017.	10798.	11283.	11870.	12557.	15230.	22234.	3.7	4.5	5.2	5.8	2.5	6.2	6.2	5.8
26 Perfumes, cosmetics	8761.	12987.	15594.	18548.	21864.	34202.	65485.	21.1	20.1	18.9	18.0	20.9	17.0	13.9	15.7
27 Other chemical industr.	23451.	15631.	18232.	21181.	24493.	36823.	68101.	16.4	16.6	16.2	15.6	15.8	15.1	13.9	14.3
28 Nonmetallic mineral pr.	35179.	30525.	31819.	33040.	34271.	37417.	45408.	4.9	4.5	3.8	3.6	6.3	3.5	3.7	7.7
29 Basic metallic industr.	22027.	61376.	66344.	71010.	75421.	109844.	261533.	9.7	8.2	7.0	6.2	13.5	10.6	18.8	14.
30 Metal products	22656.	28448.	30099.	31836.	33684.	40126.	55632.	5.9	5.8	5.8	5.8	5.6	5.9	6.7	6.1
31 Machinery	16828.	18810.	20145.	21465.	22798.	27129.	36911.	7.9	7.1	6.6	6.2	6.0	6.1	6.4	6.3
32 Electrical machinery	13287.	20446.	21504.	22558.	23919.	28463.	39701.	5.0	5.2	5.4	5.4	5.0	5.8	6.0	6.1
33 Transport equipment	35166.	18771.	20098.	21439.	22812.	28653.	40098.	7.6	7.1	6.7	6.4	8.6	5.8	7.0	7.1
34 Motor vehicles	8509.	57732.	62906.	67992.	73047.	98567.	154767.	10.1	9.0	8.1	7.4	12.3	9.4	9.4	9.4
35 Other manufacturing	128146.	9353.	10288.	11462.	12867.	18461.	33349.	7.8	10.0	11.4	12.3	3.9	12.4	12.4	12.
36 Construction	16123.	265141.	310556.	361006.	419201.	633102.	1270278.	18.6	17.1	16.2	16.1	19.4	15.3	15.3	15.3
37 Electricity	7370.	29468.	33709.	38327.	43642.	62661.	105738.	15.7	14.4	13.7	13.9	16.1	13.2	11.0	12.3
38 Gas	34067.	8907.	9462.	10087.	10783.	13359.	19985.	5.8	6.0	6.6	6.9	3.5	7.2	8.5	7.
39 Transport	7912.	46136.	48291.	50268.	52154.	60374.	84111.	5.5	4.7	4.1	4.1	8.5	4.6	6.4	6.1
40 Communications	323449.	20374.	24152.	24152.	32775.	51127.	101071.	21.1	18.5	16.9	16.1	25.0	16.2	6.5	11.7
41 Trade	59849.	360248.	375199.	381326.	386871.	401818.	428882.	2.3	1.9	1.6	1.5	1.0	2.4	1.3	1.
42 Dwellings	31492.	64954.	65654.	66228.	66707.	67778.	69141.	1.4	1.1	0.9	1.0	1.9	1.4	0.4	.6
43 Hotels and restaurants	26041.	36808.	37949.	39089.	40251.	44078.	52831.	3.3	3.1	3.0	3.0	3.8	3.0	3.7	3.3
44 Credit and insurance	60439.	33176.	35017.	36954.	39015.	46195.	63478.	5.6	5.5	5.5	5.6	6.1	5.7	6.5	6.
45 Other services		80868.	87197.	94048.	102748.	131362.	206952.	8.6	7.8	7.9	9.3	7.6	9.5	9.5	8.
T O T A L	1399462.	1925955.	2081500.	2250099.	2435370.	3115576.	4901769.	8.1	8.1	8.1	8.2	8.3	8.4	9.5	8.

233

Reference Run - Table D.1.2: Private Consumption

Sector	Millions of 1975 Pesos							Annual growth rates (per cent)							
	1975	1979	1980	1981	1982	1985	1990	79/78	80/79	81/80	82/81	80/75	85/80	90/85	90/79
1. Agriculture	55669.	65111.	68525.	71525.	74761.	86166.	114847.	4.2	5.8	4.9	4.5	4.2	4.7	5.9	5.2
2. Livestock	12218.	15512.	16419.	17378.	18406.	21977.	30738.	5.9	5.8	5.9	5.9	6.1	6.0	6.9	6.0
3. Forestry	0.	0.	0.	0.	0.	0.	0.	0.0	0.0	0.0	0.0	0.0	0.0	0.0	0.0
4. Fishing	5409.	7569.	8157.	8776.	9436.	11690.	17014.	8.1	7.8	7.6	7.5	8.6	7.5	7.8	7.6
5. Mining	0.	0.	0.	0.	0.	0.	0.	0.0	0.0	0.0	0.0	0.0	0.0	0.0	0.0
6. Quarrying	0.	0.	0.	0.	0.	0.	0.	0.0	0.0	0.0	0.0	0.0	0.0	0.0	0.0
7. Petroleum	24669.	33018.	35347.	37835.	40533.	50081.	74289.	7.2	7.0	7.1	7.1	7.5	7.2	8.2	7.7
8. Slaughter of livestock	118242.	148173.	156577.	165579.	175375.	110297.	300548.	5.7	5.7	5.9	5.9	5.8	7.4	6.5	6.
9. Milling	31441.	38213.	40096.	42101.	44260.	51685.	71207.	5.7	5.0	5.1	5.1	5.0	6.5	5.8	5.8
10. Other food processed	53807	65174.	68378.	71805.	75508.	88667.	122280.	4.9	5.0	5.2	5.2	4.9	5.3	6.6	5.9
11. Beverages	23156.	28888.	30486.	32187.	34020.	40479.	56731.	5.5	5.6	5.7	5.7	5.8	5.8	7.0	6.
12. Tobacco	5429.	7358.	7885.	8439.	9027.	11030.	15717.	7.-	7.0	7.0	7.0	7.2	6.9	7.3	7.1
13. Soft fiber textiles	5149.	7418.	8046.	8711.	9423.	11880.	17801.	8.8	8.3	8.2	8.1	8.5	9.3	8.4	8.3
14. Other textiles	0.	0.	0.	0.	0.	0.	0.	0.0	0.3	0.0	0.0	0.0	0.0	0.0	0.0
15. Wearing apparel	88006.	114605.	122157.	139127.	139127.	170805.	225954.	6.6	6.6	6.8	6.8	6.6	6.8	8.2	7.5
16. Wood and cork	10587.	14220.	15234.	16311.	17473.	21539.	31641.	7.3	7.1	7.1	7.1	7.1	7.2	8.0	7.5
17. Paper	4288.	6171.	6686.	7227.	7803.	9769.	14395.	8.7	8.1	8.0	8.0	8.3	7.9	8.1	8.
18. Printing, publishing	11099.	15390.	16590.	17868.	19521.	24110.	36274.	8.0	7.7	7.7	7.7	7.8	7.8	8.5	8.1
19. Leather	1852.	3161.	3513.	3878.	4263.	5538.	8337.	12.1	10.4	9.9	9.9	13.7	9.5	8.5	9.2
20. Rubber products	2961.	4566.	5002.	5458.	5941.	7570.	11290.	10.1	9.1	8.8	8.8	11.1	8.6	8.3	8.
21. Basic chemicals	962.	1966.	2232.	2505.	2788.	3704.	5578.	15.2	12.3	11.3	11.3	18.3	10.7	8.5	9.9
22. Synthetic fibers	0.	0.	0.	0.	0.	0.	0.	0.0	0.0	0.0	0.0	0.0	0.0	0.0	0.0
23. Fertilizers	818.	1773.	2025.	2283.	2549.	3405.	5125.	16.1	14.2	11.7	11.7	19.9	11.0	8.5	10.
24. Soaps and detergents	11386.	14259.	15046.	15879.	16764.	19828.	27235.	5.6	5.5	5.6	5.7	5.7	5.7	6.6	6.1
25. Drugs and medicines	7619.	9903.	10527.	11184.	11882.	14275.	19948.	6.4	6.2	6.2	6.3	6.7	6.3	6.9	6.6
26. Perfumes, cosmetics	16446.	21519.	22938.	24451.	26088.	31852.	46361.	6.7	6.6	6.6	6.9	6.9	6.8	7.7	6.6
27. Other chemical indust.	945.	1983.	2258.	2541.	2836.	3790.	5765.	15.6	13.9	11.6	19.0	19.0	10.9	8.7	10.2
28. Non-metallic mineral pr.	2193.	3403.	3726.	4061.	4410.	5560.	8043.	10.1	9.5	8.6	11.2	11.2	8.3	7.7	8.1
29. Basic metallic industr.	0.	0.	0.	0.	0.	0.	0.	0.0	0.0	0.0	0.0	0.0	0.0	0.0	0.0
30. Metal products	3496.	5187.	5651.	6138.	6655.	8416.	12534.	9.4	8.9	8.6	8.4	10.1	8.3	8.5	8.4
31. Machinery	660.	1516.	1738.	1964.	2195.	2920.	4286.	16.8	14.6	13.0	11.8	21.4	10.9	8.0	9.9
32. Electrical machinery	16396.	21954.	23512.	25176.	26982.	33353.	49473.	7.2	7.1	7.2	7.2	7.5	7.5	8.2	7.
33. Transport equipment	7443.	10561.	11422.	12336.	11319.	16735.	25091.	8.4	8.2	8.0	8.0	8.9	7.9	8.4	8.2
34. Motor vehicles	32846.	47619.	51845.	56395.	61345.	79218.	125382.	9.1	8.9	8.8	8.8	9.6	8.8	9.6	9.2
35. Other manufacturing	15875.	21969.	23689.	22529.	27532.	34615.	52596.	8.0	7.8	7.8	7.8	8.3	7.9	8.7	8.
36. Construction	0.	0.	0.	0.	0.	0.	0.	0.0	0.0	0.0	0.0	0.0	0.0	0.0	0.0
37. Electricity	15897.	20789.	22155.	23611.	25185.	30725.	44671.	6.6	6.6	6.7	6.7	6.9	6.9	7.8	7.2
38. Cinema	12106.	18202.	19915.	21750.	23748.	30813.	48777.	9.8	9.2	9.2	9.2	10.5	9.1	9.6	9
39. Transport	27745.	36309.	38737.	41339.	44173.	54257.	80196.	6.7	6.7	6.9	6.9	7.0	7.0	8.1	7.5
40. Communications	7312.	10699.	11632.	12623.	13692.	17405.	26512.	9.1	8.7	8.5	8.5	9.7	8.4	8.8	8.6
41. Trade	5824.	8818.	9644.	10520.	11465.	14739.	22727.	9.8	9.4	9.1	9.0	10.6	8.9	9.0	9.
42. Dwellings	27954.	35637.	37760.	40020.	42471.	51088.	72823.	6.0	6.0	6.0	6.1	6.2	6.2	7.3	6.7
43. Hotels & restaurants	6383.	8970.	9681.	10432.	11239.	14022.	20737.	8.2	7.9	7.8	7.7	8.7	7.7	8.1	6.7
44. Credit and insurance	3290.	5462.	6058.	6688.	7363.	9674.	15163.	11.7	10.9	10.4	10.1	13.0	9.8	9.4	7.9
45. Other services	73925.	102878.	111049.	119828.	129448.	163200.	252174.	6.6	6.6	6.7	7.0	7.0	7.0	7.0	9.
T O T A L	751502.	986523.	1052337.	1122602.	1198774.	1465783.	2147265.	6.7	6.7	6.8	7.0	7.0	6.9	7.0	7.

Reference Run

Table D.1.3: Government Consumption of Goods and Services

Sector	Millions of 1975 pesos							Annual growth rates (percent)							
	1975	1979	1980	1981	1982	1985	1990	79/78	80/79	81/80	82/81	80/75	85/80	90/85	90/79
1 Agriculture	77.	108.	118.	129.	142.	183.	278.	9.0	9.4	9.5	9.5	8.8	9.2	8.8	9.0
2 Livestock	0.	0.	0.	0.	0.	0.	0.	0.0	0.0	0.0	0.0	0.0	0.0	0.0	0.0
3 Forestry	0.	0.	0.	0.	0.	0.	0.	0.0	0.0	0.0	0.0	0.0	0.0	0.0	0.0
4 Fishing	0.	0.	0.	0.	0.	0.	0.	0.0	0.0	0.0	0.0	0.0	0.0	0.0	0.0
5 Mining	0.	0.	0.	0.	0.	0.	0.	0.0	0.0	0.0	0.0	0.0	0.0	0.0	0.0
6 Quarrying	0.	0.	0.	0.	0.	0.	0.	0.0	0.0	0.0	0.0	0.0	0.0	0.0	0.0
7 Petroleum	594.	829.	907.	993.	1088.	1406.	2139.	9.0	9.4	9.5	9.5	8.8	9.2	8.8	9.0
8 Slaughter of livestock	120.	168.	184.	201.	220.	285.	433.	9.0	9.4	9.5	9.5	8.8	9.2	8.8	9.0
9 Milling	0.	0.	0.	0.	0.	0.	0.	0.0	0.0	0.0	0.0	0.0	0.0	0.0	0.0
10 Other processed food	120.	168.	184.	201.	220.	285.	433.	9.0	9.4	9.5	9.5	8.8	9.2	8.8	9.0
11 Beverages	0.	0.	0.	0.	0.	0.	0.	0.0	0.0	0.0	0.0	0.0	0.0	0.0	0.0
12 Tobacco	0.	0.	0.	0.	0.	0.	0.	0.0	0.0	0.0	0.0	0.0	0.0	0.0	0.0
13 Soft fiber textiles	0.	0.	0.	0.	0.	0.	0.	0.0	0.0	0.0	0.0	0.0	0.0	0.0	0.0
14 Other textiles	0.	0.	0.	0.	0.	0.	0.	0.0	0.0	0.0	0.0	0.0	0.0	0.0	0.0
15 Wearing apparel	275.	1012.	1107.	1213.	1328.	1717.	2611.	9.0	9.4	9.5	9.5	8.8	9.2	8.8	9.0
16 Wood and cork	23.	33.	36.	39.	43.	56.	85.	9.0	9.4	9.5	9.5	8.8	9.2	8.8	9.0
17 Paper	34.	47.	52.	57.	62.	80.	122.	9.0	9.4	9.5	9.5	8.8	9.2	8.8	9.0
18 Printing, publishing	1008.	1408.	1540.	1687.	1848.	2389.	3633.	9.0	9.4	9.5	9.5	8.8	9.2	8.8	9.0
19 Leather	17.	23.	25.	28.	30.	39.	60.	9.0	9.4	9.5	9.5	8.9	9.2	8.7	9.0
20 Rubber products	1.	1.	1.	2.	2.	2.	4.	9.0	9.4	9.5	9.5	8.8	9.2	8.8	9.0
21 Basic chemicals	98.	137.	149.	164.	179.	232.	352.	9.0	9.4	9.5	9.5	8.8	9.2	8.8	9.0
22 Synthetic fibers	0.	0.	0.	0.	0.	0.	0.	0.0	0.0	0.0	0.0	0.0	0.0	0.0	0.0
23 Fertilizers	0.	0.	0.	0.	0.	0.	0.	0.0	0.0	0.0	0.0	0.0	0.0	0.0	0.0
24 Soaps and detergents	345.	482.	527.	578.	633.	818.	1244.	9.0	9.4	9.5	9.5	8.8	9.2	8.8	9.0
25 Drugs and medicines	2314.	3232.	3534.	3872.	4240.	5482.	8338.	9.0	9.4	9.5	9.5	8.8	9.2	8.7	9.0
26 Perfumes, cosmetics	0.	0.	0.	0.	0.	0.	0.	0.0	0.0	0.0	0.0	0.0	0.0	0.0	0.0
27 Other chemical indust.	0.	0.	0.	0.	0.	0.	0.	0.0	0.0	0.0	0.0	0.0	0.0	0.0	0.0
28 Nonmetallic mineral pr.	151.	210.	230.	252.	276.	357.	543.	9.0	9.4	9.5	9.5	8.8	9.2	8.8	9.0
29 Basic metallic indust.	115.	161.	176.	193.	211.	273.	416.	9.0	9.4	9.5	9.5	8.8	9.2	8.8	9.0
30 Metal products	1125.	1571.	1718.	1882.	2061.	2664.	4053.	9.0	9.4	9.5	9.5	8.8	9.2	8.8	9.0
31 Machinery	596.	833.	911.	998.	1093.	1413.	2150.	9.0	9.4	9.5	9.5	8.8	9.2	8.8	9.0
32 Electrical machinery	728.	1016.	1111.	1217.	1333.	1724.	2622.	9.0	9.4	9.5	9.5	8.8	9.2	8.8	9.0
33 Transport equipment	102.	142.	155.	170.	186.	241.	367.	9.0	9.4	9.5	9.5	8.8	9.2	8.8	9.0
34 Motor vehicles	36.	51.	55.	61.	66.	86.	130.	9.0	9.4	9.5	9.5	8.8	9.2	8.8	9.0
35 Other manufacturing	784.	1095.	1198.	1312.	1437.	1858.	2826.	9.0	9.4	9.5	9.5	8.8	9.2	8.8	9.0
36 Construction	597.	835.	913.	1000.	1095.	1416.	2153.	9.0	9.4	9.5	9.5	8.8	9.2	8.8	9.0
37 Electricity	434.	606.	663.	727.	796.	1029.	1565.	9.0	9.4	9.5	9.5	8.8	9.2	8.8	9.0
38 Cinema	27.	38.	42.	46.	50.	65.	99.	9.0	9.4	9.5	9.5	8.8	9.2	8.8	9.0
39 Transport	588.	821.	898.	983.	1077.	1392.	2118.	9.0	9.4	9.5	9.5	8.8	9.2	8.8	9.0
40 Communications	442.	617.	675.	740.	810.	1047.	1593.	9.0	9.4	9.5	9.5	8.8	9.2	8.8	9.0
41 Trade	1813.	2532.	2769.	3034.	3333.	4295.	6534.	9.0	9.4	9.5	9.5	8.8	9.2	8.8	9.0
42 Dwellings	1322.	1847.	2020.	2212.	2423.	3132.	4765.	9.0	9.4	9.5	9.5	8.8	9.2	8.8	9.0
43 Hotels and restaurants	501.	699.	765.	838.	918.	1186.	1804.	9.0	9.4	9.5	9.5	8.8	9.2	8.8	9.0
44 Credit and insurance	782.	1093.	1195.	1309.	1434.	1853.	2819.	9.0	9.4	9.5	9.5	8.8	9.2	8.8	9.0
45 Other services	1126.	1574.	1721.	1885.	2065.	2669.	4060.	9.0	9.4	9.5	9.5	8.8	9.2	8.8	9.0
T O T A L	16745.	23391.	25580.	28022.	30690.	39675.	60351.	9.0	9.4	9.5	9.5	8.8	9.2	8.8	9.0

Reference Run

Table D.1.4: Public Investment by Destination

Millions of 1975 pesos

Sector	1975	%	1979	%	1980	%	1981	%	1982	%	1985	%	1990	%
1 Agriculture	4572.	7.3	5796.	7.3	6329.	7.3	4362.	4.6	5908.	5.7	9729.	7.3	14664.	7.3
2 Livestock	626.	1.0	794.	1.0	867.	1.0	569.	.6	726.	.7	1333.	1.0	2039.	1.0
3 Forestry	376.	.6	635.	.8	964.	.8	474.	.5	518.	.5	800.	.6	1205.	.6
4 Fishing	564.	.9	397.	.5	434.	.5	759.	.8	726.	.7	1199.	.9	1808.	.9
5 Mining	188.	.3	794.	1.0	867.	1.0	948.	1.0	1037.	1.0	400.	.3	603.	.3
6 Quarrying	188.	.3	794.	1.0	867.	1.0	948.	1.0	1037.	1.0	400.	.3	603.	.3
7 Petroleum	8079.	12.9	26282.	33.1	28699.	33.1	27307.	28.8	23944.	23.1	17192.	12.9	25914.	12.9
8 Slaughter of livestock	188.	.3	238.	.3	260.	.3	284.	.3	311.	.3	400.	.3	603.	.3
9 Milling	188.	.3	238.	.3	260.	.3	284.	.3	311.	.3	400.	.3	603.	.3
10 Other processed food	188.	.3	238.	.3	260.	.3	284.	.3	311.	.3	400.	.3	603.	.3
11 Beverages	188.	.3	238.	.3	260.	.3	284.	.3	311.	.3	400.	.3	603.	.3
12 Tobacco	188.	.3	238.	.3	260.	.3	284.	.3	311.	.3	400.	.3	603.	.3
13 Soft fiber textiles	188.	.3	238.	.3	260.	.3	284.	.3	311.	.3	400.	.3	603.	.3
14 Other textiles	188.	.3	238.	.3	260.	.3	284.	.3	311.	.3	400.	.3	603.	.3
15 Wearing apparel	188.	.3	238.	.3	260.	.3	284.	.3	311.	.3	400.	.3	603.	.3
16 Wood and cork	188.	.3	238.	.3	260.	.3	284.	.3	311.	.3	400.	.3	603.	.3
17 Paper	188.	.3	238.	.3	260.	.3	284.	.7	311.	.3	400.	.3	603.	.3
18 Printing, publishing	188.	.3	238.	.3	260.	.3	284.	.3	311.	.3	400.	.3	603.	.3
19 Leather	188.	.3	238.	.3	260.	.3	284.	.3	311.	.3	400.	.3	603.	.3
20 Rubber products	188.	.3	238.	.3	260.	.3	284.	.3	311.	.3	400.	.3	603.	.3
21 Basic chemicals	188.	.3	238.	.3	260.	.3	284.	.3	311.	.3	400.	.3	603.	.3
22 Synthetic fibers	188.	.3	238.	.3	260.	.3	284.	.3	311.	.3	400.	.3	603.	.3
23 Fertilizers	2630.	4.2	1985.	2.5	2168.	2.5	2655.	2.8	8396.	8.1	5597.	4.2	8437.	4.2
24 Soaps and detergents	188.	.3	238.	.3	260.	.3	284.	.3	311.	.3	400.	.3	603.	.3
25 Drugs and medicines	188.	.3	238.	.3	260.	.3	284.	.3	311.	.3	400.	.3	603.	.3
26 Perfumes, cosmetics	188.	.3	238.	.3	260.	.3	284.	.3	311.	.3	400.	.3	603.	.3
27 Other chemical indust.	188.	.3	238.	.3	260.	.3	284.	.3	311.	.3	400.	.3	603.	.3
28 Nonmetallic mineral pr.	188.	.3	238.	.3	260.	.3	284.	.3	311.	.3	400.	.3	603.	.3
29 Basic metallic indust.	5010.	8.0	873.	1.1	954.	1.1	1043.	1.1	2695.	2.6	10661.	8.0	16071.	8.0
30 Metal products	188.	.3	238.	.3	260.	.3	284.	.3	311.	.3	400.	.3	603.	.3
31 Machinery	188.	.3	238.	.3	260.	.3	284.	.3	311.	.3	400.	.3	603.	.3
32 Electrical machinery	188.	.3	238.	.3	260.	.3	284.	.3	311.	.3	400.	.3	603.	.3
33 Transport equipment	125.	.2	159.	.2	173.	.2	190.	.2	415.	.4	267.	.2	402.	.2
34 Motor vehicles	689.	1.1	556.	.7	607.	.7	664.	.7	2177.	2.1	1466.	1.1	2210.	1.1
35 Other manufacturing	188.	.3	238.	.3	260.	.3	284.	.3	311.	.3	400.	.3	603.	.3
36 Construction	8330.	13.3	8020.	10.1	8757.	10.1	10525.	11.1	7774.	7.5	17725.	13.3	26717.	13.3
37 Electricity	6451.	10.3	8734.	11.0	9537.	11.0	11947.	12.6	13682.	13.2	13727.	10.3	20691.	10.3
38 Cinema	188.	.3	238.	.3	260.	.3	284.	.3	311.	.3	400.	.3	603.	.3
39 Transport	4885.	7.8	2382.	3.0	2601.	3.0	3034.	3.2	6323.	6.1	10395.	7.8	15669.	7.8
40 Communications	8455.	13.5	7940.	10.0	8670.	10.0	10240.	10.8	12438.	12.0	17991.	13.5	27119.	13.5
41 Trade	188.	.3	238.	.3	260.	.3	284.	.3	311.	.3	400.	.3	603.	.3
42 Dwellings	188.	.3	238.	.3	260.	.3	284.	.3	311.	.3	400.	.3	603.	.3
43 Hotels and restaurants	188.	.3	238.	.3	260.	.3	284.	.3	311.	.3	400.	.3	603.	.3
44 Credit and insurance	188.	.3	238.	.3	260.	.3	284.	.3	311.	.3	400.	.3	603.	.3
45 Other services	6012.	9.6	6352.	8.0	6936.	8.0	10904.	11.5	6841.	6.6	12794.	9.6	19285.	9.6
T O T A L	62629.	100.0	79403.	100.0	86703.	100.0	94817.	100.0	103653.	100.0	133268.	100.0	200882.	100.0

Reference Run

Table D.1.4: Public Investment by Destination (Cont.)

Annual growth rates (percent)

Sector	79/78	80/79	81/80	82/81	80/75	85/80	90/85	90/79
1 Agriculture	72.8	9.2	-31.1	35.5	6.7	9.0	8.6	8.8
2 Livestock	81.5	9.2	-34.4	27.5	6.7	9.0	8.6	8.8
3 Forestry	74.2	9.2	-31.7	9.3	13.0	2.9	8.6	6.0
4 Fishing	-32.0	9.2	75.0	-4.3	-5.1	22.6	8.6	14.8
5 Mining	8.9	9.2	9.4	9.3	35.8	-14.3	8.6	-2.5
6 Quarrying	25.1	9.2	-4.8	-12.3	28.9	-9.7	8.6	-.1
7 Petroleum	8.9	9.2	9.4	9.3	6.7	9.0	8.6	8.8
8 Slaughter of livestock	8.9	9.2	9.4	9.3	6.7	9.0	8.6	8.8
9 Milling	8.9	9.2	9.4	9.3	6.7	9.0	8.6	8.8
10 Other processed food	8.9	9.2	9.4	9.3	6.7	9.0	8.6	8.8
11 Beverages	8.9	9.2	9.4	9.3	6.7	9.0	8.6	8.8
12 Tobacco	8.9	9.2	9.4	9.3	6.7	9.0	8.6	8.8
13 Soft fiber textiles	8.9	9.2	9.4	9.3	6.7	9.0	8.6	8.8
14 Other textiles	8.9	9.2	9.4	9.3	6.7	9.0	8.6	8.8
15 Wearing apparel	8.9	9.2	9.4	9.3	6.7	9.0	8.6	8.8
16 Wood and cork	8.9	9.2	9.4	9.3	6.7	9.0	8.6	8.8
17 Paper	8.9	9.2	9.4	9.3	6.7	9.0	8.6	8.8
18 Printing, publishing	8.9	9.2	9.4	9.3	6.7	9.0	8.6	8.8
19 Leather	8.9	9.2	9.4	9.3	6.7	9.0	8.6	8.8
20 Rubber products	8.9	9.2	9.4	9.3	6.7	9.0	8.6	8.8
21 Basic chemicals	8.9	9.2	9.4	9.3	6.7	9.0	8.6	8.8
22 Synthetic fibers	8.9	9.2	9.4	9.3	6.7	9.0	8.6	8.8
23 Fertilizers	-2.8	9.2	22.5	216.2	-3.8	20.9	8.6	14.1
24 Soaps and detergents	8.9	9.2	9.4	9.3	6.7	9.0	8.6	8.8
25 Drugs and medicines	8.9	9.2	9.4	9.3	6.7	9.0	8.6	8.8
26 Perfumes, cosmetics	8.9	9.2	9.4	9.3	6.7	9.0	8.6	8.8
27 Other chemical indust.	8.9	9.2	9.4	9.3	6.7	9.0	8.6	8.8
28 Nonmetallic mineral pr.	8.9	9.2	9.4	9.3	6.7	9.0	8.6	8.8
29 Basic metallic indust.	8.9	9.2	9.4	158.4	-28.2	62.1	8.6	30.3
30 Metal products	8.9	9.2	9.4	9.3	6.7	9.0	8.6	8.8
31 Machinery	8.9	9.2	9.4	9.3	6.7	9.0	8.6	8.8
32 Electrical machinery	8.9	9.2	9.4	9.3	6.7	9.0	8.6	8.8
33 Transport equipment	8.9	9.2	9.4	118.6	6.7	9.0	8.6	13.4
34 Motor vehicles	8.9	9.2	9.4	228.0	-2.5	19.3	8.6	8.8
35 Other manufacturing	8.9	9.2	9.4	9.3	6.7	9.0	8.6	8.8
36 Construction	-.9	9.2	20.2	-26.1	1.0	15.1	8.6	11.6
37 Electricity	-4.9	9.2	25.3	14.5	8.1	7.6	8.6	8.2
38 Cinema	8.9	9.2	9.3	9.3	6.7	9.0	8.6	8.8
39 Transport	2.1	9.2	16.6	108.4	-11.8	31.9	8.6	18.7
40 Communications	.8	9.2	18.1	21.5	.5	15.7	8.6	11.8
41 Trade	8.9	9.2	9.4	9.3	6.7	9.0	8.6	8.8
42 Dwellings	8.9	9.2	9.4	9.3	6.7	9.0	8.6	8.8
43 Hotels and restaurants	8.9	9.2	9.4	9.3	6.7	9.0	8.6	8.8
44 Credit and insurance	8.9	9.2	9.4	9.3	6.7	9.0	8.6	8.8
45 Other services	-24.3	9.2	57.2	-37.3	2.9	13.0	8.6	10.6
T O T A L	8.9	9.2	9.4	9.3	6.7	9.0	8.6	8.8

Reference Run

Table D.1.5: Private Investment by Destination

Millions of 1975 pesos

Sector	1978	%	1979	%	1980	%	1981	%	1982	%	1985	%	1990	%
1 Agriculture	6946.	7.0	7579.	6.2	8478.	6.4	9527.	6.5	9677.	6.2	13734.	6.6	26323.	7.1
2 Livestock	2298.	2.3	1530.	1.3	1547.	1.2	1608.	1.1	1554.	1.0	1969.	.9	3640.	1.0
3 Forestry	229.	.2	524.	.4	688.	.5	855.	.6	909.	.6	1159.	.6	2175.	.6
4 Fishing	64.	.1	715.	.6	754.	.6	794.	.5	956.	.6	1538.	.7	3185.	.9
5 Mining	-1122.	-1.1	141.	.1	474.	.4	768.	.5	1039.	.7	1169.	.6	1313.	.4
6 Quarrying	462.	.5	745.	.6	950.	.7	1142.	.8	1335.	.9	1319.	.6	1370.	.4
7 Petroleum	11249.	11.4	22623.	18.6	29561.	22.4	36308.	25.3	41396.	26.4	41979.	20.1	53325.	14.5
8 Slaughter of livestock	33.	.0	272.	.2	322.	.2	372.	.3	424.	.3	603.	.3	1097.	.3
9 Milling	367.	.4	403.	.3	425.	.3	453.	.3	488.	.3	635.	.3	1109.	.3
10 Other processed food	928.	.9	583.	.5	567.	.4	565.	.4	576.	.4	680.	.4	1126.	.3
11 Beverages	3004.	3.0	1371.	1.1	1188.	.9	1053.	.7	962.	.6	875.	.4	1202.	.3
12 Tobacco	18.	.0	269.	.2	320.	.2	370.	.3	422.	.3	602.	.3	1096.	.3
13 Soft fiber textiles	1517.	1.5	792.	.7	732.	.6	695.	.5	679.	.4	732.	.4	1146.	.3
14 Other textiles	-152.	-.2	202.	.2	267.	.2	329.	.2	390.	.2	586.	.3	1090.	.3
15 Wearing apparel	1011.	1.0	609.	.5	588.	.4	581.	.4	589.	.4	687.	.3	1129.	.3
16 Wood and cork	109.	.1	301.	.2	345.	.3	390.	.3	438.	.3	610.	.3	1099.	.3
17 Paper	122.	.1	259.	.2	311.	.2	364.	.3	417.	.3	600.	.3	1095.	.3
18 Printing, publishing	455.	.5	430.	.4	446.	.3	469.	.3	501.	.3	642.	.3	1112.	.3
19 Leather	10.	.0	264.	.2	315.	.2	367.	.3	420.	.3	601.	.3	1096.	.3
20 Rubber products	493.	.5	447.	.4	460.	.3	480.	.3	509.	.3	646.	.3	1113.	.3
21 Basic chemicals	133.	.1	267.	.2	317.	.2	369.	.3	421.	.3	602.	.3	1096.	.3
22 Synthetic fibers	1182.	1.1	684.	.6	646.	.5	627.	.4	626.	.4	705.	.3	1136.	.3
23 Fertilizers	-6.	-.0	4032.	3.5	4359.	3.3	4378.	3.1	4665.	3.0	9252.	4.4	15646.	4.2
24 Soaps and detergents	119.	.1	306.	.3	349.	.3	393.	.3	440.	.3	611.	.3	1100.	.3
25 Drugs and medicines	-121.	-.1	190.	.2	257.	.2	321.	.2	384.	.2	583.	.3	1089.	.3
26 Perfumes, cosmetics	61.	.1	283.	.2	331.	.3	379.	.3	429.	.3	606.	.3	1098.	.3
27 Other chemical indust.	52.	.1	282.	.2	330.	.3	378.	.3	429.	.3	605.	.3	1097.	.3
28 Nonmetallic mineral pr.	1883.	1.9	923.	.8	835.	.6	775.	.5	743.	.5	764.	.4	1159.	.3
29 Basic metallic indust.	1345.	1.4	3849.	3.2	3408.	2.6	3117.	2.2	2941.	1.9	9286.	4.4	26627.	7.2
30 Metal products	534.	.5	443.	.4	456.	.3	478.	.3	507.	.3	645.	.3	1113.	.3
31 Machinery	1044.	1.1	660.	.5	628.	.5	613.	.4	614.	.4	699.	.3	1134.	.3
32 Electrical machinery	341.	.4	357.	.3	389.	.3	425.	.3	465.	.3	624.	.3	1105.	.3
33 Transport equipment	427.	.4	388.	.3	380.	.3	376.	.3	384.	.2	562.	.3	792.	.2
34 Motor vehicles	1658.	1.7	1670.	1.4	1581.	1.2	1511.	1.1	1500.	1.0	2585.	1.2	4161.	1.1
35 Other manufacturing	-309.	-.3	147.	.1	224.	.2	295.	.2	363.	.2	572.	.3	1085.	.3
36 Construction	3768.	3.8	10708.	8.8	12047.	9.1	13510.	9.4	15417.	9.8	22615.	10.8	47042.	12.8
37 Electricity	8044.	8.1	13458.	11.0	14633.	11.1	15865.	11.1	17901.	11.4	23855.	11.4	38859.	10.5
38 Cinema	83.	.1	297.	.2	342.	.3	388.	.3	436.	.3	609.	.3	1099.	.3
39 Transport	19293.	19.5	11691.	9.6	10302.	7.8	9282.	6.5	8714.	5.6	13541.	6.5	27684.	7.5
40 Communications	5956.	6.0	12812.	10.5	13713.	10.4	14742.	10.3	16282.	10.4	25180.	12.1	48593.	13.2
41 Trade	4167.	4.2	1678.	1.4	1429.	1.1	1244.	.9	1113.	.7	952.	.5	1231.	.3
42 Dwellings	14014.	14.2	5110.	4.2	4132.	3.1	3373.	2.4	2795.	1.8	1802.	.9	1560.	.4
43 Hotels and restaurants	1016.	1.0	615.	.5	592.	.4	584.	.4	592.	.4	688.	.3	1129.	.3
44 Credit and insurance	514.	.5	443.	.4	457.	.3	478.	.3	508.	.3	645.	.3	1113.	.3
45 Other services	5758.	5.8	10243.	8.4	11025.	8.4	11907.	8.3	14176.	9.1	18764.	9.0	34902.	9.5
T O T A L	98997.	100.0	121865.	100.0	131902.	100.0	143296.	100.0	156527.	100.0	108717.	100.0	368488.	100.0

Reference Run

Table D.1.5: Private Investment by Destination (Cont.)

Annual growth rates (percent)

Sector	79/78	80/79	81/80	82/81	80/75	85/80	90/85	90/79
1 Agriculture	-.8	11.9	12.4	1.6	4.1	10.1	13.9	12.0
2 Livestock	-9.1	1.1	4.0	-3.4	-7.6	4.9	13.1	8.2
3 Forestry	14.6	31.3	24.2	6.4	24.6	11.0	13.4	13.8
4 Fishing	24.2	5.4	5.4	20.4	64.0	15.3	15.7	14.5
5 Mining	*****	237.1	61.9	35.4	*****	19.8	2.3	22.5
6 Quarrying	38.3	27.6	20.2	16.9	15.5	6.8	.8	5.7
7 Petroleum	33.4	30.7	22.8	14.0	21.3	7.3	4.9	8.1
8 Slaughter of livestock	23.9	18.3	15.4	13.9	57.5	13.3	12.7	13.5
9 Milling	4.8	5.6	6.5	7.7	3.0	8.4	11.8	9.6
10 Other processsed food	-5.4	-2.8	-.4	2.0	-9.4	3.7	10.6	6.2
11 Beverages	-15.0	-13.3	-11.4	-8.6	-16.9	-5.9	6.5	-1.2
12 Tobacco	24.9	18.7	15.7	14.1	77.4	13.5	12.7	13.6
13 Soft fiber textiles	-10.2	-7.6	-5.1	-2.3	-13.6	-.0	9.4	3.4
14 Other textiles	54.3	32.0	23.0	18.5	*****	17.0	13.2	16.5
15 Wearing apparel	-6.3	-3.5	-1.1	1.4	-10.3	3.2	10.5	5.8
16 Wood and cork	17.6	14.6	13.0	12.3	25.9	12.1	12.5	12.5
17 Paper	24.0	20.2	17.0	14.6	20.5	14.0	12.8	14.0
18 Printing, publishing	2.5	3.8	5.3	6.7	-.4	7.6	11.6	9.0
19 Leather	26.3	19.7	16.2	6.4	99.5	13.8	12.8	13.8
20 Rubber products	1.4	2.9	4.4	6.1	-1.4	7.0	11.5	8.6
21 Basic chemicals	22.3	19.1	16.2	-.3	19.0	13.6	12.7	13.7
22 Synthetic fibers	-8.0	-5.5	-3.0	-.3	-11.4	1.8	10.0	4.7
23 Fertilizers	6.2	1.3	.4	6.6	*****	16.2	11.1	12.5
24 Soaps and detergents	16.7	14.0	12.6	12.1	24.0	11.9	12.5	12.3
25 Drugs and medicines	60.8	35.6	24.8	19.4	*****	17.8	13.3	17.2
26 Perfumes, cosmetics	21.4	16.8	14.5	13.3	40.3	12.9	12.6	:3.1
27 Other chemical indust.	21.8	17.0	14.6	13.4	44.9	12.7	12.6	13.2
28 Nonmetallic mineral pr.	-12.0	-9.5	-7.1	-4.2	-15.0	-1.7	8.7	2.1
29 Basic metallic indust.	-11.3	-11.4	-8.6	-5.6	20.4	22.2	23.5	19.2
30 Metal products	-1.1	3.1	4.7	6.2	-3.1	7.2	11.5	8.7
31 Machinery	-7.0	-4.9	-2.5	.3	-9.7	2.2	10.1	5.0
32 Electrical machinery	7.9	8.9	9.2	9.6	2.6	9.9	12.1	10.8
33 Transport equipment	-3.0	-2.3	-.9	2.1	-2.3	8.2	7.1	6.7
34 Motor vehicles	-5.7	-5.3	-4.5	-.7	-.9	10.3	10.0	8.7
35 Other manufacturing	143.0	52.2	31.5	23.1	*****	20.6	13.6	19.9
36 Construction	18.0	12.5	12.1	14.1	26.2	13.4	15.8	14.4
37 Electricity	14.4	8.7	8.4	12.8	12.7	10.3	10.3	10.1
38 Cinema	18.6	15.0	13.3	12.5	32.8	12.2	12.5	12.6
39 Transport	-12.7	-11.9	-9.9	-6.1	-11.8	5.6	15.4	8.2
40 Communications	-10.0	-7.0	7.5	-10.6	-18.2	12.9	14.1	12.9
41 Trade	-16.9	-14.9	-12.9	10.6	-19.3	-7.8	5.3	-2.8
42 Dwellings	-20.2	-19.1	-18.4	-17.1	-21.7	-15.3	-2.8	-10.2
43 Hotels and restaurants	-6.4	-3.7	-1.3	1.2	-10.2	3.1	10.4	5.7
44 Credit and insurance	3.1	3.1	4.6	6.2	-2.3	7.2	11.5	8.7
45 Other services	22.1	7.6	8.0	19.1	13.9	11.2	13.2	11.8
T O T A L	8.0	8.2	8.6	9.2	5.9	9.6	12.0	10.6

Reference Run

Table D.1.6: Investments by Origin

Sector	Millions of 1975 pesos							Annual growth rates (percent)							
	1975	1979	1980	1981	1982	1985	1990	79/78	80/79	81/80	82/81	80/75	85/80	90/85	90/79
1 Agriculture	4192.	4869.	5390.	5055.	5673.	8540.	14920.	21.6	10.7	-6.2	12.2	5.2	9.6	11.8	10.7
2 Livestock	1065.	846.	879.	792.	830.	1202.	2056.	9.6	3.9	-9.8	4.7	-3.8	6.5	11.3	8.4
3 Forestry	220.	422.	503.	484.	520.	713.	1230.	41.0	19.2	-3.8	7.4	18.0	7.2	11.5	10.2
4 Fishing	228.	405.	432.	565.	612.	996.	1817.	-4.1	6.8	30.8	8.3	13.6	18.2	12.8	14.6
5 Mining	-51.	55.	79.	101.	122.	93.	113.	85.5	43.5	27.9	21.0	*****	3.2	4.1	6.7
6 Quarrying	51.	120.	142.	163.	185.	134.	154.	21.4	18.1	15.0	13.5	22.8	-1.1	2.8	2.3
7 Petroleum	39.	98.	117.	127.	131.	118.	158.	28.8	19.1	9.2	2.7	24.7	.3	6.0	4.5
8 Slaughter of livestock	54.	126.	143.	162.	181.	247.	418.	16.4	13.5	12.7	11.9	21.4	11.5	11.1	11.5
9 Milling	275.	317.	339.	365.	395.	512.	847.	-1.7	6.9	7.6	8.3	4.3	8.6	10.6	9.3
10 Other processed food	162.	119.	120.	123.	129.	157.	251.	-12.2	0.8	2.5	4.9	-5.8	5.5	9.8	7.0
11 Beverages	179.	90.	81.	75.	71.	71.	101.	16.8	-10.0	-7.4	-5.3	-14.6	-2.6	7.3	1.1
12 Tobacco	21.	51.	58.	65.	73.	100.	170.	-6.4	13.7	12.1	12.3	22.6	11.5	11.2	11.6
13 Soft fiber textiles	104.	63.	61.	60.	60.	69.	107.	-25.5	-3.2	-1.6	0.0	-10.1	2.5	9.2	4.9
14 Other textiles	2.	27.	32.	37.	43.	60.	103.	13.6	18.5	15.6	16.2	71.0	13.4	11.4	13.0
15 Wearing apparel	73.	52.	52.	53.	55.	66.	106.	16.3	0.0	1.9	3.8	-6.6	4.9	9.9	6.7
16 Wood and cork	83.	150.	169.	188.	209.	282.	475.	4.7	12.7	11.2	11.2	15.3	10.8	11.0	11.0
17 Paper	43.	70.	80.	91.	102.	140.	238.	17.4	14.3	13.8	12.1	13.2	11.8	11.2	11.8
18 Printing, publishing	59.	61.	65.	69.	75.	96.	158.	3.9	6.6	6.2	8.7	2.0	8.1	10.5	9.0
19 Leather	12.	31.	35.	40.	45.	61.	104.	15.6	12.9	14.3	12.5	23.8	11.8	11.3	11.6
20 Rubber products	78.	78.	82.	87.	94.	119.	196.	-4.2	5.1	6.1	8.0	1.1	7.7	10.5	8.7
21 Basic chemicals	24.	37.	43.	48.	54.	74.	126.	13.1	16.2	11.6	12.5	12.5	11.5	11.2	11.7
22 Synthetic fibers	95.	64.	63.	63.	65.	76.	120.	27.1	-1.6	0.0	3.2	-7.9	3.8	9.6	5.9
23 Fertilizers	299.	717.	744.	802.	1489.	1693.	2745.	20.9	3.8	7.8	85.7	20.0	17.9	10.1	13.0
24 Soaps and detergents	100.	178.	199.	221.	246.	331.	557.	13.4	11.8	11.1	11.3	14.7	10.7	11.0	10.9
25 Drugs and medicines	8.	54.	66.	77.	88.	125.	215.	15.3	22.2	16.7	14.3	50.7	13.6	11.5	13.3
26 Perfumes, cosmetics	81.	170.	193.	217.	242.	329.	556.	15.5	13.5	12.4	11.5	18.9	11.3	11.1	11.4
27 Otherchemical indust.	117.	253.	287.	323.	360.	490.	828.	-8.1	13.4	12.5	11.5	19.8	11.3	11.1	11.4
28 Nonmetallic mineral pr.	174.	98.	92.	89.	89.	98.	148.	-3.7	-6.1	-3.3	0.0	-12.0	1.3	8.6	3.9
29 Basic metallic indust.	1729.	1285.	1187.	1131.	1533.	5426.	11614.	5.2	-7.6	-4.7	35.5	-7.3	35.5	16.4	22.2
30 Metal products	370.	349.	367.	391.	420.	536.	880.	9.1	5.2	6.5	7.4	-1.1	7.9	10.4	8.8
31 Machinery	30574.	40613.	44372.	48680.	53341.	71488.	120124.	9.0	9.3	9.7	9.6	7.7	10.0	10.9	10.4
32 Electrical machinery	34890.	46205.	50392.	55109.	61059.	82200.	138537.	9.0	9.1	9.4	10.8	7.6	10.3	11.0	10.4
33 Transport equipment	8828.	10838.	11846.	12986.	13290.	18541.	31444.	-2.4	9.3	9.6	2.3	6.1	9.4	11.1	10.2
34 Motor vehicles	838.	795.	781.	776.	1312.	1446.	2274.	38.0	-1.8	-0.6	69.1	-1.4	13.1	9.5	10.0
35 Other manufacturing	-4.	12.	15.	17.	20.	29.	51.	8.1	25.0	13.3	17.6	*****	14.1	12.0	14.1
36 Construction	69705.	84977.	92289.	100694.	109044.	134689.	217764.	5.9	8.6	9.1	8.3	5.8	7.9	10.1	8.9
37 Electricity	1073.	1642.	1789.	2058.	2337.	2781.	4407.	14.1	9.0	15.0	13.6	10.8	9.2	9.6	9.4
38 Cinema	48.	95.	107.	119.	132.	179.	301.	-10.5	12.6	11.2	10.9	17.4	10.8	11.0	11.1
39 Transport	725.	422.	387.	369.	451.	718.	1301.	6.3	-8.3	-4.7	22.2	-11.8	13.2	12.6	10.8
40 Communications	331.	477.	515.	575.	661.	993.	1741.	-14.4	8.0	11.7	15.0	9.2	14.0	11.9	12.5
41 Trade	1908.	839.	740.	670.	624.	592.	803.	-19.2	-11.8	-9.5	-6.9	-17.3	-4.4	6.3	-0.4
42 Dwellings	625.	235.	193.	161.	137.	97.	95.	-2.6	-17.9	-16.6	-14.9	-20.9	-12.9	-0.4	-7.9
43 Hotels and restaurants	227.	161.	161.	164.	171.	206.	327.	3.9	0.0	1.9	4.3	-6.6	5.1	9.7	6.7
44 Credit and insurance	185.	179.	189.	200.	215.	275.	451.	-1.1	5.6	5.8	7.5	0.4	7.8	10.4	8.8
45 Other services	1789.	2522.	2730.	3467.	3195.	4797.	8236.	8.3	8.2	27.0	-7.8	8.8	11.9	11.4	11.4
T O T A L	161623.	201266.	218603.	238111.	260178.	341983.	569367.	8.3	8.6	8.9	9.3	6.2	9.4	10.7	9.9

Reference Run

Table D.1.7: Imports, Exports, Balance of Trade, External Debt

Millions of 1975 pesos

		1975	1979	1980	1981	1982	1985	1990
1 Agriculture	Imports	30471	45765	49088	51570	55590	68906	97209
	Exports	7722	13343	14000	14710	15445	17880	22820
	Balance	-22749	-32422	-35079	-36860	-40145	-51026	-74389
2 Livestock	Imports	247	362	368	378	393	483	5000
	Exports	23156	22622	21764	20820	20984	13903	5000
	Balance	22850	22277	21396	20451	18984	13421	-0
3 Forestry	Imports	271	416	462	512	568	771	1274
	Exports	2014	2090	2201	2663	2596	2932	3963
	Balance	1742	1681	1730	1950	2028	2161	2680
4 Fishing	Imports	1717	1887	1982	2081	2185	2529	18
	Exports	6448	6444	4990	4604	7041	2735	15229
	Balance	-4771	-3557	-3013	-2524	-2081	4139	15211
5 Mining	Imports	1531	2031	2212	2413	2636	1559	17306
	Exports	4764	2417	1986	1740	1550	42	54
	Balance	3233	386	-225	-673	-1077	-4007	-17252
6 Quarrying	Imports	1645	2700	2460	3060	3118	5111	16673
	Exports	1879	1099	1154	1211	1272	1472	1879
	Balance	375	-1610	-1786	-1848	-1846	-3638	-14794
7 Petroleum	Imports	16747	11581	1187	11255	6247	7799	11402
	Exports	0	0	5373	5762	221R7	46477	65284
	Balance	-18747	-11581	-4186	5662	15940	38678	53882
8 Slaughter of livestock	Imports	101557	125600	131681	130028	144827	168519	230159
	Exports	14	10	20	71	22	25	0
	Balance	-101557	-125600	-131681	-130028	-144827	-168519	-230159
9 Milling	Imports	63	2497	3194	3046	4753	7615	13738
	Exports	49	2474	3174	3025	4731	7590	13762
	Balance	-14	-23	-20	-21	-22	-25	-24
10 Other processed food	Imports	12247	16675	17537	19658	220032	30980	55368
	Exports	2303	1434	1506	1581	1660	1922	2453
	Balance	-9044	-14241	-16031	-18077	-20371	-29058	-52915
11 Beverages	Imports	58	92	98	99	103	112	5787
	Exports	3342	7350	7362	7105	6605	3877	390
	Balance	3314	7250	7266	7006	6502	3764	-5397
12 Tobacco	Imports	25	38	43	49	56	81	145
	Exports	1142	2674	3521	4537	5723	10362	22595
	Balance	1117	2636	3478	4488	5667	10281	22451
13 Soft fiber textiles	Imports	857	1055	1109	1167	1228	1446	2366
	Exports	10006	9338	10104	9625	9018	6510	0
	Balance	6149	8334	8995	8458	7790	5063	-2366
14 Other textiles	Imports	155	260	301	347	400	595	1119
	Exports	2154	5040	6776	8856	11283	20649	45171
	Balance	1998	4780	6475	8509	10884	20054	44052
15 Wearing apparel	Imports	44221	62850	68431	75387	82674	109230	179798
	Exports	950	803	843	886	930	1077	1374
	Balance	-43271	-62055	-67487	-74501	-81744	-108154	-178424
16 Wood and cork	Imports	7985	8467	8274	7980	7662	6242	6237
	Exports	0	0	0	0	0	0	1156
	Balance	-7985	-8467	-8274	-7980	-7662	-6242	-5082
17 Paper	Imports	4546	9370	10611	11892	13246	18169	30211
	Exports	0	0	0	0	0	0	0
	Balance	-4546	-9370	-10611	-11892	-13246	-18169	-30211

Reference Run

Table D.1.7: Imports, Exports, Balance of Trade, External Debt (Cont.)

Millions of 1975 pesos

		1975	1979	1980	1981	1982	1985	1990
18 Printing, publishing	Imports	7979.	11316.	12342.	13457.	14686.	19197.	30825.
	Exports	0.	0.	0.	0.	0.	0.	0
	Balance	-7979.	-11316.	-12342.	-13457.	-14686.	-19197.	-30825.
19 Leather	Imports	3277.	696.	845.	1015.	1207.	1929.	3770
	Exports	27552.	7043.	8961.	11201.	13763.	23561.	49022
	Balance	24275.	6346.	8117.	10186.	12556.	21632.	45253
20 Rubber products	Imports	2475.	2384.	2754.	3157.	3607.	5403.	10337.
	Exports	1269.	0.	0.	0.	0.	0.	0
	Balance	-1269.	-2384.	-2754.	-3157.	-3607.	-5403.	-10337.
21 Basic chemicals	Imports	8581.	12143.	13378.	14700.	16132.	25339.	47615.
	Exports	5292.	2683.	1941.	1124.	222.	222.	0
	Balance	-3289.	-9459.	-11437.	-13576.	-15911.	-25339.	-47615.
22 Synthetic fibers	Imports	657.	930.	1005.	1086.	1119.	3406.	9473.
	Exports	452.	920.	718.	395.	0.	0.	0
	Balance	-206.	10.	-287.	-690.	-1119.	-3406.	-9473.
23 Fertilizers	Imports	637.	360.	431.	517.	609.	1120.	2301.
	Exports	0.	7661.	10316.	13059.	15415.	32948.	72876.
	Balance	-637.	7292.	9885.	12543.	14806.	31827.	70574.
24 Soaps and detergents	Imports	5807.	1336.	28.	31.	39.	39.	113
	Exports	3860.	7162.	478.	2534.	4860.	13642.	36149.
	Balance	177.	330.	450.	2561.	4821.	13602.	36035.
25 Drugs and medicines	Imports	3683.	177.	7492.	8620.	9378.	11664.	16628.
	Exports	10961.	6831.	347.	364.	382.	443.	565.
	Balance	-10961.	9413.	-7545.	-8256.	-8996.	-11225.	-16063.
26 Perfumes, cosmetics	Imports	1091.	0.	9377.	6907.	5441.	60.	113
	Exports	764.	-9413.	0.	0.	0.	755.	16484.
	Balance	-327.	1924.	-4377.	-6907.	-5441.	695.	16371.
27 Other chemical indust.	Imports	1861.	1772.	2228.	2571.	2953.	4306.	7547.
	Exports	2906.	-152.	2464.	3358.	4350.	8210.	16893.
	Balance	1046.	11699.	257.	787.	1397.	3904.	9306.
28 Nonmetallic mineral pr.	Imports	4683.	11600.	16701.	22533.	29432.	55326.	133779.
	Exports	5547.	7443.	9304.	9165.	10089.	13595.	-133779.
	Balance	858.	12097.	11886.	10913.	8727.	11022.	74409.
29 Basic metallic indust.	Imports	4948.	4654.	3582.	1748.	-1362.	-2573.	61000.
	Exports	6445.	7714.	8492.	9332.	11801.	22657.	36591.
	Balance	1478.	3152.	1800.	269.	0.	70572.	56541.
30 Metal products	Imports	5744.	-4562.	-5692.	-9064.	-11801.	-22657.	-56541.
	Exports	25744.	35098.	32262.	44154.	49568.	70572.	12668.
	Balance	-25744.	-35098.	-39262.	-44154.	-78272.	-70572.	-12668.
31 Machinery	Imports	42200.	5840.	64341.	70610.	78272.	105550.	177815.
	Exports	0.	0.	0.	0.	0.	0.	0
	Balance	-42200.	-5840.	-64341.	-70610.	-78272.	-105550.	-177815.
32 Electrical machinery	Imports	6703.	6228.	9205.	10561.	11096.	16326.	31972.
	Exports	0.	0.	0.	0.	0.	0.	0
	Balance	-6703.	-6228.	-9205.	-10561.	-11096.	-16326.	-31972.
33 Transport equipment	Imports	19737.	24336.	24255.	28562.	31921.	38293.	60504.
	Exports	0.	0.	0.	0.	0.	0.	0
34 Motor vehicles	Balance	-19737.	-24336.	-26255.	-28562.	-31921.	-38293.	-60504.

Reference Run

Table D.1.7: Imports, Exports, Balance of Trade, External Debt (Cont.)

Millions of 1975 pesos

Sector		1975	1979	1980	1981	1982	1985	1990
35 Other manufacturing	Imports	10218.	16504.	17656.	18735.	19800.	22897.	29852.
	Exports	0.	0.	0.	0.	0.	0.	0.
	Balance	-10218.	-16504.	-17656.	-18735.	-19800.	-22897.	-29852.
T O T A L	Imports	449867.0	585765.8	625760.8	677846.5	736118.8	970919.9	*********
	Exports	85541.4	109288.7	116520.1	134042.8	152314.1	227846.8	454154.1
	Balance	-28832.3	-19074.4	-20418.6	-21871.1	-23460.4	-29124.0	-43734.6
E x t e r n a l d e b t[a]		224849.205	405004.195	465922.285	534384.390	611281.775	902862.155	1678065.938

a) 10^9 1975 pesos; peso-dollar exchange rate (1975) = 12.50

Reference Run

Table D.1.8: Government Accounts

Millions of 1975 pesos

	1975		1979		1980		1981		1982		1985		1990	
	Value	%	Value	%	Value	%	Value	%	Value	%	Value	%	Value	%
Incomes														
Direct Taxes	52860.9	36.1	69508.6	35.4	74373.7	34.6	79509.9	33.8	85200.6	33.1	105979.3	31.9	160825.1	32.0
Indirect Taxes plus Exploitation surplus	82513.7	56.3	119508.6	60.8	132425.0	61.6	147028.9	62.5	162906.6	63.6	214772.4	64.7	327072.6	65.0
External Financing	11166.1	7.6	7438.8	3.8	8096.3	3.8	8697.0	3.7	9336.4	3.6	11338.5	3.4	15392.5	3.1
T O T A L	146540.6	100.0	196456.3	100.0	214895.0	100.0	235235.7	100.0	257443.6	100.0	332090.2	100.0	503290.2	100.0
Expenditures														
Consumption of Goods and Services	16745.2	11.4	23391.0	11.9	25580.0	11.9	28021.8	11.9	30689.7	11.9	39675.4	11.9	60350.6	11.9
Wages and Salaries	67172.9	45.8	93832.2	47.7	102613.5	47.7	112408.5	47.8	123110.8	47.8	159157.0	47.9	242094.8	47.9
Investments	62629.3	42.7	79403.3	40.4	86703.2	40.4	94817.1	40.3	103652.5	40.3	133267.7	40.1	200881.5	39.9
T O T A L	146547.3	100.0	196626.4	100.0	214896.8	100.0	235247.4	100.0	257453.0	100.0	332100.2	100.0	503326.9	100.0
Ratio Tax Revenues /GNP (percent)	15.8		16.7		17.1		17.5		17.9		18.7		19.0	
Share of Public Investment in Total Investment (percent)	38.7		39.5		39.7		39.8		39.8		39.0		35.3	

Reference Run

Table D.1.8: Government Accounts (Cont.)

Annual growth rates (percent)

	79/78	80/79	81/80	82/81	80/75	85/80	90/85	90/79
Incomes								
Direct Taxes	7.0	6.9	6.9	7.2	7.1	7.3	8.7	7.9
Indirect Taxes plus								
Exploitation Surpluses	10.2	10.8	11.0	10.8	9.9	10.2	8.8	9.6
External Financing	8.0	7.3	7.4	7.4	-6.2	7.0	6.3	6.7
T O T A L	9.0	9.3	9.5	9.4	8.0	9.1	8.7	8.9
Expenditures								
Consumption of Goods								
and Services	9.0	9.4	9.5	9.5	8.8	9.2	8.8	9.0
Wages and Salaries	9.0	9.4	9.5	9.5	8.8	9.2	8.8	9.
Investments	8.9	9.2	9.4	9.3	6.7	9.0	8.6	8.8
T O T A L	9.0	9.3	9.5	9.4	8.0	9.1	8.7	8.

Reference Run

Table D.1.9: Sectoral Employment

No. of employed persons

Sector	1975		1979		1980		1981		1982		1985		1990	
1 Agriculture	4396750.	36.4	4678382.	32.6	4765953.	32.0	4964363.	31.3	4052606.	30.4	5332888.	28.2	6451074.	25.0
2 Livestock	201470.	1.7	220992.	1.5	225240.	1.5	220430.	1.5	233371.	1.4	247576.	1.3	287176.	1.1
3 Forestry	74515.	.6	94608.	.7	103330.	.7	113691.	.7	123171.	.8	155278.	.8	234166.	.9
4 Fishing	14583.	.1	32142.	.2	38632.	.2	44055.	.3	51228.	.3	77523.	.4	146668.	.6
5 Mining	13894.	.1	9831.	.1	9315.	.1	8913.	.1	8596.	.1	7662.	.0	6079.	.0
6 Quarrying	70194.	.6	74643.	.5	74529.	.5	83130.	.5	88255.	.5	98068.	.5	69707.	.4
7 Petroleum	90859.	.7	136444.	1.0	156742.	1.1	179471.	1.2	201865.	1.2	248653.	1.3	290880.	1.1
8 Slaughter of livestock	211806.	1.8	288341.	2.0	318169.	2.1	352157.	2.3	300422.	2.4	533054.	2.8	893783.	3.5
9 Milling	190373.	1.6	226304.	1.6	235737.	1.6	245647.	1.6	256153.	1.6	292438.	1.5	377462.	1.5
10 Other processed food	130298.	1.1	128648.	.9	127137.	.9	125534.	.8	123026.	.8	119643.	.6	116497.	.5
11 Beverages	86655.	.7	67508.	.5	97218.	.7	96278.	.6	94959.	.6	90045.	.5	82657.	.3
12 Tobacco	8543.	.1	11229.	.1	12502.	.1	13464.	.1	14733.	.1	19064.	.1	78240.	.3
13 Soft fiber textile	133331.	1.1	116422.	.8	111211.	.7	105827.	.7	100578.	.6	86251.	.5	68238.	.3
14 Other textiles	23663.	.2	45167.	.3	57132.	.4	71319.	.5	87429.	.5	147178.	.8	290892.	1.1
15 Wearing apparel	289103.	2.4	261555.	1.8	257767.	1.7	244028.	1.6	235512.	1.4	212316.	1.1	184130.	.7
16 Wood and cork	205337.	1.7	356446.	2.5	405298.	2.9	457444.	2.9	512929.	2.5	649135.	3.7	1091757.	4.2
17 Paper	53737.	.4	56316.	.4	57676.	.4	59203.	.4	61169.	.4	68372.	.4	86947.	.3
18 Printing, publishing	68826.	.6	71822.	.5	72036.	.5	72208.	.4	73384.	.4	73230.	.4	76976.	.3
19 Leather	23589.	.2	44089.	.3	51697.	.3	59982.	.4	64867.	.4	98683.	.5	160150.	.6
20 Rubber products	23498.	.2	23190.	.2	22779.	.2	22332.	.2	21870.	.1	20537.	.1	18891.	.1
21 Basic chemicals	28837.	.2	24454.	.2	23775.	.2	23068.	.2	22526.	.1	21352.	.1	20602.	.1
22 Synthetic fibers	22350.	.2	27696.	.2	29418.	.2	29034.	.2	29597.	.2	31200.	.2	94820.	.1
23 Fertilizers	11249.	.1	46731.	.3	57432.	.4	68173.	.4	79707.	.5	143362.	.8	282873.	1.1
24 Soaps and detergents	7816.	.1	11284.	.1	12000.	.1	12630.	.1	13490.	.1	15088.	.1	16773.	.1
25 Drugs and medicine	48137.	.4	46547.	.3	47566.	.3	48299.	.3	49641.	.3	55215.	.3	69777.	.3
26 Perfume, cosmetics	12804.	.1	22075.	.2	25080.	.2	28226.	.2	31481.	.2	41713.	.2	60565.	.2
27 Other chemical indust.	11665.	.1	18023.	.1	20279.	.1	22277.	.1	25352.	.2	34214.	.2	52857.	.2
28 Nonmetallic mineral pr.	155949.	1.3	133570.	.9	134110.	.9	145153.	.9	140308.	.8	126026.	.7	107121.	.4
29 Basic metallic indust.	89008.	.7	139184.	1.0	139110.	.9	143270.	.9	146420.	.8	190545.	1.0	375280.	1.5
30 Metal products	185230.	1.5	229184.	1.5	229184.	1.5	237645.	1.5	266497.	1.5	276653.	1.5	347304.	1.3
31 Machinery	92135.	.8	129072.	.9	135885.	.9	147326.	.9	148593.	.9	167950.	.9	209717.	.8
32 Electrical machinery	172418.	1.4	198142.	1.4	205543.	1.4	213584.	1.4	222350.	1.4	253787.	1.3	330225.	1.3
33 Transport equipment	179056.	1.5	239816.	1.6	235431.	1.6	246607.	1.5	248318.	1.5	284635.	1.5	341979.	1.3
34 Motor vehicles	89360.	.7	125479.	.9	131610.	.9	136316.	.8	141373.	.9	160732.	.9	219358.	.9
35 Other manufacturing	236558.	2.0	300497.	2.1	342700.	2.3	395872.	2.5	460732.	2.8	736762.	3.9	1594643.	6.2
36 Construction	743613.	6.2	1382997.	9.7	1577285.	10.6	1785302.	11.5	2019009.	12.4	2814327.	14.9	4942313.	19.2
37 Electricity	72288.	.6	111338.	.8	122026.	.8	132034.	.8	145026.	.9	183143.	1.0	249521.	1.0
38 Gas	110174.	.9	137276.	1.0	146051.	1.0	157846.	1.0	170041.	1.0	215532.	1.1	332851.	1.3
39 Transport	522544.	4.3	642785.	4.6	682660.	4.6	698445.	4.5	713278.	4.4	786048.	4.2	1008892.	3.9
40 Communications	47017.	.4	87358.	.6	95444.	.6	102800.	.7	110022.	.7	134369.	.7	176655.	.7
41 Trade	1474094.	12.2	1650507.	11.6	1674665.	11.5	1694928.	10.9	1712420.	10.5	1756470.	9.3	1836087.	7.1
42 Dwellings	8024.	.1	8708.	.1	8802.	.1	8879.	.1	8943.	.1	9087.	.0	9270.	.0
43 Hotels and restaurants	293307.	2.4	303953.	2.1	304008.	2.0	303039.	2.0	303703.	2.0	303877.	1.6	313364.	1.2
44 Credit and insurance	158119.	1.3	206631.	1.4	219571.	1.5	232287.	1.5	247059.	1.5	299593.	1.6	425780.	1.7
45 Other services	1008378.	8.3	1070156.	7.5	1088969.	7.3	1108416.	7.1	1142796.	7.0	1227977.	6.5	1448004.	5.6
T O T A L	12090755.	100.0	14270834.	100.0	14490695.	100.0	15565595.	100.0	16279723.	100.0	18007250.	100.0	25798803.	100.0

Table D.1.9: Sectoral Employment (Cont.)

Annual growth rates (percent)

Sector	79/78	80/79	81/80	82/81	80/75	85/80	90/85	90/79
1 Agriculture	1.4	1.9	2.1	1.8	1.6	2.3	3.9	3.0
2 Livestock	1.7	1.9	2.0	1.6	2.3	1.9	3.0	2.4
3 Forestry	6.7	9.2	10.0	8.3	6.8	8.5	8.6	8.6
4 Fishing	21.9	16.3	14.3	16.3	21.4	15.0	13.6	14.5
5 Mining	-6.3	-5.3	-4.3	-3.6	-7.7	-3.8	-4.5	-4.3
6 Quarrying	4.2	5.2	5.0	6.2	2.3	4.5	.3	2.7
7 Petroleum	13.5	14.9	14.5	12.5	11.5	9.7	3.2	7.1
8 Slaughter of livestock	9.8	10.3	10.7	10.9	8.5	10.9	10.9	10.8
9 Milling	4.2	4.2	4.2	4.3	4.4	4.4	5.2	4.8
10 Other processed food	-1.0	-1.2	-1.0	-1.3	-.5	-1.2	-.5	-.9
11 Beverages	.4	-.4	-1.0	-1.4	2.3	-1.5	-1.7	-1.5
12 Tobacco	9.1	9.5	9.5	9.4	7.5	9.2	8.2	8.7
13 Soft fiber textiles	-4.3	-4.6	-4.8	-5.0	-3.6	-5.0	-4.6	-4.8
14 Other textiles	27.4	26.6	24.7	22.4	19.3	20.8	14.6	18.5
15 Wearing apparel	-3.2	-3.4	-3.5	-3.5	-2.7	-3.4	-2.8	-3.1
16 Wood and cork	14.3	13.6	12.9	12.1	14.6	11.5	9.3	10.7
17 Paper	2.0	2.4	2.8	3.2	1.6	3.5	4.9	4.0
18 Printing, publishing	.3	.3	.7	.7	.9	.3	.9	.6
19 Leather	18.2	17.3	16.0	14.8	17.0	13.8	10.2	12.4
20 Rubber products	-1.5	-1.6	-2.0	-2.1	-.6	-2.1	-1.7	-1.8
21 Basic chemicals	-3.4	-3.1	-2.7	-2.3	-3.8	-2.1	-.7	-1.5
22 Synthetic fibers	3.3	2.6	2.2	1.9	4.9	1.9	2.2	2.1
23 Fertilizers	28.7	22.7	18.9	16.9	38.5	20.1	14.6	17.8
24 Soaps and detergents	8.2	7.1	6.1	5.7	9.1	2.1	2.1	3.6
25 Drugs and medicines	.7	1.5	2.2	2.8	-.4	3.2	4.8	3.7
26 Perfumes, cosmetics	14.6	13.6	12.6	11.5	14.4	10.7	7.7	9.6
27 Other chemical indust.	12.7	12.5	12.1	11.6	11.7	11.0	9.1	10.3
28 Nonmetallic mineral pr.	-2.1	-2.7	-3.1	-3.3	-.8	-3.4	-3.2	-3.2
29 Basic metallic indust.	5.7	4.1	3.0	2.3	9.3	4.5	14.5	9.8
30 Metal products	3.8	3.7	3.7	3.7	4.4	3.8	4.7	4.2
31 Machinery	6.1	5.3	4.7	4.1	8.1	4.3	4.5	4.5
32 Electrical machinery	3.6	3.7	3.9	4.1	3.4	4.3	5.4	4.8
33 Transport equipment	4.4	3.9	3.6	3.2	5.4	4.1	3.7	3.9
34 Motor vehicles	5.9	4.8	4.6	3.3	8.1	5.2	5.3	5.2
35 Other manufacturing	11.8	14.0	15.5	16.4	7.7	16.5	16.7	16.4
36 Construction	15.5	14.0	13.2	13.1	16.2	12.3	11.9	12.3
37 Electricity	10.9	9.6	8.3	9.1	11.0	4.5	6.4	7.6
38 Gas	6.6	7.0	7.4	7.7	5.0	8.0	9.1	8.4
39 Transport	3.8	3.0	2.4	2.1	5.5	2.9	5.1	3.9
40 Communications	11.6	9.3	7.7	7.0	15.2	7.1	5.6	6.6
41 Trade	1.8	1.6	1.2	1.6	2.6	1.0	.9	1.0
42 Dwellings	1.4	1.1	.7	.7	1.9	.6	.4	.3
43 Hotels and restaurants	.7	.0	-.0	-.1	.7	-.0	.6	.3
44 Credit and insurance	6.4	6.3	6.2	6.3	6.2	6.4	7.3	6.8
45 Other services	2.5	1.6	1.8	3.1	1.5	2.4	3.4	2.8
	4.7	4.3	4.5	4.4	4.3	4.9	6.4	5.5

Reference Run

Table D.1.10: Employment by Socio-economic Group

Thousands of persons

Socio-economic group	1975	%	1979	%	1980	%	1981	%	1982	%	1985	%	1990	%
1. Entr. Empl. Prof. (H)	911814	7.5	1105756	7.7	1159349	7.8	1216340	7.8	1278948	7.9	1506427	8.0	2094047	8.1
2. Entr. Empl. Prof. (M)	2375891	19.7	2863614	20.1	2999032	20.1	3143313	20.2	3301183	20.3	3874800	20.5	5358732	20.8
3. Entr. Empl. Prof. (L)	3182601	26.3	3788233	26.5	3956084	26.6	4135215	26.6	4329457	26.6	5036389	26.6	6871096	26.6
4. Workers	2083406	17.2	2583270	18.1	2724735	18.3	2874904	18.5	3041898	18.7	3664029	19.3	5200082	20.2
5. Peasants (H-M)	190128	1.6	202592	1.4	206484	1.4	210946	1.4	214795	1.3	231656	1.2	280828	1.1
6. Peasants (L)	639764	5.3	681701	4.8	694799	4.7	709812	4.6	722766	4.4	779499	4.1	944961	3.7
7. Landless Workers	2707151	22.4	3054219	21.4	3159211	21.2	3275065	21.0	3390676	20.8	3832449	20.3	5049056	19.6
T O T A L	12090755	100.0	14279834	100.0	14899695	100.0	15565595	100.0	16279723	100.0	18907250	100.0	25798803	100.0

Reference Run

Table D.1.10: Employment b Socio-economic Group (Cont.)

Annual growth rates (percent)

Socio-economic group	79/78	80/79	81/80	82/81	80/75	85/80	90/85	90/79
1. Entr. Empl. Prof. (H)	4.9	4.8	4.9	5.1	4.9	5.4	6.8	6.0
2. Entr. Empl. Prof. (M)	4.7	4.7	4.9	5.0	4.8	5.3	6.7	5.9
3. Entr. Empl. Prof. (L)	4.4	4.4	4.5	4.7	4.8	4.9	6.4	5.6
4. Workers	5.6	5.5	5.5	4.7	5.5	6.0	7.4	6.6
5. Peasants (H-M)	1.4	1.9	2.2	1.8	1.7	2.3	3.9	3.0
6. Peasants (L)	1.4	1.9	2.2	1.8	1.7	2.3	3.0	3.0
7. Landless Workers	3.0	3.4	3.7	3.5	3.1	3.9	5.7	4.7
Landless Workers	4.2	4.3	4.5	4.6	4.3	4.9	6.4	5.5

Reference Run

Table D.1.11: Income by Socio-economic Group

Millions of 1975 pesos

Socio-economic group	1975	%	1979	%	1980	%	1981	%	1982	%	1985	%	1990	%
1. Entr. Empl. Prof. (H)	207101	24.9	270332	24.6	288113	24.6	307200	24.5	328162	24.5	402089	24.2	590768	23.7
2. Entr. Empl. Prof. (M)	240733	28.9	307376	28.0	325145	27.7	343979	27.5	364403	27.2	435565	26.3	611918	24.6
3. Entr. Empl. Prof. (L)	133698	16.1	165706	15.1	173716	14.8	182071	14.5	191111	14.2	222513	13.4	303715	12.2
4. Workers	166963	20.0	255205	23.3	282626	24.1	312676	25.0	346165	25.8	469614	28.3	804924	32.4
5. Peasants (H-M)	25723	3.1	29993	2.7	31241	2.7	32602	2.6	33988	2.5	39346	2.4	54058	2.2
6. Peasants (L)	15676	1.9	18117	1.7	18857	1.6	19673	1.6	20488	1.5	23658	1.4	32318	1.3
7. Landless Workers	42945	5.2	50111	4.6	52223	4.5	54536	4.4	56871	4.2	65737	4.0	89749	3.6
	832838	100.1	1096839	100.0	1171919	100.0	1252737	100.1	1341188	99.9	1658522	100.0	2487451	100.0

Reference Run

Table D.1.11: Income by Socio-economic Group (Cont.)

Socio-economic group	Annual growth rates (percent)							
	79/75	80/79	81/80	82/81	90/75	85/80	90/85	90/79
1. Entr. Empl. Prof. (H)	6.4	7.4	6.6	6.6	6.9	6.9	8.0	7.4
2. Entr. Empl. Prof. (M)	5.9	5.4	5.7	5.5	6.2	6.0	7.0	6.5
3. Entr. Empl. Prof. (L)	5.0	4.4	4.8	5.0	5.4	5.1	6.0	5.7
4. Workers	11.0	10.7	10.6	10.7	11.1	10.7	11.4	11.0
5. Peasants (H-M)	3.8	4.7	4.4	4.3	4.0	4.7	4.6	5.5
6. Peasants (L)	3.6	4.1	4.3	4.1	3.9	4.6	4.6	5.4
7. Landless Workers	3.8	4.2	4.4	4.3	4.0	4.7	6.4	5.4
T O T A L	6.0	6.6	6.2	7.1	7.1	7.2	8.4	7.7

Reference Run

Table D.1.12: Average Income by Socio-economic Group, Gini Coefficient and Welfare Indicators

Socio-economic group	Thousands of 1975 pesos							Annual growth rates (percent)							
	1975	1979	1980	1981	1982	1985	1990	79/79	80/79	81/80	82/81	90/75	85/80	90/85	90/79
1. Entr.Empl.Prof.(H)	227.	244.	249.	253.	257.	267.	282.	1.7	2.0	1.6	1.6	1.4	1.1	1.3	
2. Entr.Empl.Prof.(M)	101.	107.	108.	109.	110.	112.	114.	.9	.9	.9	.7	.4			
3. Entr.Empl.Prof.(L)	42.	44.	44.	44.	44.	44.	44.	2.3	0.0	0.0	0.0	0.0	0.0	0.0	
4. Workers	80.	99.	104.	109.	114.	129.	155.	5.1	5.1	4.8	4.6	4.4	3.7	4.2	
5. Peasants (H-M)	135.	148.	151.	155.	158.	170.	192.	2.1	2.0	2.6	1.9	2.3	2.5	2.	
6. Peasants (L)	25.	27.	27.	29.	29.	30.	34.	3.8	3.7	0.0	1.6	1.1	1.1	
7. Landless Workers	16.	16.	17.	17.	17.	17.	18.	0.0	6.3	0.0	0.0	1.2	0.0	1.1	
T O T A L	69.	77.	79.	80.	82.	88.	96.	2.2	2.2	2.1	1.8	2.3	1.9	1.8	1.9
Welfare indicators															
Gini Coefficient	.416	.413	.417	.410	.417	.414	.415	.06	.06	.06	.06	.06	.06	.06	.06
Efficiency-equity[a]	.486	.644	.690	.739	.788	.972	1.455								
Equal weights								2.4	2.2	1.7	1.2	2.1	1.4	1.4	1 5
Poverty weighted								2.9	2.9	2.3	1.5	2.5	1.8	1.9	1.9

a) 10^{12} 1975 pesos

D.2: Case One

Case One

Table D.2.1: Sectoral Gross Output

	Millions of 1978 pesos							Annual growth rates (percent)							
Sector	1978	1979	1980	1981	1982	1985	1990	79/78	80/79	81/80	82/81	83/82	88/83	93/88	93/82
1 Agriculture	169963	177434	185284	193426	202644	239663	341055	4.4	4.4	4.4	4.4	4.7	6.5	6.4	7.3
2 Livestock	98463	101150	103682	106346	109305	120178	146681	2.5	2.5	2.6	2.8	2.7	3.7	5.4	4.4
3 Forestry	8611	9286	10254	11491	12967	19381	37746	7.9	10.4	12.1	12.8	11.4	14.4	13.9	14.1
4 Fishing	6861	8387	9918	11729	13883	22914	48808	22.2	18.3	18.3	17.9	19.1	17.3	15.2	16.5
5 Mining	23870	24661	25473	26437	27573	32007	44123	3.3	3.3	3.8	4.3	3.0	5.9	7.8	6.5
6 Quarrying	14645	15822	19660	19660	22351	33445	64706	7.9	10.3	12.6	13.7	11.7	14.3	13.8	14.1
7 Petroleum	112845	138870	173598	213327	257438	412777	812625	23.3	25.0	22.9	20.6	22.0	15.5	13.8	14.9
8 Slaughter of livestock	40194	44045	47989	53309	59173	81128	140646	9.6	8.9	10.3	10.7	10.3	11.4	11.9	11.6
9 Milling	138910	142135	145123	85743	92173	154437	176464	7.9	7.6	7.5	7.6	7.6	8.2	9.6	8.8
10 Other processed food	58626	62597	66827	150097	72845	149403	94437	2.6	6.1	6.7	6.9	7.6	3.7	5.2	4.3
11 Beverages	55857	58528	59635	70070	75172	80300	202311	10.8	12.0	12.0	4.0	5.2	3.2	3.9	3.5
12 Tobacco	56687	58886	60853	62675	64497	77366	702441	3.7	3.3	3.0	2.9	2.8	13.6	13.4	13.6
13 Soft fiber textiles	4896	6397	8831	12136	16361	34124	84341	30.7	38.0	37.4	34.7	34.3	23.2	4.6	3.8
14 Other textiles	104906	113971	118297	122553	126195	134167	165910	4.6	3.8	3.2	3.6	3.3	3.3	17.2	21.1
15 Wearing apparel	17251	20134	23810	28301	33644	56973	113973	15.7	18.3	18.9	18.9	18.2	16.7	14.7	3.9
16 Wood and cork	35111	37736	38994	42124	44204	50811	66205	7.5	6.0	5.3	4.9	5.7	5.0	4.5	15.9
17 Paper	25886	26936	28231	29795	31580	38516	47348	4.3	4.8	5.5	6.0	5.7	7.6	6.4	5.6
18 Printing, publishing	11055	11122	13401	14642	33731	44159	114210	17.3	18.8	19.2	19.0	18.2	16.6	9.3	8.7
19 Leather	18638	12254	13401	14642	15915	20395	31723	10.2	9.4	8.7	9.2	8.9	9.6	9.9	9.3
20 Rubber products	18638	18743	19159	19684	20302	23387	31994	1.8	2.2	2.7	3.6	2.9	5.6	7.7	6.4
21 Basic chemicals	17311	18671	19901	21094	22290	26213	35630	7.0	6.0	5.7	6.3	5.9	5.9	7.3	6.5
22 Other chemical indust.	4744	6717	9389	12876	17313	34095	90713	40.4	39.8	37.2	34.4	34.5	23.4	17.2	21.2
23 Synthetic fibers	12928	15562	19041	23686	28562	47010	108560	20.4	22.4	24.2	22.4	21.8	18.4	15.4	17.3
24 Soaps and detergents	11571	16625	16324	16400	17217	21018	32741	-5.1	-1.8	1.7	3.7	.7	8.7	11.0	9.5
25 Drugs and medicines	16660	13618	16712	20830	25869	46676	103335	17.7	22.7	24.6	24.2	16.7	19.5	19.5	18.2
26 Perfumes, cosmetics	22621	22621	26365	30930	36318	57738	116785	15.1	16.5	17.3	17.4	16.7	15.9	14.3	15.3
27 Other chemical indust.	53423	56492	59143	61442	63750	70361	84652	5.7	4.7	4.1	3.6	4.3	3.5	4.6	3.9
28 Nonmetallic mineral pr.	84604	93350	101466	109908	114965	149026	188407	11.1	9.0	7.6	6.8	8.1	6.0	7.1	6.5
29 Basic metallic indust.	47410	50639	53088	57186	60591	72302	101926	6.8	6.4	4.1	6.0	6.3	6.5	6.0	7.2
30 Metal products	28556	31049	33522	35901	38240	45927	44311	6.2	7.8	7.1	6.5	7.3	6.5	7.0	7.1
31 Machinery	40753	44146	47185	50144	53034	63353	84470	9.3	6.9	6.3	5.8	6.6	5.8	7.2	6.4
32 Electrical machinery	30005	33936	36843	30707	43540	63517	82504	9.8	8.6	8.0	6.9	8.2	8.5	9.9	9.0
33 Transport equipment	82863	91484	100382	109355	117950	146199	213418	10.4	9.7	8.9	8.9	7.5	8.6	8.6	8.0
34 Motor vehicles	19920	22345	24867	27644	30554	41604	70667	12.1	11.3	10.8	10.9	11.2	11.0	11.5	11.2
35 Other manufacturing	277659	328838	391804	460110	560024	933574	1970095	18.4	19.2	19.7	20.6	19.2	17.2	15.0	16.4
36 Construction	35726	41207	47286	54303	62670	95377	145036	15.3	14.8	14.8	15.2	15.1	14.6	13.7	14.3
37 Electricity	16634	17339	18173	19146	20290	24776	37048	4.2	4.8	5.4	6.0	5.6	4.7	9.4	4.3
38 Gas	76224	80614	84359	87324	90000	100505	121393	5.8	4.7	4.1	3.6	4.3	3.5	4.7	4.0
39 Transport	18771	22843	27659	33677	40443	58674	147272	21.7	21.1	21.0	20.8	21.0	17.8	15.2	16.8
40 Communications	627753	646181	667076	675678	596072	715574	76495	2.9	2.5	3.1	1.7	2.1	3.5	1.7	1.5
41 Trade	99027	99581	100063	100646	101797	101797	1035848	.6	.5	.4	.4	.4	.3	.5	4.4
42 Dwellings	75772	78605	81005	83418	85856	92479	109646	3.7	3.2	2.9	2.7	3.0	3.0	4.2	3.5
43 Hotels and restaurants	62024	65324	69657	72171	75232	88247	121516	5.3	5.1	5.1	5.1	5.9	17.2	7.5	6.6
44 Credit and insurance	120359	128079	137841	146818	165567	212625	354014	7.2	6.9	7.7	8.5	7.9	10.4	11.4	10.7
T O T A L	2934464	3158700	3407244	3664756	3993126	5153810	8235858	7.6	7.0	8.1	8.4	8.1	9.4	10.5	9.8

Case One

Table D.2.2: Private Consumption

| | Millions of 1978 pesos | | | | | | | Annual growth rates (percent) | | | | | | | |
Sector	1978	1979	1980	1981	1982	1985	1990	77/78	80/79	81/80	82/81	83/78	88/83	93/88	93/82
1 Agriculture	93914.	98113.	102634.	107558.	112940.	132783.	183735.	4.5	4.6	4.8	5.0	4.8	6.1	7.9	6.7
2 Livestock	25362.	26691.	28109.	29642.	31305.	37357.	52620.	5.2	5.3	5.5	5.6	5.5	6.6	7.9	7.1
3 Forestry	0.	0.	0.	0.	0.	0.	0.	0.0	0.0	0.0	0.0	0.0	0.0	0.0	0.0
4 Fishing	14020.	14855.	15742.	16695.	17720.	21374.	30352.	6.0	6.0	6.1	6.1	6.8	6.8	8.0	7.3
5 Mining	0.	0.	0.	0.	0.	0.	0.	0.0	0.0	0.0	0.0	0.0	0.0	0.0	0.0
6 Quarrying	0.	0.	0.	0.	0.	0.	0.	0.0	0.0	0.0	0.0	0.0	0.0	0.0	0.0
7 Petroleum	56301.	59922.	63810.	68045.	72665.	89724.	134099.	6.4	6.5	6.6	6.8	6.7	7.8	9.2	8.4
8 Slaughter of livestock	228116.	241095.	255096.	270420.	287219.	349690.	513334.	5.7	5.8	6.0	6.2	6.0	7.4	8.9	8.0
9 Milling	57982.	60815.	63854.	67160.	70773.	84130.	118529.	4.8	5.0	5.2	5.4	6.0	6.5	8.0	7.1
10 Other processed food	97046.	101904.	107146.	112873.	119157.	142507.	203151.	5.0	5.4	5.6	5.6	5.2	6.7	8.3	7.4
11 Beverages	45445.	47851.	50434.	53342.	56309.	67613.	96694.	5.3	5.4	5.7	5.8	5.4	6.8	8.3	7.4
12 Tobacco	13371.	14110.	14894.	15736.	16642.	19874.	27757.	5.5	5.6	5.7	5.8	5.6	6.5	7.6	7.0
13 Soft fiber textiles	13893.	14784.	15737.	16770.	17887.	21920.	31958.	6.4	6.6	6.6	6.7	6.6	7.4	8.5	7.9
14 Other textiles	0.	0.	0.	0.	0.	0.	0.	0.0	0.0	0.0	0.0	0.0	0.0	0.0	0.0
15 Wearing apparel	182180.	193815.	206433.	220294.	235525.	292287.	441526.	6.1	6.2	6.3	6.9	6.7	8.0	9.5	8.6
16 Wood and cork	24494.	25989.	27595.	29342.	31247.	38221.	56018.	6.1	6.2	6.3	6.5	6.4	7.4	8.8	8.0
17 Paper	11833.	12551.	13313.	14133.	15016.	18163.	25845.	6.1	6.1	6.3	6.2	6.9	6.9	8.0	7.4
18 Printing, publishing	27040.	28828.	30752.	32850.	35137.	43524.	65066.	6.6	6.7	6.8	7.0	7.9	7.9	9.2	8.4
19 Leather	7637.	7836.	8328.	8850.	9404.	11314.	15732.	6.4	6.3	6.3	6.3	6.6	6.6	7.3	6.9
20 Rubber products	9566.	10167.	10803.	11482.	12208.	14766.	20894.	6.3	6.3	6.3	6.3	6.8	6.8	7.8	7.2
21 Basic chemicals	5421.	5755.	6102.	6465.	6844.	8110.	10832.	6.2	6.0	5.9	5.9	6.0	5.9	6.2	6.0
22 Synthetic fibers	0.	0.	0.	0.	0.	0.	0.	0.0	0.0	0.0	0.0	0.0	0.0	0.0	0.0
23 Fertilizers	5137.	5450.	5774.	6112.	6463.	7627.	10081.	6.1	5.9	5.8	5.7	5.7	6.0	6.0	5.8
24 Soaps and detergents	23095.	24237.	25451.	26760.	28176.	33305.	46112.	4.9	5.1	5.3	5.3	6.2	6.2	7.6	6.8
25 Drugs and medicines	17052.	17947.	18896.	19916.	21014.	24962.	34697.	5.2	5.3	5.4	5.5	6.3	6.3	7.6	6.8
26 Perfumes, cosmetics	35311.	37426.	39704.	42188.	44900.	54870.	80515.	6.0	6.1	6.3	6.4	7.4	7.4	8.8	8.0
27 Other chemical indust.	5515.	5864.	6228.	6608.	7007.	8344.	11257.	6.3	6.3	6.1	6.0	6.0	6.0	6.5	6.2
28 Nonmetallic mineral pr.	7477.	7900.	8342.	8807.	9300.	10990.	14821.	5.7	5.6	5.6	5.6	5.9	5.9	6.7	6.2
29 Basic metallic indust.	0.	0.	0.	0.	0.	0.	0.	0.0	0.0	0.0	0.0	0.0	0.0	0.0	0.0
30 Metal products	10397.	11037.	11717.	12448.	13235.	16043.	22860.	6.2	6.2	6.2	6.3	7.0	7.0	8.0	7.4
31 Machinery	4674.	4942.	5217.	5499.	5788.	6713.	8527.	5.8	5.4	5.4	5.3	5.0	5.0	4.9	5.0
32 Electrical machinery	36682.	39013.	41527.	44275.	47277.	58333.	86884.	6.4	6.6	6.6	6.8	7.8	7.8	9.1	8.3
33 Transport equipment	19630.	20911.	22281.	23764.	25371.	31215.	46027.	6.5	6.6	6.7	6.8	7.6	7.6	8.8	8.1
34 Motor vehicles	82695.	89157.	96195.	103955.	112487.	144236.	227819.	7.8	7.9	8.1	8.2	9.1	9.1	10.3	9.6
35 Other manufacturing	37603.	40182.	42973.	46032.	49379.	61727.	93756.	6.9	6.9	7.1	7.3	8.2	8.2	9.5	8.7
36 Construction	0.	0.	0.	0.	0.	0.	0.	0.0	0.0	0.0	0.0	0.0	0.0	0.0	0.0
37 Electricity	34361.	36401.	38596.	40988.	43599.	53207.	77920.	5.9	6.0	6.2	6.4	7.4	7.4	8.8	7.9
38 Cinema	34119.	36729.	39548.	42634.	46009.	58465.	90888.	7.7	7.7	7.8	7.9	8.8	8.8	8.9	9.2
39 Transport	58002.	61640.	65586.	69921.	74680.	92344.	138377.	6.3	6.4	6.6	6.8	7.9	7.9	9.3	8.4
40 Communications	20169.	21557.	23041.	24650.	26391.	32708.	48748.	6.9	6.9	7.0	7.1	7.8	7.8	9.1	8.3
41 Trade	17178.	18394.	19694.	21104.	22630.	28153.	42120.	7.1	7.2	7.2	7.2	7.9	7.9	9.1	8.4
42 Dwellings	56467.	59681.	63126.	66873.	70948.	85886.	124380.	5.7	5.8	5.9	6.1	7.1	7.1	8.6	7.7
43 Hotels and restaurants	16386.	17413.	18509.	19693.	20972.	25580.	37092.	6.3	6.3	6.4	6.5	7.3	7.3	8.5	7.8
44 Credit and insurance	11720.	12572.	13482.	14463.	15521.	19307.	28699.	7.3	7.2	7.3	7.3	7.9	7.9	8.9	8.3
45 Other services	175201.	187904.	201655.	216756.	233309.	294749.	456512.	7.3	7.3	7.5	7.6	8.6	8.6	9.9	9.1
T O T A L	1622223.	1721438.	1828328.	1945002.	2072454.	2542123.	3756282.	6.1	6.2	6.4	6.6	7.6	7.6	9.0	8.1

Case One

Table D.2.3: Government Consumption of Goods and Services

	Millions of 1978 pesos							Annual growth rates (percent)						
Sector	1978	1979	1980	1981	1982	1985	1990	78/79	79/79	81/80	82/81	83/79	88/83	93/98
1 Agriculture	135.	147.	162.	170.	194.	265.	443.	9.4	10.2	10.4	10.4	10.1	10.5	11.2
2 Livestock	0.	0.	0.	0.	0.	0.	0.	0.0	0.0	0.0	0.0	0.0	0.0	0.0
3 Forestry	0.	0.	0.	0.	0.	0.	0.	0.0	0.0	0.0	0.0	0.0	0.0	0.0
4 Fishing	0.	0.	0.	0.	0.	0.	0.	0.0	0.0	0.0	0.0	0.0	0.0	0.0
5 Mining	0.	0.	0.	0.	0.	0.	0.	0.0	0.0	0.0	0.0	0.0	0.0	0.0
6 Quarrying	0.	0.	0.	0.	0.	0.	0.	0.0	0.0	0.0	0.0	0.0	0.0	0.0
7 Petroleum	1034.	1131.	1246.	1374.	1519.	2039.	3406.	9.4	10.2	10.4	10.4	10.1	10.5	11.2
8 Slaughter of livestock	210.	229.	253.	279.	308.	413.	689.	9.4	10.2	10.4	10.4	10.1	10.5	11.2
9 Milling	0.	0.	0.	0.	0.	0.	0.	0.0	0.0	0.0	0.0	0.0	0.0	0.0
10 Other processed food	710.	229.	253.	279.	308.	413.	689.	9.4	10.2	10.4	10.4	10.1	10.5	11.2
11 Beverages	0.	0.	0.	0.	0.	0.	0.	0.0	0.0	0.0	0.0	0.0	0.0	0.0
12 Tobacco	0.	0.	0.	0.	0.	0.	0.	0.0	0.0	0.0	0.0	0.0	0.0	0.0
13 Soft fiber textiles	0.	0.	0.	0.	0.	0.	0.	0.0	0.0	0.0	0.0	0.0	0.0	0.0
14 Other textiles	1262.	1381.	1522.	1679.	1854.	2489.	4151.	9.4	10.2	10.4	10.4	10.1	10.5	11.2
15 Wearing apparel	41.	45.	49.	54.	60.	81.	134.	9.4	10.2	10.4	10.4	10.1	10.5	11.2
16 Wood and cork	52.	64.	71.	78.	87.	116.	194.	9.4	10.2	10.4	10.4	10.1	10.5	11.2
17 Paper	1756.	1922.	2117.	2337.	2579.	3463.	5775.	9.4	10.2	10.4	10.4	10.1	10.5	11.2
18 Printing, publishing	299.	32.	35.	39.	43.	57.	95.	9.4	10.2	10.4	10.4	10.1	10.5	11.2
19 Leather	2.	2.	2.	2.	2.	2.	6.	0.0	0.0	0.0	0.0	0.0	0.0	0.0
20 Rubber products	170.	186.	205.	227.	250.	335.	560.	9.4	10.2	10.4	10.4	10.1	10.5	11.2
21 Basic chemicals	0.	0.	0.	0.	0.	0.	0.	0.0	0.0	0.0	0.0	0.0	0.0	0.0
22 Synthetic fibers	0.	0.	0.	0.	0.	0.	0.	0.0	0.0	0.0	0.0	0.0	0.0	0.0
23 Fertilizers	0.	0.	0.	0.	0.	0.	0.	0.0	0.0	0.0	0.0	0.0	0.0	0.0
24 Soaps and detergents	601.	658.	725.	801.	883.	1186.	1977.	9.4	10.2	10.4	10.4	10.1	10.5	11.2
25 Drugs and medicines	4031.	4410.	4858.	5362.	5919.	7944.	13253.	9.4	10.2	10.4	10.4	10.1	10.5	11.2
26 Perfumes, cosmetics	0.	0.	0.	0.	0.	0.	0.	0.0	0.0	0.0	0.0	0.0	0.0	0.0
27 Other chemical indust.	0.	0.	0.	0.	0.	0.	0.	0.0	0.0	0.0	0.0	0.0	0.0	0.0
28 Nonmetallic mineral pr.	262.	287.	316.	349.	385.	517.	863.	9.4	10.2	10.4	10.4	10.1	10.5	11.2
29 Basic metallic indust.	201.	220.	242.	267.	295.	394.	661.	9.4	10.2	10.4	10.4	10.1	10.5	11.2
30 Metal products	1959.	2143.	2361.	2606.	2877.	3863.	6442.	9.4	10.2	10.4	10.4	10.1	10.5	11.2
31 Machinery	1039.	1137.	1253.	1383.	1526.	2049.	3417.	9.4	10.2	10.4	10.4	10.1	10.5	11.2
32 Electrical machinery	1267.	1387.	1528.	1686.	1861.	2499.	4167.	9.4	10.2	10.4	10.4	10.1	10.5	11.2
33 Transport equipment	177.	194.	214.	236.	260.	349.	583.	9.4	10.2	10.4	10.4	10.1	10.5	11.2
34 Motor vehicles	63.	69.	76.	84.	93.	124.	207.	9.4	10.2	10.4	10.4	10.1	10.5	11.2
35 Other manufacturing	1366.	1495.	1647.	1818.	2006.	2694.	4492.	9.4	10.2	10.4	10.4	10.1	10.5	11.2
36 Construction	1041.	1139.	1255.	1385.	1529.	2052.	3423.	9.4	10.2	10.4	10.4	10.1	10.5	11.2
37 Electricity	756.	828.	912.	1006.	1111.	1492.	2487.	9.4	10.2	10.4	10.4	10.1	10.5	11.2
38 Gas	48.	52.	58.	63.	70.	94.	157.	9.4	10.2	10.4	10.4	10.1	10.5	11.2
39 Transport	1624.	1120.	1234.	1362.	1504.	2019.	3366.	9.4	10.2	10.4	10.4	10.1	10.5	11.2
40 Communications	770.	842.	928.	1024.	1131.	1518.	2532.	9.4	10.2	10.4	10.4	10.1	10.5	11.2
41 Trade	3158.	3456.	3807.	4202.	4638.	6228.	10385.	9.4	10.2	10.4	10.4	10.1	10.5	11.2
42 Dwellings	2303.	2520.	2776.	3064.	3382.	4542.	7573.	9.4	10.2	10.4	10.4	10.1	10.5	11.2
43 Hotels and restaurants	872.	954.	1051.	1160.	1281.	1720.	2866.	9.4	10.2	10.4	10.4	10.1	10.5	11.2
44 Credit and insurance	1363.	1491.	1643.	1813.	2001.	2687.	4481.	9.4	10.2	10.4	10.4	10.1	10.5	11.2
45 Other services	1963.	2147.	2365.	2611.	2882.	3870.	6453.	9.4	10.2	10.4	10.4	10.1	10.5	11.2
T O T A L	29174.	31918.	35163.	38811.	42840.	57425.	95922.	9.4	10.2	10.4	10.4	10.1	10.5	11.2

Case One

Table D.2.4: Public Investment by Destination

Millions of 1978 pesos

Sector	1978	%	1979	%	1980	%	1981	%	1982	%	1985	%	1990	%
1 Agriculture	6528	4.6	11306	7.3	14294	8.4	17086	9.6	22489	10.9	30015	10.9	49672	10.9
2 Livestock	851	.6	1540	1.0	1472	1.1	2246	1.2	2476	1.2	3304	1.2	5468	1.2
3 Forestry	710	.5	1239	.8	1831	.9	1684	.9	2063	1.0	2754	1.0	4557	1.0
4 Fishing	1135	.8	774	.5	851	.5	937	.5	1238	.6	1652	.6	2734	.6
5 Mining	1419	1.0	1540	1.0	1472	1.1	2061	1.1	2270	1.1	3029	1.1	5013	1.1
6 Quarrying	1419	1.0	1540	1.0	1772	1.1	2061	1.1	2270	1.1	3029	1.1	5013	1.1
7 Porcelain	40869	28.8	51258	33.1	51300	30.2	50960	27.2	49517	24.0	66089	24.0	109369	24.0
8 Slaughter of livestock	426	.3	465	.3	510	.3	562	.3	619	.3	826	.3	1367	.3
9 Milling	426	.3	465	.3	510	.3	562	.3	619	.3	826	.3	1367	.3
10 Other processed food	426	.3	465	.3	510	.3	562	.3	619	.3	826	.3	1367	.3
11 Beverage	426	.3	465	.3	510	.3	562	.3	619	.3	826	.3	1367	.3
12 Tobacco	426	.3	465	.3	510	.3	562	.3	619	.3	826	.3	1367	.3
13 Soft fiber textiles	426	.3	465	.3	510	.3	562	.3	619	.3	826	.3	1367	.3
14 Other textiles	426	.3	465	.3	510	.3	562	.3	619	.3	826	.3	1367	.3
15 Wearing apparel	426	.3	465	.3	510	.3	562	.3	619	.3	826	.3	1367	.3
16 Wood and cork	426	.3	465	.3	510	.3	562	.3	619	.3	826	.3	1367	.3
17 Paper	426	.3	465	.3	510	.3	562	.3	619	.3	826	.3	1367	.3
18 Printing, publishing	426	.3	465	.3	510	.3	562	.3	619	.3	826	.3	1367	.3
19 Leather	426	.3	465	.3	510	.3	562	.3	619	.3	826	.3	1367	.3
20 Rubber products	426	.3	465	.3	510	.3	562	.3	619	.3	826	.3	1367	.3
21 Basic chemicals	426	.3	465	.3	510	.3	562	.3	619	.3	826	.3	1367	.3
22 Synthetic fibers	426	.3	465	.3	510	.3	562	.3	619	.3	826	.3	1367	.3
23 Fertilizers	3973	2.9	3971	2.6	4254	2.5	4871	2.6	5571	2.7	7435	2.7	12304	2.7
24 Soaps and detergents	426	.3	465	.3	510	.3	562	.3	619	.3	826	.3	1367	.3
25 Drugs and medicine	426	.3	465	.3	510	.3	562	.3	619	.3	826	.3	1367	.3
26 Perfumes, cosmetics	426	.3	465	.3	510	.3	562	.3	619	.3	826	.3	1367	.3
27 Other chemical indust.	426	.3	465	.3	510	.3	562	.3	619	.3	826	.3	1367	.3
28 Nonmetallic mineral pr.	1561	1.1	1703	1.1	1872	1.1	2248	1.2	2270	1.1	3029	1.1	5013	1.1
29 Basic metallic indust.	426	.3	465	.3	510	.3	562	.3	619	.3	826	.3	1367	.3
30 Metal products	426	.3	465	.3	510	.3	562	.3	619	.3	826	.3	1367	.3
31 Machinery	426	.3	465	.3	510	.3	562	.3	619	.3	826	.3	1367	.3
32 Electrical machinery	426	.3	465	.3	510	.3	562	.3	619	.3	826	.3	1367	.3
33 Transport equipment	284	.2	310	.2	340	.2	375	.2	419	.3	826	.3	1367	.3
34 Motor vehicles	993	.7	1084	.7	1191	.7	1311	.7	1444	.7	1928	.7	3190	.7
35 Other manufacturing	426	.3	465	.3	510	.3	562	.3	619	.3	826	.3	1367	.3
36 Construction	15752	11.1	15441	10.1	17757	10.3	19859	10.6	22489	10.9	30015	10.9	49672	10.9
37 Electricity	17480	12.6	17034	11.0	19229	11.3	21733	11.6	24552	11.9	32769	11.9	54229	11.9
38 Gases	426	.3	465	.3	510	.3	562	.3	619	.3	826	.3	1367	.3
39 Transport	4541	3.2	4644	3.0	5275	3.1	5808	3.1	6602	3.2	8812	3.2	14582	3.2
40 Communications	15326	10.8	16548	10.8	17757	10.3	20047	10.7	22695	11.0	30291	11.0	50127	11.0
41 Trade	426	.3	465	.3	510	.3	562	.3	619	.3	826	.3	1367	.3
42 Dwellings	426	.3	465	.3	510	.3	562	.3	619	.3	826	.3	1367	.3
43 Hotels and restaurants	426	.3	465	.3	510	.3	562	.3	619	.3	826	.3	1367	.3
44 Credit and insurance	426	.3	465	.3	510	.3	562	.3	619	.3	826	.3	1367	.3
45 Other services	16310	11.5	12380	8.0	14464	8.5	16862	9.0	19807	9.6	26435	9.6	43747	9.6
TOTAL	141005	100.0	154859	100.0	170165	100.0	187353	100.0	206372	100.0	275369	100.0	455702	100.0

Case One

Table D.2.4: Public Investment by Destination (Cont.)

Annual growth rates (percent)

Sector	79/78	80/79	81/80	82/81	M3/78	88/83	93/88	93/82
1 Agriculture	73.2	26.4	25.8	25.6	30.5	10.3	11.1	10.6
2 Livestock	81.9	20.9	20.1	10.1	26.2	10.3	11.1	10.6
3 Forestry	74.6	23.6	10.1	22.4	26.2	10.3	11.1	10.6
4 Fishing	-31.8	9.9	10.1	32.1	3.7	10.3	11.1	10.6
5 Mining	9.1	20.9	10.1	10.1	12.0	10.3	11.1	10.6
6 Quarrying	9.1	20.9	10.1	10.1	12.0	10.3	11.1	10.6
7 Petroleum	25.4	.3	-.8	-2.8	5.0	10.3	11.1	10.6
8 Slaughter of livestock	9.1	9.9	10.1	10.1	9.9	10.3	11.1	10.6
9 Milling	9.1	9.9	10.1	10.1	9.9	10.3	11.1	10.6
10 Other processed food	9.1	9.9	10.1	10.1	9.9	10.3	11.1	10.6
11 Beverages	9.1	9.9	10.1	10.1	9.9	10.3	11.1	10.6
12 Tobacco	9.1	9.9	10.1	10.1	9.9	10.3	11.1	10.6
13 Soft fiber textiles	9.1	9.9	10.1	10.1	9.9	10.3	11.1	10.6
14 Other textiles	9.1	9.9	10.1	10.1	9.9	10.3	11.1	10.6
15 Wearing apparel	9.1	9.9	10.1	10.1	9.9	10.3	11.1	10.6
16 Wood and cork	9.1	9.9	10.1	10.1	9.9	10.3	11.1	10.6
17 Paper	9.1	9.9	10.1	10.1	9.9	10.3	11.1	10.6
18 Printing, publishing	9.1	9.9	10.1	10.1	9.9	10.3	11.1	10.6
19 Leather	9.1	9.9	10.1	10.1	9.9	10.3	11.1	10.6
20 Rubber products	9.1	9.9	10.1	10.1	9.9	10.3	11.1	10.6
21 Basic chemicals	9.1	9.9	10.1	10.1	9.9	10.3	11.1	10.6
22 Synthetic fibers	9.1	9.9	10.1	10.1	9.9	10.3	11.1	10.6
23 Fertilizers	-2.6	9.9	14.5	14.4	9.1	10.3	11.1	10.6
24 Soaps and detergents	9.1	9.9	10.1	10.1	9.9	10.3	11.1	10.6
25 Drugs and medicines	9.1	9.9	10.1	10.1	9.9	10.3	11.1	10.6
26 Perfumes, cosmetics	9.1	9.9	10.1	10.1	9.9	10.3	11.1	10.6
27 Other chemical indust.	9.1	9.9	10.1	10.1	9.9	10.3	11.1	10.6
28 Nonmetallic mineral pr.	9.1	9.9	10.1	10.1	9.9	10.3	11.1	10.6
29 Basic metallic indust.	9.1	9.9	20.1	.6	9.9	10.3	11.1	10.6
30 Metal products	9.1	9.9	10.1	10.1	9.9	10.3	11.1	10.6
31 Machinery	9.1	9.9	10.1	10.1	9.9	10.3	11.1	10.6
32 Electrical machinery	9.1	9.9	10.1	10.1	9.9	10.3	11.1	10.6
33 Transport equipment	9.1	9.9	10.1	65.2	19.1	10.3	11.1	10.6
34 Motor vehicles	9.1	9.9	10.1	10.1	9.9	10.3	11.1	10.6
35 Other manufacturing	9.1	9.9	10.1	10.1	9.9	10.3	11.1	10.6
36 Construction	-.7	12.1	13.3	13.2	9.5	10.3	11.1	10.6
37 Electricity	-4.7	12.9	13.0	13.0	8.4	10.3	11.1	10.6
38 Gases	9.1	9.9	10.1	10.1	9.9	10.3	11.1	10.6
39 Transport	2.3	13.5	10.1	13.7	8.9	10.3	11.1	10.6
40 Communications	1.0	13.2	14.4	13.2	10.3	10.3	11.1	10.6
41 Trade	9.1	9.9	10.1	10.1	9.9	10.3	11.1	10.6
42 Dwellings	9.1	9.9	10.1	10.1	9.9	10.3	11.1	10.6
43 Hotels and restaurants	9.1	9.9	10.1	10.1	9.9	10.3	11.1	10.6
44 Credit and insurance	9.1	9.9	10.1	10.1	9.9	10.3	11.1	10.6
45 Other services	-24.1	16.8	16.6	17.5	6.0	10.3	11.1	10.6
T O T A L	9.1	9.9	10.1	10.1	9.9	10.3	11.1	10.6

Case One

Table D.2.5: Private Investment by Destination

Millions of 1978 pesos

Sector	1978	%	1979	%	1980	%	1981	%	1982	%	1985	%	1990	%
1 Agriculture	25137.	17.0	21968.	13.2	20219.	10.8	21085.	10.0	23420.	9.8	36615.	10.5	71868.	10.8
2 Livestock	3326.	2.2	2713.	1.6	2612.	1.4	2733.	1.3	3003.	1.3	4233.	1.2	7976.	1.2
3 Forestry	721.	.5	814.	.5	1089.	.6	1443.	.7	1803.	.8	3205.	.9	6544.	1.0
4 Fishing	242.	.2	609.	.4	786.	.4	955.	.5	1111.	.5	1934.	.6	3930.	.6
5 Mining	1416.	1.0	1353.	.8	1590.	.8	2010.	1.0	2373.	1.0	3709.	1.1	7258.	1.1
6 Quarrying	173.	.1	704.	.4	1158.	.6	1641.	.8	2108.	.9	3588.	1.0	7219.	1.1
7 Petroleum	22602.	15.3	32599.	19.6	44784.	23.9	55313.	26.2	63636.	26.7	86458.	24.9	160105.	24.1
8 Slaughter of livestock	345.	.2	408.	.2	487.	.3	583.	.3	676.	.3	1024.	.3	1983.	.3
9 Milling	660.	.4	666.	.4	680.	.4	724.	.3	784.	.3	1073.	.3	1999.	.3
10 Other processed food	691.	.5	655.	.4	721.	.4	739.	.3	796.	.3	1079.	.3	2001.	.3
11 Beverages	3794.	2.6	3233.	1.9	2620.	1.4	2136.	1.0	1860.	.8	1560.	.4	2154.	.3
12 Tobacco	170.	.1	287.	.2	391.	.2	512.	.2	623.	.3	1000.	.3	2035.	.3
13 Soft fiber textiles	1532.	1.0	1284.	.8	1110.	.6	1059.	.5	1034.	.4	1186.	.3	1964.	.3
14 Other textiles	-821.	-.1	95.	.1	248.	.1	406.	.2	543.	.2	964.	.3	2048.	.3
15 Wearing apparel	1825.	1.2	1482.	.9	1279.	.7	1180.	.6	1126.	.5	1228.	.4	1975.	.3
16 Wood and cork	151.	.1	271.	.2	388.	.2	507.	.2	619.	.3	999.	.3	2042.	.3
17 Paper	1704.	1.2	1368.	.8	1218.	.6	1126.	.5	1086.	.5	1210.	.3	1981.	.3
18 Printing, publishing	274.	.2	351.	.2	475.	.3	562.	.3	662.	.3	1018.	.3	1976.	.3
19 Leather	164.	.1	289.	.2	403.	.2	516.	.2	627.	.3	1002.	.3	2008.	.3
20 Rubber products	787.	.5	765.	.5	818.	.4	802.	.4	846.	.4	1101.	.3	1962.	.3
21 Basic chemicals	28.	.0	99.	.1	201.	.1	398.	.2	531.	.2	959.	.3	2029.	.3
22 Synthetic fibers	1359.	.9	1150.	.7	1059.	.6	1003.	.5	994.	.4	1169.	.3	2029.	.3
23 Fertilizers	-243.	-.2	1285.	.8	2479.	1.3	3689.	1.7	4818.	2.0	8640.	2.5	17666.	2.7
24 Soaps and detergents	101.	.1	231.	.1	354.	.2	483.	.2	601.	.3	991.	.3	1973.	.3
25 Drugs and medicines	-1218.	-.8	-730.	-.4	-267.	-.1	-18.	-.0	228.	.1	822.	.2	1919.	.3
26 Perfumes, cosmetics	-16.	-.0	154.	.1	313.	.2	446.	.2	574.	.2	978.	.3	1969.	.3
27 Other chemical indust.	166.	.1	284.	.2	402.	.2	516.	.2	626.	.3	1002.	.3	1976.	.3
28 Nonmetallic mineral pr.	2327.	1.6	1914.	1.1	1641.	.9	1427.	.7	1317.	.6	1315.	.4	2076.	.3
29 Basic metallic indust.	7252.	4.9	6213.	3.7	5447.	2.9	4783.	2.3	4564.	1.9	4707.	1.4	7574.	1.1
30 Metal products	906.	.6	875.	.5	849.	.5	842.	.4	875.	.4	1114.	.3	2012.	.3
31 Machinery	1278.	.9	1173.	.7	1090.	.6	1012.	.5	1005.	.4	1173.	.3	2031.	.3
32 Electrical machinery	1482.	1.0	1245.	.7	1153.	.6	1064.	.5	1041.	.4	1190.	.3	2036.	.3
33 Transport equipment	966.	.7	889.	.5	878.	.5	758.	.4	737.	.3	1046.	.3	1990.	.3
34 Motor vehicles	2718.	1.8	2742.	1.6	2670.	1.4	2390.	1.1	2379.	1.0	2753.	.8	4743.	.7
35 Other manufacturing	570.	.4	575.	.3	602.	.3	672.	.3	743.	.3	1055.	.3	1993.	.3
36 Construction	5353.	3.6	10363.	6.2	14316.	7.6	17998.	8.5	21932.	9.2	36011.	10.4	71678.	10.8
37 Electricity	10806.	7.3	14778.	8.9	17964.	9.6	21581.	10.2	25387.	10.6	39973.	11.5	78463.	11.8
38 Cinema	254.	.2	340.	.2	428.	.2	542.	.3	645.	.3	1010.	.3	1979.	.3
39 Transport	24093.	16.3	20005.	12.0	17160.	9.2	14851.	7.0	13687.	5.7	13856.	4.0	22086.	3.3
40 Communications	7044.	4.8	10967.	6.6	14433.	7.7	18216.	8.6	22137.	9.3	36344.	10.5	72336.	10.9
41 Trade	4652.	3.1	3918.	2.4	3240.	1.7	2552.	1.2	2181.	.9	1706.	.5	2200.	.3
42 Dwellings	3810.	2.6	3217.	1.9	2740.	1.5	2178.	1.0	1897.	.8	1578.	.5	2159.	.3
43 Hotels and restaurants	1692.	1.1	1397.	.8	1226.	.7	1134.	.5	1092.	.5	1213.	.3	2043.	.3
44 Credit and insurance	795.	.5	769.	.5	789.	.4	793.	.4	837.	.4	1097.	.3	2007.	.3
45 Other services	6282.	4.2	10845.	6.5	13269.	7.1	16092.	7.6	19138.	8.0	31622.	9.1	63099.	9.5
T O T A L	148091.	100.0	166624.	100.0	187511.	100.0	211412.	100.0	238699.	100.0	347511.	100.0	663041.	100.0

254

Case One

Table D.2.5: Private Investment by Destination (Cont.)

Annual growth rates (percent)

Sector	79/78	80/79	81/80	82/81	83/78	88/83	93/88	93/82
1 Agriculture	-12.6	-8.0	4.3	11.1	1.7	15.1	14.2	14.8
2 Livestock	-18.4	-3.7	4.6	9.8	.1	13.0	13.8	13.2
3 Forestry	12.8	33.8	32.5	25.0	25.5	17.2	14.4	16.6
4 Fishing	151.5	29.1	21.5	16.3	41.4	17.0	14.4	16.3
5 Mining	-4.5	17.5	26.4	18.1	14.4	14.9	14.1	14.7
6 Quarrying	306.0	64.4	41.7	28.4	71.6	16.4	14.3	16.0
7 Petroleum	44.2	37.4	23.5	15.0	25.4	12.1	13.7	12.7
8 Slaughter of livestock	18.5	19.4	19.5	16.0	17.7	12.4	14.1	14.3
9 Milling	.9	2.1	6.4	8.3	5.5	14.3	13.8	12.8
10 Other processed food	-5.2	10.1	2.5	7.7	4.8	12.2	13.7	12.6
11 Beverages	-14.8	-19.0	-18.5	-12.9	-15.0	1.2	11.2	4.5
12 Tobacco	69.2	35.9	31.1	21.6	34.2	15.4	14.2	15.1
13 Soft fiber textiles	-16.2	-13.6	-4.6	-2.3	-7.3	8.8	13.1	10.1
14 Other textiles	*****	161.2	63.9	33.6	*****	17.1	14.4	16.6
15 Wearing apparel	-18.2	-14.3	-7.7	-4.6	-9.3	7.7	12.9	10.5
16 Wood and cork	-79.1	43.3	30.7	22.2	37.3	15.5	14.2	15.2
17 Paper	-19.7	-11.0	-7.5	-3.6	-8.5	8.1	13.0	9.6
18 Printing, publishing	28.3	35.3	18.4	17.7	23.0	14.6	14.4	14.5
19 Leather	75.4	39.7	28.2	21.4	35.2	15.3	14.2	15.1
20 Rubber products	-2.8	7.0	-2.0	5.5	3.0	11.4	13.6	12.0
21 Basic chemicals	250.7	102.6	98.1	33.6	88.3	17.4	14.5	16.8
22 Synthetic fibers	-15.4	-7.9	-5.3	-.9	-5.5	9.3	13.2	10.5
23 Fertilizers	*****	92.8	48.8	30.6	*****	17.3	14.4	16.7
24 Soaps and detergents	128.6	53.2	36.5	24.4	48.2	15.8	14.3	15.5
25 Drugs and medicines	-40.1	-63.4	-93.4	*****	*****	26.5	15.3	26.0
26 Perfumes, cosmetics	*****	103.1	42.3	28.8	*****	16.4	14.3	16.0
27 Other chemical indust.	70.3	41.6	28.1	21.4	34.8	15.3	14.2	15.1
28 Nonmetallic mineral pr.	-17.8	-14.3	-13.0	-7.8	-11.4	5.6	12.4	7.7
29 Basic metallic indust.	-14.3	-12.3	-12.2	-4.6	-9.3	6.3	12.6	8.3
30 Metal products	-3.4	-3.0	-.8	3.9	.6	11.0	13.5	11.7
31 Machinery	-8.2	-7.1	-7.1	-.7	-4.2	9.2	13.2	10.0
32 Electrical machinery	-16.0	-7.3	-7.8	-2.1	-6.5	8.7	13.1	10.0
33 Transport equipment	-7.9	-1.3	-13.6	-2.8	-3.3	13.4	13.9	13.4
34 Motor vehicles	.9	-3.6	-10.5	-.5	-2.2	9.0	13.1	10.2
35 Other manufacturing	.9	4.6	11.6	10.6	7.8	13.1	13.9	13.3
36 Construction	93.6	38.1	25.7	21.9	37.5	15.8	14.3	15.5
37 Electricity	36.8	21.6	20.1	17.6	22.5	15.1	14.2	14.9
38 Cinema	33.7	26.0	26.5	19.0	24.4	15.0	14.1	14.8
39 Transport	-17.0	-14.2	-13.5	-7.8	-11.3	6.0	12.5	8.0
40 Communications	55.7	31.6	26.2	21.5	30.4	15.8	14.3	15.5
41 Trade	-15.8	-17.3	-21.2	-14.5	-16.2	1.7	10.5	3.1
42 Dwellings	-15.6	-14.9	-20.5	-12.9	-14.8	1.0	11.1	4.4
43 Hotels and restaurants	-17.4	-12.3	-7.5	-3.7	-8.3	8.1	13.0	9.5
44 Credit and insurance	-3.3	2.7	.4	5.6	2.6	11.6	13.6	12.1
45 Other services	72.7	22.3	21.3	18.9	29.6	16.0	14.3	15.6
TOTAL	12.5	12.5	12.8	12.9	12.8	13.6	13.9	13.7

Case One

Table D.2.6: Investment by Origin

Sector	Millions of 1978 pesos								Annual growth rates (percent)							
	1978	1979	1980	1981	1982	1983	1985	1990	79/78	80/78	81/80	82/81	83/78	88/83	93/88	93/82
1 Agriculture	11556.	12111.	12663.	13711.	14793.	24953.	4424.	5.1	3.7	13.2	17.5	10.4	12.9	12.9	12.9
2 Livestock	1520.	1551.	1633.	1711.	1994.	2763.	4894.	2.0	5.2	11.1	10.0	7.8	11.8	12.7	12.1
3 Forestry	521.	747.	954.	1130.	1407.	2160.	4041.	43.5	27.7	19.4	23.6	25.8	14.0	13.0	13.8
4 Fishing	501.	503.	596.	685.	855.	1305.	2426.	.4	18.3	15.6	24.1	14.7	13.8	13.0	13.7
5 Mining	167.	171.	204.	240.	308.	724.	2.3	19.3	17.6	14.0	13.2	12.8	12.9	12.9	12.9
6 Quarrying	124.	176.	234.	341.	616.	954.	41.5	34.5	22.2	18.2	26.1	13.6	13.0	13.5	
7 Petroleum	137.	168.	197.	213.	224.	305.	539.	32.1	14.7	10.5	6.5	14.4	11.4	12.6	11.8
8 Slaughter of livestock	191.	215.	245.	282.	319.	456.	824.	13.3	14.3	14.7	13.1	13.7	12.5	12.7	12.7
9 Milling	162.	560.	585.	637.	694.	940.	1666.	4.1	5.3	8.0	9.1	7.3	11.5	12.7	11.9
10 Other processed food	162.	162.	169.	160.	205.	274.	488.	.7	10.0	5.6	8.8	6.8	11.4	12.7	11.8
11 Beverages	207.	207.	175.	151.	139.	134.	197.	-12.4	-15.3	-13.8	-8.1	-11.0	4.2	11.1	6.4
12 Tobacco	60.	75.	80.	107.	124.	143.	334.	-26.3	19.8	19.2	15.6	19.0	13.1	12.3	13.1
13 Soft fiber textiles	113.	107.	90.	56.	71.	109.	203.	-10.7	-7.3		2.0	-2.4	9.4	13.0	10.3
14 Other textiles	21.	34.	46.	66.	71.	125.	208.	62.2	35.6	27.7	20.0	31.5	13.9	13.1	13.8
15 Wearing apparel	137.	119.	100.	106.	145.	175.	208.	-13.1	-8.6	-2.6		-4.3	8.7	12.9	9.8
16 Wood and cork	161.	205.	251.	298.	345.	503.	932.	27.5	22.2	19.0	15.8	19.7	13.1	13.0	13.2
17 Paper	290.	257.	236.	230.	245.	245.	477.	-14.0	-5.7	-2.3		-3.6	9.0	12.2	10.0
18 Printing, publishing	64.	75.	91.	173.	118.	170.	308.	16.6	20.8	14.1	13.9	15.7	12.7	12.7	12.8
19 Leather	36.	46.	58.	64.	76.	112.	204.	27.6	21.3	18.1	15.5	19.3	13.0	13.0	13.1
20 Rubber products	138.	140.	151.	155.	167.	220.	385.	1.4	8.1	2.6	7.4	5.6	11.0	12.6	11.5
21 Basic chemicals	34.	42.	53.	71.	85.	132.	246.	24.2	26.2	34.9	19.8	24.3	14.1	13.1	13.9
22 Synthetic fibers	123.	111.	108.	168.	111.	138.	234.	-9.6	-2.8	-.3	3.1	-2.7	9.7	12.4	10.5
23 Fertilizers	435.	588.	768.	976.	1184.	1833.	3417.	38.2	30.6	27.1	21.4	26.7	14.0	13.1	13.9
24 Soaps and detergents	-172.	229.	393.	342.	399.	594.	1092.	32.1	24.3	20.9	16.7	21.7	13.3	13.3	13.3
25 Drugs and medicines	-101.	-34.	31.	69.	108.	209.	417.	-66.5		123.9	55.6		17.7	13.5	17.1
26 Perfumes, cosmetics	134.	202.	269.	330.	390.	590.	1091.	51.2	33.1	22.3	18.4	27.6	13.6	13.0	13.5
27 Other chemical indust.	288.	365.	445.	525.	606.	890.	1628.	26.5	21.9	18.1	15.5	19.2	13.0	12.9	13.1
28 Nonmetallic mineral pr.	231.	260.	191.	167.	163.	180.	289.	-13.6	-9.6	-2.7	-6.7	-6.1	7.4	11.9	8.8
29 Basic metallic indust.	2307.	2153.	1951.	1912.	1859.	2104.	3424.	-10.2	-7.5	-3.9	-2.8	-4.6	7.8	12.0	9.1
30 Metal products	683.	698.	720.	766.	905.	1733.	.6	1.5	3.3	6.4	3.9	10.7	12.5	11.3	
31 Machinery	545111.	637761.	712729.	806419.	899011.	1263351.	2272800.	12.6	12.5	12.1	11.8	12.2	12.8	12.8	12.5
32 Electrical machinery	640564.	721394.	810788.	903031.	1014411.	1423371.	2560015.	12.6	12.4	12.1	11.7	12.1	12.8	12.9	12.4
33 Transport equipment	16142.	17904.	20035.	22777.	25945.	37027.	67182.	10.9	12.2	13.4	13.9	12.6	12.8	12.8	12.7
34 Motor vehicles	1335.	1366.	1378.	1321.	1365.	1671.	2832.	3.1	.9	3.3	3.3	1.6	9.5	12.3	10.4
35 Other manufacturing	30.	31.	33.	37.	41.	56.	101.	4.4	7.0	10.9	10.4	8.7	11.9	12.7	12.2
36 Construction	120617.	133973.	148946.	165021.	182608.	263473.	4536883.	11.1	11.1	10.9	10.7	11.0	12.0	12.7	12.3
37 Electricity	2123.	2354.	2752.	3205.	3696.	5383.	9819.	10.9	16.9	16.5	15.3	14.7	12.9	12.7	13.0
38 Clothes	120.	142.	166.	195.	224.	325.	592.	18.3	16.7	17.6	14.5	16.1	12.9	12.9	13.0
39 Transport	850.	740.	673.	620.	609.	640.	1100.	-13.9	-9.0	-7.9	-1.8	-6.5	7.6	11.9	8.9
40 Communications	515.	608.	735.	880.	1031.	1533.	2817.	18.3	20.8	19.7	17.2	18.2	13.3	12.9	13.3
41 Trade	2296.	1919.	1643.	1364.	1226.	1100.	1562.	-13.7	-14.4	-17.0	-10.1	-12.5	2.6	10.7	5.3
42 Dwellings	185.	162.	143.	121.	111.	106.	155.	-13.1	-11.7	-15.7	-8.7	-10.8	4.0	11.1	6.3
43 Hotels and restaurants	407.	352.	328.	320.	323.	385.	445.	-12.1	-6.7	-2.3	.9	-3.4	9.0	12.2	9.9
44 Credit and insurance	331.	324.	342.	356.	383.	506.	887.	-2.0	5.4	4.2	7.5	5.3	11.0	11.5	11.5
45 Other services	3475.	3532.	4215.	5009.	5920.	8825.	16741.	2.8	19.4	18.8	18.2	14.7	13.4	13.0	13.3
T O T A L	288003.	321480.	357673.	398782.	445018.	622876.	1118736.	10.9	11.3	11.5	11.6	11.4	12.2	12.8	12.4

Case One

Table D.2.7: Imports, Exports, Balance of Trade, External Debt

Millions of 1978 pesos

S E C T O R		1974	1979	1980	1981	1983	1985	2000
1 Agriculture	Imports	37092	38789	40492	43914	47775	57693	76072
	Exports	12707	13342	16009	14710	15445	17490	29822
	Balance	-24385	-25447	-24477	-29194	-32330	-39541	-53752
2 Livestock	Imports	418	434	457	489	523	668	971
	Exports	52285	52645	51691	50378	49895	42980	27096
	Balance	52867	52211	51234	49889	48373	42332	26125
3 Forestry	Imports	594	656	731	815	908	1252	2265
	Exports	4995	5011	5235	5609	6075	9572	16303
	Balance	4402	4353	4504	4794	5116	7260	14098
4 Fishing	Imports	1797	1887	13717	12681	12025	7490	35
	Exports	14021	13546	13717	12681	12025	7490	9113
	Balance	-12224	-11659	-11730	-10600	-9840	-5370	9077
5 Mining	Imports	3393	3781	12167	4563	4905	6471	10247
	Exports	12282	12234	12167	12261	12436	13467	16873
	Balance	8889	8457	8425	7698	7451	6996	6626
6 Quarrying	Imports	3036	3269	3607	3735	3984	4861	7082
	Exports	4842	4844	5156	5834	6777	11090	23941
	Balance	1806	1576	1658	2099	2793	6229	16859
7 Petroleum	Imports	34415	23799	8676	9347	10075	12726	19471
	Exports	0	0	1087	20451	41773	112420	288345
	Balance	-34415	-23799	-7651	11704	31697	99700	268874
8 Slaughter of livestock	Imports	190212	199603	200548	220298	231833	274102	383273
	Exports	0	0	0	0	0	0	0
	Balance	-190212	-199603	-200548	-220298	-231833	-274102	-383273
9 Milling	Imports	1806	138	28	30	31	35	45
	Exports	1806	-138	1535	3147	4836	10629	25702
	Balance	0	-139	1507	3117	4805	10594	25657
10 Other processed food	Imports	3597	2802	6324	10693	14350	30452	72434
	Exports	1971	1434	1506	1581	1660	1922	2453
	Balance	-1626	-1368	-4818	-9112	-12690	-28530	-69982
11 Beverages	Imports	164	154	164	171	178	196	7138
	Exports	10418	12232	13354	13674	13301	9117	390
	Balance	10272	12078	13190	13604	13123	8921	-6748
12 Tobacco	Imports	56	67	69	78	89	131	248
	Exports	1928	2750	4031	5618	7611	15926	39932
	Balance	1872	2728	3962	5540	7523	15796	39685
13 Soft fiber textiles	Imports	1711	1782	1375	1944	2063	2426	3377
	Exports	16956	16979	16712	16172	15448	12197	2990
	Balance	15224	15196	14437	14207	13385	9771	-387
14 Other textiles	Imports	369	353	410	479	561	892	1811
	Exports	3327	4680	6431	10011	13964	30717	78708
	Balance	3019	4327	6022	9532	13403	29825	76897
15 Wearing apparel	Imports	8017	8755	65010	107332	119257	165021	292421
	Exports	765	803	643	846	930	1077	1374
	Balance	-80282	-87882	-96375	-106446	-118327	-164845	-291047
16 Wood and cork	Imports	18552	15902	19105	19001	18667	16763	10026
	Exports	0	0	0	0	0	0	0
	Balance	-18657	-18092	-19105	-19001	-18667	-16763	-10026
17 Paper	Imports	11453	11896	13797	14056	15633	22277	40818
	Exports	-11453	-11895	-13707	-14056	-15633	-22277	-40818
	Balance							

Case One

Table D.2.7: Imports, Exports, Balance of Trade, External Debt (Cont.)

Millions of 1978 pesos

SECTOR		1978	1979	1980	1981	1982	1985	1990
18 Printing, publishing	Imports	18935.	20761.	22687.	24682.	26810.	34374.	53327.
	Exports	0.	0.	0.	0.	0.	0.	0.
	Balance	-18935.	-20761.	-22687.	-24682.	-26810.	-34374.	-53327.
19 Leather	Imports	1030.	1204.	1425.	1693.	2009.	3264.	6722.
	Exports	6918.	8975.	11719.	15126.	19214.	35752.	82186.
	Balance	5888.	7772.	10294.	13432.	17205.	32488.	75464.
20 Rubber products	Imports	5806.	5948.	6209.	6527.	6979.	8933.	14227.
	Exports	0.	0.	0.	0.	0.	0.	0.
	Balance	-5806.	-5948.	-6209.	-6527.	-6979.	-8933.	-14227.
21 Basic chemicals	Imports	12340.	13241.	14408.	15857.	18421.	30475.	62574.
	Exports	4118.	3086.	1907.	577.	0.	0.	0.
	Balance	-8223.	-10154.	-12501.	-15280.	-18421.	-30475.	-62574.
22 Synthetic fibers	Imports	1341.	1464.	1591.	1731.	1879.	4755.	14873.
	Exports	1351.	1516.	1390.	1042.	476.	0.	0.
	Balance	10.	52.	-201.	-689.	-1402.	-4755.	-14873.
23 Fertilizers	Imports	4507.	3329.	1497.	306.	410.	857.	2138.
	Exports	0.	0.	0.	1356.	4856.	20462.	66499.
	Balance	-4507.	-3329.	-1497.	1050.	4446.	19606.	64362.
24 Soaps and detergents	Imports	11820.	10515.	8467.	5701.	2164.	75.	165.
	Exports	0.	0.	0.	0.	0.	12880.	56277.
	Balance	-11820.	-10515.	-8467.	-5701.	-2164.	12806.	56112.
25 Drugs and medicines	Imports	9592.	11898.	13829.	15406.	16866.	20873.	28473.
	Exports	315.	330.	347.	364.	382.	443.	565.
	Balance	-9277.	-11567.	-13482.	-15041.	-16484.	-20430.	-27908.
26 Perfumes, cosmetics	Imports	24677.	24886.	24226.	22759.	20620.	10486.	165.
	Exports	0.	0.	0.	0.	0.	0.	20804.
	Balance	-24677.	-24886.	-24226.	-22759.	-20620.	-10486.	20640.
27 Other chemical indust.	Imports	3239.	2857.	2772.	3221.	3747.	5814.	11476.
	Exports	0.	0.	582.	1960.	3663.	10644.	30653.
	Balance	-3239.	-2857.	-2190.	-1260.	-84.	4831.	19178.
28 Nonmetallic mineral pr.	Imports	2376.	3531.	10143.	18935.	29896.	76243.	207992.
	Exports	3426.	0.	0.	0.	0.	0.	0.
	Balance	1049.	-3531.	-10143.	-18935.	-29896.	-76243.	-207992.
29 Basic metallic indust.	Imports	8751.	9877.	11035.	12308.	13683.	26710.	98549.
	Exports	15455.	17041.	16932.	15203.	12113.	2197.	2804.
	Balance	6704.	7164.	5897.	2896.	-1571.	-24513.	-95745.
30 Metal products	Imports	9568.	10573.	11691.	12908.	14263.	25613.	71593.
	Exports	10786.	10225.	9111.	7299.	4848.	0.	0.
	Balance	1218.	-348.	-2580.	-5609.	-9415.	-25613.	-71593.
31 Machinery	Imports	46746.	53449.	61355.	70334.	80434.	120181.	231409.
	Exports	0.	0.	0.	0.	0.	0.	0.
	Balance	-46746.	-53449.	-61355.	-70334.	-80434.	-120181.	-231409.
32 Electrical machinery	Imports	76981.	85634.	95719.	107075.	119756.	169636.	308610.
	Exports	0.	0.	0.	0.	0.	0.	0.
	Balance	-76981.	-85634.	-95719.	-107075.	-119756.	-169636.	-308610.
33 Transport equipment	Imports	13270.	14141.	15644.	17772.	20737.	30407.	56082.
	Exports	0.	0.	0.	0.	0.	0.	0.
	Balance	-13270.	-14141.	-15644.	-17772.	-20737.	-30407.	-56082.
34 Motor vehicles	Imports	44563.	46627.	49063.	52155.	56405.	74664.	127395.
	Exports	0.	0.	0.	0.	0.	0.	0.
	Balance	-44563.	-46627.	-49063.	-52155.	-56405.	-74664.	-127395.

Case One

Table D.2.7: Imports, Exports, Balance of Trade, External Debt (Cont.)

Millions of 1978 pesos

SECTOR	1978	1979	1980	1981	1982	1985	1990
35 Other manufacturing							
Imports	23440.	24115.	24959.	25967.	27046.	31055.	41233.
Exports	0.	0.	0.	0.	0.	0.	0.
Balance	-23440.	-24115.	-24959.	-25967.	-27046.	-31055.	-41233.
TOTAL							
Imports	876367.	915774.	967375.	1044990.	1136438.	1527835.	2722436.
Exports	169267.	170062.	178243.	205442.	236838.	372852.	815829.
Balance	-19211.	-20531.	-21979.	-23576.	-25335.	-31886.	-49182.
External debt [a]	675735.811	763852.348	862229.334	972042.354	1094596.246	1554279.352	2752302.669

a) 10^9 1978 pesos; peso-dollar exchange rate (1978) = 22.72

Case One

Table D.2.8: Government Accounts

Millions of 1978 pesos

	1978 Value	%	1979 Value	%	1980 Value	%	1981 Value	%	1982 Value	%	1985 Value	%	1990 Value	%
Incomes														
Direct Taxes	108896.	35.4	115906.	34.5	123488.	33.4	131947.	32.3	141397.	31.4	177391.	29.5	273696.	27.3
Indirect Taxes plus Exploitation Surplus	189394.	61.6	210443.	62.6	236042.	63.8	264882.	64.9	296627.	66.0	410780.	68.2	707072.	70.7
External Financing	9407.	3.1	9858.	2.9	10540.	2.8	11105.	2.7	11174.	2.6	14208.	2.3	20040.	2.0
TOTAL	307698.	100.0	336207.	100.0	370070.	100.0	407934.	100.0	449698.	100.0	602280.	100.0	1000808.	100.0
Expenditures														
Consumption of Goods and Services	29174.	9.5	31918.	9.5	35163.	9.5	38811.	9.5	42840.	9.5	57525.	9.6	95922.	9.6
Wages and Salaries	136617.	44.4	149468.	44.5	164665.	44.5	181748.	44.5	200615.	44.6	269383.	44.7	449192.	44.9
Investments	141905.	46.1	154859.	46.1	170165.	46.0	187353.	46.0	206322.	45.9	275369.	45.7	455702.	45.5
TOTAL	307696.	100.0	336245.	100.0	369992.	100.0	407912.	100.0	449777.	100.0	602277.	100.0	1000816.	100.0
Ratio Tax Revenues /GNP (percent)	16.4		16.8		17.4		17.9		18.4		19.8		21.6	
Share of Public Investment in Total Investment (percent)	48.9		48.2		47.6		47.0		46.4		44.2		40.7	

Case One

Table D.2.8: Government Accounts (Cont.)

Annual growth rates (percent)

	79/75	75/76	91/86	83/91	93/78	88/83	93/88	93/82
Incomes								
Direct Taxes	6.4	6.5	6.5	7.2	6.9	8.5	9.9	9.0
Indirect Taxes plus Exploitation Surpluses	11.1	12.2	12.2	12.0	11.8	11.4	11.7	11.4
External Financing	4.0	4.0	5.4	5.1	5.8	6.9	8.3	7.5
T O T A L	6.2	10.1	10.2	10.2	10.0	10.4	11.2	10.7
Expenditures								
Consumption of Goods and Services	9.4	10.2	10.4	10.4	10.1	10.5	11.2	10.8
Wages and Salaries	9.4	10.2	10.4	10.4	10.1	10.5	11.2	10.8
Investments	9.1	9.9	10.1	10.1	9.9	10.3	11.1	10.6
T O T A L	9.3	10.0	10.2	10.3	10.0	10.4	11.1	10.7

Case One

Table D.2.9: Sectoral Employment

No. of employed persons

Sector	1978	%	1979	%	1980	%	1981	%	1982	%	1985	%	1990	%
1 Agriculture	4326056.	35.2	4966052.	34.7	5111513.	34.2	5259752.	33.6	5431518.	33.1	6151767.	31.6	8145389.	29.9
2 Livestock	235243.	1.7	239379.	1.7	243559.	1.6	247972.	1.6	252991.	1.5	272042.	1.4	324320.	1.2
3 Forestry	97255.	.7	102975.	.7	111649.	.7	122838.	.8	136101.	.8	192530.	1.0	342112.	1.3
4 Fishing	20958.	.2	25005.	.2	28865.	.2	33326.	.2	38341.	.2	59139.	.3	111665.	.4
5 Mining	16785.	.1	16026.	.1	15297.	.1	14673.	.	14143.	.1	12959.	.1	12043.	.
6 Quarrying	74827.	.5	76306.	.5	79586.	.5	84709.	.5	91020.	.6	115005.	.6	167845.	.6
7 Petroleum	111783.	.8	130176.	.9	153637.	1.0	178331.	1.1	203085.	1.2	274035.	1.4	404689.	1.5
8 Slaughter of livestock	258979.	1.9	283369.	2.0	310977.	2.1	342513.	2.2	378652.	2.3	517234.	2.7	889318.	3.3
9 Milling	178691.	1.3	188949.	1.3	199285.	1.3	209864.	1.3	221081.	1.3	260571.	1.3	358333.	1.3
10 Other processed food	149889.	1.1	146937.	1.0	143950.	1.0	141279.	.9	138761.	.8	132886.	.7	130122.	.5
11 Beverages	98271.	.7	100755.	.7	101979.	.7	102024.	.7	101227.	.6	96899.	.5	90110.	.3
12 Tobacco	10764.	.1	11454.	.1	12354.	.1	13424.	.1	14681.	.1	19340.	.1	30247.	.1
13 Soft fiber textiles	137364.	1.0	131797.	.9	125793.	.8	119662.	.8	113734.	.7	97794.	.5	78762.	.3
14 Other textiles	18776.	.1	24180.	.2	32500.	.2	44541.	.3	59144.	.4	118256.	.6	273858.	1.0
15 Wearing apparel	354262.	2.6	346532.	2.4	336477.	2.3	325290.	2.1	313889.	1.9	281544.	1.4	242215.	.9
16 Wood and cork	247510.	1.8	279258.	1.8	319233.	2.1	366792.	2.3	421509.	2.6	622201.	3.2	1088730.	4.0
17 Paper	65295.	.5	69384.	.5	72706.	.5	75715.	.5	78559.	.5	87280.	.4	107454.	.4
18 Printing, publishing	81571.	.6	79944.	.6	78732.	.5	78082.	.5	77766.	.5	78692.	.4	85839.	.3
19 Leather	41081.	.3	46385.	.3	53052.	.4	60878.	.4	69750.	.4	101724.	.5	174049.	.6
20 Rubber products	25411.	.2	25466.	.2	25333.	.2	25174.	.2	24889.	.2	24003.	.1	23245.	.1
21 Basic chemicals	34528.	.3	32769.	.2	31222.	.2	29900.	.2	28872.	.2	26817.	.1	25814.	.1
22 Synthetic fibers	25241.	.2	26348.	.2	27181.	.2	27888.	.2	28516.	.2	30400.	.2	35087.	.1
23 Fertilizers	9056.	.1	12612.	.1	17487.	.1	23790.	.2	31727.	.2	64901.	.3	155829.	.6
24 Soaps and detergents	8357.	.1	9058.	.1	9479.	.1	11025.	.1	12148.	.1	15420.	.1	19929.	.1
25 Drugs and medicines	45717.	.3	42157.	.3	40216.	.3	39732.	.3	40038.	.2	44821.	.2	62287.	.2
26 Perfumes, cosmetics	13239.	.1	14742.	.1	17117.	.1	20187.	.1	23721.	.1	36255.	.2	62043.	.2
27 Other chemical indust.	14121.	.1	15674.	.1	17623.	.1	19943.	.1	22590.	.1	32238.	.2	54471.	.2
28 Nonmetallic mineral pr.	191645.	1.4	189126.	1.3	184785.	1.2	179443.	1.1	173498.	1.1	155577.	.8	132539.	.5
29 Basic metal indust.	114757.	.8	122786.	.9	128856.	.9	133532.	.9	137325.	.8	145969.	.8	163733.	.6
30 Metal products	215070.	1.6	225199.	1.6	234937.	1.6	244412.	1.6	253874.	1.5	285778.	1.5	364330.	1.3
31 Machinery	113218.	.8	121161.	.8	128423.	.9	135195.	.9	141556.	.9	161478.	.8	207531.	.8
32 Electrical machinery	225256.	1.6	240634.	1.7	253656.	1.7	265839.	1.7	277283.	1.7	312842.	1.6	395205.	1.4
33 Transport equipment	224675.	1.6	239294.	1.7	251991.	1.7	264020.	1.7	273770.	1.7	314260.	1.6	415957.	1.5
34 Motor vehicles	133621.	.8	120657.	.8	127329.	.9	131415.	.9	138415.	.8	152637.	.8	183396.	.7
35 Other manufacturing	298911.	2.2	347464.	2.4	400914.	2.7	460758.	2.9	529575.	3.2	803723.	4.1	1635472.	6.0
36 Construction	869169.	6.3	1002304.	7.0	1163100.	7.8	1355667.	8.7	1578337.	9.6	2425062.	12.5	4491155.	16.4
37 Electricity	86410.	.6	95493.	.7	104990.	.7	115711.	.7	127734.	.8	170978.	.9	267816.	1.0
38 Cinema	134140.	1.0	140894.	1.0	148801.	1.0	157970.	1.0	168693.	1.0	210762.	1.1	327410.	1.2
39 Transport	630797.	4.6	656240.	4.6	675803.	4.5	691882.	4.4	705150.	4.3	741493.	3.8	825091.	3.0
40 Communications	60170.	.4	67488.	.5	75313.	.5	84015.	.5	93544.	.6	124364.	.6	173361.	.6
41 Trade	1543361.	11.3	1582031.	11.1	1614202.	10.8	1640510.	10.5	1660992.	10.1	1709033.	8.8	1793543.	6.6
42 Dwellings	7162.	.1	7202.	.1	7217.	.	7268.	.	7294.	.	7362.	.	7492.	.
43 Hotels and restaurants	380695.	2.8	383225.	2.7	383651.	2.6	382945.	2.4	381702.	2.3	378041.	1.9	383824.	1.4
44 Credit and insurance	202849.	1.5	215085.	1.5	227591.	1.5	240855.	1.5	254785.	1.6	304276.	1.6	430895.	1.6
45 Other services	1083268.	7.9	1095515.	7.7	1104887.	7.4	1122714.	7.2	1149248.	7.0	1274559.	6.6	1598900.	5.9
TOTAL	13696233.	100.0	14295492.	100.0	14934169.	100.0	15635452.	100.0	16421232.	100.0	19444948.	100.0	27287455.	100.0

Case One

Table D.2.9: Sectoral Employment (Cont.)

Annual growth rates (percent)

Sector	79/78	80/79	81/80	82/81	83/78	88/83	93/88	93/82
1 Agriculture	2.9	2.9	2.9	3.3	3.2	5.0	6.8	5.7
2 Livestock	1.8	1.7	1.8	2.0	1.9	3.0	4.6	3.6
3 Forestry	5.9	8.4	10.0	10.8	9.4	12.3	11.8	12.1
4 Fishing	19.3	15.4	15.5	15.0	16.2	14.5	12.4	13.7
5 Mining	-4.5	-4.5	-4.1	-3.6	-4.0	-2.0	-.4	-1.5
6 Quarrying	-2.0	4.3	6.4	7.5	5.6	8.1	7.5	7.8
7 Petroleum	16.5	12.0	16.1	13.9	15.2	9.0	7.4	8.5
8 Slaughter of livestock	9.4	9.7	10.1	10.6	10.1	11.2	11.7	11.4
9 Milling	5.7	5.5	5.3	5.3	5.5	6.1	7.4	6.6
10 Other processed food	-2.0	-2.0	-1.9	-1.8	-1.9	-1.0	.5	-.3
11 Beverages	2.5	1.2	1.2	-.8	.3	-1.6	-.9	-1.2
12 Tobacco	6.4	7.9	8.7	9.4	8.4	9.5	9.1	9.4
13 Soft fiber textiles	-4.1	-4.6	-4.9	-5.0	-4.7	-4.6	-3.4	-4.1
14 Other textiles	28.8	36.1	35.4	32.8	32.4	21.5	15.5	19.4
15 Wearing apparel	-2.2	-2.9	-3.3	-3.5	-3.1	-3.3	-2.2	-2.8
16 Wood and cork	12.8	14.3	14.9	14.9	14.3	12.8	10.9	12.1
17 Paper	6.3	4.8	4.1	3.8	4.5	3.8	5.2	4.4
18 Printing, publishing	-2.0	-1.5	-.8	-.4	-.9	1.1	2.7	1.7
19 Leather	12.9	14.4	14.8	14.6	14.1	12.3	10.4	11.6
20 Rubber products	-.2	-.5	-.6	-1.1	-.7	-1.0	-.0	-.6
21 Basic chemicals	-5.1	-4.7	-4.2	-3.4	-4.1	-1.6	.4	-.8
22 Synthetic fibers	4.4	3.2	2.6	2.3	2.9	2.4	3.8	3.0
23 Fertilizers	39.3	38.7	36.0	33.4	35.4	22.4	16.3	20.2
24 Soaps and detergents	8.4	10.2	10.5	10.2	9.7	6.6	3.9	5.6
25 Drugs and medicines	-7.8	-4.6	-1.2	-.8	-2.1	5.6	7.8	6.3
26 Perfumes, cosmetics	11.4	16.1	17.9	17.5	15.8	13.0	9.7	11.2
27 Other chemical indust.	11.0	12.4	13.2	13.3	12.6	11.8	10.3	11.0
28 Nonmetallic mineral pr.	-1.3	-2.3	-2.9	-3.3	-2.7	-3.5	-2.4	-3.0
29 Basic metallic indust.	7.0	4.9	3.6	2.8	4.1	2.0	3.1	2.5
30 Metal products	4.7	4.3	4.0	3.9	4.2	4.4	5.9	5.1
31 Machinery	7.0	6.0	5.3	4.7	5.5	4.7	6.0	5.3
32 Electrical machinery	6.8	5.4	4.8	4.3	5.5	4.7	5.7	4.9
33 Transport equipment	6.5	5.3	4.8	3.7	5.0	5.2	6.6	5.8
34 Motor vehicles	6.2	6.5	4.8	3.7	4.7	3.4	4.5	3.9
35 Other manufacturing	16.2	15.4	14.9	14.9	15.3	15.1	15.6	15.3
36 Construction	15.3	16.0	16.6	16.4	16.1	14.1	12.0	13.3
37 Electricity	10.5	9.9	10.2	10.4	10.3	9.8	9.0	9.5
38 Cinema	5.0	5.6	6.2	6.8	6.2	8.5	10.2	9.1
39 Transport	4.0	3.0	2.4	1.9	2.6	1.8	2.9	2.3
40 Communications	12.2	11.6	11.6	11.3	11.5	8.5	6.2	7.6
41 Trade	2.5	2.0	1.6	1.2	1.7	.9	1.3	1.1
42 Dwellings	.6	.5	.4	-.3	-.4	.3	1.5	.4
43 Hotels and restaurants	-.7	.1	-.2	-.3	-.0	-.1	1.1	-.4
44 Credit and insurance	6.0	5.8	5.8	5.8	5.9	6.6	8.2	7.3
45 Other services	1.1	.9	1.6	2.4	1.8	4.2	5.2	4.5
T O T A L	4.4	4.5	4.7	5.0	4.8	6.4	7.9	7.0

Case One

Table D.2.10: Employment by Socio-Economic Group

Thousands of persons

Socio-economic group	1978	%	1979	%	1980	%	1981	%	1982	%	1985	%	1990	%
1. Entr. Empl. Prof. (H)	1043482	7.6	1092622	7.6	1144599	7.7	1202033	7.7	1265673	7.7	1505938	7.7	2122406	7.8
2. Entr. Empl. Prof. (M)	2711369	19.8	2836569	19.8	2969233	19.9	3115710	19.9	3278374	20.0	3894657	20.0	5478685	20.1
3. Entr. Empl. Prof. (L)	3612138	26.4	3770856	26.4	3938770	26.4	4123370	26.4	4328790	26.4	5112015	26.3	7133230	26.1
4. Workers	2407249	17.6	2531739	17.7	2664767	17.8	2813239	18.0	2977912	18.1	3595088	18.5	5168712	18.9
5. Peasants (H-M)	208979	1.5	215068	1.5	221425	1.5	227936	1.5	235483	1.4	267129	1.4	354621	1.3
6. Peasants (L)	703195	5.1	723684	5.1	745075	5.0	766983	4.9	792379	4.8	898864	4.6	1193265	4.4
7. Landless Workers	3009822	22.0	3124954	21.9	3250300	21.8	3386181	21.7	3542620	21.6	4171256	21.5	5836537	21.4
T O T A L	13696233	100.0	14295492	100.0	14934169	100.0	15635452	100.0	16421232	100.0	19444948	100.0	27287455	100.0

Case One

Table D.2.10: Employment by Socio-economic Group (Cont.)

Annual growth rates (percent)

Socio-economic group	79/78	80/79	81/80	82/81	83/78	88/83	93/88	93/82
1. Entr. Empl. Prof. (H)	4.7	4.8	5.0	5.3	5.1	6.5	7.9	7.1
2. Entr. Empl. Prof. (M)	4.6	4.7	4.9	5.2	5.0	6.5	7.9	7.0
3. Entr. Empl. Prof. (L)	4.4	4.5	4.7	5.0	4.8	6.3	7.7	6.9
4. Workers	5.2	5.3	5.6	5.9	5.6	7.0	8.3	7.5
5. Peasants (H-M)	2.9	3.0	2.9	3.3	3.2	5.1	6.9	5.8
6. Peasants (L)	2.9	3.0	2.9	3.3	3.2	5.1	6.9	5.8
7. Landless Workers	3.8	4.0	4.2	4.6	4.4	6.3	7.8	6.9
T O T A L	4.4	4.5	4.7	5.0	4.8	6.4	7.9	7.0

Case One

Table D.2.11: Income by Socio-economic Group

Millions of 1978 pesos

Socio-economic group	1978	%	1979	%	1980	%	1981	%	1982	%	1985	%	1990	%
1. Entr. Empl. Prof. (H)	429343	24.0	456801	24.3	486487	24.3	519096	24.2	554799	24.1	686590	23.9	1032570	23.5
2. Entr. Empl. Prof. (M)	502878	28.6	532153	28.3	563023	28.1	596125	27.8	631609	27.5	760124	26.5	1092717	24.9
3. Entr. Empl. Prof. (L)	271985	15.4	285335	15.2	299040	14.9	313558	14.6	329040	14.3	385192	13.4	530410	12.1
4. Workers	373330	21.2	411886	21.9	455735	22.7	505689	23.6	561941	24.5	776677	27.0	1352929	30.8
5. Peasants (H-M)	56137	3.2	58695	3.1	61378	3.1	64246	3.0	67494	2.9	80566	2.8	116440	2.7
6. Peasants (L)	32881	1.9	34439	1.8	36093	1.8	37860	1.8	39869	1.7	48023	1.7	70496	1.6
7. Landless Workers	93943	5.3	98107	5.2	102553	5.1	107353	5.0	112804	4.9	134661	4.7	194591	4.4
T O T A L	1760498	99.8	1877414	99.8	2004310	100.0	2143927	100.0	2297557	99.9	2871833	100.0	4390153	100.0

Case One

Table D.2.11: Income by Socio-economic Group (Cont.)

Annual growth rates (percent)

Socio-economic group		79/78	80/79	81/80	82/81	83/78	80/83	93/88	93/82
1. Entr. Empl. Prof.	(H)	6.4	6.5	6.7	6.9	6.7	7.9	9.4	8.5
2. Entr. Empl. Prof.	(M)	5.8	5.8	5.9	6.0	5.9	6.9	8.5	7.6
3. Entr. Empl. Prof.	(L)	4.9	4.8	4.9	4.9	4.9	6.0	7.7	6.7
4. Workers		10.3	10.6	11.0	11.1	10.9	11.6	12.0	11.7
5. Peasants (H-M)		4.6	4.8	4.7	5.1	4.9	6.9	8.7	7.6
6. Peasants (L)		4.7	4.8	4.9	5.3	5.1	7.2	9.0	7.6
7. Landless Workers		4.4	4.5	4.7	5.1	4.9	6.9	8.7	7.6
T O T A L		6.6	5.8	7.0	7.2	7.0	8.3	9.7	8.9

Case One

Table D.2.12: Average Income by Socio-economic Group, Gini Coefficient and Welfare Indicators

		Thousands of 1978 pesos							Annual growth rates (percent)							
Socio-economic group		1978	1979	1980	1981	1982	1985	1990	79/78	80/79	81/80	82/81	83/78	88/83	93/88	93/82
1. Entr. Empl. Prof.	(H)	411.	418.	425.	432.	438.	456.	487.	1.7	1.7	1.6	1.4	1.6	1.3	1.4	1.3
2. Entr. Empl. Prof.	(M)	185.	188.	190.	191.	193.	195.	199.	1.6	1.1	.5	1.0	1.0	.4	.5	.5
3. Entr. Empl. Prof.	(L)	75.	76.	76.	76.	76.	75.	74.	1.3	0.0	0.0	0.0	.3	-.3	-.3	-.2
4. Workers		155.	163.	171.	180.	189.	216.	262.	5.2	4.9	5.3	5.0	5.0	4.3	3.4	3.9
5. Peasants (H-M)		269.	273.	277.	282.	287.	302.	328.	1.5	1.5	1.8	1.8	1.6	1.7	1.7	1.7
6. Peasants (L)		47.	48.	48.	49.	50.	53.	59.	2.1	1.0	2.1	2.0	1.6	2.2	2.0	2.1
7. Landless Workers		31.	31.	32.	32.	32.	32.	33.	0.0	3.2	0.0	0.0	.6	.6	.6	.6
T O T A L		129.	131.	134.	137.	140.	148.	161.	2.0	1.8	1.9	1.9	1.9	1.7	1.6	1.6
Welfare indicators																
Gini Coefficient		.413	.411	.410	.410	.409	.411	.414	.13	.13	.13	.13	.13	.13	.13	.13
Efficiency-equity [a]		1.033	1.109	1.186	1.274	1.371	1.720	2.659								
Equal weights									2.1	1.8	1.5	1.5	1.7	1.3	1.1	1.2
Poverty weighted									2.4	2.2	2.0	2.0	2.1	1.8	1.5	1.7

a) 10^{12} 1978 pesos

D.3: Status-Quo-Plus-Oil Scenario

Status-Quo-Plus-Oil Scenario

Table D.3.1: Sectoral Gross Output

Sector	Millions of 1978 pesos							Annual growth rates (percent)						
	1978	1979	1980	1981	1982	1985	1990	79/78	80/79	81/80	82/81	85/82	90/85	90/78
1 Agriculture	169963.	177731.	185903.	193960.	202411.	232066.	304522.	4.6	4.6	4.3	4.4	4.5	5.6	4.9
2 Livestock	99669.	101249.	103887.	106570.	109408.	119497.	145783.	2.6	2.6	2.6	2.7	3.0	4.0	3.2
3 Forestry	8611.	9313.	10323.	11534.	12962.	18707.	34992.	8.2	10.8	11.7	12.4	12.7	13.3	12.4
4 Fishing	6963.	8448.	10050.	11950.	14164.	22755.	46744.	21.3	19.0	18.9	18.5	17.2	15.5	17.1
5 Mining	14665.	24692.	25539.	26503.	27625.	31940.	44406.	23.1	3.4	3.8	4.2	4.8	7.0	5.5
6 Quarrying	14665.	15868.	17579.	19757.	22395.	33251.	64469.	8.2	10.8	12.4	13.4	14.7	14.1	14.1
7 Petroleum	1125405.	139916.	176181.	220047.	271930.	490490.	1071800.	24.7	25.9	24.9	23.6	21.7	16.6	17.0
8 Slaughter of livestock	40194.	44199.	48757.	53984.	60006.	83425.	149804.	10.0	10.3	10.7	11.2	11.9	12.5	12.2
9 Milling	68700.	74351.	80247.	86481.	93242.	117069.	183907.	7.9	7.9	7.8	7.8	7.9	9.4	8.3
10 Other processed food	138910.	142655.	146423.	150580.	154993.	171062.	213657.	2.7	2.6	2.8	2.9	3.4	4.6	3.6
11 Beverages	58626.	63151.	67151.	70535.	73470.	91354.	96738.	7.7	6.3	5.0	4.2	3.9	5.7	4.4
12 Tobacco	15969.	17594.	19797.	22445.	25612.	38369.	74417.	10.0	12.5	13.4	14.1	14.4	14.0	14.5
13 Soft fibre textiles	56687.	58975.	61023.	62931.	64847.	71104.	86363.	4.0	3.5	3.1	3.0	3.1	4.0	4.1
14 Other textiles	4896.	6456.	9005.	12467.	16898.	35435.	91556.	31.7	39.5	38.5	35.5	27.9	21.0	21.7
15 Wearing apparel	108996.	114169.	118676.	122816.	126867.	139698.	170011.	4.7	3.9	3.5	3.3	3.3	5.0	4.2
16 Wood and cork	17291.	20249.	24091.	28798.	34418.	57129.	121763.	17.1	19.0	19.5	19.5	18.5	16.3	16.6
17 Paper	35111.	37840.	40193.	42422.	44515.	51634.	59856.	7.8	6.2	5.5	4.9	5.0	3.0	4.5
18 Printing, publishing	25826.	26980.	28333.	29971.	31848.	39229.	59093.	4.5	5.0	5.8	6.3	7.2	8.0	6.6
19 Leather	17055.	20123.	24057.	29171.	35515.	70092.	122017.	18.0	19.6	21.3	21.7	25.4	11.8	8.8
20 Rubber products	11122.	12299.	13495.	14701.	16120.	23883.	33287.	10.6	9.7	8.9	9.7	14.0	6.9	9.4
21 Basic chemicals	18408.	18757.	19193.	19746.	20492.	23683.	33170.	2.9	2.3	2.9	3.8	4.9	7.3	5.0
22 Synthetic fibers	17311.	18725.	20007.	21259.	22513.	26683.	36900.	8.2	6.8	6.0	5.9	6.6	6.7	6.4
23 Fertilizers	4784.	6794.	9592.	13252.	17816.	36935.	92392.	42.0	41.2	38.1	34.4	27.6	20.1	27.9
24 Soaps and detergents	12928.	15667.	19304.	23838.	29337.	51829.	114334.	21.2	23.2	23.5	23.1	20.6	17.5	21.2
25 Drugs and medicines	17524.	16509.	16281.	16549.	17218.	21269.	35240.	-5.3	-1.9	1.8	3.9	7.4	10.6	6.0
26 Perfumes, cosmetics	11571.	13699.	16935.	21251.	26550.	48771.	112993.	18.4	23.6	25.5	24.9	22.4	18.4	19.8
27 Other chemical indust.	19640.	22739.	26651.	31434.	37102.	59901.	124593.	15.7	17.2	17.9	18.0	17.3	15.0	16.1
28 Nonmetallic mineral pr.	43423.	56614.	59374.	61880.	64211.	71202.	84422.	6.0	4.9	4.2	3.8	3.7	3.4	5.8
29 Basic metallic indust.	84504.	93722.	102459.	110568.	118195.	141697.	195622.	11.6	9.3	7.9	6.9	6.3	6.6	6.9
30 Metal products	47410.	50767.	54152.	57601.	61181.	73779.	104036.	7.1	6.7	6.4	6.2	6.4	7.1	6.8
31 Machinery	28566.	31189.	33723.	36209.	38647.	45835.	64635.	9.2	8.1	7.4	6.7	5.8	7.1	7.0
32 Electrical machinery	40743.	44281.	47448.	50541.	53580.	63517.	87660.	8.7	7.2	6.5	6.0	5.9	6.6	6.8
33 Transport equipment	30905.	34056.	37081.	40162.	43047.	52334.	74653.	10.2	8.9	8.3	7.2	6.7	7.3	7.5
34 Motor vehicles	82863.	91631.	101080.	110441.	119472.	149606.	222934.	10.8	10.3	9.3	8.2	7.9	9.2	8.5
35 Other manufacturing	19930.	22441.	25073.	27899.	31066.	42806.	74522.	12.6	11.7	11.3	11.3	11.6	12.2	11.8
36 Construction	277659.	330873.	396764.	474601.	570646.	945293.	2093061.	19.2	19.9	19.6	20.2	18.4	17.2	18.4
37 Electricity	34726.	41425.	47776.	55127.	63566.	96393.	187604.	16.6	15.3	15.4	15.3	14.7	14.3	14.3
38 Gas	16634.	17367.	18238.	19264.	20452.	25572.	34681.	4.4	5.0	5.6	6.2	7.9	10.0	14.3
39 Transport	76228.	80788.	84718.	88281.	91562.	101321.	127716.	6.0	4.8	4.2	3.7	3.6	4.8	4.1
40 Communications	18771.	23005.	28038.	34035.	41070.	69628.	155716.	22.6	21.9	21.4	20.7	19.5	17.5	16.7
41 Trade	637763.	646913.	663635.	677606.	689661.	719066.	775416.	7.1	2.6	2.1	1.7	2.2	1.5	1.6
42 Dwellings	99027.	99603.	100104.	100547.	100923.	101930.	103881.	.6	.5	.4	.3	.3	.4	.4
43 Hotels and restaurants	75622.	78717.	81312.	83762.	86128.	93723.	112663.	4.3	5.0	6.0	6.4	6.4	4.6	3.8
44 Credit and insurance	67034.	65455.	66930.	72605.	76655.	90130.	134061.	2.0	5.3	5.3	5.4	5.9	8.1	7.0
45 Other services	120369.	129322.	138589.	149340.	161680.	209676.	361095.	7.4	7.2	7.8	8.3	9.7	11.1	10.2
T O T A L	2934644.	3167618.	3424957.	3717376.	4040742.	5264815.	8611327.	7.9	8.2	8.5	8.7	8.5	9.8	10.3

Status-Quo-Plus-Oil Scenario

Table D.3.2: Private Consumption

Sector	Millions of 1978 pesos							Annual growth rates (percent)								
	1978	1979	1980	1981	1982	1985	1990	79/78	80/79	81/80	82/81	83/82	88/83	93/88	93/90	93/83
1 Agriculture	93914	98258	102948	108051	113613	134027	147483	4.6	4.8	5.0	5.0	5.0	5.3	3.0	7.0	7.0
2 Livestock	25362	26733	28201	29785	31499	37707	53646	5.4	5.5	5.6	5.6	6.3	6.7	8.3	8.3	7.4
3 Forestry	0	0	0	0	0	0	0	0.0	0.0	0.0	0.0	0.0	0.0	0.0	0.0	0.0
4 Fishing	14020	14879	15795	16780	17841	21646	31224	6.1	6.2	6.2	6.3	7.1	7.6	8.5	8.5	7.7
5 Mining	0	0	0	0	0	0	0	0.0	0.0	0.0	0.0	0.0	0.0	0.0	0.0	0.0
6 Quarrying	0	0	0	0	0	0	0	0.0	0.0	0.0	0.0	0.0	0.0	0.0	0.0	0.0
7 Petroleum	56391	60057	64104	68514	73326	91112	134629	4.7	6.7	6.9	6.9	9.1	9.7	9.7	9.7	9.7
8 Slaughter of livestock	228115	241589	256170	272123	289586	354434	572904	5.9	6.0	6.2	7.6	7.6	9.3	9.3	9.3	8.3
9 Milling	57902	60913	64067	67486	71206	84834	120459	5.1	5.2	5.3	5.4	6.3	6.6	9.3	9.3	7.3
10 Other processed food	97646	102078	107525	113442	119940	143590	207108	5.1	5.3	5.5	5.4	5.5	6.9	8.5	8.5	7.6
11 Beverages	45445	47934	50615	53525	56692	68307	93714	5.5	5.6	5.7	5.8	6.0	7.0	8.0	8.0	7.7
12 Tobacco	13371	14130	14938	15804	16736	20053	28297	5.7	5.7	5.9	5.8	6.8	7.0	8.0	8.0	7.6
13 Soft fiber textiles	13893	14810	15795	16863	18030	22204	32867	6.6	6.7	6.8	6.9	7.7	7.7	9.0	9.2	8.2
14 Other textiles	0	0	0	0	0	0	0	0.0	0.0	0.0	0.0	0.0	0.0	0.0	0.0	0.0
15 Wearing apparel	182180	194265	207413	221867	237745	296976	453350	6.6	6.8	7.0	7.2	7.0	8.3	10.6	10.6	9.4
16 Wood and cork	24494	26039	27704	29516	31488	38710	57530	6.3	6.4	6.5	6.7	4.6	7.7	9.2	9.2	8.3
17 Paper	11833	12570	13356	14201	15111	18363	26470	6.2	6.3	6.4	6.4	7.1	8.2	8.4	8.4	7.4
18 Printing, publishing	27047	28890	30888	33060	35449	44204	67246	6.8	6.9	7.0	7.2	7.1	8.2	9.7	9.7	8.8
19 Leather	9366	9846	10350	10886	11535	14637	16126	6.5	6.4	6.4	6.4	6.8	8.0	7.7	7.2	7.2
20 Rubber products	5421	5760	10836	11535	12284	14036	21429	6.4	6.1	6.5	6.5	7.1	8.2	8.2	8.2	6.2
21 Basic chemicals	0	0	6112	6481	6867	8161	10997	6.3	6.1	6.0	6.0	6.5	7.1	6.5	6.5	6.2
22 Synthetic fibers	0	0	0	0	0	0	0	0.0	0.0	0.0	0.0	0.0	0.0	0.0	0.0	0.0
23 Fertilizers	5137	5454	5783	6125	6481	7646	10109	5.2	6.0	5.9	5.8	5.8	6.2	4.0	4.0	6.2
24 Soaps and detergents	23195	24271	25526	26876	28332	33578	46885	5.1	5.2	5.3	5.4	5.8	7.1	7.9	7.9	6.3
25 Drugs and medicines	17092	17971	18952	20007	21132	25173	35315	5.1	5.4	5.6	5.7	6.5	6.5	7.9	7.9	7.1
26 Perfumes, cosmetics	35311	37500	39865	42446	45267	56626	82970	6.2	6.3	6.5	6.6	7.7	7.7	9.3	9.3	8.1
27 Other chemical indust.	5531	5870	6230	6627	7036	8603	11465	6.4	6.3	6.2	6.1	6.0	7.7	8.0	8.0	6.5
28 Nonmetallic mineral pr.	7417	7907	8359	8834	9337	11059	15025	5.8	5.7	5.7	5.7	6.0	6.0	6.8	6.8	6.3
29 Basic metallic indust.	0	0	0	0	0	0	0	0.0	0.0	0.0	0.0	0.0	0.0	0.0	0.0	0.0
30 Metal products	10397	11053	11753	12504	13317	16196	23288	6.3	6.3	6.4	6.5	6.4	7.1	8.3	8.3	7.6
31 Machinery	4474	4944	5221	5505	5797	6733	6580	5.2	5.6	5.4	5.3	5.5	5.0	5.1	5.1	4.0
32 Electrical machinery	36682	39096	41709	44567	47603	59236	80755	6.6	6.7	6.9	6.8	6.9	8.1	9.6	10.7	8.8
33 Transport equipment	19630	20954	22373	23912	25580	31662	47433	6.7	6.8	6.9	7.0	7.3	7.9	9.3	9.6	8.5
34 Motor vehicles	82695	89410	96740	104853	113810	147359	238056	8.1	8.2	8.4	8.5	9.5	10.9	10.9	10.1	10.1
35 Other manufacturing	37603	40276	43170	46366	49860	62821	92294	7.1	7.2	7.4	7.5	8.6	10.0	10.0	9.2	9.2
36 Construction	0	0	0	0	0	0	0	0.0	0.0	0.0	0.0	0.0	0.0	0.0	0.0	0.0
37 Electricity	34361	36472	38751	41233	43948	53093	80035	6.1	6.2	6.4	6.6	7.6	8.3	9.2	8.3	8.3
38 Gas	34119	36827	39762	42980	46507	60605	94570	7.9	8.0	8.1	8.0	9.1	10.5	10.5	10.5	8.3
39 Transport	58002	61774	65876	70390	75362	93745	142794	6.5	6.6	6.8	7.0	7.6	9.2	9.7	9.7	8.8
40 Communications	20169	21604	23144	24817	26635	33223	50623	7.1	7.1	7.2	7.3	8.2	9.6	9.6	9.6	8.6
41 Trade	17178	18434	19782	21248	22840	28655	43764	7.3	7.3	7.4	7.5	8.3	9.7	9.7	9.7	8.9
42 Dwellings	56467	59797	63377	67270	71529	89717	128606	5.9	6.0	6.2	6.3	6.7	7.4	9.1	9.1	8.1
43 Hotels and restaurants	16386	17465	18578	19805	21133	26943	32260	6.5	6.6	6.6	6.7	7.5	7.5	9.0	9.5	8.1
44 Credit and insurance	11720	12598	13538	14556	15568	19646	29824	7.5	7.5	7.5	7.9	8.3	7.5	9.5	9.5	8.8
45 Other services	175201	186400	202754	216549	235010	308084	476603	7.5	7.6	7.8	7.9	8.0	10.5	10.5	10.5	9.6
T O T A L	1622223	1725004	1836090	1957635	2088002	2679324	3973246	6.3	6.4	6.6	6.8	6.8	7.8	9.4	8.5	8.5

Status-Quo-Plus-Oil Scenario

Table D.3.3: Government Consumption of Goods and Services

Sector	Millions of 1978 pesos							Annual growth rates (percent)							
	1978	1979	1980	1981	1982	1985	1990	79/78	80/79	81/80	82/81	83/78	86/83	93/86	93/82
1 Agriculture	135.	148.	153.	181.	202.	282.	504.	9.8	10.6	11.0	11.3	10.9	12.1	12.7	12.3
2 Livestock	0.	0.	0.	0.	0.	0.	0.	0.0	0.0	0.0	0.0	0.0	0.0	0.0	0.0
3 Forestry	0.	0.	0.	0.	0.	0.	0.	0.0	0.0	0.0	0.0	0.0	0.0	0.0	0.0
4 Fishing	0.	0.	0.	0.	0.	0.	0.	0.0	0.0	0.0	0.0	0.0	0.0	0.0	0.0
5 Mining	0.	0.	0.	0.	0.	0.	0.	0.0	0.0	0.0	0.0	0.0	0.0	0.0	0.0
6 Quarrying	0.	0.	0.	0.	0.	0.	0.	0.0	0.0	0.0	0.0	0.0	0.0	0.0	0.0
7 Petroleum	1034.	1135.	1255.	1394.	1552.	2166.	3471.	9.8	10.6	11.0	11.3	10.9	12.1	12.7	12.3
8 Slaughter of livestock	210.	230.	254.	282.	314.	439.	784.	9.8	10.6	11.0	11.3	10.9	12.1	12.7	12.3
9 Milling	0.	0.	0.	0.	0.	0.	0.	0.0	0.0	0.0	0.0	0.0	0.0	0.0	0.0
10 Other processed food	210.	230.	254.	282.	314.	439.	784.	9.8	10.6	11.0	11.3	10.9	12.1	12.7	12.3
11 Beverages	0.	0.	0.	0.	0.	0.	0.	0.0	0.0	0.0	0.0	0.0	0.0	0.0	0.0
12 Tobacco	0.	0.	0.	0.	0.	0.	0.	0.0	0.0	0.0	0.0	0.0	0.0	0.0	0.0
13 Soft fiber textiles	0.	0.	0.	0.	0.	0.	0.	0.0	0.0	0.0	0.0	0.0	0.0	0.0	0.0
14 Other textiles	0.	0.	0.	0.	0.	0.	0.	0.0	0.0	0.0	0.0	0.0	0.0	0.0	0.0
15 Wearing apparel	1262.	1366.	1532.	1701.	1894.	2644.	4725.	9.8	10.6	11.0	11.3	10.9	12.1	12.7	12.3
16 Wood and cork	41.	45.	60.	55.	86.	129.	153.	9.8	10.6	11.0	11.3	10.9	12.1	12.7	12.3
17 Paper	59.	65.	72.	79.	88.	129.	221.	9.8	10.6	11.0	11.3	10.9	12.1	12.7	12.3
18 Printing, publishing	1756.	1928.	2132.	2347.	2636.	3672.	6574.	9.8	10.6	11.0	11.3	10.9	12.1	12.7	12.3
19 Leather	29.	32.	35.	39.	43.	61.	108.	9.8	10.6	11.0	11.3	10.9	12.1	12.7	12.3
20 Rubber products	2.	2.	2.	2.	2.	6.	6.	9.8	10.6	11.0	11.3	10.9	12.1	12.7	12.3
21 Basic chemicals	170.	187.	207.	230.	256.	357.	638.	9.8	10.6	11.0	11.3	10.9	12.1	12.7	12.3
22 Synthetic fibers	0.	0.	0.	0.	0.	0.	0.	0.0	0.0	0.0	0.0	0.0	0.0	0.0	0.0
23 Fertilizers	0.	0.	0.	0.	0.	0.	0.	0.0	0.0	0.0	0.0	0.0	0.0	0.0	0.0
24 Soap and detergents	601.	660.	730.	811.	902.	1260.	2251.	9.8	10.6	11.0	11.3	10.9	12.1	12.7	12.3
25 Drugs and medicines	4031.	4425.	4893.	5432.	6049.	8443.	15087.	9.8	10.6	11.0	11.3	10.9	12.1	12.7	12.3
26 Perfumes, cosmetics	0.	0.	0.	0.	0.	0.	0.	0.0	0.0	0.0	0.0	0.0	0.0	0.0	0.0
27 Other chemical indust.	0.	0.	0.	0.	0.	0.	0.	0.0	0.0	0.0	0.0	0.0	0.0	0.0	0.0
28 Nonmetallic mineral pr.	262.	288.	318.	354.	394.	550.	982.	9.8	10.6	11.0	11.3	10.9	12.1	12.7	12.3
29 Basic metallic indust.	201.	221.	244.	271.	302.	421.	752.	9.8	10.6	11.0	11.3	10.9	12.1	12.7	12.3
30 Metal products	1959.	2151.	2378.	2641.	2940.	4104.	7333.	9.8	10.6	11.0	11.3	10.9	12.1	12.7	12.3
31 Machinery	1247.	1391.	1530.	1708.	1902.	2655.	3890.	9.8	10.6	11.0	11.3	10.9	12.1	12.7	12.3
32 Electrical machinery	177.	195.	215.	238.	266.	371.	663.	9.8	10.6	11.0	11.3	10.9	12.1	12.7	12.3
33 Transport equipment	63.	69.	77.	85.	95.	132.	236.	9.8	10.6	11.0	11.3	10.9	12.1	12.7	12.3
34 Motor vehicles	1364.	1500.	1659.	1841.	2050.	2862.	5114.	9.8	10.6	11.0	11.3	10.9	12.1	12.7	12.3
35 Other manufacturing	1041.	1143.	1264.	1403.	1562.	2180.	3896.	9.8	10.6	11.0	11.3	10.9	12.1	12.7	12.3
36 Construction	756.	830.	918.	1019.	1135.	1584.	2831.	9.8	10.6	11.0	11.3	10.9	12.1	12.7	12.3
37 Electricity	48.	52.	56.	64.	72.	100.	179.	9.8	10.6	11.0	11.3	10.9	12.1	12.7	12.3
38 Cinema	1024.	1124.	1243.	1380.	1536.	2145.	3832.	9.8	10.6	11.0	11.3	10.9	12.1	12.7	12.3
39 Transport	770.	845.	935.	1039.	1158.	1613.	2882.	9.8	10.6	11.0	11.3	10.9	12.1	12.7	12.3
40 Communications	3154.	3467.	3836.	4257.	4740.	6616.	11822.	9.8	10.6	11.0	11.3	10.9	12.1	12.7	12.3
41 Trade	2303.	2529.	2796.	3104.	3456.	4825.	8621.	9.8	10.6	11.0	11.3	10.9	12.1	12.7	12.3
42 Dwellings	872.	958.	1059.	1176.	1309.	1827.	3265.	9.8	10.6	11.0	11.3	10.9	12.1	12.7	12.3
43 Hotels and restaurants	1363.	1496.	1654.	1837.	2045.	2855.	5101.	9.8	10.6	11.0	11.3	10.9	12.1	12.7	12.3
44 Credit and insurance	1043.	2155.	2382.	2645.	2945.	4111.	7346.	9.8	10.6	11.0	11.3	10.9	12.1	12.7	12.3
45 Other services															
T O T A L	29174.	32027.	35414.	39320.	43778.	61109.	100196.	9.8	10.6	11.0	11.3	10.9	12.1	12.7	12.3

Status-Quo-Plus-Oil Scenario

Table D.3.4: Public Investment by Destination

Millions of 1978 pesos

Sector	1977	%	1979	%	1980	%	1981	%	1982	%	1985	%	1990	%
1 Agriculture	6737	4.6	11776	7.3	12966	7.3	14337	7.3	15901	7.3	21967	7.3	38759	7.3
2 Livestock	665	.4	1613	1.0	1774	1.0	1964	1.0	2175	1.0	3009	1.0	5309	1.0
3 Forestry	738	.5	1200	.7	1471	.8	1571	.8	1743	.8	2407	.8	4748	.8
4 Fishing	1120	.8	907	.5	938	.5	982	.5	1042	.5	1505	.5	2655	.5
5 Mining	1475	1.0	1613	1.0	1776	1.0	1964	1.0	2178	1.0	3009	1.0	5309	1.0
6 Quarrying	1475	1.0	1613	1.0	1776	1.0	1964	1.0	2178	1.0	3009	1.0	5309	1.0
7 Petroleum	42494	28.8	53302	33.1	58791	33.1	65008	33.1	72099	33.1	99605	33.1	175742	33.1
8 Slaughter of livestock	443	.3	484	.3	533	.3	589	.3	653	.3	903	.3	1593	.3
9 Milling	443	.3	484	.3	533	.3	589	.3	653	.3	903	.3	1593	.3
10 Other processed food	443	.3	484	.3	533	.3	589	.3	653	.3	903	.3	1593	.3
11 Beverages	443	.3	484	.3	533	.3	589	.3	653	.3	903	.3	1593	.3
12 Tobacco	443	.3	484	.3	533	.3	589	.3	653	.3	903	.3	1593	.3
13 Soft fiber textiles	443	.3	484	.3	533	.3	589	.3	653	.3	903	.3	1593	.3
14 Other textiles	443	.3	484	.3	533	.3	589	.3	653	.3	903	.3	1593	.3
15 Wearing apparel	443	.3	484	.3	533	.3	589	.3	653	.3	903	.3	1593	.3
16 Wood and cork	443	.3	484	.3	533	.3	589	.3	653	.3	903	.3	1593	.3
17 Paper	443	.3	484	.3	533	.3	589	.3	653	.3	903	.3	1593	.3
18 Printing, publishing	443	.3	484	.3	533	.3	589	.3	653	.3	903	.3	1593	.3
19 Leather	443	.3	484	.3	533	.3	589	.3	653	.3	903	.3	1593	.3
20 Rubber products	443	.3	484	.3	533	.3	589	.3	653	.3	903	.3	1593	.3
21 Basic chemicals	443	.3	484	.3	533	.3	589	.3	653	.3	903	.3	1593	.3
22 Synthetic fibers	443	.3	484	.3	533	.3	589	.3	653	.3	903	.3	1593	.3
23 Fertilizers	4131	2.8	4033	2.5	4440	2.5	4910	2.5	5446	2.5	7523	2.5	13274	2.5
24 Soaps and detergents	443	.3	484	.3	533	.3	589	.3	653	.3	903	.3	1593	.3
25 Drugs and medicines	443	.3	484	.3	533	.3	589	.3	653	.3	903	.3	1593	.3
26 Perfumes, cosmetics	443	.3	484	.3	533	.3	589	.3	653	.3	903	.3	1593	.3
27 Other chemical indust.	443	.3	484	.3	533	.3	589	.3	653	.3	903	.3	1593	.3
28 Nonmetallic mineral pr.	443	.3	484	.3	533	.3	589	.3	653	.3	903	.3	1593	.3
29 Basic metallic indust.	1623	1.1	1774	1.1	1954	1.1	2160	1.1	2396	1.1	3310	1.1	5840	1.1
30 Metal products	443	.3	484	.3	533	.3	589	.3	653	.3	903	.3	1593	.3
31 Machinery	443	.3	484	.3	533	.3	589	.3	653	.3	903	.3	1593	.3
32 Electrical machinery	443	.3	484	.3	533	.3	589	.3	653	.3	903	.3	1593	.3
33 Transport equipment	255	.2	333	.2	355	.2	393	.2	436	.2	602	.2	1062	.2
34 Motor vehicles	1033	.7	1120	.7	1243	.7	1370	.7	1527	.7	2106	.7	3717	.7
35 Other manufacturing	443	.3	484	.3	533	.3	589	.3	653	.3	903	.3	1593	.3
36 Construction	16378	11.1	16292	10.1	17939	10.1	19876	10.1	22000	10.1	30393	10.1	53625	10.1
37 Electricity	13591	12.6	17743	11.0	19536	11.0	21606	11.0	23961	11.0	33101	11.0	58404	11.0
38 Cinema	443	.3	484	.3	533	.3	589	.3	653	.3	903	.3	1593	.3
39 Transport	4722	3.2	4839	3.0	5328	3.0	5932	3.0	6555	3.0	9027	3.0	15928	3.0
40 Communications	15935	10.8	16130	10.0	17762	10.0	19646	10.0	21782	10.0	30092	10.0	53094	10.0
41 Trade	443	.3	484	.3	533	.3	589	.3	653	.3	903	.3	1593	.3
42 Dwellings	443	.3	484	.3	533	.3	589	.3	653	.3	903	.3	1593	.3
43 Hotels and restaurants	443	.3	484	.3	533	.3	589	.3	653	.3	903	.3	1593	.3
44 Credit and insurance	443	.3	484	.3	533	.3	589	.3	653	.3	903	.3	1593	.3
45 Other services	16965	11.5	12906	8.0	14200	8.0	15712	8.0	17425	8.0	24074	8.0	42476	8.0
TOTAL	147649	100.0	161304	100.0	177615	100.0	196400	100.0	217823	100.0	300922	100.0	530944	100.0

Status-Quo-Plus-Oil Scenario

Table D.3.4: Public Investment by Destination (Cont.)

Sector		79/78	80/79	81/80	82/81	83/82	88/83	93/88	97/93
				Annual growth rates (percent)					
1	Agriculture	73.5	10.1	10.6	10.0	21.1	11.7	12.4	12.0
2	Livestock	82.2	10.1	10.6	10.0	22.3	11.7	12.4	12.0
3	Forestry	74.9	10.1	10.6	10.0	21.3	11.7	12.4	12.0
4	Fishing	-31.7	10.1	10.6	10.0	.5	11.7	12.4	12.0
5	Mining	9.3	10.1	10.6	10.0	10.4	11.7	12.4	12.0
6	Quarrying	9.3	10.1	10.6	10.0	10.4	11.7	12.4	12.0
7	Petroleum	25.6	10.1	10.6	10.0	13.5	11.7	12.4	12.0
8	Slaughter of livestock	9.3	10.1	10.6	10.0	10.4	11.7	12.4	12.0
9	Milling	9.3	10.1	10.6	10.0	10.4	11.7	12.4	12.0
10	Other processed food	9.3	10.1	10.6	10.0	10.4	11.7	12.4	12.0
11	Beverages	9.3	10.1	10.6	10.0	10.4	11.7	12.4	12.0
12	Tobacco	9.3	10.1	10.6	10.0	10.4	11.7	12.4	12.0
13	Soft fiber textiles	9.3	10.1	10.6	10.0	10.4	11.7	12.4	12.0
14	Other textiles	9.3	10.1	10.6	10.0	10.4	11.7	12.4	12.0
15	Wearing apparel	9.3	10.1	10.6	10.0	10.4	11.7	12.4	12.0
16	Wood and cork	9.3	10.1	10.6	10.0	10.4	11.7	12.4	12.0
17	Paper	9.3	10.1	10.6	10.0	10.4	11.7	12.4	12.0
18	Printing, publishing	9.3	10.1	10.6	10.0	10.4	11.7	12.4	12.0
19	Leather	9.3	10.1	10.6	10.0	10.4	11.7	12.4	12.0
20	Rubber products	9.3	10.1	10.6	10.0	10.4	11.7	12.4	12.0
21	Basic chemicals	9.3	10.1	10.6	10.0	10.4	11.7	12.4	12.0
22	Synthetic fibers	9.3	10.1	10.6	10.0	10.4	11.7	12.4	12.0
23	Fertilizers	-2.4	10.1	10.6	10.0	7.9	11.7	12.4	12.0
24	Soaps and detergents	9.3	10.1	10.6	10.0	10.4	11.7	12.4	12.0
25	Drugs and medicines	9.3	10.1	10.6	10.0	10.4	11.7	12.4	12.0
26	Perfumes, cosmetics	9.3	10.1	10.6	10.0	10.4	11.7	12.4	12.0
27	Other chemical indust.	9.3	10.1	10.6	10.0	10.4	11.7	12.4	12.0
28	Nonmetallic mineral pr.	9.3	10.1	10.6	10.0	10.4	11.7	12.4	12.0
29	Basic metallic indust.	9.3	10.1	10.6	10.0	10.4	11.7	12.4	12.0
30	Metal products	9.3	10.1	10.6	10.0	10.4	11.7	12.4	12.0
31	Machinery	9.3	10.1	10.6	10.0	10.4	11.7	12.4	12.0
32	Electrical machinery	9.3	10.1	10.6	10.0	10.4	11.7	12.4	12.0
33	Transport equipment	9.3	10.1	10.6	10.0	10.4	11.7	12.4	12.0
34	Motor vehicles	9.3	10.1	10.6	10.0	10.4	11.7	12.4	12.0
35	Other manufacturing	9.3	10.1	10.6	10.0	10.4	11.7	12.4	12.0
36	Construction	-4.6	10.1	10.6	10.0	9.4	11.7	12.4	12.0
37	Electricity	9.3	10.1	10.6	10.0	2.5	11.7	12.4	12.0
38	Cinema	9.3	10.1	10.6	10.0	10.4	11.7	12.4	12.0
39	Transport	2.5	10.1	10.6	13.5	9.0	11.7	12.4	12.0
40	Communications	1.2	10.1	10.6	10.0	8.7	11.7	12.4	12.0
41	Trade	9.3	10.1	10.6	10.0	10.4	11.7	12.4	12.0
42	Dwellings	9.3	10.1	10.6	13.3	10.4	11.7	12.4	12.0
43	Hotels and restaurants	9.3	10.1	10.6	10.0	10.4	11.7	12.4	12.0
44	Credit and insurance	9.3	10.1	10.6	10.0	10.4	11.7	12.4	12.0
45	Other services	-23.0	11.1	10.6	10.0	2.7	11.7	12.4	12.0
	T O T A L	9.3	10.1	10.4	10.0	10.4	11.7	12.4	12.0

Status-Quo-Plus-Oil Scenario

Table D.3.5: Private Investment by Destination

Millions of 1978 pesos

Sector	1977	%	1978	%	1979	%	1980	%	1981	%	1982	%	1985	%	1990	%
1 Agriculture	26137.	17.0	22842.	13.1	22862.	13.1	21186.	10.8	21490.	9.6	22472.	8.9	28828.	7.8	53026.	7.4
2 Livestock	3458.	2.3	3629.	1.8	2629.	1.6	3739.	1.4	2813.	1.3	2970.	1.2	3904.	1.1	7250.	1.0
3 Forestry	750.	.5	451.	.3	651.	.4	1145.	.6	1455.	.7	1776.	.7	2851.	.8	5717.	.8
4 Fishing	252.	.2	441.	.3	441.	.3	829.	.4	1009.	.5	1176.	.5	1813.	.5	3543.	.5
5 Mining	1473.	1.0	1421.	.8	1421.	.8	1678.	.9	2058.	.9	2342.	.9	3638.	1.0	7169.	1.0
6 Quarrying	120.	.1	742.	.4	742.	.4	1221.	.6	1567.	.7	2099.	.8	3510.	.9	7130.	1.0
7 Petroleum	23501.	15.3	34178.	19.6	34178.	19.6	47132.	23.9	60275.	27.0	73375.29.	.1	117925.	31.8	236543.32.	.9
8 Slaughter of livestock	358.	.2	428.	.2	428.	.2	512.	.3	615.	.3	715.	.3	1092.	.3	2151.	.3
9 Milling	686.	.4	605.	.4	605.	.4	714.	.4	753.	.3	829.	.3	1143.	.3	2166.	.3
10 Other processed food	718.	.5	684.	.4	684.	.4	756.	.4	779.	.3	842.	.3	1149.	.3	2168.	.3
11 Beverages	3945.	2.6	3358.	1.9	3358.	1.9	2734.	1.4	2244.	1.0	1962.	.8	1657.	.4	2323.	.3
12 Tobacco	177.	.1	302.	.2	302.	.2	412.	.2	541.	.2	660.	.3	1056.	.3	2143.	.3
13 Soft fiber textiles	1593.	1.0	1330.	.8	1330.	.8	1164.	.6	1116.	.5	1094.	.4	1263.	.3	2203.	.3
14 Other textiles	-84.	-.1	102.	.1	102.	.1	263.	.1	420.	.2	575.	.2	1028.	.3	2131.	.3
15 Wearing apparel	1497.	1.0	1554.	.9	1554.	.9	1340.	.7	1243.	.6	1191.	.5	1307.	.4	2216.	.3
16 Wood and cork	157.	.1	284.	.2	284.	.2	400.	.2	535.	.2	655.	.3	1064.	.3	2143.	.3
17 Paper	1772.	1.2	1426.	.8	1426.	.8	1276.	.6	1197.	.5	1148.	.5	1248.	.3	2211.	.3
18 Printing, publishing	284.	.2	368.	.2	368.	.2	490.	.3	593.	.3	701.	.3	1085.	.3	2149.	.3
19 Leather	171.	.1	303.	.2	303.	.2	428.	.2	545.	.2	664.	.3	1068.	.3	2144.	.3
20 Rubber products	819.	.5	798.	.5	798.	.5	866.	.4	844.	.4	804.	.3	1073.	.3	2176.	.3
21 Basic chemicals	29.	.1	138.	.1	138.	.1	217.	.1	471.	.2	664.	.2	1023.	.3	2130.	.3
22 Synthetic fibers	1413.	.9	1190.	.7	1190.	.7	1119.	.6	1056.	.5	1051.	.4	1244.	.3	2197.	.3
23 Fertilizers	-252.	-.2	1366.	.8	1366.	.8	2624.	1.3	3900.	1.7	5031.	2.0	8676.	2.3	17796.	2.5
24 Soaps and detergents	105.	.1	244.	.1	244.	.1	374.	.2	511.	.2	637.	.3	1056.	.3	2140.	.3
25 Drugs and medicines	-1267.	-.8	-756.	-.4	-756.	-.4	-279.	-.1	-17.	-.0	242.	.1	877.	.2	2086.	.3
26 Perfumes, cosmetics	-17.	-.0	163.	.1	163.	.1	330.	.2	471.	.2	608.	.2	1043.	.3	2136.	.3
27 Other chemical indust.	173.	.1	299.	.2	299.	.2	424.	.2	544.	.2	663.	.3	1068.	.3	2144.	.3
28 Normetallic mineral pr.	2420.	1.6	1992.	1.1	1992.	1.1	1716.	.9	1503.	.7	1341.	.5	1398.	.4	2244.	.3
29 Basic metallic indust.	7540.	4.9	6644.	3.7	6644.	3.7	5693.	2.9	5031.	2.3	4341.	1.9	4986.	1.3	8179.	1.1
30 Metal products	942.	.6	917.	.5	917.	.5	1140.	.6	987.	.4	1057.	.4	1186.	.3	2180.	.3
31 Machinery	1339.	.9	1221.	.7	1221.	.7	1207.	.6	1055.	.5	1061.	.4	1246.	.3	2199.	.3
32 Electrical machinery	1541.	1.0	1297.	.7	1297.	.7	1207.	.6	1120.	.5	1101.	.4	1267.	.3	2204.	.3
33 Transport equipment	1004.	.7	925.	.5	925.	.5	915.	.5	797.	.4	778.	.3	864.	.2	1475.	.2
34 Motor vehicles	2426.	1.6	2850.	1.6	2850.	1.6	2784.	1.4	2512.	1.1	2510.	1.0	2928.	.8	5135.	.7
35 Other manufacturing	533.	.4	601.	.3	601.	.3	633.	.3	709.	.3	786.	.3	1124.	.3	2161.	.3
36 Construction	5566.	3.6	10879.	6.2	10879.	6.2	15066.	7.6	18862.	8.5	22727.	9.0	34141.	9.8	72226.	10.0
37 Electricity	11236.	7.3	15492.	8.9	15492.	8.9	18995.	9.6	22570.	10.1	26267.	10.4	40045.	10.8	78870.	11.0
38 Cinema	264.	.2	356.	.2	356.	.2	451.	.2	572.	.3	683.	.3	1077.	.3	2145.	.3
39 Transport	25052.	16.3	20816.	12.0	20816.	12.0	17037.	9.1	15558.	7.0	14323.	5.7	14170.	3.8	22498.	3.1
40 Communications	7324.	4.8	11514.	6.6	11514.	6.6	15202.	7.7	19032.	8.5	22745.	9.0	35893.	9.7	71554.	10.0
41 Trade	4637.	3.1	4068.	2.3	4068.	2.3	3377.	1.7	2479.	1.0	2200.	.9	1810.	.5	2369.	.3
42 Dwellings	3062.	2.5	3342.	1.9	3342.	1.9	2855.	1.4	2287.	1.0	2000.	.8	1674.	.5	2328.	.3
43 Hotels and restaurants	1759.	1.1	1455.	.8	1455.	.8	1284.	.7	1194.	.5	1154.	.5	1291.	.3	2211.	.3
44 Credit and insurance	827.	.5	802.	.5	802.	.5	827.	.4	835.	.4	845.	.3	1160.	.3	2174.	.3
45 Other services	6531.	4.2	11394.	6.5	11394.	6.5	13079.	7.1	16444.	7.5	19239.	7.6	29193.	7.9	57391.	8.0
T O T A L	153991.	100.0	174168.	100.0	174168.	100.0	196944.	100.0	223062.	100.0	252531.	100.0	370283.	100.0	718894.	100.0

269

Status-Quo-Plus-Oil Scenario

Table D.3.5: Private Investment by Destination (Cont.)

Sector	79/78	80/79	81/80	82/81	83/78	86/83	93/88	93/82
					Annual growth rates (percent)			
1 Agriculture	-12.5	-7.3	1.4	4.4	-1.8	11.4	14.0	12.1
2 Livestock	-18.2	-3.1	2.7	5.6	-1.5	11.8	14.1	12.5
3 Forestry	13.5	34.5	27.2	27.0	22.9	15.6	14.7	15.4
4 Fishing	154.8	29.3	21.8	16.6	40.3	14.8	14.6	14.8
5 Mining	-3.5	18.0	22.6	16.8	13.3	14.7	14.6	14.7
6 Quarrying	311.3	64.8	36.6	15.8	69.7	16.3	14.8	16.0
7 Petroleum	45.4	37.9	77.9	75.9	79.0	15.6	14.7	15.5
8 Slaughter of livestock	19.3	19.9	19.9	21.7	18.2	14.7	14.6	14.7
9 Milling	1.3	2.7	6.0	16.4	5.0	12.8	14.3	13.2
10 Other processed food	-4.9	10.5	3.1	8.6	5.2	12.5	14.2	13.1
11 Beverages	-14.9	-18.6	-17.9	-12.6	-14.7	1.5	11.7	4.9
12 Tobacco	71.0	36.5	31.3	22.0	34.7	15.7	11.7	15.5
13 Soft fiber textiles	-16.0	-13.0	44.2	-2.0	-6.9	9.1	13.6	10.4
14 Other textiles	*****	159.0	63.3	33.9	*****	17.5	14.9	17.0
15 Wearing apparel	-10.1	-13.8	7.2	-4.2	-8.9	8.0	13.4	9.6
16 Food and cork	81.1	43.6	30.9	72.5	37.8	15.8	14.7	15.6
17 Paper	-19.5	-10.5	-7.0	-3.3	-8.2	8.4	13.5	10.0
18 Printing, publishing	29.5	35.5	18.0	18.1	23.5	14.9	14.4	14.9
19 Leather	77.1	40.1	28.5	21.7	35.7	15.6	14.7	15.5
20 Rubber products	-2.5	7.3	-1.4	-3.3	3.3	11.7	14.1	12.5
21 Basic chemicals	267.3	100.9	94.7	33.7	89.1	17.7	14.9	17.2
22 Synthetic fibers	-15.2	-7.4	-4.4	-.1	-5.2	9.6	13.7	10.8
23 Fertilizers	*****	92.0	48.6	29.0	*****	16.8	14.8	16.5
24 Soaps and detergents	131.6	53.4	36.6	24.7	48.8	16.2	14.8	15.9
25 Drugs and medicines	-40.3	-63.1	-93.8	*****	*****	26.9	15.8	26.5
26 Perfumes, cosmetics	*****	102.2	42.5	79.1	*****	16.8	14.8	16.4
27 Other chemical indust.	-17.5	41.9	78.4	21.8	35.4	4.7	14.7	8.1
28 Nonmetallic mineral pr.	-14.3	-13.9	-12.5	-7.4	-11.1	5.9	12.9	8.1
29 Basic metallic indust.	-3.2	-11.9	-11.4	-5.7	-9.2	6.8	13.2	8.8
30 Metal products	-3.2	-2.5	-.3	.9	.9	11.3	14.0	12.1
31 Machinery	-6.1	-6.7	-.5	-.4	-3.9	9.5	13.7	10.7
32 Electrical machinery	-15.6	-1.1	-12.9	-1.8	-6.2	9.0	13.6	10.4
33 Transport equipment	-7.0	-2.3	-.8	-2.4	-4.9	8.2	13.5	9.8
34 Motor vehicles	1.4	5.2	12.0	-.1	-1.9	9.3	13.7	10.6
35 Other manufacturing	95.5	35.5	25.2	11.0	8.2	13.4	14.4	13.7
36 Construction	37.9	22.0	19.4	20.5	37.0	15.4	14.7	15.3
37 Electricity	35.0	26.6	26.7	16.3	22.0	14.7	14.6	14.7
38 Climate	-16.9	-13.8	-13.3	10.4	24.9	15.3	14.6	15.2
39 Transport	57.2	39.0	35.2	-7.9	-11.3	5.5	12.8	7.8
40 Communications	-15.6	-17.0	25.2	19.5	29.6	15.3	14.6	15.2
41 Trade	-15.4	-14.6	-20.6	-14.2	-15.9	-.5	11.0	3.5
42 Dwellings	-17.3	-14.4	-10.0	-12.6	-14.5	1.2	11.6	4.7
43 Hotels and restaurants	-3.1	-11.6	-7.0	-3.3	-8.0	8.4	13.5	9.9
44 Credit and insurance	74.4	22.7	19.2	15.5	27.7	11.9	14.1	12.5
45 Other services						14.6	14.5	14.6
T O T A L	13.1	13.1	13.3	13.3	13.2	13.9	14.5	14.1

Status-Quo-Plus-Oil Scenario

Table D.3.6: Investments by Origin

Sector	Millions of 1978 pesos							Annual growth rates (percent)							
	1978	1979	1980	1981	1982	1985	1990	79/78	80/79	81/80	82/81	83/7P	8A/83	93/8R	93/A2
1 Agriculture	11904.	12608.	12431.	13038.	13950.	18490.	33410.	5.2	-1.4	4.9	7.0	4.8	11.5	13.4	12.1
2 Livestock	1581.	1616.	1643.	1739.	1874.	2516.	4572.	2.2	1.7	5.8	7.8	5.3	11.8	13.4	12.3
3 Forestry	542.	779.	934.	1102.	1281.	1914.	3627.	43.9	19.9	18.0	16.2	22.1	13.8	13.7	13.9
4 Fishing	521.	527.	425.	725.	825.	1206.	2270.	1.1	18.6	16.0	13.8	12.5	13.4	13.7	13.4
5 Mining	174.	179.	204.	237.	265.	397.	736.	2.9	13.8	16.4	13.4	11.9	13.3	13.7	13.5
6 Quarrying	129.	184.	234.	263.	334.	408.	970.	42.2	27.3	21.2	17.8	24.8	14.2	13.8	14.1
7 Petroleum	132.	175.	212.	261.	291.	435.	825.	32.7	21.0	18.3	16.1	20.4	13.8	13.7	13.9
8 Slaughter of livestock	197.	224.	757.	756.	337.	491.	971.	13.8	14.7	15.1	13.7	14.2	13.3	13.7	13.5
9 Milling	559.	584.	617.	649.	734.	1013.	1861.	4.4	5.7	5.5	9.6	7.8	13.8	13.5	13.9
10 Other processed food	168.	169.	187.	194.	217.	250.	545.	-12.4	-15.0	-13.3	-7.7	-10.6	4.9	12.0	7.2
11 Beverages	246.	215.	193.	159.	131.	197.	374.	-26.9	20.2	19.6	16.2	19.5	13.3	13.5	12.6
12 Tobacco	62.	79.	94.	113.	146.	143.	219.	-10.5	-6.9	.5	2.5	-2.0	12.0	13.1	7.2
13 Soft fiber textiles	124.	111.	104.	104.	107.	132.	232.	63.3	35.8	28.0	20.6	32.2	10.2	13.1	13.9
14 Other textiles	22.	36.	49.	62.	75.	118.	232.	-12.9	-8.1	-2.2	.6	-3.9	14.7	13.9	11.1
15 Wearing apparel	143.	124.	114.	112.	112.	135.	232.	28.1	22.5	19.4	16.4	20.2	9.4	13.0	14.6
16 Wood and cork	167.	214.	253.	314.	364.	549.	1042.	-13.8	-5.3	-1.8	1.4	-3.2	13.7	13.7	10.5
17 Paper	310.	267.	253.	243.	252.	307.	532.	13.8	21.1	14.6	14.5	16.7	9.7	13.1	13.9
18 Printing, publishing	47.	78.	95.	109.	125.	183.	364.	24.7	21.6	16.5	16.1	19.8	13.5	13.1	10.8
19 Leather	37.	48.	58.	64.	80.	129.	228.	1.7	8.3	3.2	2.0	6.0	13.8	13.7	13.6
20 Rubber products	144.	146.	154.	163.	176.	237.	430.	25.4	26.7	34.9	3.6	24.9	13.4	13.4	13.9
21 Basic chemicals	45.	44.	55.	75.	90.	142.	275.	-9.3	-2.2	-.5	2.6	-.5	14.8	13.9	12.3
22 Synthetic fibers	128.	116.	113.	114.	119.	149.	262.	39.2	30.8	24.7	18.9	25.8	14.4	13.8	14.7
23 Fertilizers	446.	615.	805.	1006.	1194.	1847.	3542.	32.8	24.6	21.3	17.3	22.2	14.4	13.8	11.3
24 Soaps and detergents	175.	238.	296.	360.	427.	641.	1221.	-67.0	-8.0	125.0	56.5	21.3	14.1	14.3	14.4
25 Drugs and medicines	-105.	-215.	32.	73.	114.	226.	467.	52.1	33.4	22.8	19.0	26.2	18.6	14.3	17.0
26 Perfumes, cosmetics	130.	212.	282.	347.	412.	636.	1210.	27.1	22.2	18.5	16.1	19.7	14.4	13.8	14.3
27 Other chemical indust.	300.	301.	466.	552.	641.	940.	1820.	-13.5	-9.2	-7.0	-2.2	-6.3	13.8	13.7	13.9
28 Nonmetallic mineral pr.	240.	208.	189.	176.	172.	193.	322.	-10.1	-7.2	-5.9	-.7	-4.4	8.7	12.7	9.5
29 Basic metallic indust.	247.	221.	2080.	1956.	1943.	2251.	3813.	.8	1.9	3.8	6.9	4.4	8.7	12.9	10.0
30 Metal products	710.	716.	730.	757.	810.	1072.	1935.	13.1	13.2	12.9	12.8	12.9	13.1	13.6	12.1
31 Machinery	58662.	66549.	75304.	84990.	95842.	137814.	257378.	13.1	13.1	12.8	12.7	12.9	13.1	13.6	13.3
32 Electrical machinery	66597.	75293.	85169.	96110.	108360.	155783.	290916.	13.1	13.1	12.9	12.7	12.9	13.1	13.6	13.3
33 Transport equipment	16784.	18681.	20760.	23237.	26043.	37125.	69103.	11.3	11.1	11.9	12.1	11.8	12.9	13.6	13.2
34 Motor vehicles	1377.	1421.	1438.	1387.	1440.	1797.	3160.	3.1	1.2	-3.5	3.8	2.0	10.3	13.2	11.2
35 Other manufacturing	31.	33.	35.	39.	43.	61.	113.	4.8	7.4	11.4	10.9	9.2	12.7	13.6	13.0
36 Construction	1285414.	1398817.	1567633.	1759885.	1976695.	2827855.	5270527.	-67.0	12.3	12.3	12.3	12.1	13.3	13.6	13.2
37 Electricity	2207.	2459.	2845.	3270.	3716.	5413.	10158.	11.4	15.7	14.9	13.7	13.8	13.3	13.6	13.5
38 Cinema	125.	149.	174.	206.	236.	350.	662.	18.9	17.1	18.0	15.1	16.7	13.1	13.7	13.7
39 Transport	893.	770.	698.	643.	676.	696.	1153.	-13.8	-9.3	-7.8	-2.8	-6.7	7.8	12.7	9.3
40 Communications	535.	636.	758.	889.	1024.	1518.	2867.	18.9	19.2	17.3	15.1	17.0	13.6	13.7	13.7
41 Trade	2313.	1994.	1712.	1432.	1293.	1188.	1735.	-13.8	-14.1	-16.4	-9.7	-12.1	3.3	11.6	6.8
42 Dwellings	194.	168.	149.	127.	117.	113.	173.	-13.1	-11.5	-15.1	-7.8	-10.5	4.7	12.0	7.0
43 Hotels and restaurants	416.	367.	343.	337.	342.	415.	719.	-11.9	-6.3	-1.9	1.4	-3.0	9.7	13.1	10.7
44 Credit and insurance	334.	338.	358.	375.	405.	545.	991.	1.3	5.7	4.7	8.0	5.8	11.9	13.4	12.3
45 Other services	3572.	3693.	4285.	4921.	5573.	8097.	15178.	3.4	16.0	14.9	13.2	12.1	13.5	13.4	13.4
T O T A L	301526.	335469.	374556.	419359.	470350.	671200.	1249831.	11.3	11.7	12.0	12.2	11.9	12.9	13.6	13.2

Status-Quo-Plus-Oil Scenario

Table D.3.7: Imports, Exports, Balance of Trade, External Debt

Millions of 1978 pesos

S E C T O R		1978	1979	1980	1981	1982	1985	1990
1 Agriculture	Imports	37550.	39282.	40362.	43066.	46537.	61556.	104513.
	Exports	12707.	13342.	14009.	14710.	15445.	17880.	22820.
	Balance	-24843.	-25940.	-26352.	-28356.	-31092.	-43676.	-81693.
2 Livestock	Imports	423.	430.	458.	483.	513.	628.	944.
	Exports	53230.	52571.	51635.	50254.	49510.	41113.	19861.
	Balance	52807.	52132.	51176.	49774.	47997.	40484.	18918.
3 Forestry	Imports	594.	460.	737.	857.	923.	1290.	2332.
	Exports	4075.	4098.	5272.	5615.	6031.	7786.	12816.
	Balance	4391.	4328.	4535.	4790.	5108.	6487.	10484.
4 Fishing	Imports	1707.	1887.	1902.	2081.	2185.	2579.	37.
	Exports	14041.	13587.	13171.	12507.	11809.	8292.	6153.
	Balance	-12263.	-11650.	-11100.	-10516.	-9625.	-5763.	6115.
5 Mining	Imports	3303.	3777.	4199.	4613.	5055.	6632.	10761.
	Exports	12275.	12277.	12103.	12230.	12367.	13178.	15959.
	Balance	8685.	9333.	7904.	7616.	7313.	6547.	5197.
6 Quarrying	Imports	3034.	3333.	3516.	3752.	4018.	4921.	7254.
	Exports	4837.	4349.	5178.	5778.	6622.	10534.	22518.
	Balance	1803.	1561.	1662.	2017.	2604.	5613.	15263.
7 Petroleum	Imports	3437.	2337.	5722.	6417.	6622.	12982.	203A8.
	Exports	-3447.	-2337.	-6445.	24425.	51368.	162565.	483079.
	Balance	190219.	190953.	210331.	150008.	41100.	149583.	462720.
8 Slaughter of livestock	Imports	0.	0.	0.	291478.	233330.	276761.	390619.
	Exports	-190213.	-10996.	-213331.	-271478.	-23333A.	-276761.	0.
	Balance	1054.	0.	28.	30.	31.	36.	-390619.
9 Milling	Imports	-1535.	-40.	1477.	3403.	5259.	12004.	46.
	Exports	1071.	2905.	1648.	3373.	5228.	11969.	30525.
	Balance	3603.	1434.	6559.	10632.	14755.	30794.	30479.
10 Other processed food	Imports	1619.	-1472.	1506.	1581.	1660.	1922.	72986.
	Exports	144.	155.	164.	-4851.	-13095.	-28477.	2453.
	Balance	1040.	1330.	1347.	172.	180.	199.	-70533.
11 Beverages	Imports	1045.	1615.	1711.	13933.	13440.	9430.	6967.
	Exports	55.	65.	70.	13661.	13311.	9732.	390.
	Balance	1375.	2431.	4140.	78.	90.	135.	-6577.
12 Tobacco	Imports	1860.	2749.	4670.	5819.	7937.	16908.	263.
	Exports	1711.	1795.	1882.	5740.	7846.	16772.	43590.
	Balance	16951.	16994.	16712.	1976.	2079.	2465.	43327.
13 Soft fiber textiles	Imports	15240.	15189.	14230.	14159.	15416.	12954.	3507.
	Exports	300.	355.	434.	14187.	13337.	9589.	2276.
	Balance	3327.	4733.	7491.	496.	571.	914.	-1232.
14 Other textiles	Imports	3016.	4378.	6476.	10323.	14485.	32348.	1889.
	Exports	-1663.	655.	975A3.	9437.	13914.	31434.	85034.
	Balance	765.	803.	843.	108408.	120814.	169372.	83145.
15 Wearing apparel	Imports	8028A.	98429.	96719.	884.	930.	1077.	304027.
	Exports	18663.	16998.	19111.	-107522.	-119884.	-168296.	1374.
	Balance	0.	0.	0.	18959.	18502.	16655.	-302653.
16 Wood and cork	Imports	-18663.	-18998.	-19111.	-18049.	0.	0.	9430.
	Exports	11465.	11916.	12950.	1415A.	-18502.	-15555.	4045.
	Balance	-11465.	-11916.	-12950.	-1415A.	15783.	22661.	-5385.
17 Paper	Imports							42329.
	Exports							0.
	Balance							-42328.

Status-Quo-Plus-Oil Scenario

Table D.3.7: Imports, Exports, Balance of Trade, External Debt (Cont.)

Millions of 1978 pesos

SECTOR		1978	1979	1980	1981	1982	1983	1990
18 Printing, publishing	Imports	18937.	20828.	22827.	24904.	27126.	35077.	55573.
	Exports	0.	0.	0.	0.	0.	0.	0.
	Balance	-18937.	-20828.	-22827.	-24904.	-27126.	-35077.	-55573.
19 Leather	Imports	1030.	1211.	1442.	1773.	2055.	3900.	7176.
	Exports	6916.	9064.	11941.	15523.	19037.	37513.	84590.
	Balance	5886.	7853.	10499.	13800.	17782.	34123.	81433.
20 Rubber products	Imports	5812.	5950.	6315.	6534.	6680.	6643.	13902.
	Exports	0.	0.	0.	0.	0.	0.	0.
	Balance	-5812.	-5950.	-6315.	-6534.	-6680.	-6643.	-13902.
21 Basic chemicals	Imports	12340.	13266.	14475.	15984.	18877.	31705.	65879.
	Exports	4116.	3042.	1811.	409.	0.	0.	0.
	Balance	-8224.	-10224.	-12665.	-15574.	-18877.	-31705.	-65879.
22 Synthetic fibers	Imports	1341.	1459.	1602.	1747.	1902.	5020.	16007.
	Exports	1346.	1518.	1393.	1017.	424.	0.	0.
	Balance	5.	59.	-209.	-730.	-1478.	-5020.	-16007.
23 Fertilizers	Imports	4524.	3295.	1366.	314.	472.	871.	3177.
	Exports	0.	0.	0.	1661.	5312.	21144.	68465.
	Balance	-4524.	-3295.	-1366.	1347.	4890.	20773.	66280.
24 Soaps and detergents	Imports	0.	0.	0.	314.	1637.	1478.	177.
	Exports	11826.	11826.	10461.	5385.	14552.	14474.	62676.
	Balance	11826.	11826.	10461.	5385.	14552.	14474.	62501.
25 Drugs and medicines	Imports	958.	1197.	8305.	5613.	21350.	21350.	29525.
	Exports	315.	330.	347.	964.	443.	382.	56.
	Balance	-9273.	-11645.	-13627.	-15249.	-16755.	-20907.	-28960.
26 Perfumes, cosmetics	Imports	2466.	2489.	24183.	22625.	20341.	9312.	177.
	Exports	0.	0.	0.	0.	0.	0.	0.
	Balance	-24682.	-24691.	-24183.	-22525.	-20341.	-9312.	25801.
27 Other chemical indust.	Imports	3251.	7946.	3600.	3274.	9836.	6103.	256625.
	Exports	-3251.	-2864.	660.	2134.	3905.	11955.	125465.
	Balance	2377.	3714.	-2140.	-1133.	159.	5857.	35734.
28 Nonmetallic mineral pr.	Imports	3417.		10622.	19713.	30872.	77250.	23189.
	Exports	1040.	-3714.	-10622.	-19711.	-30872.	-77250.	211063.
	Balance	8014.	9932.	11266.	12691.	14273.	26982.	-211063.
29 Basic metallic indust.	Imports	16423.	17077.	17000.	15372.	12261.	2197.	99140.
	Exports	6608.	7095.	5736.	2881.	-2012.	-24785.	2804.
	Balance	9700.	10785.	11959.	13374.	14774.	25891.	-96336.
30 Metal products	Imports	18990.	10336.	9190.	7383.	5013.	0.	72284.
	Exports	1191.	-430.	-2760.	-5880.	-9761.	-25891.	0.
	Balance	48997.	56210.	64599.	74903.	86414.	132066.	-72284.
31 Machinery	Imports	-40937.	-56210.	-64599.	-74903.	-86414.	-258891.	263470.
	Exports	79839.	89800.	99867.	112409.	126839.	132066.	0.
	Balance	-40937.	-56210.	-64599.	-74903.	-86414.	-132066.	-72284.
32 Electrical machinery	Imports	79839.	89800.	99867.	112453.	126839.	183355.	344820.
	Exports	0.	0.	0.	0.	0.	0.	0.
	Balance	-79839.	-89800.	-99867.	-112453.	-126839.	-183355.	-344820.
33 Transport equipment	Imports	13512.	14974.	16424.	18137.	20712.	32068.	66703.
	Exports	0.	0.	0.	0.	0.	0.	0.
	Balance	-12638.	-14974.	-16424.	-18137.	-20712.	-32068.	-66703.
34 Motor vehicles	Imports	44615.	44750.	46759.	25641.	56947.	75940.	131913.
	Exports	0.	0.	0.	0.	0.	0.	0.
	Balance	-44615.	-46759.	-46759.	-25641.	-56987.	-75940.	-131913.

Status-Quo-Plus-Oil Scenario

Table D.3.7: Imports, Exports, Balance of Trade, External Debt (Cont.)

Millions of 1978 pesos

		1978	1979	1980	1981	1982	1985	1990
35 Other manufacturing	Imports	23441.	24135.	25005.	26040.	27160.	31343.	42200.
	Exports	0.	0.	0.	0.	0.	0.	0.
	Balance	-23441.	-24135.	-25005.	-26040.	-27160.	-31343.	-42200.
TOTAL	Imports	882927.	924511.	973351.	1068902.	1157823.	1586350.	2920707.
	Exports	160211.	170307.	180330.	210063.	248620.	429130.	1037537.
	Balance	-30743.	-32841.	-35258.	-38035.	-40994.	-52130.	-82350.
External debt [a]		687268.438	746949.532	903721.448	1031564.893	1175763.310	1723501.149	3188503.967

a) 10^9 1978 pesos; peso-dollar exchange rate (1978)= 22.72

Status-Quo-Plus-Oil Scenario

Table D.3.8: Government Accounts

Millions of 1978 pesos

	1978 Value	%	1979 Value	%	1980 Value	%	1981 Value	%	1982 Value	%	1985 Value	%	1990 Value	%
Incomes														
Direct Taxes	108896.	34.7	116195.	33.0	124694.	32.0	132472.	31.6	142596.	30.6	179216.	27.7	278789.	24.2
Indirect Taxes plus Exploitation Surplus	169304.	61.4	211290.	62.3	249158.	64.1	305073.	64.1	445598.	65.4	837777.	68.8		72.7
External Financing	15105.	4.8	15855.	4.4	16728.	4.4	17858.	4.3	19088.	4.1	23313.	3.6	35212.	3.1
TOTAL	313305.	100.0	342320.	100.0	378882.	100.0	415888.	100.0	466707.	100.0	648127.	100.0	1151697.	100.0
Expenditures														
Consumption of Goods and Services	29174.	9.3	32027.	9.3	35414.	9.3	39320.	9.4		9.4	61109.	9.4	109196.	9.5
Wages and Salaries	136617.	43.6	149070.	43.7	165840.	43.8	184130.	43.8	205310.	43.9	286165.	44.1	511350.	44.4
Investments	147549.	47.1	161304.	47.1	177615.	47.0	196400.	46.9	217823.	46.8	300922.	46.4	530944.	46.1
TOTAL	313340.	100.0	343210.	100.0	373876.	100.0	419950.	100.0	466011.	100.0	648195.	100.0	1151490.	100.0
Ratio Tax Revenues/GNP (percent)	16.4		16.8		17.4		18.0		18.7		20.7		23.8	
Share of Public Investment in Total Investment (percent)	48.9		48.1		47.4		46.8		46.3		44.8		42.5	

Status-Quo-Plus-Oil Scenario

Table D.3.8: Government Accounts (Cont.)

Annual growth rates (percent)

	79/78	80/79	81/80	82/81	83/74	84/83	93/88	93/83
Incomes								
Direct Taxes	6.7	6.8	7.1	7.3	7.1	6.6	10.2	9.2
Indirect Taxes plus Exploitation Surpluses	11.6	12.6	13.1	13.3	12.8	13.5	13.5	13.5
External Financing	5.0	5.5	6.8	6.9	6.0	7.8	9.5	8.4
TOTAL	9.5	10.3	10.8	11.2	10.6	11.9	12.6	12.1
Expenditures								
Consumption of Goods and Services	9.8	10.6	11.0	11.3	10.9	12.1	12.7	12.3
Wages and Salaries	9.8	10.6	11.6	11.3	10.9	12.1	12.7	12.3
Investments	9.3	10.1	10.6	10.9	10.4	11.7	12.4	12.0
TOTAL	9.6	10.4	10.8	11.1	10.7	11.9	12.6	12.2

Status-Quo-Plus-Oil Scenario

Table D.3.9: Sectoral Employment

No. of employed persons

Sector	1978	%	1979	%	1980	%	1981	%	1982	%	1985	%	1990	%
1 Agriculture	4826056	35.2	4974367	34.7	5128591	34.2	5274260	33.5	6425257	32.8	5056779	30.4	7369399	27.3
2 Livestock	235243	1.7	239612	1.7	244041	1.6	248493	1.6	253228	1.5	270560	1.6	317909	1.2
3 Forestry	97255	.7	103272	.7	112397	.7	123295	.8	136044	.8	185838	1.0	317149	1.2
4 Fishing	20958	.?	25186	.?	29250	.?	33954	.?	39050	.2	58710	.3	105944	.4
5 Mining	16785	.1	16046	.1	15338	.1	14710	.1	14170	.1	12948	.?	12033	.0
6 Quarrying	74827	.5	76528	.5	80133	.5	85122	.5	91200	.5	114338	.6	167231	.6
7 Petroleum	111783	.8	131156	.9	155923	1.0	183862	1.2	214518	1.3	318098	1.6	533758	2.0
8 Slaughter of livestock	258975	1.0	284355	2.0	313205	2.1	346273	2.2	384308	2.3	531880	2.7	939675	3.5
9 Milling	178691	1.3	185409	1.3	200420	1.3	211670	1.3	223645	1.4	266731	1.4	375169	1.4
10 Other processed food	149899	1.1	147065	1.0	144246	1.0	141734	.0	139300	.?	134108	.?	134455	.5
11 Beverages	98271	.7	101733	.7	102472	.7	102700	.7	102067	.6	98171	.?	92311	.3
12 Tobacco	10764	.1	11498	.?	12456	.?	13560	.?	14937	.?	19972	.?	37131	.1
13 Soft fiber textiles	137364	1.0	131903	.?	126146	.6	120150	.?	114351	.?	98798	.?	80651	.3
14 Other textiles	18776	.1	24485	.?	33560	.2	45700	.3	61160	.4	124194	.6	285122	1.1
15 Wearing apparel	354262	2.6	347133	2.4	337563	2.2	326789	2.1	315796	1.9	244644	1.5	248190	.9
16 Wood and cork	247510	1.8	280869	2.0	322996	2.?	373234	2.?	431206	2.?	646526	3.3	1163148	4.3
17 Paper	65295	.5	69576	.5	73070	.5	76252	.5	70281	.?	80149	.?	111110	.4
18 Printing, publishing	81571	.6	80075	.6	79017	.4	78543	.5	78424	.5	80149	.4	89593	.3
19 Leather	41081	.3	46647	.3	53691	.4	61042	.4	71371	.4	105713	.5	185946	.7
20 Rubber products	25411	.2	25559	.?	25531	.?	25231	.?	25224	.?	24588	.?	24391	.1
21 Basic chemicals	34528	.3	32793	.?	31278	.?	29994	.?	29014	.?	27157	.?	26722	.1
22 Synthetic fibers	25241	.?	26425	.?	27326	.?	28101	.?	28901	.?	30945	.2	36416	.1
23 Fertilizers	9456	.1	12756	.?	17633	.?	24481	.?	32649	.?	66009	.3	158712	.6
24 Soaps and detergents	8357	.1	9119	.?	10177	.?	11240	.?	12465	.?	16074	.?	21351	.1
25 Drugs and medicines	45737	.3	42067	.3	40110	.?	39650	.4	40040	.?	45359	.2	65054	.2
26 Perfumes, cosmetics	13239	.1	14530	.?	17347	.?	20595	.?	24346	.?	37827	.2	66548	.2
27 Other chemical indust.	14121	.1	15756	.?	17414	.?	20264	.?	23077	.?	33446	.2	58112	.2
28 Nonmetallic mineral pr.	191645	1.4	184536	1.3	185606	1.2	180439	1.1	174728	1.1	157480	.8	135937	.5
29 Basic metallic indust.	114757	.8	123277	.9	129785	.?	134825	.9	138760	.8	148495	.8	169649	.6
30 Metal products	215070	1.6	225771	1.6	229192	.0	246189	1.4	256347	1.6	291054	1.5	379032	1.4
31 Machinery	113218	.8	121554	.8	129192	.9	136365	.9	143137	.?	164473	.8	215993	.8
32 Electrical machinery	225256	1.6	241375	1.7	250671	1.7	267944	1.7	290137	1.7	318526	1.6	410127	1.5
33 Transport equipment	224675	1.6	240164	1.7	253671	1.7	266436	1.7	277000	1.7	307317	1.6	375365	1.4
34 Motor vehicles	113621	.?	121109	.?	128216	.?	134730	.?	140193	.?	156049	.8	191574	.7
35 Other manufacturing	269911	2.?	346558	2.4	404233	2.7	466359	3.0	534072	3.3	926869	4.3	1727011	6.4
36 Construction	869165	6.3	1009546	7.?	1177640	7.3	1377866	8.8	1605694	9.7	2454477	12.6	4554059	16.9
37 Electricity	86410	.6	95951	.7	106678	.?	117662	.7	122554	.8	172708	.9	271519	1.0
38 Gas	134140	1.0	141122	1.0	149337	1.0	155299	1.0	170174	1.0	214686	1.1	341841	1.3
39 Transport	530707	4.0	657640	4.?	776432	4.5	695471	4.4	705616	4.3	747513	3.8	835172	3.1
40 Communications	60176	.4	67966	.?	76345	.5	85424	.5	95016	.6	125001	.6	177894	.7
41 Trade	1543341	11.3	1583325	11.1	1617432	10.8	1645100	10.5	1667000	10.1	1719070	8.8	1813794	6.7
42 Dwellings	7162	.1	7204	.?	7340	.0	7272	.?	7299	.0	7372	.0	7513	.0
43 Hotels and restaurants	380695	2.8	383734	2.7	384764	2.6	386434	2.4	383669	2.3	381679	2.0	392392	1.5
44 Credit and insurance	202849	1.5	215517	1.5	228605	1.5	242302	1.5	256873	1.6	300213	1.6	446949	1.7
45 Other services	1083266	7.9	1058636	7.7	1111067	7.4	1256769	7.2	1154258	7.0	1256842	6.5	1535758	5.7
TOTAL	13596233	100.0	14331365	100.0	15010067	100.0	15738254	100.0	16532723	100.0	19438884	100.0	27008886	100.0

Status-Quo-Plus-Oil Scenario

Table D.3.9: Sectoral Employment (Cont.)

Annual growth rates (percent)

Sector	74/71	../..	81/80	82/81	83/78	88/83	93/88	93/82
1 Agriculture	3.1	3.1	2.8	2.9	3.0	3.7	5.5	4.4
2 Livestock	4.0	3.1	1.0	1.0	1.9	2.7	4.4	3.4
3 Forestry	6.2	6.6	9.7	10.3	9.2	11.2	11.4	11.2
4 Fishing	20.2	16.1	16.1	15.6	16.6	13.4	12.1	13.0
5 Mining	-4.4	-4.4	-4.1	-3.7	-4.9	-2.7	-.3	-1.4
6 Quarrying	2.3	4.7	4.2	7.1	5.6	7.9	7.8	7.8
7 Petroleum	17.3	18.9	17.9	16.7	17.2	12.3	9.5	11.3
8 Slaughter of livestock	9.0	10.1	10.6	11.0	10.5	11.8	12.4	12.0
9 Milling	6.0	5.4	5.6	5.7	5.8	6.5	8.0	7.1
10 Other processed food	-1.0	-1.0	-1.7	-1.7	-1.7	-.7	1.0	-.6
11 Beverages	2.4	1.4	.7	-.4	.6	-1.4	-1.6	-1.0
12 Tobacco	6.4	8.3	9.2	9.9	8.9	10.1	9.8	10.0
13 Soft fiber textiles	-3.0	-4.4	-4.6	-4.8	-4.5	-4.4	-3.1	-3.8
14 Other textiles	30.0	37.6	36.5	33.4	33.4	22.1	16.1	20.0
15 Wearing apparel	-2.7	-2.4	-3.2	-3.4	-3.0	-3.1	-1.8	-2.6
16 Wood and cork	13.6	15.6	15.4	15.6	14.9	13.4	11.5	12.7
17 Paper	6.4	5.0	4.4	4.0	4.7	4.1	5.7	4.8
18 Printing, publishing	-1.2	-1.2	-.6	-.1	-.7	1.5	3.3	2.2
19 Leather	13.9	15.1	15.4	15.2	14.6	12.9	11.0	12.2
20 Rubber products	-.6	-.6	-.6	-.3	-.7	-.6	.6	-.1
21 Basic chemicals	-5.0	-4.4	-4.1	-4.4	-3.9	-1.2	.9	-.4
22 Synthetic fibers	4.7	3.4	2.8	2.5	3.2	2.8	4.3	3.4
23 Fertilizers	40.0	40.0	37.0	33.4	36.1	22.1	16.6	20.2
24 Soaps and detergents	9.1	10.9	11.2	10.8	10.4	7.2	4.5	6.2
25 Drugs and medicines	-6.0	-4.7	-1.1	1.0	-2.1	6.2	8.6	7.0
26 Perfumes, cosmetics	12.6	17.0	18.7	18.2	14.6	13.7	10.3	12.4
27 Other chemical indust.	11.6	13.1	13.6	13.9	13.2	12.4	11.0	11.8
28 Nonmetallic mineral pr.	-1.1	-2.1	-2.7	-3.2	-2.5	-3.2	-2.1	-2.7
29 Basic metallic indust.	7.4	5.2	3.9	2.9	4.4	2.3	3.6	2.9
30 Metal products	5.4	5.2	4.5	4.1	4.4	4.8	6.5	5.5
31 Machinery	7.4	6.3	5.5	5.0	5.0	5.1	6.5	5.7
32 Electrical machinery	7.2	5.7	5.0	4.5	5.4	4.7	6.2	5.3
33 Transport equipment	6.0	6.6	5.1	4.0	5.0	3.7	5.0	4.3
34 Motor vehicles	5.5	5.9	5.1	4.0	5.1	3.8	5.1	4.4
35 Other manufacturing	16.7	15.4	16.4	15.4	15.7	15.6	16.3	15.9
36 Construction	16.0	16.6	17.0	16.6	14.6	14.1	12.2	13.4
37 Electricity	11.1	10.6	10.6	10.5	10.6	9.7	9.2	9.5
38 Gas	5.2	5.2	6.4	7.1	6.4	8.0	10.8	9.7
39 Transport	4.3	3.2	2.5	2.0	2.7	1.9	3.1	2.4
40 Communications	13.0	12.3	11.9	11.2	11.7	8.3	6.4	7.6
41 Trade	2.6	2.1	1.7	1.3	1.4	1.0	1.5	1.2
42 Dwellings	.4	.4	.4	.4	.4	.3	.5	.4
43 Hotels and restaurants	4.2	.2	-.1	-.2	.4	.1	1.5	.7
44 Credit and insurance	6.2	6.0	6.0	6.0	6.1	7.0	8.8	7.7
45 Other services	1.4	1.1	1.7	2.2	1.8	3.5	4.0	4.0
T O T A L	4.6	4.7	4.9	5.0	4.9	4.2	7.8	6.8

Status-Quo-Plus-Oil Scenario

Table D.3.10: Employment by Socio-economic Group

Thousands of persons

Socio-economic group	1 9 7 8	%	1 9 7 9	%	1 9 8 0	%	1 9 8 1	%	1 9 8 2	%	1 9 8 5	%	1 9 9 0	%
1. Entr. Empl. Prof. (H)	1043482.	7.6	1095596.	7.6	1150894.	7.7	1211275.	7.7	1277186.	7.7	1519458.	7.8	2150868.	8.0
2. Entr. Empl. Prof. (M)	2711369.	19.8	2844153.	19.8	2985284.	19.9	3138992.	19.9	3306739.	20.0	3923074.	20.2	5528933.	20.5
3. Entr. Empl. Prof. (L)	3612138.	26.4	3730442.	26.4	3959020.	26.4	4151945.	26.4	4361867.	26.4	5131329.	26.4	7136649.	26.4
4. Workers	2407249.	17.6	2539356.	17.7	2680981.	17.9	2837978.	18.0	3010668.	18.2	3648814.	18.8	5309449.	19.7
5. Peasants (H-M)	208979.	1.5	215429.	1.5	222169.	1.5	228568.	1.5	235221.	1.4	258707.	1.3	321071.	1.2
6. Peasants (L)	703195.	5.1	724899.	5.1	747577.	5.0	769109.	4.9	791495.	4.8	870525.	4.5	1080375.	4.0
7. Landless Workers	3009822.	22.0	3131474.	21.9	3264143.	21.7	3401390.	21.6	3549546.	21.5	4086976.	21.0	5481541.	20.3
T O T A L	13696233.	100.0	14331348.	100.0	15010057.	100.0	15739256.	100.0	16532723.	100.0	19438884.	100.0	27008886.	100.0

Status-Quo-Plus-Oil Scenario

Table D.3.10: Employment by Socio-economic Group (Cont.)

Annual growth rates (percent)

Socio-economic group	79/78	80/79	81/80	82/81	83/78	88/83	93/88	93/82
1. Entr. Empl. Prof. (H)	5.0	5.0	5.2	5.4	5.3	6.6	8.2	7.2
2. Entr. Empl. Prof. (M)	4.9	5.0	5.1	5.3	5.2	6.5	8.1	7.1
3. Entr. Empl. Prof. (L)	4.7	4.7	4.9	5.1	4.9	6.2	7.8	6.8
4. Workers	5.5	5.6	5.9	6.1	5.9	7.2	8.7	7.8
5. Peasants (H-M)	3.1	3.1	2.9	2.9	3.0	3.8	5.6	4.5
6. Peasants (L)	3.1	3.1	2.9	2.9	3.0	3.8	5.6	4.5
7. Landless Workers	4.0	4.2	4.2	4.4	4.3	5.4	7.1	6.1
T O T A L	4.6	4.7	4.9	5.0	4.9	6.2	7.8	6.8

Status-Quo-Plus-Oil Scenario

Table D.3.11: Income by Socio-economic Group

Millions of 1978 pesos

Socio-economic group	1 9 7 8	%	1 9 7 9	%	1 9 8 0	%	1 9 8 1	%	1 9 8 2	%	1 9 8 5	%	1 9 9 0	%
1. Entr. Empl. Prof. (H)	429343.	24.4	457893.	24.3	488862.	24.3	523020.	24.2	560607.	24.2	701377.	24.0	1082273.	23.8
2. Entr. Empl. Prof. (M)	502878.	28.6	533317.	28.3	565507.	28.1	600208.	27.8	637658.	27.5	775175.	26.5	1141995.	25.1
3. Entr. Empl. Prof. (L)	271985.	15.4	285866.	15.2	300154.	14.9	315259.	14.6	331306.	14.3	389196.	13.3	541609.	11.9
4. Workers	373330.	21.2	413419.	22.0	459188.	22.8	511508.	23.7	570580.	24.6	797816.	27.3	1424069.	31.3
5. Peasants (H-M)	56137.	3.2	58797.	3.1	61593.	3.1	64467.	3.0	67553.	2.9	78693.	2.7	108060.	2.4
6. Peasants (L)	32881.	1.9	34511.	1.8	36224.	1.8	37984.	1.8	39870.	1.7	46664.	1.6	64540.	1.4
7. Landless Workers	93943.	5.3	98272.	5.2	102906.	5.1	107722.	5.0	112931.	4.9	131915.	4.5	182300.	4.0
T O T A L	1760498.	100.0	1882064.	99.9	2014436.	100.1	2160168.	100.1	2320505.	100.1	2920837.	99.9	4544845.	99.9

Status-Quo-Plus-Oil Scenario

Table D.3.11: Income by Socio-economic Group (Cont.)

Socio-economic group		Annual growth rates (percent)							
		79/73	80/79	81/80	82/81	83/82	88/83	93/88	93/82
1. Entr. Empl. Prof. (H)		6.6	6.6	7.0	7.3	7.0	8.4	10.1	9.1
2. Entr. Empl. Prof. (M)		6.1	6.3	6.6	6.2	6.2	7.4	9.2	8.1
3. Entr. Empl. Prof. (L)		5.1	5.0	5.0	5.1	5.0	6.1	8.0	6.9
4. Workers		10.7	11.1	11.1	11.4	11.5	11.3	12.6	12.3
5. Peasants (H-M)		4.7	4.6	4.7	4.6	4.8	5.9	7.7	6.6
6. Peasants (L)		4.9	5.0	5.0	4.0	5.0	5.0	7.9	6.8
7. Landless Workers		4.4	4.7	4.7	4.7	4.8	6.0	7.9	6.7
T O T A L		6.5	7.0	7.7	7.4	7.4	7.3	8.6	10.2	9.2

Status-Quo-Plus-Oil Scenario

Table D.3.12: Average Income by Socio-economic Group, Gini Coefficient and Welfare Indicators

Socio-economic group	Thousands of 1978 pesos							Annual growth rates (percent)								
	1978	1979	1980	1981	1982	1985	1990	79/78	80/79	81/80	82/81	83/82	88/83	93/88	93/84	93/82
1. Entr.Empl.Prof. (H)	411.	418.	425.	432.	439.	462.	503.	1.7	1.7	1.6	1.6	1.7	1.7	1.7	1.7	1.7
2. Entr.Empl.Prof. (M)	185.	188.	189.	191.	193.	198.	207.	.5	.9	1.0	1.0	.9	1.0	1.0	.9
3. Entr.Empl.Prof. (L)	75.	76.	76.	76.	76.	76.	76.	.0	.0	.0	0.0	0.0	0.0	0.7	0.2
4. Workers	165.	153.	171.	180.	190.	219.	248.	4.0	5.3	5.4	5.1	4.5	5.7	4.1	1.5
5. Peasants (H-M)	269.	273.	277.	282.	287.	304.	337.	1.5	1.8	1.8	1.7	2.0	2.1	2.3	1.9
6. Peasants (L)	47.	48.	48.	49.	49.	54.	60.	2.1	2.1	2.0	1.6	2.2	2.6	2.3
7. Landless Workers	31.	31.	32.	32.	32.	32.	33.	0.0	3.2	0.0	.5	.6	.4	.6	.5
T O T A L	129.	131.	134.	137.	140.	150.	168.	2.0	1.8	2.0	1.9	2.0	2.0	2.0	2.0	2.0
Welfare indicators																
Gini Coefficient	.413	.411	.411	.410	.409	.411	.415	.20	.20	.20	.20	.20	.20	.20	.20	.20
Efficiency-equity[a]	1.033	1.106	1.182	1.265	1.358	1.692	2.573									
Equal weights								2.1	1.7	1.6	1.7	1.6	1.7	1.6	1.4	1.5
Poverty weighted								2.4	2.2	2.1	2.2	2.0	2.0	1.8	1.9

a) 10^{12} 1978 pesos

New Development Strategy

Table D.4.1: Sectoral Gross Output

Sector	Millions of 1978 pesos							Annual growth rates (percent)							
	1978	1979	1980	1981	1982	1985	.990	79/78	80/79	81/80	82/81	83/78	88/83	93/88	93/82
1 Agriculture	169963.	171165.	186863.	208161.	234518.	347615.	691178.	4.2	5.5	11.4	12.7	9.4	14.5	15.2	14.7
2 Livestock	98669.	100405.	102342.	104327.	106481.	114609.	137953.	1.8	1.9	1.9	2.1	2.0	3.1	5.2	3.9
3 Forestry	8611.	9225.	10174.	11275.	12549.	17591.	32374.	7.1	10.3	10.8	11.3	10.2	12.4	13.9	13.0
4 Fishing	6863.	8612.	10137.	13742.	18436.	40590.	116552.	25.5	17.7	35.6	34.2	28.8	26.6	20.4	24.2
5 Mining	23870.	24593.	25344.	26183.	27150.	30904.	41843.	3.0	3.1	3.3	3.7	3.4	5.3	8.0	6.4
6 Quarrying	14665.	16049.	17818.	19923.	22374.	32073.	60526.	9.4	11.0	11.8	12.3	11.4	13.1	14.3	13.6
7 Petroleum	112585.	139328.	174104.	200309.	227202.	313472.	517115.	23.8	25.0	15.1	13.4	17.7	10.5	11.6	11.2
8 Slaughter of livestock	40194.	43859.	47941.	61012.	78614.	165082.	468933.	9.1	9.3	27.3	28.9	20.3	25.8	20.3	23.5
9 Milling	63706.	73342.	77920.	91343.	109141.	195867.	499822.	6.6	6.4	17.2	19.5	13.9	21.5	19.0	20.3
10 Other processed food	139910.	141992.	144879.	160467.	181035.	277700.	541106.	2.1	2.1	10.8	12.8	8.3	15.6	12.5	14.1
11 Beverages	58626.	61359.	63558.	65316.	66840.	71617.	84041.	4.7	3.6	2.8	2.3	3.1	2.7	4.5	3.5
12 Tobacco	15859.	17642.	19781.	22248.	25111.	36365.	63303.	11.2	12.1	12.5	12.9	12.3	13.4	14.4	13.8
13 Soft fiber textiles	56687.	58248.	59608.	60873.	62187.	66912.	80208.	2.8	2.3	2.2	2.2	2.3	3.0	5.1	3.9
14 Other textiles	4896.	7062.	10002.	13609.	17927.	35232.	86290.	44.3	41.6	36.1	31.7	36.2	21.8	12.1	20.6
15 Wearing apparel	108996.	112424.	115303.	126382.	140737.	207313.	358090.	3.1	2.6	9.6	11.4	7.8	12.6	12.1	12.4
16 Wood and cork	17251.	20381.	24157.	37060.	54560.	140898.	444695.	18.1	18.5	53.4	47.2	34.9	30.7	21.5	27.3
17 Paper	35111.	36940.	38470.	44624.	52038.	81326.	160026.	5.2	4.1	16.0	16.6	11.6	20.4	14.8	15.0
18 Printing, publishing	25826.	26927.	28181.	32336.	37918.	65365.	161833.	4.3	4.7	14.7	17.3	11.8	20.4	18.6	19.4
19 Leather	17055.	20222.	24044.	26482.	33599.	53693.	112459.	18.6	18.9	18.5	18.0	18.3	16.7	15.9	16.2
20 Rubber products	11122.	12034.	12950.	13930.	14960.	18813.	29825.	8.2	7.6	7.6	7.4	7.7	8.7	11.2	9.7
21 Basic chemicals	18408.	18820.	19313.	19897.	20625.	23548.	32202.	2.2	2.6	3.0	3.7	3.1	5.4	8.2	6.6
22 Synthetic fibers	17311.	18296.	19172.	20025.	20905.	24099.	33110.	5.7	4.8	4.5	4.4	4.8	5.6	8.2	6.7
23 Fertilizers	4784.	7339.	10397.	14077.	18422.	35670.	86376.	53.4	41.7	35.4	30.9	37.4	21.4	17.9	20.3
24 Soaps and detergents	12928.	15920.	19606.	23346.	29015.	49043.	107783.	23.1	23.2	22.1	21.2	21.9	17.9	16.6	17.5
25 Drugs and medicines	17524.	17376.	17724.	18489.	19490.	23847.	37094.	-.8	2.0	4.3	5.4	3.4	8.1	10.9	9.2
26 Perfumes, cosmetics	11571.	14239.	17758.	22052.	27075.	47050.	105767.	23.1	24.7	24.2	22.8	23.2	18.6	16.9	18.1
27 Other chemical indust.	19668.	22833.	26641.	31079.	36194.	56286.	115051.	16.1	16.7	16.5	16.5	16.4	15.5	16.9	15.6
28 Nonmetallic mineral pr.	53423.	55461.	57131.	58616.	60034.	64878.	97916.	3.8	3.0	2.6	2.4	2.9	4.3	18.4	10.3
29 Basic metallic indust.	84004.	90363.	95826.	100815.	105639.	122380.	171130.	7.6	6.0	5.2	4.8	5.7	5.7	11.3	8.1
30 Metal products	47410.	49939.	52445.	54992.	57692.	67725.	139385.	5.3	5.0	4.9	4.9	5.1	8.7	27.6	16.6
31 Machinery	28556.	30412.	32151.	33848.	35573.	41816.	85768.	6.5	5.7	5.3	5.1	5.6	8.6	27.5	16.5
32 Electrical machinery	40753.	43174.	45293.	47354.	49439.	56933.	98673.	5.9	4.9	4.5	4.4	4.9	5.7	26.4	14.6
33 Transport equipment	30905.	33076.	35092.	37116.	39057.	45944.	108146.	7.8	6.1	5.8	5.2	5.9	9.7	32.8	19.3
34 Motor vehicles	82863.	89295.	95708.	102121.	108461.	131336.	236772.	7.8	7.2	6.7	6.2	6.8	8.5	20.5	13.6
35 Other manufacturing	19930.	22010.	24172.	26481.	29063.	38934.	110529.	10.4	9.8	9.6	9.7	9.9	14.6	34.9	23.0
36 Construction	276659.	333517.	397092.	465544.	542879.	841155.	1681104.	20.1	19.1	17.2	16.6	17.8	15.4	13.4	14.6
37 Electricity	35726.	41221.	46981.	53042.	59832.	85772.	157431.	15.4	14.0	12.9	12.8	13.5	12.9	12.5	12.7
38 Cinema	16634.	17342.	18156.	19081.	20148.	24321.	36509.	4.3	4.7	5.1	5.6	5.1	7.4	10.1	8.5
39 Transport	76228.	79153.	81515.	83606.	85580.	92269.	110489.	3.8	3.0	2.6	2.4	2.8	3.0	5.0	3.9
40 Communications	18771.	23035.	27802.	32877.	38629.	60782.	124330.	22.7	20.7	18.3	17.5	19.2	16.1	13.5	15.0
41 Trade	627763.	639052.	647892.	654955.	660723.	678039.	721784.	1.8	1.4	1.1	.9	1.2	1.0	1.8	1.4
42 Dwellings	99027.	99373.	99650.	99881.	100076.	100682.	102253.	.3	.3	.2	.2	.2	.2	.5	.3
43 Hotels and restaurants	75772.	77748.	79434.	81004.	82596.	88261.	104102.	2.6	2.2	2.0	2.0	2.2	2.7	4.6	3.5
44 Credit and insurance	62024.	64678.	67332.	70121.	73094.	84230.	116108.	4.3	4.1	4.1	4.2	4.3	5.7	8.3	6.8
45 Other services	120559.	129616.	138134.	146853.	156706.	195581.	300593.	7.7	6.6	6.3	6.7	6.9	8.6	8.7	8.5
	2934454.	3140900.	3365992.	3659479.	4000322.	5393621.	9714775.	7.0	7.2	8.7	9.3	8.4	11.5	14.1	12.5

New Development Strategy

Table D.4.2: Private Consumption

Sector	Millions of 1978 pesos							Annual growth rates (percent)							
	1978	1979	1980	1981	1982	1985	1990	79/78	80/79	81/80	82/81	83/78	88/83	93/88	93/82
1 Agriculture	99572.	103693.	108138.	114015.	120748.	148010.	229415.	4.1	4.3	5.4	5.9	5.2	8.1	11.0	9.3
2 Livestock	28091.	29440.	30880.	32746.	34878.	43362.	68314.	4.8	4.9	6.0	6.5	5.8	8.5	11.3	9.6
3 Forestry	0.	0.	0.	0.	0.	0.	0.	0.0	0.0	0.0	0.0	0.0	0.0	0.0	0.0
4 Fishing	14143.	14917.	15729.	16701.	17785.	21947.	33764.	5.5	5.4	6.2	6.5	6.0	8.1	10.7	9.1
5 Mining	0.	0.	0.	0.	0.	0.	0.	0.0	0.0	0.0	0.0	0.0	0.0	0.0	0.0
6 Quarrying	0.	0.	0.	0.	0.	0.	0.	0.0	0.0	0.0	0.0	0.0	0.0	0.0	0.0
7 Petroleum	53725.	56865.	60215.	64447.	69288.	88727.	147364.	5.8	5.9	7.0	7.5	6.9	9.6	12.5	10.8
8 Slaughter of livestock	243369.	255745.	269023.	286432.	306535.	388207.	636963.	5.1	5.2	6.5	7.0	6.3	9.3	12.3	10.5
9 Milling	67181.	70203.	73454.	77841.	82917.	103488.	165186.	4.5	4.6	6.0	6.5	5.7	8.7	11.6	9.9
10 Other processed food	103026.	112988.	118375.	125689.	134179.	168712.	273054.	4.6	4.8	6.2	6.8	5.9	9.0	11.8	10.1
11 Beverages	49917.	52322.	54911.	58353.	62324.	78347.	126350.	4.8	4.9	6.2	6.8	6.0	9.0	11.8	10.1
12 Tobacco	14270.	15000.	15777.	16755.	17859.	22147.	34341.	5.1	5.2	6.2	7.2	6.0	8.3	11.5	10.3
13 Soft fiber textiles	14267.	15112.	16009.	17108.	18345.	23153.	37020.	5.9	5.9	6.9	7.7	7.2	8.9	11.5	10.0
14 Other textiles	186141.	196833.	208348.	223263.	240469.	310284.	523928.	5.7	5.9	7.2	7.7	6.9	9.9	12.9	11.1
15 Wearing apparel	24658.	26027.	27493.	29369.	31513.	40040.	65288.	5.6	5.6	6.8	7.3	6.6	9.3	12.0	10.4
16 Wood and cork	12481.	13181.	13919.	14814.	15816.	19667.	30561.	5.6	5.6	6.4	7.6	6.6	8.3	10.9	9.4
17 Paper	26262.	27846.	29535.	31642.	34041.	43562.	71943.	6.0	5.9	7.1	7.6	7.0	9.5	12.3	10.7
18 Printing, publishing	9341.	9894.	10473.	11152.	11901.	14712.	22438.	6.0	5.9	6.5	6.3	6.3	7.4	9.5	8.3
19 Leather	7139.	7571.	8019.	8527.	9078.	11083.	16332.	6.0	5.8	6.5	6.7	6.4	8.0	10.4	9.0
20 Rubber products	5415.	5738.	6072.	6437.	6827.	8181.	11428.	5.9	5.8	6.5	6.0	6.0	6.5	7.9	7.1
21 Basic chemicals	5127.	5430.	5743.	6087.	6454.	7722.	10700.	6.0	4.6	6.0	6.0	6.0	6.4	7.6	6.9
22 Synthetic fibers	0.	0.	0.	0.	0.	0.	0.	0.0	0.0	0.0	0.0	0.0	0.0	0.0	0.0
23 Fertilizers	5255.	5577.	5909.	6272.	6658.	7996.	11197.	5.9	5.8	5.8	6.2	6.0	8.1	10.8	9.2
24 Soaps and detergents	24921.	26058.	27269.	28840.	30630.	37715.	58330.	4.6	4.6	6.0	6.4	5.6	8.1	10.8	9.3
25 Drugs and medicines	18142.	19023.	19961.	21158.	22514.	27828.	43120.	4.9	5.5	6.0	6.4	5.8	8.2	12.0	10.3
26 Perfumes, cosmetics	36974.	38983.	41128.	43851.	46964.	59393.	96564.	5.4	5.5	6.5	6.1	6.1	9.1	12.0	10.3
27 Other chemical indust.	5255.	5577.	5909.	6272.	6658.	7996.	11197.	6.1	6.0	6.1	6.1	6.1	6.6	8.0	7.2
28 Nonmetallic mineral pr.	7849.	8270.	8709.	9224.	9787.	11859.	17280.	5.4	5.3	6.1	5.8	5.8	7.2	9.1	8.0
29 Basic metallic indust.	0.	0.	0.	0.	0.	0.	0.	0.0	0.0	0.0	0.0	0.0	0.0	0.0	0.0
30 Metal products	10954.	11582.	12249.	13074.	14001.	17571.	27627.	5.7	5.8	6.7	7.1	6.6	8.6	11.0	9.6
31 Machinery	4716.	4982.	5253.	5541.	5840.	6828.	8935.	5.6	5.4	5.5	5.4	5.5	5.4	6.0	5.7
32 Electrical machinery	37430.	39578.	41871.	44763.	48066.	61266.	100880.	5.7	5.8	6.9	7.4	6.7	9.4	12.3	10.4
33 Transport equipment	19490.	20652.	21891.	23437.	25192.	32118.	52539.	6.0	6.0	7.1	7.5	6.9	9.4	12.1	10.4
34 Motor vehicles	68736.	73874.	79387.	86174.	93932.	125080.	220660.	7.5	7.5	8.5	9.0	8.4	11.0	13.8	12.1
35 Other manufacturing	35002.	37206.	39562.	42498.	45848.	59212.	99456.	6.3	6.3	7.4	7.3	7.3	9.9	12.7	11.0
36 Construction	0.	0.	0.	0.	0.	0.	0.	0.0	0.0	0.0	0.0	0.0	0.0	0.0	0.0
37 Electricity	35901.	37828.	39888.	42537.	45572.	57720.	94025.	5.4	5.4	6.6	7.1	6.4	9.2	12.0	10.3
38 Cinema	29360.	31456.	33696.	36492.	39684.	52453.	91052.	7.1	7.1	8.3	8.7	8.1	10.7	13.4	11.7
39 Transport	60681.	64115.	67801.	72535.	77976.	99891.	166232.	5.7	5.7	7.0	7.5	6.8	9.6	12.5	10.8
40 Communications	17817.	18953.	20148.	21564.	23150.	29323.	47417.	6.4	6.3	7.0	7.4	7.0	9.1	11.9	10.2
41 Trade	15046.	16040.	17086.	18327.	19716.	25103.	40802.	6.6	6.5	7.3	7.2	7.2	9.2	12.0	10.3
42 Dwellings	58464.	61443.	64583.	68450.	72840.	90309.	142656.	5.1	5.1	6.0	6.4	5.9	8.5	11.5	9.7
43 Hotels and restaurants	16492.	17441.	18441.	19644.	20993.	26225.	41364.	5.8	5.7	6.5	6.9	6.4	8.6	11.3	9.7
44 Credit and insurance	9204.	9853.	10533.	11315.	12179.	15444.	24609.	7.1	6.9	7.6	7.6	7.4	8.9	11.4	10.0
45 Other services	145049.	154776.	165158.	178077.	192867.	252490.	435418.	6.7	6.7	7.8	8.3	7.7	10.4	13.3	11.6
TOTAL	1626609.	1716495.	1812638.	1935150.	2075401.	2637178.	4324822.	5.5	5.6	6.8	7.2	6.6	9.3	12.2	10.5

New Development Strategy

Table D.4.3: Government Consumption of Goods and Services

Sector	Millions of 1978 pesos							Annual growth rates (percent)							
	1978	1979	1980	1981	1982	1985	1990	79/78	80/79	81/80	82/81	83/78	88/83	93/88	93/82
1 Agriculture	184.	199.	216.	234.	255.	336.	576.	8.1	8.6	8.6	8.9	8.7	10.4	13.1	11.5
2 Livestock	0.	0.	0.	0.	0.	0.	0.	0.0	0.0	0.0	0.0	0.0	0.0	0.0	0.0
3 Forestry	0.	0.	0.	0.	0.	0.	0.	0.0	0.0	0.0	0.0	0.0	0.0	0.0	0.0
4 Fishing	0.	0.	0.	0.	0.	0.	0.	0.0	0.0	0.0	0.0	0.0	0.0	0.0	0.0
5 Mining	0.	0.	0.	0.	0.	0.	0.	0.0	0.0	0.0	0.0	0.0	0.0	0.0	0.0
6 Quarrying	0.	0.	0.	0.	0.	0.	0.	0.0	0.0	0.0	0.0	0.0	0.0	0.0	0.0
7 Petroleum	1412.	1526.	1658.	1801.	1962.	2583.	4422.	8.1	8.6	8.6	8.9	8.7	10.4	13.1	11.5
8 Slaughter of livestock	286.	309.	336.	355.	397.	523.	896.	8.1	8.6	8.6	8.9	8.7	10.4	13.1	11.5
9 Milling	0.	0.	0.	0.	0.	0.	0.	0.0	0.0	0.0	0.0	0.0	0.0	0.0	0.0
10 Other processed food	286.	309.	336.	355.	397.	523.	896.	8.1	8.6	8.6	8.9	8.7	10.4	13.1	11.5
11 Beverages	0.	0.	0.	0.	0.	0.	0.	0.0	0.0	0.0	0.0	0.0	0.0	0.0	0.0
12 Tobacco	0.	0.	0.	0.	0.	0.	0.	0.0	0.0	0.0	0.0	0.0	0.0	0.0	0.0
13 Soft fiber textiles	0.	0.	0.	0.	0.	0.	0.	0.0	0.0	0.0	0.0	0.0	0.0	0.0	0.0
14 Other textiles	0.	0.	0.	0.	0.	0.	0.	0.0	0.0	0.0	0.0	0.0	0.0	0.0	0.0
15 Wearing apparel	1723.	1863.	2024.	2198.	2395.	3153.	5398.	8.1	8.6	8.6	8.9	8.7	10.4	13.1	11.5
16 Wood and cork	56.	60.	66.	71.	78.	102.	175.	8.1	8.6	8.6	8.9	8.7	10.4	13.1	11.5
17 Paper	80.	87.	95.	103.	112.	147.	252.	8.1	8.6	8.6	8.9	8.7	10.4	13.1	11.5
18 Printing, publishing	2398.	2592.	2816.	3059.	3332.	4387.	7510.	8.1	8.6	8.6	8.9	8.7	10.4	13.1	11.5
19 Leather	40.	43.	46.	50.	55.	72.	124.	8.1	8.6	8.6	8.9	8.7	10.4	13.1	11.5
20 Rubber products	2.	3.	3.	3.	3.	4.	7.	8.1	8.6	8.6	8.9	8.7	10.4	13.1	11.5
21 Basic chemicals	233.	251.	273.	297.	323.	426.	728.	8.1	8.6	8.6	8.9	8.7	10.4	13.1	11.5
22 Synthetic fibers	0.	0.	0.	0.	0.	0.	0.	0.0	0.0	0.0	0.0	0.0	0.0	0.0	0.0
23 Fertilizers	0.	0.	0.	0.	0.	0.	0.	0.0	0.0	0.0	0.0	0.0	0.0	0.0	0.0
24 Soaps and detergents	821.	888.	964.	1047.	1141.	1502.	2571.	8.1	8.6	8.6	8.9	8.7	10.4	13.1	11.5
25 Drugs and medicines	5502.	5949.	6463.	7020.	7646.	10068.	17235.	8.1	8.6	8.6	8.9	8.7	10.4	13.1	11.5
26 Perfumes, cosmetics	0.	0.	0.	0.	0.	0.	0.	0.0	0.0	0.0	0.0	0.0	0.0	0.0	0.0
27 Other chemical indust.	0.	0.	0.	0.	0.	0.	0.	0.0	0.0	0.0	0.0	0.0	0.0	0.0	0.0
28 Nonmetallic mineral pr.	358.	387.	421.	457.	498.	655.	1122.	8.1	8.6	8.6	8.9	8.7	10.4	13.1	11.5
29 Basic metallic indust.	274.	297.	322.	350.	381.	502.	860.	8.1	8.6	8.6	8.9	8.7	10.4	13.1	11.5
30 Metal products	2674.	2892.	3141.	3412.	3716.	4894.	8377.	8.1	8.6	8.6	8.9	8.7	10.4	13.1	11.5
31 Machinery	1419.	1534.	1666.	1810.	1971.	2596.	4444.	8.1	8.6	8.6	8.9	8.7	10.4	13.1	11.5
32 Electrical machinery	1730.	1871.	2032.	2207.	2404.	3166.	5420.	8.1	8.6	8.6	8.9	8.7	10.4	13.1	11.5
33 Transport equipment	242.	262.	284.	309.	336.	443.	758.	8.1	8.6	8.6	8.9	8.7	10.4	13.1	11.5
34 Motor vehicles	86.	93.	101.	110.	120.	157.	270.	8.1	8.6	8.6	8.9	8.7	10.4	13.1	11.5
35 Other manufacturing	1865.	2017.	2191.	2380.	2592.	3413.	5842.	8.1	8.6	8.6	8.9	8.7	10.4	13.1	11.5
36 Construction	1421.	1536.	1669.	1813.	1975.	2600.	4451.	8.1	8.6	8.6	8.9	8.7	10.4	13.1	11.5
37 Electricity	1033.	1116.	1213.	1317.	1435.	1889.	3234.	8.1	8.6	8.6	8.9	8.7	10.4	13.1	11.5
38 Cinema	65.	70.	76.	83.	91.	119.	204.	8.1	8.6	8.6	8.9	8.7	10.4	13.1	11.5
39 Transport	1398.	1511.	1642.	1783.	1942.	2557.	4378.	8.1	8.6	8.6	8.9	8.7	10.4	13.1	11.5
40 Communications	1051.	1137.	1235.	1341.	1461.	1923.	3293.	8.1	8.6	8.6	8.9	8.7	10.4	13.1	11.5
41 Trade	4312.	4662.	5064.	5501.	5991.	7889.	13506.	8.1	8.6	8.6	8.9	8.7	10.4	13.1	11.5
42 Dwellings	3144.	3399.	3693.	4011.	4369.	5753.	9849.	8.1	8.6	8.6	8.9	8.7	10.4	13.1	11.5
43 Hotels and restaurants	1191.	1287.	1399.	1519.	1655.	2179.	3730.	8.1	8.6	8.6	8.9	8.7	10.4	13.1	11.5
44 Credit and insurance	1860.	2011.	2185.	2374.	2585.	3404.	5828.	8.1	8.6	8.6	8.9	8.7	10.4	13.1	11.5
45 Other services	2679.	2897.	3147.	3418.	3723.	4902.	8392.	8.1	8.6	8.6	8.9	8.7	10.4	13.1	11.5
T O T A L	39824.	43058.	46775.	50810	55341.	72869.	124745.	8.1	8.6	8.6	8.9	8.7	10.4	13.1	11.5

New Development Strategy

Table D.4.4: Public Investment by Destination

Millions of 1978 pesos

Sector	1976	%	1977	%	1978	%	1979	%	1980	%	1981	%	1982	%	1985	%	1990	%
1 Agriculture	8320	4.6	14276	7.1	38230	18.0	41999	18.2	46247	18.4	6281	19.0	106513	18.8				
2 Livestock	1085	.6	1954	1.0	2126	1.0	2308	1.0	2513	1.0	3310	1.0	5466	1.0				
3 Forestry	904	.5	1564	.5	1700	.8	1846	.8	2011	.8	2448	.8	4532	.8				
4 Fishing	1447	.8	978	.5	2762	1.3	3231	1.4	3770	1.8	5957	1.8	10198	1.8				
5 Mining	1809	1.0	1954	1.0	2126	1.0	2308	1.0	2513	1.0	3310	1.0	5466	1.0				
6 Quarrying	1809	1.0	1954	1.0	2126	1.0	2308	1.0	2513	1.0	3310	1.0	5466	1.0				
7 Petroleum	52091	28.8	64730	33.1	36115	17.1	36922	16.0	37702	15.0	39716	12.0	67707	12.0				
8 Slaughter of livestock	543	.3	587	.3	2337	1.1	2764	1.2	3267	1.3	5295	1.6	9065	1.6				
9 Milling	543	.3	587	.3	2337	1.1	2764	1.2	3267	1.3	5295	1.6	9065	1.6				
10 Other processed food	543	.3	587	.3	4461	.2	5077	.2	5781	.3	8605	2.6	9065	1.6				
11 Beverages	543	.3	587	.3	637	.3	692	.3	754	.3	993	.3	1700	.3				
12 Tobacco	543	.3	587	.3	637	.3	692	.3	754	.3	993	.3	1700	.3				
13 Soft fiber textiles	543	.3	587	.3	637	.3	692	.3	754	.3	993	.3	1700	.3				
14 Other textiles	543	.3	587	.3	637	.3	692	.3	754	.3	993	.3	1700	.3				
15 Wearing apparel	543	.3	507	.3	5077	.2	5077	.2	5781	.3	5295	1.6	9065	1.6				
16 Wood and cork	543	.3	587	.3	2337	1.1	2764	1.2	3267	1.3	5295	1.6	9065	1.6				
17 Paper	543	.3	587	.3	4461	.2	4616	.2	4776	1.9	5295	1.6	9065	1.6				
18 Printing, publishing	543	.3	587	.3	2337	1.1	2764	1.2	3267	1.3	5295	1.6	9065	1.6				
19 Leather	543	.3	587	.3	637	.3	692	.3	754	.3	993	.3	1700	.3				
20 Rubber products	543	.3	587	.3	637	.3	692	.3	754	.3	993	.3	1700	.3				
21 Basic chemicals	543	.3	587	.3	637	.3	692	.3	754	.3	993	.3	1700	.3				
22 Synthetic fibers	543	.3	587	.3	637	.3	692	.3	754	.3	993	.3	1700	.3				
23 Fertilizers	5044	2.8	4449	2.5	5311	2.5	5769	2.5	6284	2.5	8274	2.5	14164	2.5				
24 Soaps and detergents	543	.3	587	.3	637	.3	692	.3	754	.3	993	.3	1700	.3				
25 Drugs and medicines	543	.3	587	.3	637	.3	692	.3	754	.3	993	.3	1700	.3				
26 Perfumes, cosmetics	543	.3	587	.3	637	.3	692	.3	754	.3	993	.3	1700	.3				
27 Other chemical indust.	543	.3	587	.3	637	.3	692	.3	754	.3	993	.3	1700	.3				
28 Nonmetallic mineral pr.	543	.3	587	.3	637	.3	692	.3	754	.3	993	.3	1700	.3				
29 Basic metallic indust.	1990	1.1	2151	1.1	2538	1.1	2765	1.1	3641	1.1	10198	1.8						
30 Metal products	543	.3	587	.3	637	.3	692	.3	754	.3	993	.3	10198	1.8				
31 Machinery	543	.3	587	.3	637	.3	692	.3	754	.3	993	.3	10198	1.8				
32 Electrical machinery	543	.3	587	.3	637	.3	692	.3	754	.3	993	.3	10198	1.8				
33 Transport equipment	362	.2	391	.2	475	.2	462	.2	503	.2	662	.2	9632	1.7				
34 Motor vehicles	1266	.7	1369	.7	1697	.7	1615	.7	1759	.7	2317	.7	17464	2.2				
35 Other manufacturing	543	.3	587	.3	637	.3	692	.3	754	.7	993	.7	10198	1.8				
36 Construction	20077	11.1	19765	10.1	19332	9.1	21000	9.1	22872	9.1	30117	9.1	40726	7.1				
37 Electricity	22790	12.6	21511	11.0	21244	10.0	23076	10.0	25134	10.0	33095	10.0	45325	8.0				
38 Cinema	543	.3	587	.3	637	.3	692	.3	754	.3	993	.3	1700	.3				
39 Transport	5788	3.2	5007	3.0	6373	3.0	6923	3.0	7540	3.0	9929	3.0	16997	3.0				
40 Communications	19534	10.8	19556	10.0	19120	9.0	20769	9.0	22671	9.0	33095	10.0	39559	7.0				
41 Trade	543	.3	587	.3	637	.3	692	.3	754	.3	993	.3	1700	.3				
42 Dwellings	543	.3	587	.3	637	.3	692	.3	754	.3	993	.3	1700	.3				
43 Hotels and restaurants	543	.3	587	.3	637	.3	692	.3	754	.3	993	.3	1700	.3				
44 Credit and insurance	543	.3	587	.3	637	.3	692	.3	754	.3	993	.3	1700	.3				
45 Other services	20800	11.5	15665	8.0	14771	7.0	16615	7.2	18599	7.4	26476	8.0	28328	5.0				
T O T A L	180871	100.0	195550	100.0	212439	100.0	230765	100.0	251343	100.0	330955	100.0	566561	100.0				

New Development Strategy

Table D.4.4: Public Investment by Destination (Cont.)

Annual growth rates (percent)

Sector	79/78	80/79	81/80	82/81	83/78	88/83	93/88	93/82
1 Agriculture	71.6	167.9	9.8	10.1	43.8	10.6	13.1	11.6
2 Livestock	80.2	8.6	8.6	8.9	20.4	20.4	13.1	11.5
3 Forestry	73.0	8.6	8.6	8.9	19.4	10.4	13.1	11.5
4 Fishing	-32.4	182.4	17.0	16.7	24.9	13.0	13.1	13.4
5 Mining	8.1	8.6	8.6	8.9	8.7	10.4	13.1	11.5
6 Quarrying	8.1	8.6	8.6	8.9	8.7	10.4	13.1	11.5
7 Petroleum	24.3	-44.2	2.2	2.1	-5.9	7.1	13.1	9.3
8 Slaughter of livestock	8.1	298.3	18.5	18.0	47.9	13.4	13.1	13.6
9 Milling	8.1	298.3	18.5	18.0	47.9	13.4	13.1	13.6
10 Other processed food	8.1	660.4	13.8	13.9	64.8	1.8	13.1	7.9
11 Beverages	8.1	8.6	8.6	8.9	8.7	10.4	13.1	11.5
12 Tobacco	8.1	8.6	8.6	8.9	8.7	10.4	13.1	11.5
13 Soft fiber textiles	8.1	8.6	8.6	8.9	8.7	10.4	13.1	11.5
14 Other textiles	8.1	8.6	8.6	8.9	8.7	10.4	13.1	11.5
15 Wearing apparel	8.1	660.4	13.8	13.9	64.8	1.8	13.1	7.9
16 Wood and cork	8.1	298.3	18.5	18.0	47.9	13.4	13.1	13.6
17 Paper	8.1	660.4	13.5	3.5	55.6	7.8	13.1	9.8
18 Printing, publishing	8.1	298.3	18.5	18.0	47.9	13.4	13.1	13.6
19 Leather	8.1	8.6	8.6	8.9	8.7	10.4	13.1	11.5
20 Rubber products	8.1	8.6	8.6	8.9	8.7	10.4	13.1	11.5
21 Basic chemicals	8.1	8.6	8.6	8.9	8.7	10.4	13.1	11.5
22 Synthetic fibers	-3.5	8.6	8.6	8.9	8.7	10.4	13.1	11.5
23 Fertilizers	8.1	8.6	8.6	8.9	6.3	10.4	13.1	11.5
24 Soaps and detergents	8.1	8.6	8.6	8.9	8.7	10.4	13.1	11.5
25 Drugs and medicines	8.1	8.6	8.6	8.9	8.7	10.4	13.1	11.5
26 Perfumes, cosmetics	8.1	8.6	8.6	8.9	8.7	10.4	13.1	11.5
27 Other chemical indust.	8.1	8.6	8.6	8.9	8.7	10.4	13.1	11.5
28 Nonmetallic mineral pr.	8.1	8.6	8.6	8.9	8.7	45.7	33.0	36.1
29 Basic metallic indust.	8.1	8.6	8.6	8.9	8.7	12.4	33.0	21.0
30 Metal products	8.1	8.6	8.6	8.9	8.7	45.7	33.0	36.1
31 Machinery	8.1	8.6	8.6	8.9	8.7	45.7	33.0	36.1
32 Electrical machinery	8.1	8.6	8.6	8.9	8.7	45.7	33.0	36.1
33 Transport equipment	8.1	8.6	8.6	8.9	8.7	55.3	34.3	40.8
34 Motor vehicles	8.1	8.6	8.6	8.9	8.7	30.3	29.0	27.6
35 Other manufacturing	8.1	8.6	8.6	8.9	8.7	45.7	33.0	36.1
36 Construction	-1.6	-2.1	8.6	8.9	4.5	8.4	3.4	6.1
37 Electricity	-5.6	-1.2	8.6	8.9	3.8	8.6	4.5	6.8
38 Cinema	8.1	8.6	8.6	8.9	8.7	10.4	13.1	11.5
39 Transport	1.4	-2.2	8.6	8.9	7.3	10.4	13.1	6.1
40 Communications	.1	8.6	> 8.6	8.9	4.8	8.4	3.2	6.1
41 Trade	8.1	8.6	8.6	8.9	8.7	10.4	13.1	11.5
42 Dwellings	8.1	8.6	8.6	8.9	8.7	10.4	13.1	11.5
43 Hotels and restaurants	8.1	8.6	8.6	8.9	8.7	10.4	13.1	11.5
44 Credit and insurance	8.1	8.6	8.6	8.9	8.7	10.4	13.1	11.5
45 Other services	-24.8	-4.9	11.7	11.9	.1	6.0	-1.0	3.3
T O T A L	8.1	8.6	8.6	8.9	8.7	10.4	13.1	11.5

New Development Strategy

Table D.4.5: Private Investment by Destination

Millions of 1978 pesos

Sector	1978	%	1979	%	1980	%	1981	%	1982	%	1985	%	1990	%
1 Agriculture	6943.	9.6	6376.	7.2	6898.	6.9	13859.	11.6	21058.	14.7	45124.	18.0	116086.	18.7
2 Livestock	1857.	2.5	1305.	1.5	1217.	1.2	1317.	1.1	1517.	1.1	2532.	1.0	6228.	1.0
3 Forestry	396.	.5	446.	.5	634.	.6	853.	.7	1089.	.8	1989.	.8	4975.	.8
4 Fishing	134.	.2	400.	.5	495.	.5	1010.	.8	1568.	1.1	3843.	1.5	11047.	1.8
5 Mining	782.	1.0	735.	.8	886.	.9	1155.	1.0	1405.	1.0	2499.	1.0	6221.	1.0
6 Quarrying	96.	.1	479.	.6	773.	.8	1066.	.9	1354.	.9	2485.	1.0	6218.	1.0
7 Petroleum	12486.	16.7	15243.	22.2	27163.	27.2	28015.	23.4	28924.	20.1	37235.	14.8	76321.	12.3
8 Slaughter of livestock	190.	.3	230.	.3	278.	.3	751.	.6	1273.	.9	3339.	1.3	9802.	1.6
9 Milling	365.	.5	349.	.4	348.	.4	790.	.7	1298.	.9	3346.	1.3	9803.	1.6
10 Other processed food	382.	.5	339.	.4	371.	.4	1299.	1.1	2290.	1.6	5729.	2.3	11469.	1.8
11 Beverages	2096.	2.8	1536.	1.8	1060.	1.1	779.	.7	700.	.5	831.	.3	1884.	.3
12 Tobacco	94.	.1	177.	.2	243.	.2	329.	.3	412.	.3	747.	.3	1866.	.3
13 Soft fiber textiles	846.	1.1	623.	.7	488.	.5	476.	.4	503.	.4	774.	.3	1872.	.3
14 Other textiles	-45.	-.1	89.	.1	192.	.2	300.	.3	393.	.3	742.	.3	1865.	.3
15 Wearing apparel	1006.	1.3	715.	.8	550.	.6	1416.	1.2	2362.	1.6	5750.	2.3	10395.	1.7
16 Wood and cork	83.	.1	169.	.2	244.	.2	731.	.6	1261.	.9	3335.	1.3	9801.	1.6
17 Paper	941.	1.3	655.	.8	534.	.5	1402.	1.2	2236.	1.6	4382.	1.7	10045.	1.6
18 Printing, publishing	151.	.2	203.	.2	280.	.3	747.	.6	1271.	.9	3338.	1.3	9802.	1.6
19 Leather	91.	.1	178.	.2	250.	.3	331.	.3	413.	.3	747.	.3	1866.	.3
20 Rubber products	435.	.6	394.	.5	413.	.4	412.	.3	466.	.3	763.	.3	1869.	.3
21 Basic chemicals	16.	.0	81.	.1	155.	.2	293.	.2	387.	.3	740.	.3	1864.	.3
22 Synthetic fibers	751.	1.0	562.	.6	482.	.5	463.	.4	496.	.3	772.	.3	1871.	.3
23 Fertilizers	-134.	-.2	1013.	1.2	1791.	1.8	2617.	2.2	3347.	2.3	6200.	2.5	15543.	2.5
24 Soaps and detergents	-56.	-.1	151.	.2	231.	.2	322.	.3	407.	.3	746.	.3	1865.	.3
25 Drugs and medicines	-673.	-.9	-280.	-.3	38.	.0	190.	.2	327.	.2	722.	.3	1860.	.3
26 Perfumes, cosmetics	-9.	-.0	117.	.1	221.	.2	312.	.3	402.	.3	744.	.3	1865.	.3
27 Other chemical indust.	92.	.1	175.	.2	250.	.3	331.	.3	413.	.3	747.	.3	1866.	.3
28 Nonmetallic mineral pr.	1286.	1.7	912.	1.1	694.	.7	580.	.5	571.	.4	794.	.3	6405.	1.0
29 Basic metallic indust.	4006.	5.4	3000.	3.5	2368.	2.4	2010.	1.7	2023.	1.4	2889.	1.2	7800.	1.3
30 Metal products	500.	.7	447.	.5	413.	.4	421.	.4	471.	.3	764.	.3	6399.	1.0
31 Machinery	706.	.9	583.	.7	505.	.5	469.	.4	502.	.3	773.	.3	6401.	1.0
32 Electrical machinery	819.	1.1	605.	.7	522.	.5	481.	.4	508.	.4	775.	.3	5425.	.9
33 Transport equipment	534.	.7	440.	.5	410.	.4	339.	.3	353.	.2	521.	.2	5778.	.9
34 Motor vehicles	1501.	2.0	1390.	1.6	1272.	1.3	1112.	.9	1189.	.8	1810.	.7	8897.	1.4
35 Other manufacturing	315.	.4	305.	.4	315.	.3	372.	.3	439.	.3	755.	.3	6396.	1.0
36 Construction	2957.	3.9	6465.	7.5	8995.	8.9	10891.	9.1	13075.	9.1	22826.	9.1	52759.	8.5
37 Electricity	5970.	8.0	8629.	10.0	10477.	10.5	12455.	10.4	14650.	10.2	25167.	10.0	57723.	9.3
38 Cinema	140.	.2	199.	.2	254.	.3	337.	.3	416.	.3	748.	.3	1866.	.3
39 Transport	13310.	17.8	9558.	11.0	7272.	7.3	5968.	5.0	5817.	4.0	7967.	3.2	18768.	3.0
40 Communications	3891.	5.2	6624.	7.6	8763.	8.8	10823.	9.0	12953.	9.0	22581.	9.0	52562.	8.5
41 Trade	2570.	3.4	1850.	2.1	1310.	1.3	898.	.8	778.	.5	854.	.3	1890.	.3
42 Dwellings	2105.	2.8	1525.	1.8	1132.	1.1	795.	.7	713.	.5	835.	.3	1885.	.3
43 Hotels and restaurants	935.	1.2	673.	.8	536.	.5	498.	.4	518.	.4	778.	.3	1873.	.3
44 Credit and insurance	439.	.6	395.	.5	395.	.4	408.	.3	462.	.3	762.	.3	1869.	.3
45 Other services	3470.	4.6	6689.	7.7	7990.	8.0	9217.	7.7	10646.	7.4	19064.	7.6	40494.	6.5
T O T A L	74867.	100.0	86649.	100.0	100008.	100.0	119640.	100.0	143657.	100.0	250862.	100.0	621360.	100.0

New Development Strategy

Table D.4.5: Private Investment by Destination (Cont.)

Sector	Annual growth rates (percent)							
	79/78	80/79	81/80	82/81	83/78	88/83	93/88	93/82
1 Agriculture	-9.6	9.9	100.9	51.9	32.6	23.0	20.2	22.8
2 Livestock	-29.0	-6.7	8.2	15.2	-.6	19.6	19.8	19.5
3 Forestry	12.0	42.0	34.7	27.6	27.5	20.9	-19.9	20.6
4 Fishing	198.0	23.9	104.0	55.2	75.4	27.8	20.6	25.6
5 Mining	-6.1	20.6	30.4	21.6	16.9	20.5	19.9	20.3
6 Quarrying	400.1	61.3	37.9	27.1	77.2	20.9	19.9	20.7
7 Petroleum	54.1	41.2	3.1	3.2	19.6	12.4	18.8	14.6
8 Slaughter of livestock	20.7	20.8	170.7	69.5	57.8	29.1	20.7	26.6
9 Milling	-4.3	-.3	127.3	64.3	38.8	28.9	20.7	26.4
10 Other processed food	-11.1	9.5	249.8	76.3	54.3	23.3	13.5	20.6
11 Beverages	-26.7	-31.0	-26.5	-10.1	-19.9	14.0	19.4	14.9
12 Tobacco	88.1	37.5	35.7	25.1	40.1	20.7	19.9	20.5
13 Soft fiber textiles	-26.4	-21.6	-2.5	5.7	-7.8	18.3	19.7	18.4
14 Other textiles	*****	115.6	56.5	31.0	*****	21.3	19.9	21.0
15 Wearing apparel	-29.0	-23.1	157.3	66.8	27.4	17.8	17.8	19.9
16 Wood and cork	102.0	44.6	200.0	72.5	86.0	29.2	20.7	20.7
17 Paper	-30.4	-18.5	162.6	59.5	26.2	18.7	20.7	20.4
18 Printing, publishing	34.6	37.8	166.5	70.2	65.3	29.1	20.7	20.7
19 Leather	95.6	40.9	32.3	24.9	41.1	20.7	19.8	20.5
20 Rubber products	-9.4	4.8	-.3	13.1	4.5	19.2	19.9	19.2
21 Basic chemicals	417.3	92.5	88.9	31.8	99.3	21.5	19.9	21.2
22 Synthetic fibers	-25.2	-14.2	-4.0	7.2	-5.7	18.5	19.7	18.5
23 Fertilizers	*****	76.8	46.1	27.9	*****	21.0	19.9	20.8
24 Soaps and detergents	169.4	63.2	39.4	26.6	55.2	20.9	19.9	20.7
25 Drugs and medicines	-58.5	*****	406.4	71.9	*****	23.3	20.0	23.1
26 Perfumes, cosmetics	*****	88.8	41.1	28.7	*****	21.0	19.9	20.8
27 Other chemical indust.	90.3	43.0	32.2	24.9	40.7	20.7	19.9	20.5
28 Nonmetallic mineral pr.	-29.1	-23.8	-16.5	-1.6	-13.9	32.8	50.4	37.8
29 Basic metallic indust.	-25.1	-21.1	-15.1	.7	-11.4	17.1	33.0	23.2
30 Metal products	-10.7	-7.5	-7.1	11.8	1.7	35.7	50.5	40.2
31 Machinery	-17.4	-13.5	-7.1	7.0	-4.4	34.7	50.5	39.4
32 Electrical machinery	-26.1	-13.8	-7.9	5.7	-7.0	16.2	73.3	38.9
33 Transport equipment	-17.5	-6.9	-17.3	4.2	-6.1	39.7	54.6	43.2
34 Motor vehicles	-7.4	-8.5	-12.5	6.9	-2.4	26.2	40.9	31.2
35 Other manufacturing	-3.2	3.4	18.1	17.9	10.7	36.7	50.6	41.1
36 Construction	118.6	37.6	22.4	20.1	39.7	20.3	13.8	17.3
37 Electricity	44.5	21.4	18.9	17.6	23.9	19.5	14.8	17.3
38 Cinema	41.6	28.0	32.4	23.6	29.4	20.6	19.9	20.4
39 Transport	-28.2	-23.9	-17.9	-2.5	-14.3	16.4	19.6	16.8
40 Communications	70.2	32.3	23.5	19.7	31.9	20.8	13.3	17.3
41 Trade	-28.0	-29.2	-31.4	-13.3	-22.0	12.5	19.2	14.7
42 Dwellings	-27.5	-25.8	-29.8	-10.3	-19.7	13.7	19.3	14.7
43 Hotels and restaurants	-28.0	-20.3	-7.2	4.0	-9.3	18.0	19.7	18.1
44 Credit and insurance	-10.0	-1.2	3.3	13.4	4.2	19.1	19.8	19.3
45 Other services	92.8	19.5	15.4	15.5	29.8	20.1	10.9	15.8
TOTAL	15.7	15.4	19.6	20.1	18.2	20.1	19.9	20.0

New Development Strategy

Table D.4.6: Investments by Origin

Sector	Millions of 1978 pesos							Annual growth rates (percent)							
	1978	1979	1980	1981	1982	1985	1990	79/78	80/79	81/80	82/81	83/78	88/83	93/88	93/82
1 Agriculture	5556.	7481.	16430.	20333.	24499.	39314.	81026.	34.6	119.6	23.8	20.5	39.1	15.7	16.8	16.4
2 Livestock	1065.	1187.	1216.	1319.	1467.	2126.	4329.	11.6	2.5	8.5	9.1	11.2	14.4	16.6	15.2
3 Forestry	474.	762.	849.	983.	1128.	1688.	3461.	54.3	16.0	15.7	14.8	22.1	14.8	16.6	15.6
4 Fishing	575.	501.	1185.	1544.	1943.	3567.	7733.	-12.9	136.5	30.2	25.9	33.1	18.8	16.9	18.4
5 Mining	153.	159.	178.	204.	231.	343.	701.	3.8	11.9	15.0	13.1	11.4	14.7	16.6	15.5
6 Quarrying	149.	190.	226.	263.	302.	452.	927.	27.8	19.0	16.4	14.7	18.4	14.8	16.6	15.6
7 Petroleum	129.	168.	127.	130.	133.	154.	289.	30.0	-24.6	2.6	2.6	1.3	9.6	16.1	11.9
8 Slaughter of livestock	180.	201.	643.	866.	1117.	2124.	4641.	11.4	220.2	34.7	29.0	50.8	19.5	17.0	18.9
9 Milling	449.	463.	1329.	1762.	2260.	4277.	9340.	3.1	186.9	32.6	28.3	44.5	19.4	17.0	18.8
10 Other processed food	134.	134.	701.	925.	1170.	2078.	2977.	-19.5	-20.0	31.9	26.6	60.8	12.1	13.3	13.1
11 Beverages	148.	119.	95.	82.	81.	102.	201.	-19.9	421.9	-13.3	-1.2	-10.5	12.1	16.4	13.3
12 Tobacco	64.	76.	88.	102.	117.	174.	357.	-12.9	15.3	16.1	14.1	15.9	13.9	16.5	15.5
13 Soft fiber textiles	85.	74.	69.	71.	77.	108.	218.	-35.7	-7.0	3.8	7.6	-1.0	13.6	16.5	14.8
14 Other textiles	30.	41.	51.	61.	70.	106.	217.	35.7	22.7	19.7	15.6	21.5	15.0	16.6	15.7
15 Wearing apparel	95.	79.	306.	396.	497.	674.	1187.	-16.0	284.9	29.6	25.4	45.1	8.3	16.6	12.8
16 Wood and cork	175.	211.	720.	977.	1263.	2408.	5264.	20.6	241.7	35.6	29.4	55.5	19.5	17.0	18.9
17 Paper	208.	174.	699.	842.	982.	1355.	2675.	-16.3	302.3	20.5	16.5	39.9	12.4	16.4	14.3
18 Printing, publishing	64.	73.	241.	323.	418.	794.	1736.	13.9	231.3	34.3	29.1	52.4	16.6	17.0	18.9
19 Leather	39.	47.	54.	62.	71.	106.	217.	20.7	16.1	14.1	14.1	16.0	14.8	16.6	15.5
20 Rubber products	111.	112.	120.	126.	139.	200.	264.	-0.3	7.1	5.1	10.5	6.9	14.2	16.5	15.1
21 Basic chemicals	41.	49.	59.	73.	84.	128.	246.	19.6	18.8	24.4	15.7	18.7	18.7	16.6	15.8
22 Synthetic fibers	89.	79.	77.	80.	86.	122.	452.	-11.2	-2.5	3.2	8.2	1.4	14.0	16.5	14.8
23 Fertilizers	562.	673.	810.	958.	1098.	1650.	3387.	19.7	20.3	18.1	14.8	17.3	14.8	16.6	15.6
24 Soaps and detergents	196.	241.	284.	332.	380.	568.	1166.	23.2	17.7	16.8	14.5	17.3	15.7	16.7	16.3
25 Drugs and medicines	-17.	39.	86.	112.	137.	218.	452.	****	119.8	30.8	22.5	****	15.7	16.6	16.3
26 Perfumes, cosmetics	174.	230.	281.	328.	378.	568.	1166.	31.9	22.0	15.1	15.1	19.9	16.6	16.6	15.6
27 Other chemical indust.	309.	371.	432.	498.	568.	847.	1736.	20.0	16.5	15.3	14.1	16.0	14.8	16.6	15.5
28 Nonmetallic mineral pr.	154.	126.	112.	107.	111.	150.	1395.	-18.0	-16.5	-4.5	4.1	-4.8	40.8	39.5	36.9
29 Basic metallic indust.	1631.	1401.	1280.	1237.	1302.	1776.	4896.	-14.1	-8.7	-3.3	5.3	-2.8	14.5	33.0	22.0
30 Metal products	535.	530.	539.	571.	628.	901.	8514.	-1.7	6.0	6.0	10.0	5.6	14.2	39.5	37.8
31 Machinery	51677.	57407.	62700.	70220.	78983.	115543.	239556.	11.1	9.2	12.0	12.5	11.6	14.7	17.0	15.6
32 Electrical machinery	58454.	64971.	70702.	79149.	88787.	129602.	269206.	11.1	8.8	11.8	12.3	11.4	14.7	17.1	15.6
33 Transport equipment	13718.	15358.	20339.	23783.	27659.	42290.	83848.	12.0	32.4	16.9	16.3	18.5	14.6	15.5	15.2
34 Motor vehicles	988.	985.	985.	974.	1052.	1473.	7626.	-.3	-1.1	-1.1	8.1	3.1	28.7	33.9	29.2
35 Other manufacturing	26.	27.	29.	32.	36.	52.	498.	4.0	6.8	11.8	12.0	9.5	42.5	39.5	38.2
36 Construction	108250.	119011.	119951.	131552.	145630.	208720.	410800.	9.9	.8	9.7	10.7	8.5	13.1	14.4	14.4
37 Electricity	2128.	2230.	2347.	2629.	2944.	4311.	7626.	4.8	5.2	12.0	12.0	9.3	13.3	10.2	11.9
38 Cinema	121.	139.	158.	182.	207.	308.	631.	15.0	-13.5	15.4	13.7	14.3	14.7	16.6	15.5
39 Transport	573.	463.	409.	387.	401.	537.	1073.	-19.2	-11.5	-5.5	3.6	-5.5	13.2	16.5	14.1
40 Communications	539.	602.	641.	727.	818.	1281.	2121.	11.8	6.5	13.3	12.6	11.4	13.8	8.9	11.5
41 Trade	1363.	1067.	853.	697.	671.	809.	1572.	21.7	-20.1	-18.3	-3.6	-12.8	11.4	16.3	12.7
42 Dwellings	116.	93.	78.	65.	65.	80.	158.	-20.2	-16.2	-15.9	-1.4	-10.4	12.0	16.3	13.2
43 Hotels and restaurants	279.	238.	222.	225.	240.	335.	675.	-14.7	-6.8	1.4	6.9	-1.1	13.8	16.5	14.6
44 Credit and insurance	258.	258.	271.	289.	320.	461.	939.	-4.0	5.1	6.6	10.6	6.8	14.3	15.1	15.1
45 Other services	3689.	3395.	3475.	3926.	4445.	6922.	10461.	-8.0	2.4	13.0	13.0	6.7	12.2	6.0	9.6
T O T A L	255736.	282205.	312445.	350402.	394098.	581813.	1187913.	10.4	10.7	12.1	12.7	11.8	14.6	16.6	15.4

New Development Strategy

Table D.4.7: Imports, Exports, Balance of Trade, External Debt

Millions of 1978 pesos

SECTOR		1978	1979	1980	1981	1982	1985	1990
1 Agriculture	Imports	36829	39470	47218	45795	43202	30475	27627
	Exports	12707	13342	14009	14710	15445	17880	64755
	Balance	-24122	-26127	-33208	-31085	-27757	-12595	37129
2 Livestock	Imports	386	406	421	446	476	10408	152877
	Exports	50981	49576	48182	42283	34196	3917	5000
	Balance	50595	49170	47761	41837	33720	-6491	-147877
3 Forestry	Imports	594	653	720	807	907	4912	32484
	Exports	5042	4933	5204	4438	3238	0	0
	Balance	4448	4279	4484	3631	2331	-4912	-32484
4 Fishing	Imports	14218	13360	13528	11866	9437	25	63
	Exports	1797	1887	1982	2081	2185	5962	57296
	Balance	-12421	-11473	-11547	-9786	-7252	5937	57234
5 Mining	Imports	3353	3703	4009	4324	4666	5947	14273
	Exports	12296	12345	12418	12554	12761	13661	14180
	Balance	8903	8641	8409	8230	8095	7714	-93
6 Quarrying	Imports	3036	3220	3398	3589	3794	4565	7603
	Exports	4818	5078	5621	6406	7381	11410	22455
	Balance	1782	1858	2223	2817	3587	6845	14852
7 Petroleum	Imports	32218	20605	8533	9099	9716	12005	19138
	Exports	0	0	5173	13803	21149	33513	24419
	Balance	-32218	-20605	-3360	4704	11433	21508	5281
8 Slaughter of livestock	Imports	205531	214521	224463	229509	232860	231678	187441
	Exports	0	0	0	0	0	0	0
	Balance	-205531	-214521	-224463	-229509	-232860	-231678	-187441
9 Milling	Imports	10916	10170	10387	3975	31	39	66
	Exports	0	0	0	0	5381	55434	243406
	Balance	-10916	-10170	-10387	-3975	5350	55395	243341
10 Other processed food	Imports	10769	14242	18763	14371	7136	4059	7917
	Exports	1366	1434	1506	1581	1660	39359	141778
	Balance	-9403	-12808	-17257	-12789	-5476	35350	133861
11 Beverages	Imports	144	151	156	161	166	306	390
	Exports	6035	6279	5821	4073	1560	10413	46794
	Balance	5891	6128	5665	3912	1394	10107	46404
12 Tobacco	Imports	56	62	70	78	89	128	244
	Exports	1025	2009	3292	4688	6342	12896	32417
	Balance	969	1947	3222	4610	6254	12768	32173
13 Soft fiber textiles	Imports	1711	1780	1851	2004	2195	0	0
	Exports	16617	16294	15726	13074	9543	10076	56083
	Balance	14906	14514	13874	11070	7348	10076	56083
14 Other textiles	Imports	309	358	416	492	582	955	2162
	Exports	3318	5326	8079	11405	15386	31288	78102
	Balance	3009	4969	7663	10914	14804	30333	75940
15 Wearing apparel	Imports	85427	93103	102404	107068	110909	118103	190975
	Exports	765	803	843	886	930	1077	1374
	Balance	-84662	-92300	-101561	-106183	-109979	-117027	-189601
16 Wood and cork	Imports	18749	18905	19245	11589	2834	4674	10420
	Exports	0	0	0	0	2548	64933	295087
	Balance	-18749	-18905	-19245	-11589	-286	60259	284667
17 Paper	Imports	12032	12865	14592	13970	13156	12997	27221
	Exports	0	0	0	0	0	1994	12368
	Balance	-12032	-12865	-14592	-13970	-13156	-11004	-14853

New Development Strategy

Table D.4.7: Imports, Exports, Balance of Trade, External Debt (Cont.)

Millions of 1978 pesos

SECTOR		1978	1979	1980	1981	1982	1985	1990
18 Printing, publishing	Imports	18797.	20380.	22185.	21878.	20740.	11324.	2476.
	Exports	0.	0.	0.	0.	0.	0.	31957.
	Balance	-18797.	-20380.	-22185.	-21878.	-20740.	-11324.	29481.
19 Leather	Imports	1030.	1216.	1440.	1702.	2004.	3192.	6670.
	Exports	7133.	9418.	12259.	15564.	19407.	34639.	79818.
	Balance	6103.	8202.	10819.	13862.	17403.	31447.	73148.
20 Rubber products	Imports	5556.	5836.	6212.	6774.	7484.	10399.	19737.
	Exports	0.	0.	0.	0.	0.	0.	0.
	Balance	-5556.	-5836.	-6212.	-6774.	-7484.	-10399.	-19737.
21 Basic chemicals	Imports	12340.	13403.	14673.	16151.	18569.	30870.	66905.
	Exports	4054.	3108.	2069.	747.	0.	0.	0.
	Balance	-8286.	-10295.	-12604.	-15405.	-18569.	-30870.	-66905.
22 Synthetic fibers	Imports	1341.	1445.	1551.	1893.	3491.	10740.	31733.
	Exports	1385.	1246.	870.	0.	0.	0.	0.
	Balance	44.	-199.	-680.	-1893.	-3491.	-10740.	-31733.
23 Fertilizers	Imports	4634.	2807.	595.	334.	437.	844.	2041.
	Exports	0.	0.	0.	2264.	5397.	17865.	54939.
	Balance	-4634.	-2807.	-595.	1930.	4960.	17021.	52898.
24 Soaps and detergents	Imports	13889.	12226.	9966.	7434.	4420.	74.	164.
	Exports	0.	0.	0.	0.	0.	7570.	42728.
	Balance	-13889.	-12226.	-9966.	-7434.	-4420.	7496.	42564.
25 Drugs and medicines	Imports	12237.	13951.	15356.	16716.	18136.	23297.	37605.
	Exports	315.	330.	347.	364.	382.	443.	565.
	Balance	-11922.	-13621.	-15009.	-16352.	-17754.	-22854.	-37040.
26 Perfumes, cosmetics	Imports	26381.	25854.	24620.	23199.	21455.	14554.	164.
	Exports	0.	0.	0.	0.	0.	0.	5234.
	Balance	-26381.	-25854.	-24620.	-23199.	-21455.	-14554.	5070.
27 Other chemical indust.	Imports	3000.	2490.	2803.	3251.	3770.	5819.	11754.
	Exports	0.	0.	1074.	2251.	3613.	8840.	23288.
	Balance	-3000.	-2490.	-1729.	-1000.	-157.	3021.	11533.
28 Nonmetallic mineral pr.	Imports	2377.	5489.	13063.	21716.	31758.	71222.	165616.
	Exports	3036.	0.	0.	0.	0.	0.	0.
	Balance	659.	-5489.	-13063.	-21716.	-31758.	-71222.	-165616.
29 Basic metallic indust.	Imports	8672.	9716.	10310.	11277.	12354.	28116.	106409.
	Exports	16069.	15558.	13238.	10391.	6595.	2197.	2804.
	Balance	7397.	5841.	2928.	-886.	-5759.	-25919.	-103605.
30 Metal products	Imports	9131.	9972.	10700.	11679.	12847.	30818.	52298.
	Exports	9225.	7850.	5866.	3201.	0.	0.	0.
	Balance	94.	-2122.	-4834.	-8478.	-12847.	-30818.	-52298.
31 Machinery	Imports	42234.	48126.	53912.	62018.	71544.	111081.	221527.
	Exports	0.	0.	0.	0.	0.	0.	0.
	Balance	-42234.	-48126.	-53912.	-62018.	-71544.	-111081.	-221527.
32 Electrical machinery	Imports	72595.	80268.	87608.	98305.	110918.	163751.	324787.
	Exports	0.	0.	0.	0.	0.	0.	0.
	Balance	-72595.	-80268.	-87608.	-98305.	-110918.	-163751.	-324787.
33 Transport equipment	Imports	10770.	12124.	17025.	20881.	25568.	44326.	63450.
	Exports	0.	0.	0.	0.	0.	0.	0.
	Balance	-10770.	-12124.	-17025.	-20881.	-25568.	-44326.	-63450.
34 Motor vehicles	Imports	30290.	32206.	34462.	38008.	42712.	63137.	110356.
	Exports	0.	0.	0.	0.	0.	0.	0.
	Balance	-30290.	-32206.	-34462.	-38008.	-42712.	-63137.	-110356.

New Development Strategy

Table D.4.7: Imports, Exports, Balance of Trade, External Debt (Cont.)

Millions of 1978 pesos

SECTOR		1978	1979	1980	1981	1982	1985	1990
35 Other manufacturing	Imports	21334.	21968.	22721.	23956.	25409.	31564.	19693.
	Exports	0.	0.	0.	0.	0.	0.	9388.
	Balance	-21334.	-21968.	-22721.	-2356.	-25409.	-31564.	-10305.
TOTAL	Imports	858698.	894732.	951583.	989997.	1036753.	1370273.	2604214.
	Exports	157982.	156817.	163581.	166764.	175101.	365182.	1243749.
	Balance	10.	11.	12.	13.	14.	18.	32.
External debt[a]		656514.100	722165.510	794382.061	873820.267	961202.294	1279360.253	2060422.481

a) 10^9 1978 pesos; peso-dollar exchange rate (1978) = 22.72

New Development Strategy

Table D.4.8: Government Accounts

Millions of 1978 pesos

	1978 Value	%	1979 Value	%	1980 %	Value	1981 %	Value	1982 %	Value	1985 Value	%
Incomes												
Direct Taxes	217783.	53.5	230687.	52.4	244403.	51.1	262778.	50.6	284255.	50.2	372988.	50.1
Indirect Taxes plus Exploitation Surplus	189394.	46.5	209556.	47.6	233846.	48.1	256731.	49.4	281583.	49.8	372075.	49.9
External financing	0.	0.0	0.	0.0	0.	0.0	0.	0.0	0.	0.0	0.	0.0
TOTAL	407187.	100.0	440253.	100.0	478254.	100.0	519510.	100.0	565838.	100.0	745062.	100.0
Expenditures												
Consumption of Goods and Services	39824.	9.8	43058.	9.8	46775.	9.8	50810.	9.8	55341.	9.8	72869.	9.8
Wages and Salaries	186491.	45.8	201636.	45.8	219040.	45.8	237935.	45.8	259154.	45.8	341239.	45.8
Investments	180871.	44.4	195559.	44.4	212439.	44.4	230765.	44.4	251343.	44.4	330955.	44.4
TOTAL	407187.	100.0	440253.	100.0	478254.	100.0	519510.	100.0	565838.	100.0	745062.	100.0
Ratio Tax Revenues /GNP (percent)	22.4		22.8		23.4		23.6		23.8		24.1	
Share of Public Investment in Total Invest-ment (percent)	70.7		69.3		68.0		65.9		63.6		56.9	

(1985: Value 649118. 50.9 / 626534. 49.1 / 0. 0.0 / 01275472. 100.0 and 124745. 9.8 / 584166. 45.8 / 566561. 44.4 / 01275472. 100.0; Ratio 24.1; Share 47.7 — for year 1990)

New Development Strategy

Table D.4.8: Government Accounts (Cont.)

Annual growth rates (percent)

	79/78	80/79	81/80	82/81	83/78	88/83	93/88	93/83
Incomes								
Direct Taxes plus	5.9	5.9	7.5	8.2	7.3	10.6	13.3	11.7
Exploitation Surpluses	10.6	11.6	9.8	9.7	10.3	10.2	12.8	11.3
External Financing	0.0	0.0	0.0	0.0	0.0	0.0	0.0	0.9
T O T A L	8.1	8.6	8.6	8.9	8.7	10.4	13.1	11.5
Expenditures								
Consumption of Goods and Services	8.1	8.6	8.6	8.9	8.7	10.4	13.1	11.5
Wages and Salaries	8.1	8.6	8.4	8.9	8.7	10.4	13.1	11.5
Investments	8.1	8.6	8.6	8.9	8.7	10.4	13.1	11.5
T O T A L	8.1	8.6	8.6	8.9	8.7	10.4	13.1	11.5

New Development Strategy

Table D.4.9: Sectoral Employment

No. of employed persons

Sector	1977	%	1979	%	1980	%	1981	%	1982	%	1985	%	1990	%
1 Agriculture	4676356	34.7	4965537	34.8	5155078	34.7	5660421	35.4	6285939	36.1	6922771	38.1	16507315	38.9
2 Livestock	235243	1.7	237615	1.7	240411	1.6	243265	1.5	246453	1.4	259435	1.1	300919	.7
3 Forestry	97255	.7	102305	.7	110775	.7	120531	.8	131708	.8	174754	.7	293428	.7
4 Fishing	20958	.2	25676	.2	29503	.2	39044	.2	51137	.3	104742	.4	266655	.6
5 Mining	16785	.1	15082	.1	15271	.1	14533	.1	13926	.1	12512	.1	11421	.0
6 Quarrying	74927	.5	77400	.5	81222	.5	85840	.5	91116	.5	102269	.5	157003	.4
7 Petroleum	111763	.8	130606	.9	154085	1.0	167371	1.0	179233	1.0	208108	.9	257524	.6
8 Slaughter of livestock	256970	1.9	282716	2.0	3079064	2.1	391344	2.4	503486	2.9	1052492	4.5	2967219	7.0
9 Milling	173601	1.3	186473	1.3	194617	1.3	223571	1.4	261780	1.5	442119	1.9	1019633	2.4
10 Other processed food	149999	1.1	146297	1.0	142724	1.0	151040	.9	169810	.9	217839	.9	3379095	.8
11 Beverages	98271	.7	98135	.7	96900	.7	95102	.6	92857	.5	86421	.4	80195	.2
12 Tobacco	10764	.1	11529	.1	12446	.1	13477	.1	14645	.1	18929	.1	29843	.1
13 Soft fiber textiles	137364	1.0	130366	.9	123219	.8	116222	.7	109660	.6	99266	.4	74903	.2
14 Other textiles	18772	.1	24696	.2	37264	.3	49975	.3	64886	.4	122096	.5	278152	.7
15 Wearing apparel	354242	2.6	341424	2.4	327960	2.2	336278	2.1	350318	2.0	422445	1.8	522754	1.2
16 Wood and cork	247510	1.8	282676	2.0	323082	2.2	480310	3.0	683554	3.9	1594536	6.8	4247955	10.0
17 Paper	65295	.5	67921	.5	69036	.5	80710	.5	92481	.5	130697	.6	259731	.6
18 Printing, publishing	91571	.6	79018	.6	78594	.5	84760	.5	93372	.5	133548	.6	242232	.6
19 Leather	41601	.3	44847	.3	53651	.4	61187	.4	69477	.4	99071	.4	171340	.4
20 Rubber products	25411	.2	25010	.2	24478	.2	23951	.1	23396	.1	22161	.1	21854	.1
21 Basic chemicals	34528	.2	32904	.2	31473	.2	30224	.2	29202	.2	27002	.1	25982	.1
22 Synthetic fibers	25241	.2	25420	.2	26185	.2	26670	.2	26744	.2	27948	.1	32605	.1
23 Fertilizers	9056	.1	13779	.1	10364	.1	11300	.1	33759	.2	63801	.3	148378	.3
24 Soaps and detergents	8357	.1	9266	.1	10275	.1	11300	.1	12328	.1	15211	.1	19783	.0
25 Drugs and medicines	45737	.3	44641	.3	43666	.3	44254	.3	45324	.3	50855	.2	68477	.2
26 Perfumes, cosmetics	13239	.1	15414	.1	18190	.1	21371	.1	24827	.1	36545	.2	67298	.1
27 Other chemical indust.	14171	.1	15431	.1	17807	.1	20039	.1	22513	.1	31428	.1	53663	.1
28 Nonmetallic mineral pr.	191645	1.4	185675	1.3	178499	1.2	170911	1.1	163361	.9	143493	.6	153307	.4
29 Basic metallic indust.	114757	.8	118856	.8	121354	.8	122932	.8	124077	.7	129252	.5	148577	.4
30 Metal products	215070	1.6	222098	1.6	228645	1.5	235037	1.5	241727	1.4	267353	1.1	490225	1.2
31 Machinery	113218	.8	118524	.8	123169	.8	127464	.8	131681	.8	147025	.6	276544	.7
32 Electrical machinery	225256	1.6	235342	1.7	243484	1.6	251049	1.6	258446	1.5	295510	1.2	461203	1.1
33 Transport equipment	224675	1.6	233235	1.6	240016	1.6	246233	1.5	251325	1.5	269795	1.2	445230	1.1
34 Motor vehicles	113821	.8	117766	.8	121402	.8	124589	.7	127270	.7	137170	.6	203616	.5
35 Other manufacturing	298011	2.2	342251	2.4	389707	2.6	442662	2.8	503692	2.9	752079	3.2	2558011	6.0
36 Construction	869160	6.3	1016566	7.1	1178515	7.9	1345336	8.4	1527563	8.8	2784995	9.3	3822011	9.0
37 Electricity	86410	.6	95526	.7	104312	.7	112837	.7	121069	.7	153759	.7	227061	.5
38 Gas	134140	1.0	140921	1.0	148668	1.0	157634	1.0	167511	1.0	206888	.9	327642	.8
39 Transport	630797	4.6	644349	4.5	652788	4.4	658635	4.1	663224	3.8	680731	2.9	950978	1.8
40 Communications	60170	.4	68055	.5	75701	.5	82510	.5	89368	.5	110069	.5	149732	.4
41 Trade	1543361	11.3	1564580	11.0	1579620	10.6	1590195	9.9	1597524	9.2	1619010	6.9	1647902	4.0
42 Dwellings	7162	.1	7187	.1	7207	.0	7274	.0	7238	.0	7282	.0	7395	.0
43 Hotels and restaurants	360695	2.6	370040	2.7	375790	2.5	371863	2.3	367936	2.1	359245	1.5	367557	.9
44 Credit and insurance	202840	1.5	212050	1.5	223198	1.5	234015	1.5	245586	1.4	288783	1.2	417090	1.0
45 Other services	1083246	7.9	1100924	7.7	1107738	7.5	1110875	6.9	1118686	6.4	1173474	5.0	1344999	3.2
T o t a l	13696233	100.0	14235139	100.0	14846305	100.0	16009879	100.0	17424960	100.0	23404477	100.0	42399337	100.0

New Development Strategy

Table D.4.9: Sectoral Employment (Cont.)

Annual growth rates (percent)

Sector	79/78	80/79	81/80	82/81	83/78	88/83	93/88	93/82
1 Agriculture	2.7	4.0	9.8	11.0	7.8	12.8	12.6	13.1
2 Livestock	1.0	1.7	1.2	1.3	1.2	2.3	4.4	3.2
3 Forestry	5.2	8.3	8.8	9.3	8.2	10.4	11.7	11.0
4 Fishing	22.6	14.9	32.3	31.0	25.8	23.5	17.7	21.2
5 Mining	-4.8	-4.8	-4.5	-4.7	-4.4	-2.7	-.7	-1.7
6 Quarrying	3.4	4.9	5.7	6.1	5.3	6.9	8.0	7.4
7 Petroleum	16.8	18.0	8.6	7.1	11.2	4.4	5.4	4.9
8 Slaughter of livestock	9.0	9.1	27.1	28.7	20.1	25.6	20.1	23.3
9 Milling	4.8	4.3	14.9	17.1	11.7	19.1	14.6	17.9
10 Other processed food	-2.4	-7.4	5.8	7.8	3.5	10.5	7.5	9.0
11 Beverages	-1.1	-1.2	-1.9	-2.4	-1.6	-2.0	-.3	-1.3
12 Tobacco	7.1	8.0	8.3	8.7	8.2	9.2	10.2	9.6
13 Soft fiber textiles	-5.1	-5.5	-5.7	-5.6	-5.5	-4.9	6.4	4.1
14 Other textiles	42.2	39.6	34.1	29.8	34.2	20.0	-3.0	-4.1
15 Wearing apparel	-3.5	-4.1	2.5	4.2	.9	5.4	16.4	18.9
16 Wood and cork	14.2	14.6	48.3	42.3	30.4	26.3	4.8	5.1
17 Paper	4.0	3.0	14.7	15.3	10.3	13.7	17.4	23.1
18 Printing, publishing	-2.0	-1.7	-1.7	10.2	5.1	13.1	13.5	12.7
19 Leather	14.1	14.4	14.0	13.5	13.8	11.9	11.6	11.9
20 Rubber products	-1.6	-2.1	-2.2	-2.3	-2.1	-1.1	11.4	-.7
21 Basic chemicals	-4.7	-4.4	-4.0	-3.4	-3.9	-1.7	-.1	-.7
22 Synthetic fibers	2.3	1.4	1.1	1.0	1.4	2.2	-.1	3.3
23 Fertilizers	52.2	40.5	34.3	29.8	34.3	20.4	4.4	19.3
24 Soaps and detergents	10.9	10.9	10.0	9.1	9.8	6.1	17.0	5.8
25 Drugs and medicines	-3.7	-.9	1.4	2.4	.5	5.1	5.0	6.1
26 Perfumes, cosmetics	16.4	18.0	17.5	16.2	16.6	12.2	7.7	11.7
27 Other chemical indust.	12.0	12.6	12.5	12.3	12.3	11.4	10.6	11.5
28 Nonmetallic mineral pr.	-3.1	-4.3	-4.3	-4.4	-4.0	-2.6	11.5	3.0
29 Basic metallic indust.	3.6	7.1	1.3	.9	1.8	1.8	10.5	14.1
30 Metal products	3.3	3.0	2.8	2.8	3.0	6.5	7.2	14.3
31 Machinery	4.7	3.9	3.5	3.3	3.4	6.8	25.1	14.5
32 Electrical machinery	4.5	3.5	3.1	3.0	3.4	4.3	25.3	13.0
33 Transport equipment	3.8	2.9	2.6	2.1	2.7	6.4	24.7	15.6
34 Motor vehicles	3.4	3.1	2.4	2.2	2.8	4.4	29.4	9.2
35 Other manufacturing	14.5	13.9	13.6	13.8	13.9	18.8	15.4	27.5
36 Construction	17.0	15.9	14.2	13.5	14.7	12.3	39.9	11.6
37 Electricity	10.5	9.2	8.2	6.4	8.8	8.2	10.5	9.4
38 Cinema	5.1	4.5	5.9	4.1	5.9	8.3	7.4	6.4
39 Transport	2.1	1.3	.9	.7	1.2	1.3	11.6	2.7
40 Communications	13.1	11.2	9.0	8.3	9.8	7.0	3.3	6.0
41 Trade	1.4	1.0	.7	.5	.8	.6	4.7	1.0
42 Dwellings	.3	.3	.2	.2	.2	.2	1.4	.
43 Hotels and restaurants	.4	-.9	-1.0	-1.1	-.9	-.3	.	.5
44 Credit and insurance	5.0	4.8	4.8	4.9	5.0	6.4	1.5	7.5
45 Other services	1.6	.6	.3	.7	.9	2.5	2.6	2.4
T O T A L	3.9	4.3	7.8	8.8	6.9	11.4	14.8	12.8

New Development Strategy

Table D.4.10: Employment by Socio-economic Group

Thousands of persons

Socio-economic group	1978	%	1979	%	1980	%	1981	%	1982	%	1985	%	1990	%
1. Entr. Empl. Prof. (H)	1043682	7.6	1086462	7.6	1131504	7.6	1209601	7.6	1304011	7.5	1705162	7.3	3054516	7.2
2. Entr. Empl. Prof. (M)	2711349	19.8	2821393	19.8	2938410	19.8	3146871	19.7	3399491	19.5	4472925	19.1	8031051	18.9
3. Entr. Empl. Prof. (L)	3612138	26.4	3751828	26.4	3903845	26.3	4189064	26.2	4536160	26.0	6012784	25.7	10796730	25.5
4. Workers	2607249	17.7	2517774	17.7	2630030	17.7	2809513	17.5	3024927	17.4	3936866	16.8	7106720	16.8
5. Peasants (H-M)	268974	1.9	214741	1.5	232259	1.5	245010	1.5	271918	1.6	385330	1.6	711532	1.7
6. Peasants (L)	703195	5.1	722541	5.1	751244	5.1	824435	5.1	914979	5.3	1296597	5.5	2394239	5.6
7. Landless Workers	3009822	22.0	3120900	21.9	3268013	22.0	3585385	22.4	3973475	22.8	5595413	23.9	10307049	24.3
T O T A L	13636233	100.0	14235139	100.0	14846305	100.0	16009879	100.0	17424960	100.0	23404477	100.0	42399337	100.0

New Development Strategy

Table D.4.10: Employment by Socio-economic Group (Cont.)

Annual growth rates (percent)

Socio-economic group		79/78	80/79	81/80	82/81	83/78	86/83	93/88	93/82
1. Entr. Empl. Prof.	(H)	4.1	6.9	7.8	4.3	10.7	15.4	12.6	
2. Entr. Empl. Prof.	(M)	4.1	7.1	8.0	6.4	10.9	15.3	12.7	
3. Entr. Empl. Prof.	(L)	3.0	7.3	8.3	6.5	11.1	14.9	12.6	
4. Workers		4.6	6.8	7.7	6.4	10.7	16.1	12.9	
5. Peasants (H-M)		2.8	9.7	11.0	7.8	12.8	13.5	13.0	
6. Peasants (L)		2.8	9.7	11.0	7.8	12.8	13.5	13.0	
7. Landless Workers		3.7	9.7	10.8	8.1	12.6	13.6	13.0	
T O T A L		3.9	4.3	7.8	6.9	11.4	14.8	12.8	

New Development Strategy

Table D.4.11: Income by Socio-economic Group

Millions of 1978 pesos

Socio-economic group	1978	%	1979	%	1980	%	1981	%	1982	%	1985	%	1990	%
1. Entr. Empl. Prof. (H)	733234	14.0	752280	14.0	2671504	14.0	284803	13.9	304766	13.7	383911	13.3	624127	12.6
2. Entr. Empl. Prof. (M)	496943	29.2	522715	29.0	544405	28.7	578909	28.2	611090	27.6	748730	25.9	1162629	23.5
3. Entr. Empl. Prof. (L)	351211	20.6	365435	20.3	340423	19.4	398694	19.4	419430	18.9	503504	17.4	756416	15.3
4. Workers	374948	22.0	412186	22.9	453224	23.7	504081	24.5	562784	25.4	800122	27.7	1540633	31.1
5. Peasants (H-M)	23301	1.4	24300	1.3	25504	1.3	27983	1.4	31054	1.4	44426	1.5	86134	1.7
6. Peasants (L)	42850	2.5	44418	2.5	47327	2.5	52626	2.6	59204	2.7	87706	3.0	175423	3.6
7. Landless Workers	173094	10.3	181510	10.1	207704	10.3	207704	10.1	228730	10.3	310551	11.1	600620	12.1
T O T A L	1761466	99.9	1803144	100.1	1912646	100.1	2054790	100.1	2219058	100.1	2888040	99.9	4946182	99.9

New Development Strategy

Table D.4.11: Income by Socio-economic Group (Cont.)

Annual growth rates (percent)

Socio-economic group	79/78	80/79	81/80	82/81	83/78	88/83	93/88	93/82
1. Entr. Empl. Prof. (H)	5.9	5.9	6.6	7.0	6.6	9.0	12.3	10.3
2. Entr. Empl. Prof. (M)	5.1	5.0	5.6	5.9	5.6	8.0	11.3	9.3
3. Entr. Empl. Prof. (L)	4.2	4.0	4.8	5.2	4.8	7.4	10.4	8.6
4. Workers	9.9	10.0	11.2	11.6	11.0	13.1	15.6	14.1
5. Peasants (H-M)	4.3	5.0	9.7	11.0	8.3	13.6	14.9	14.0
6. Peasants (L)	4.6	5.6	11.2	12.5	9.4	14.6	15.3	14.8
7. Landless Workers	4.3	5.0	9.0	10.1	7.9	12.8	14.2	13.3
T O T A L	6.0	6.1	7.4	8.0	7.2	10.3	13.2	11.4

New Development Strategy

Table D.4.12: Average Income by Socio-economic Group, Gini Coefficient and Welfare Indicators

	Thousands of 1978 pesos							Annual growth rates (percent)							
Socio-economic group	1978	1979	1980	1981	1982	1985	1990	79/78	80/79	81/80	82/81	83/78	88/83	93/88	93/82
1. Entr. Empl. Prof. (H)	228.	232.	236.	235.	234.	225.	204.	1.8	1.7	-.4	-.4	.3	-1.5	-2.8	-2.1
2. Entr. Empl. Prof. (M)	183.	185.	187.	184.	180.	167.	145.	1.1	1.1	-1.6	-2.2	-.8	-2.6	-3.3	-2.9
3. Entr. Empl. Prof. (L)	97.	98.	97.	95.	92.	84.	70.	1.0	-1.0	-2.1	-3.2	-1.5	-3.3	-4.0	-3.5
4. Workers	156.	164.	172.	179.	186.	203.	217.	5.1	4.9	4.1	3.9	4.2	2.3	-.5	1.1
5. Peasants (H-M)	111.	113.	114.	114.	114.	115.	121.	1.8	.9	0.0	0.0	.5	.7	1.3	.9
6. Peasants (L)	61.	62.	63.	64.	65.	68.	73.	1.6	1.6	1.6	1.6	1.6	1.5	1.6	1.6
7. Landless Workers	58.	58.	58.	58.	58.	57.	58.	0.0	0.0	0.0	0.0	-.3	.3	.3	.2
T O T A L	124.	127.	129.	128.	127.	123.	117.	2.0	1.6	.2	-.0	.7	-.4	-1.3	-.8
Welfare indicators															
Gini Coefficient	.260	.261	.264	.263	.264	.266	.263	-.37	-.37	-.37	-.37	-.37	-.37	-.37	-.37
Efficiency-equity[a]	1.259	1.333	1.408	1.515	1.633	2.120	3.645								
Equal weights								1.8	1.2	.1	-.4	.4	-.8	-1.7	-1.2
Poverty weighted								2.2	1.7	1.0	.6	1.1	.1	-.9	-.3

a) 10^{12} 1978 pesos

REFERENCES

Aceituno, G., 1980, Los ingresos del sector publico: tendencias recientes, Economía Mexicana 2, 163-178.

Adelman, I. and S. Robinson, 1978, Income Distribution Policy in Developing Countries. A Case Study of Korea (Stanford University Press, Stanford).

Ahluwalia, M.S. and H.B. Chenery, 1974, The Economic Framework, in: Chenery et al., 1974, Ch. II.

Allen, R.G.D., 1957, Mathematical Economics (Macmillan, London).

Altimir, O., 1974, La medición de la población economicamente activa de México, 1950-1970, Demografía y Economía 1, 50-83.

Altimir, O., 1977, Income Distribution Estimates from Household Surveys and Population Censuses in Latin America: An Assessment of Reliability. Economic Commission for Latin America and Development Research Center, World Bank (Mimeograph).

Anonymous, 1981, SAM: The Mexican food system, IFDA (International Foundation for Development Alternatives) Dossier 25, 17-30.

Arrow, K. and S. Chang, 1978, Optimal Pricing, Use and Exploration of Uncertain Natural Resource Stocks, Technical Report No. 31, Department of Economics, Harvard University.

Bacharach, M., 1970, Biproportional Matrices and Input-Output Change (Cambridge University Press, Cambridge).

Bale, M.D. and E. Lutz, 1981, Price Distortions in Agriculture and Their Effects: An International Comparison, American Journal of Agricultural Economics 1, 8-22.

Barker, T., V. Borooah, R.van der Ploeg, A. Winters, 1980, The Cambridge Multisectoral Model: An Instrument for National Economic Policy Analysis, Journal of Policy Modeling 3, 319-343.

Barker, T. and V. Brailovsky, eds., 1981, Oil or Industry? (Academic Press, London).

Barkin, D., 1971, La persistencia de la pobreza en México: un análisis económico estructural, in: Wionczek, ed., 1971, pp. 186-207.

Bell, C.L.G. and J.H. Duloy, 1974, Formulating a Strategy, in: Chenery et al., 1974, Ch. V.

Beltrán del Río, A., 1973, A Macroeconometric Model for Mexico: Specifications and Simulations, Ph.D. dissertation, University of Pennsylvania.

Beltrán del Río, A., 1980, El síndrome del petróleo mexicano: Primeros síntomas, medidas preventivas y pronósticos, Comercio Exterior 6, 556-569.

Bergsman, J., 1980, Income Distribution and Poverty in Mexico, Staff Working Paper No. 395, World Bank.

Bergsman, J. and A.S. Manne, 1966, An Almost Consistent Intertemporal Model for India's Fourth and Fifth Plans, in: Adelman, I. and E. Thorbecke, eds., 1966, The Theory and Design of Economic Development (Johns Hopkins University Press, Baltimore).

Blackorby, C. and D. Donaldson, 1978, Measures of Relative Equality and Their Meaning in Terms of Social Welfare, Journal of Economic Theory 18, 59-80.

Blitzer, C., P.B. Clark and L. Taylor, eds., 1975, Economy-Wide Models and Development Planning (Oxford University Press, London).

Bohm, D., 1980, Wholeness and the implicate order (Routledge, London).

Brailovsky, V., 1981, Industrialization and Oil in Mexico: A Long-term Perspective, in: T. Barker and V. Brailovsky, eds., 1981.

Bródy, A., 1970, Proportions, Prices and Planning (North-Holland, Amsterdam).

Cambridge, Department of Applied Economics, 1962-1974, A Programme for Growth, Volumes I to XII (Chapman and Hall, London).

Carter, A., 1970, Structural Change in the American Economy (Harvard University Press, Cambridge, Mass.).

Centro de Investigaciones Agrarias (CIA), 1974, Estructura Agraria y Desarrollo Agrícola en México (Fondo de Cultura Económica, México).

Centro de Investigación y Docencia Económicas (CIDE), 1980, The Mexican economy: recent development and future prospects, Cambridge Journal of Economics 4, 177-197.

Chakravarty, S., 1969, Capital and Development Planning (MIT Press, Cambridge, Mass.).

Chenery, H.B., M.S. Ahluwalia, C.L.G. Bell, J.H. Duloy and R. Jolly, 1974, Redistribution with Growth (Oxford University Press, Oxford).

Chiang, A.C., 1974, Fundamental Methods of Mathematical Economics (McGraw-Hill, Tokio).

Chichilnisky, G. and L. Taylor, 1980, Agriculture and the Rest of the Economy: Macroconnections and Policy Restraints, American Journal of Agricultural Economics, 303-309.

Clark, P.B., 1975, Intersectoral Consistency and Macroeconomic Planning, in: Blitzer et al., eds., 1975.

Cline, W.R., 1972, Potential Effects of Income Redistribution on Economic Growth: Latin American Cases (Praeger, New York).

Cline, W.R., 1975, Distribution and Development: A Survey of Literature, Journal of Development Economics 1, 359-400.

Corden, W.M. and J.P. Neary, 1982, Booming Sector and De-Industrialization in a Small Open Economy, The Economic Journal 92, 825-848.

Dasgupta, P.S. and G.M. Heal, 1979, Economic Theory and Exhaustible Resources (Cambridge University Press, Cambridge).

Deaton, A., 1975, Models and Projections of Demand in Post-War Britain (Chapman and Hall, London).

Departamento de Planeación, 1981, Sumario Estadístico, Comercio Exterior 3, 353-360.

Departamento de Planeación, 1982, Sumario Estadístico, Comercio Exterior 4, 474-480.

Díaz Serrano, J., 1980, Informe de Petróleos Mexicanos 1979, Comercio Exterior 4, 386-394.

Domar, E.D., 1946, Capital Expansion, Rate of Growth, and Employment, Econometrica 2, 137-147.

Dovring, F., 1970, Land Reform and Productivity in Mexico, Land Economics 3, 264-274. (For a Spanish version, see Solís, ed., 1973, 34-54.)

Esteva, G., 1978, Y si los campesinos existen? Comercio Exterior 6, 699-713.

Esteva, G., 1980, Qué hay detrás de la crisis rural, Comercio Exterior 7, 675-683.

Evans, M.K. and L.R. Klein, 1968, The Wharton Econometric Forecasting Model, Econometrics Research Unit, Wharton School of Finance and Commerce, University of Pennsylvania.

Fajnzylber, F. and T. Martínez Tarragó, 1976, Las empresas transnacionales (Fondo de Cultura Económica, México).

FitzGerald, E.V.K., 1977, Patterns of Saving and Investment in Mexico: 1939-76, Working Papers No. 30, Centre of Latin American Studies, University of Cambridge.

Fox, K.A., and E. Thorbecke, 1965, Specification of Structures and Data Requirements, in: B.G. Hickman, ed., Quantitative Planning of Economic Policy (The Brookings Institution, Washington).

Franchet, Y., R.A. Inman and A.S. Manne, 1973, Numerical data for multisector planning, in: Goreux and Manne, eds., 1973.

Frisch, R., 1962, Preface to the Oslo Channel Model: A Survey of Types of Economic Forecasting and Programming, in: R. Geary, ed., Europe's Future in Figures (North-Holland, Amsterdam).

Frisch, R., 1965, General Outlook on a Method of Advanced and Democratic Macroeconomic Planning, Memorandum from the Institute of Economics at the University of Oslo.

Fullerton, D., Y. Kodrzycki Henderson, J.B. Shoven, 1981, A Comparison of Methodologies in Empirical General Equilibrium Models of Taxation, Woodrow Wilson School, Princeton University, Discussion Paper 19.

Georgescu-Roegen, N., 1974, Dynamic Models and Economic Growth, in: N. Georgescu-Roegen, 1976, Energy and Economic Myths (Pergamon, New York).

Gómez Oliver, L., 1978, Crisis agrícola, crisis de campesinos, Comercio Exterior 6, 714-727.

Goreux, L.M. and A.S. Manne, eds., 1973, Multilevel Planning: Case Studies in Mexico (North-Holland, Amsterdam).

Graaff, J., 1977, Equity and Efficiency as Components of the General Welfare, South African Journal of Economics 4, 362-375.

Grandmont, J.M., 1977, Temporary General Equilibrium Theory, Econometrica 3, 535-572.

Griffin, K., 1974, The Political Economy of Agrarian Change (Macmillan, London).

Griffin, K., 1978, International Inequality and National Poverty (Macmillan, London).

Gutiérrez, R., 1979, La balanza petrolera de México 1970-1982, Comercio Exterior 8, 839-850.

Hansen, B., 1966, Lectures in Economic Theory I (Studentlitteratur, Lund).

Hansen, B., 1967, The Economic Theory of Fiscal Policy (Allen and Unwin, London).

Harrod, R.F., 1936, The Trade Cycle (Oxford University Press, Oxford).

Hernández Laos, E. and J. Córdoba Chávez, 1979, Estructura de la distribución del ingreso en México, Comercio Exterior 5, 505-520.

Hewitt de Alcántara, C., 1976, Modernizing Mexican Agriculture, United Nations Research Institute for Social Development, Geneva.

Hotelling, H., 1931, The Economics of Exhaustible Resources, Journal of Political Economy 2, 137-175.

International Labour Office (ILO), 1966, Measurement of Under-employment, Geneva.

International Labour Office (ILO), 1973, Strategies for Employ-ment Promotion, Geneva.

International Labour Office (ILO), 1976, Employment, Growth and Basic Needs: A One World Problem, Geneva.

International Labour Office (ILO), 1978, Year Book of Labour Statistics, Geneva.

International Monetary Fund (IMF), 1981, International Financial Statistics Year Book, Washington, D.C.

Johansen, L., 1973, The Rate of Growth in Dynamic Input-Output Models: Some Observations Along Lines Suggested by O. Lange and A. Bródy, Jahrbuch der Wirtschaft Osteuropas 4 (Günter Olzog Verlag, Munich).

Johansen, L., 1977, Lectures on Macroeconomic Planning, Part One, General Aspects (North-Holland, Amsterdam).

Johansen, L., 1978, Lectures on Macroeconomic Planning, Part Two, Decentralization, Planning under Uncertainty (North-Holland, Amsterdam).

Jorgenson, D.W., 1961, The Structure of Multi-Sector Dynamic Models, International Economic Review 3, 276-293.

Junankar, P.N., 1972, Investment: Theories and Evidence (Mac-millan, London).

Kaldor, N., 1956, Alternative Theories of Distribution, Review of Economic Studies 1-2, 83-100.

Kaldor, N., 1964, Las reformas al sistema fiscal en México, Comercio Exterior 4, 265-267. (Reprinted in: Solís, ed., 1973.)

Kaldor, N., 1981, The Energy Issues, in: Barker and Brailovsky, eds., 1981.

Kalecki, M., 1954, Theory of Economic Dynamics (Allen and Unwin, London).

Kalecki, M., 1970, Problems of Financing Economic Development in a Mixed Economy, in: M. Kalecki, 1972, Selected Essays on the Economic Growth of the Socialist and the Mixed Economy (Cambridge University Press, Cambridge). (The original 1963 Polish version was published in Ekonomista 6, 1114-1124.)

Kalifa, S., 1976, Income Distribution in Mexico, Ph.D. dissertation, University of Cornell.

Katouzian, M.A.H., 1978, Oil versus Agriculture: A Case of Dual Resource Depletion in Iran, Journal of Peasant Studies 3, 347-369.

Katouzian, M.A.H., 1979, The Political Economy of Oil Exporting Countries, Peuples Méditerranéens 8, 3-22.

Kendrick, D., 1981, Stochastic Control for Economic Models (McGraw-Hill, New York).

Kmenta, J., 1971, Elements of Econometrics (Macmillan, New York).

Kuznets, S., 1955, Economic Growth and Income Inequality, American Economic Review 1, 1-28.

Lange, O., 1957, Some Observations on Input-Output Analysis, Sankhya 4, 305-336.

Lange, O., 1970, Introduction to Economic Cybernetics (Pergamon, Oxford).

Lao Tzu, 1963, Tao te ching (Penguin classics).

Leontief, W., 1951, The Structure of the American Economy, 1919-1939 (Oxford University Press, New York).

Leontief, W., 1953, Dynamic Analysis, in: Leontief et al., Studies on the Structure of the American Economy (Oxford University Press, New York).

Lluch, C., 1973, The extended linear expenditure system, European Economic Review 4, 21-32.

Lluch, C., A.A. Powell and R.A. Williams, 1977, Patterns in Household Demand and Saving (Oxford University Press, London).

Lundberg, E., 1937, Studies in the Theory of Economic Expansion, Stockholm University, Institute for Social Sciences, Stockholm Economic Studies No. 6.

Lydall, H., 1977, Income Distribution During the Process of Development, International Labour Office, World Employment Programme Research Working Paper No. 52, Geneva.

302

Mexico, 1969, Cuentas nacionales y acervos de capital 1950-1967,
   Banco de México.

Mexico, 1971, IX Censo General de Población 1970, Secretaría
   de Industria y Comercio, Dirección de Estadística.

Mexico, 1975, V Censo Agrícola-Ganadero y Ejidal, Secretaría de
   Industria y Comercio, Dirección General de Estadística.

Mexico, 1977, Indicadores ecomómicos 1, Banco de México.

Mexico, 1978a, La estructura de la oferta y la demanda en México
   1975: Matrices de relaciones intersectoriales, Secretaría
   de Patrimonio y Fomento Industrial.

Mexico, 1978b, Producto interno bruto y gasto 1960-1975, Banco de
   México.

Mexico, 1978c, Acervos y formación de capital 1960-1975, Banco de
   México.

Mexico, 1979a, Producto interno bruto y gasto 1970-1978, Banco de
   México.

Mexico, 1979b, Indicadores económicos 1, Banco de México.

Mexico, 1979c, Plan Nacional de Desarrollo Industrial, Secretaría
   de Patrimonio y Fomento Industrial.

Mexico, 1979d, Programa Nacional del Empleo 1980/82, Secretaría
   de Trabajo y Previsión Social.

Mexico, 1980a, Producto interno bruto y gasto 1970-1979, Banco de
   México.

Mexico, 1980b, Plan Global de Desarrollo 1980-1982, Secretaría de
   Programación y Presupuesto.

Mexico, 1980c, Informe Anual 1979, Banco de México.

Mexico, 1981, Informe Anual 1980, Banco de México.

Mexico, n.d.a, Matriz de Insumo-Producto de México Año 1970,
   Secretaría de Programación y Presupuesto, Banco de México,
   PNUD-ONU.

Mexico, n.d.b, Encuesta Nacional de Ingresos y Gastos de los
   Hogares 1977, Informe metodológico, Secretaría de Programa-
   ción y Presupuesto, Coordinación del Sistema Nacional de
   Información.

Mikesell, R.F. and J.E. Zinser, 1973, The Nature of the Savings
   Function in Developing Countries: A Survey of the Theoretical
   and Empirical Literature, Journal of Economic Literature 1,
   1-26.

Miyasawa, K. and S. Masegi, 1963, Interindustry Analysis and the
    Structure of Income Distribution, Metroeconomica 2-3, 89-103.

Miyasawa, K., 1976, Input-Output Analysis and the Structure of
    Income Distribution (Springer, Berlin).

Montes de Oca, R.E. and F. Rello, 1982, Hacia un proyecto alimen-
    tario diferente, Comercio Exterior 2, 172-180.

Morawetz, D., 1974, Employment Implications of Industrialization
    in Developing Countries: A Survey, The Economic Journal 84,
    491-542.

Morishima, M., 1973, Marx's Economics. A Dual Theory of Value
    and Growth (Cambridge University Press, Cambridge).

Mújica Vélez, R., 1979, Las zonas de riego: acumulación y mar-
    ginalidad, Comercio Exterior 4, 404-410.

Myrdal, G., 1981, Need for Reforms in Underdeveloped Countries,
    in: S. Grassman and E. Lundberg, eds., The World Economic
    Order: Past and Prospects (Macmillan, London).

Naylor, T.A., 1971, Computer Simulation Experiments with Models
    of Economic Systems (John Wiley, New York).

Nguyen, D.T. and M.L. Martínez Saldívar, 1979, The effects of
    land reform on agricultural production, employment and income
    distribution: A statistical study of Mexican states, 1959-69,
    The Economic Journal 89, 624-635.

Nordhaus, W. and J. Tobin, 1972, Is growth obsolete?, in: Eco-
    nomic Growth: Fiftieth anniversary colloquium (NBER/Columbia
    University Press, New York).

Ortiz Mena, A., 1966, Contenido y Alcances de la Política Fiscal,
    Actividad Económica en Latinoamerica 75, 6-18 (Reprinted
    in Solís, ed., 1973).

Ortiz Mena, A., 1970, Desarrollo estabilizador: una década de
    estrategia económica en México, El Trimestre Económico 146,
    417-449.

Paukert, F., J. Skolka and J. Maton, 1976, Redistribution of
    Income, Patterns of Consumption and Employment: A Case Study
    of the Philippines, in: K.R.Polenske and J. Skolka, eds.,
    Advances in Input-Output Analysis (Ballinger, Cambridge,
    Mass.),

Pemex, 1981, La actividad petrolera de México en 1980, Comercio
    Exterior 4, 446-454.

Preston, R.S., 1975, The input-output sector of the Wharton annual
    and industry forecasting model, in: G. Fromm and L.R. Klein,
    eds., The Brookings Model: Perspective and Recent Develop-
    ments (North-Holland, Amsterdam).

Prigogine, I., 1980, From Being to Becoming. Time and Complexity
    in the Physical Sciences (W.H. Freeman, San Francisco).

304

Programa Regional del Empleo para América Latina y el Caribe
(PREALC), 1975, Opciones de Políticas y Creación de Empleo
Productivo en México, International Labour Office, México.

Pyatt, G., J. Bharier, R.M. Lindley, R.M. Mabro and Y. Sabolo,
1973, A Methodology for Macro-Economic Projections, Mission
Working Paper No. 12, International Labour Office, Geneva
(Mimeograph).

Pyatt, G. and A. Roe, 1977, Social Accounting for Development
Planning, with Special Reference to Sri Lanka (Cambridge
University Press, London).

Pyatt, G. and J.I. Round, 1977, Social Accounting Matrices for
Development Planning, Review of Income and Wealth 4, 339-364.

Pyatt, G. and E. Thorbecke, 1976, Planning Techniques for a
Better Future, International Labour Office, Geneva.

Ramírez Hernández, J. and A. Chávez, 1981, Situación alimentaria
de México, Comercio Exterior 4, 385-390.

Rendón, T., 1976, Utilización de Mano de Obra en la Agricultura
Mexicana 1940-1973, Demografía y Economía 3.

Reyes Osorio, S. and S. Eckstein, 1971, El Desarrollo polarizado
de la agricultura mexicana, in: Wionczek, ed., 1971.

Reynolds, C.W., 1979, Labor Market Relations for the United
States and Mexico and Current Migration Controversies, Food
Research Institute Studies 2, 121-151.

Sabau, H., 1980, Estimación de un sistema lineal de ingreso-gasto
para el caso de México, Centro de Investigación y Docencia
Económicas, México (Unpublished).

Sección Nacional, 1980a, El SAM, principio de una estrategia,
Comercio Exterior 7, 684-689.

Sección Nacional, 1980b, La balanza comercial de productos
agrícolas, Comercio Exterior 7, 689-695.

Sen, A., 1979, The Welfare Basis of Real Income Comparisons:
A Survey, Journal of Economic Literature 1, 1-45.

Serra Puche, J.J., 1979, A Computational General Equilibrium
Model for the Mexican Economy: An Analysis of Fiscal Policies, Ph.D. dissertation, Yale University.

Singh, A., 1981, Comments on Chapter 5, in: T. Barker and
V. Brailovsky, eds., 1981.

Slater, L.J., 1972, More Fortran Programs for Economists (Cambridge University Press, London).

Snyder, D.W., 1974, Econometric Studies of Household Saving Behaviour in Developing Countries: A Survey, Journal of Development Studies 10, 139-153.

Solís, L., 1970, La realidad económica mexicana: retrovisión y perspectivas (Siglo Veintiuno, Mexico).

Solís, L., ed., 1973, La economía mexicana, 1.análisis por sectores y distribución (Fondo de Cultura Económica, Mexico).

Solís, L., 1977, A Monetary Will-O'-The Wisp: Pursuit of Equity Through Deficit Spending, International Labour Office, Geneva.

Solís, L., 1980, Alternativas para el desarrollo (Joaquín Mortiz, Mexico).

Stavenhagen, R., 1977, Basic Needs, Peasants and the Strategy for Rural Development, in: M. Nerfin, ed., Another Development: Approaches and Strategies (The Dag Hammarskjöld Foundation, Uppsala).

Stone, R., 1954, Linear Expenditure Systems and Demand Analysis, An Application to the Pattern of British Demand, Economic Journal 255, 511-527.

Stewart, J.R., 1978, Potential Effects of Income Redistribution on Economic Growth: An Expanded Estimating Procedure Applied to Mexico, Economic Development and Cultural Change 3, 467-485.

Streeten, P.P., 1979, Basic Needs: Premises and Promises, Journal of Policy Modeling 1, 136-146.

Sunkel, O., 1960, Inflation in Chile: An Unorthodox Approach, International Economic Papers 10, 107-131.

Svennilson, I., 1938, Ekonomisk planering: teoretiska studier (Almqvist & Wiksell, Uppsala).

Svennilson, I., 1965, Planning in a Market Economy. Weltwirtschaftliches Archiv 2, 184-200.

Taylor, L., 1975, Theoretical Foundations and Technical Implications, in: Blitzer et al., eds., 1975.

Tello, C., 1979, La política económica en México 1970-1976 (Siglo Veintiuno, Mexico).

Tsukui, J., 1968, Application of a Turnpike Theorem to Planning for Efficient Accumulation: An Example for Japan, Econometrica 1, 172-186.

Tsukui, J. and Y. Murakami, 1979, Turnpike Optimality in Input-Output Systems (North-Holland, Amsterdam).

306

United Nations, Statistical Office, 1968, A System of National
    Accounts, Studies in Methods, Series F, No. 2, Rev. 3,
    New York.

United Nations, Economic Commision for Asia and the Far East
    (ECAFE), 1970, Sectoral Output and Employment Projections
    for the Second Development Decade, Development Programming
    Series No. 8, Bangkok.

van Ginneken, W., 1980, Socio-economic Groups and Income Distribu-
    tion in Mexico (Croom Helm, London).

Vío Grossi, F., 1980, Economías campesinas, cambio agrario y
    movimientos campesinos en América Latina, Comercio Exterior
    7, 699-708.

Vossenaar, R., 1977, El Análisis de los Efectos de Políticas Re-
    distributivas en Base a un Modelo de Insumo-Producto con
    Estratificación Tecnológica: Un Estudio de Caso Aplicado
    a México, Universidad Católica de Chile, Cuadernos de
    Economía 14, 121-159.

Warman, A., 1979, Desarrollo capitalista o campesino en el campo
    mexicano, Comercio Exterior 4, 399-403.

Weil, S., 1950, La connaissance surnaturelle (Gallimard, Paris).

Whitehead, L., 1980, Mexico from Bust to Boom: A Political Evalua-
    tion of the 1976-1979 Stabilization Programme, World De-
    velopment 11, 843-864.

Wionczek, M., ed., 1971, La sociedad mexicana: presente y futuro
    (Fondo de Cultura Económica, México).

World Bank, 1981, World Development Report 1981, Washington.

World Bank, 1982, World Development Report 1982, Washington.

Yates, P.L., 1978, El campo mexicano (El Caballito, México).
    English version, 1981, Mexico's Agricultural Dilemma
    (University of Arizona Press, Tuscon).

Yates, P.L., 1981, Mexican Land Reform, 1959-1969: A Comment,
    The Economic Journal 363, 745-752.

INDEX

For Product Safety Concerns and Information please contact our EU
representative GPSR@taylorandfrancis.com
Taylor & Francis Verlag GmbH, Kaufingerstraße 24, 80331 München, Germany

www.ingramcontent.com/pod-product-compliance
Lightning Source LLC
Chambersburg PA
CBHW061135220326
41599CB00025B/4242